TEACHER'S EDITION

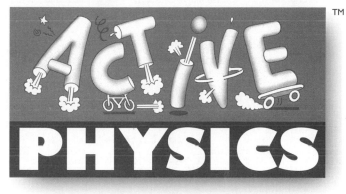

ACTIVE PHYSICS™

Arthur Eisenkraft, Ph.D.

Active Physics has been developed in association
with the
American Association of Physics Teachers (AAPT)
and the
American Institute of Physics (AIP)

TRANSPORTATION

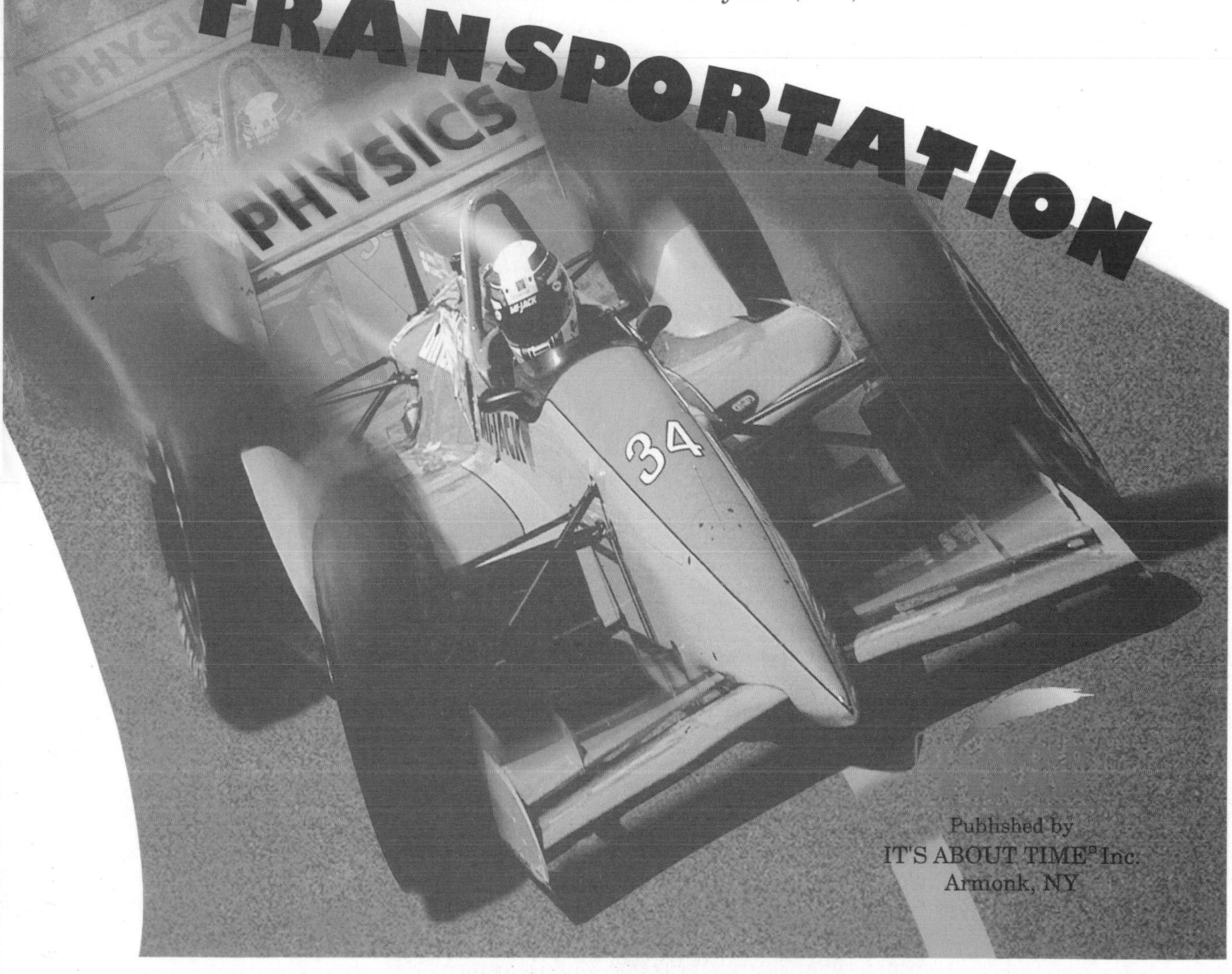

Published by
IT'S ABOUT TIME® Inc.
Armonk, NY

Published in 1999 by

It's About Time, Inc.

84 Business Park Drive, Armonk, NY 10504
Phone (914) 273-2233 Fax (914) 273-2227
Toll Free (888) 698-TIME
http://www.Its-About-Time.com

Publisher
Laurie Kreindler

Project Director
Dr. Arthur Eisenkraft

Project Manager
Ruta Demery

Design
John Nordland

Production Manager
Barbara Zahm

Studio Manager
Leslie Jander

Cover Illustration
Steven Belcher

Student's Edition Illustrations and Photos

Chapter 1: Tomas Bunk pages 4, 10, 17, 22, 26, 40 & 46; ©Ford Photomedia pages 3 & 13; Michael Gadomski/PhotoReseachers; Corel page 44; Nick Gunderson/Tony Stone. **Chapter 2:** Tomas Bunk pages 62, 67, 73, 76, 79, 84, 93, 95, 100; page 59 & 60 Nicholas Pinturas/Tony Stone; page 64 AP Photos; page 69 Aldo Torelli/Tony Stone; page 83 Donald Johnston/Tony Stone. **Chapter 3:** Tomas Bunk pages 107, 110, 124, 134, 142, 148, 153 & 157; NASA photos pages 122, 135, 136, 138, 139, 145, 159; Royal Observatory, Edinburgh/PhotoResearchers; NASA/PhotoResearchers; Star Trek©1991 Paramount Pictures. All other photos PhotoDisc©1998.

Teacher's Edition Illustrations

Kathleen Bowen, Robert Hansmann, Cathy Vidal

All student activities in this textbook have been designed to be as safe as possible, and have been reviewed by professionals specifically for that purpose. As well, appropriate warnings concerning potential safety hazards are included where applicable to particular activities. However, responsibility for safety remains with the student, the classroom teacher, the school principal, and the school board.

Printed and bound in the United States of America

ISBN 1-891629-11-5

2 3 4 5 D 02 01 00 99

This project was supported, in part, by the
National Science Foundation
Opinions expressed are those of the authors and not necessarily those of the Foundation

TABLE OF CONTENTS

Acknowledgments

Project Director

Arthur Eisenkraft teaches physics and serves as science coordinator in the Bedford Public Schools in N.Y. Dr. Eisenkraft is the author of numerous science and educational publications. He holds a US Patent for a laser vision testing system and was featured in *Scientific American.*

Dr. Eisenkraft is chair of the Duracell Science Scholarship Competition; chair of the Toyota TAPESTRY program giving grants to science teachers; and chair of the Toshiba/NSTA ExploraVisions Awards competition for grades K-12. He is co-author of a contest column and serves on the advisory board of *Quantum* magazine, a collaborative effort of the US and Russia. In 1993, he served as Executive Director for the XXIV International Physics Olympiad after being Academic Director for the United States Team for six years. He served on the content committee and helped write the National Science Education Standards of the NRC (National Research Council).

Dr. Eisenkraft received the Presidential Award for Excellence in Science Teaching at the White House in 1986, and the AAPT Distinguished Service Citation for "excellent contributions to the teaching of physics" in 1989. In 1991 he was recognized by the Disney Corporation as Science Teacher of the Year in their American Teacher Awards program. In 1993 he received an Honorary Doctor of Science degree from Rensselaer Polytechnic Institute.

Primary and Contributing Authors

Communication

Richard Berg
University of Maryland
College Park, MD

Ron DeFronzo
Eastbay Ed. Collaborative
Attleboro, MA

Harry Rheam
Eastern Senior High School
Atco, NJ

John Roeder
The Calhoun School
New York, NY

Patty Rourke
Potomac School
McLean, VA

Larry Weathers
The Bromfield School
Harvard, MA

Home

Jon L. Harkness
Active Physics Regional Coordinator
Wausau, WI

Douglas A. Johnson
Madison West High School
Madison, WI

John J. Rusch
University of Wisconsin, Superior
Superior, WI

Ruta Demery
Blue Ink Editing
Stayner, ON

Hugh Brown
Atlas Communications
St. Albert, AB

Medicine

Russell Hobbie
University of Minnesota
St. Paul, MN

Terry Goerke
Hill-Murray High School
St. Paul, MN

John Koser
Wayzata High School
Plymouth, MN

Ed Lee
WonderScience, Associate Editor
Silver Spring, MD

Predictions

Ruth Howes
Ball State University
Muncie, IN

Chris Chiaverina
New Trier Township High School
Crystal Lake, IL

Charles Payne
Ball State University
Muncie, IN

Ceanne Tzimopoulos
Omega Publishing
Medford, MA

Sports

Howard Brody
University of Pennsylvania
Philadelphia, PA

Mary Quinlan
Radnor High School
Radnor, PA

Carl Duzen
Lower Merion High School
Havertown, PA

Jon L. Harkness
Active Physics Regional Coordinator
Wausau, WI

David Wright
Tidewater Comm. College
Virginia Beach, VA

Transportation

Ernest Kuehl
Lawrence High School
Cedarhurst, NY

Robert L. Lehrman
Bayside, NY

Salvatore Levy
Roslyn High School
Roslyn, NY

Tom Liao

SUNY Stony Brook
Stony Brook, NY

Bob Ritter
University of Alberta
Edmonton, AB, CA

Principal Investigators

Bernard V. Khoury
American Association of Physics Teachers

Dwight Edward Neuenschwander
American Institute of Physics

Consultants

Peter Brancazio
Brooklyn College of CUNY
Brooklyn, NY

Robert Capen
Canyon del Oro High School
Tucson, AZ

Carole Escobar

Earl Graf
SUNY Stony Brook
Stony Brook, NY

Jack Hehn
American Association of Physics Teachers
College Park, MD

Donald F. Kirwan
Louisiana State University
Baton Rouge, LA

Gayle Kirwan
Louisiana State University
Baton Rouge, LA

James La Porte
Virginia Tech
Blacksburg, VA

Charles Misner
University of Maryland
College Park, MD

Robert F. Neff
Suffern, NY

Ingrid Novodvorsky
Mountain View High School
Tucson, AZ

John Robson
University of Arizona
Tucson, AZ

Mark Sanders
Virginia Tech
Blacksburg, VA

Brian Schwartz
Brooklyn College of CUNY
New York, NY

Bruce Seiger
Wellesley High School
Newburyport, MA

Clifford Swartz
SUNY Stony Brook
Setauket, NY

Barbara Tinker
The Concord Consortium
Concord, MA

Robert E. Tinker
The Concord Consortium
Concord, MA

Joyce Weiskopf
Herndon, VA

Donna Willis
American Association of Physics Teachers
College Park, MD

Safety Reviewer

Gregory Puskar
University of West Virginia
Morgantown, WV

Equity Reviewer

Leo Edwards
Fayetteville State University
Fayetteville, NC

Spreadsheet and MBL

Ken Appel
Yorktown High School
Peekskill, NY

Physics at Work

Barbara Zahm
Zahm Productions
New York, NY

Physics InfoMall

Brian Adrian
Bethany College
Lindsborg, KS

Unit Reviewers

George A. Amann
F.D. Roosevelt High School
Rhinebeck, NY

Patrick Callahan
Catasaugua High School
Center Valley, PA

Beverly Cannon
Science and Engineering Magnet High School
Dallas, TX

Barbara Chauvin

Elizabeth Chesick
The Baldwin School
Haverford, PA 19041

Chris Chiaverina
New Trier Township High School
Crystal Lake, IL

Andria Erzberger
Palo Alto Senior High School
Los Altos Hills, CA

Elizabeth Farrell Ramseyer
Niles West High School
Skokie, IL

Mary Gromko
President of Council of State Science Supervisors
Denver, CO

Thomas Guetzloff

Jon L. Harkness
Active Physics Regional Coordinator
Wausau, WI

Dawn Harman
Moon Valley High School
Phoenix, AZ

James Hill
Piner High School
Sonoma, CA

Bob Kearney

Claudia Khourey-Bowers
McKinley Senior High School

Steve Kliewer
Bullard High School
Fresno, CA

Ernest Kuehl
Roslyn High School
Cedarhurst, NY

Jane Nelson
University High School
Orlando, FL

John Roeder
The Calhoun School
New York, NY

Patty Rourke
Potomac School
McLean, VA

Gerhard Salinger
Fairfax, VA

Irene Slater
La Pietra School for Girls

Pilot Test Teachers

John Agosta

Donald Campbell
Portage Central High School
Portage, MI

John Carlson
Norwalk Community
Technical College
Norwalk, CT

Veanna Crawford
Alamo Heights High School
New Braunfels

Janie Edmonds
West Milford High School
Randolph, NJ

Eddie Edwards
Amarillo Area Center for
Advanced Learning
Amarillo, TX

Arthur Eisenkraft
Fox Lane High School
Bedford, NY

Tom Ford

Bill Franklin

Roger Goerke
St. Paul, MN

Tom Gordon
Greenwich High School
Greenwich, CT

Ariel Hepp

John Herrman
College of Steubenville
Steubenville, OH

Linda Hodges

Ernest Kuehl
Lawrence High School
Cedarhurst, NY

Fran Leary
Troy High School
Schenectady, NY

Harold Lefcourt

Cherie Lehman
West Lafayette High School
West Lafayette, IN

Kathy Malone
Shady Side Academy
Pittsburgh, PA

Bill Metzler
Westlake High School
Thornwood, NY

Elizabeth Farrell Ramseyer
Niles West High School
Skokie, IL

Daniel Repogle
Central Noble High School
Albion, IN

Evelyn Restivo
Maypearl High School
Maypearl, TX

Doug Rich
Fox Lane High School
Bedford, NY

John Roeder
The Calhoun School
New York, NY

Tom Senior
New Trier Township High School
Highland Park, IL

John Thayer
District of Columbia Public Schools
Silver Spring, MD

Carol-Ann Tripp
Providence Country Day
East Providence, RI

Yvette Van Hise
High Tech High School
Freehold, NJ

Jan Waarvick

Sandra Walton
Dubuque Senior High School
Dubuque, IA

Larry Wood
Fox Lane High School
Bedford, NY

Field Test Coordinator

Marilyn Decker
Northeastern University
Acton, MA

Field Test Workshop Staff

John Carlson

Marilyn Decker

Arthur Eisenkraft

Douglas Johnson

John Koser

Ernest Kuehl

Mary Quinlan

Elizabeth Farrell Ramseyer

John Roeder

Field Test Evaluators

Susan Baker-Cohen

Susan Cloutier

George Hein

Judith Kelley

all from Lesley College,
Cambridge, MA

Field Test Teachers and Schools

Rob Adams
Polytech High School
Woodside, DE

Benjamin Allen
Falls Church High School
Falls Church, VA

Robert Applebaum
New Trier High School
Winnetka, IL

Joe Arnett
Plano Sr. High School
Plano, TX

Bix Baker
GFW High School
Winthrop, MN

Debra Beightol
Fremont High School
Fremont, NE

Patrick Callahan
Catasaugua High School
Catasaugua, PA

George Coker
Bowling Green High School
Bowling Green, KY

Janice Costabile
South Brunswick High School
Monmouth Junction, NJ

Stanley Crum
Homestead High School
Fort Wayne, IN

Russel Davison
Brandon High School
Brandon, FL

Christine K. Deyo
Rochester Adams High School
Rochester Hills, MI

Jim Doller
Fox Lane High School
Bedford, NY

Jessica Downing
Esparto High School
Esparto, CA

Douglas Fackelman
Brighton High School
Brighton, CO

Rick Forrest
Rochester High School
Rochester Hills, MI

Mark Freeman
Blacksburg High School
Blacksburg, VA

Jonathan Gillis
Enloe High School
Raleigh, NC

Karen Gruner
Holton Arms School
Bethesda, MD

Larry Harrison
DuPont Manual High School
Louisville, KY

Alan Haught
Weaver High School
Hartford, CT

Steven Iona
Horizon High School
Thornton, CO

Phil Jowell
Oak Ridge High School
Conroe, TX

Deborah Knight
Windsor Forest High School
Savannah, GA

Thomas Kobilarcik
Marist High School
Chicago, IL

Sheila Kolb
Plano Senior High School
Plano, TX

Todd Lindsay
Park Hill High School
Kansas City, MO

Malinda Mann
South Putnam High School
Greencastle, IN

Steve Martin
Maricopa High School
Maricopa, AZ

Nancy McGrory
North Quincy High School
N. Quincy, MA

David Morton
Mountain Valley High School
Rumford, ME

Charles Muller
Highland Park High School
Highland Park, NJ

Fred Muller
Mercy High School
Burlingame, CA

Vivian O'Brien
Plymouth Regional High School
Plymouth, NH

Robin Parkinson
Northridge High School
Layton, UT

Donald Perry
Newport High School
Bellevue, WA

Francis Poodry
Lincoln High School
Philadelphia, PA

John Potts
Custer County District High School
Miles City, MT

Doug Rich
Fox Lane High School
Bedford, NY

John Roeder
The Calhoun School
New York, NY

Consuelo Rogers
Maryknoll Schools
Honolulu, HI

Lee Rossmaessler, Ph.D
Mott Middle College High School
Flint, MI

John Rowe
Hughes Alternative Center
Cincinnati, OH

Rebecca Bonner Sanders
South Brunswick High School
Monmouth Junction, NJ

David Schlipp
Narbonne High School
Harbor City, CA

Eric Shackelford
Notre Dame High School
Sherman Oaks, CA

Robert Sorensen
Springville-Griffith Institute and
Central School
Springville, NY

Teresa Stalions
Crittenden County High School
Marion, KY

Roberta Tanner
Loveland High School
Loveland, CO

Anthony Umelo
Anacostia Sr. High School
Washington, D.C.

Judy Vondruska
Mitchell High School
Mitchell, SD

Deborah Waldron
Yorktown High School
Arlington, VA

Ken Wester
The Mississippi School for
Mathematics and Science
Columbus, MS

Susan Willis
Conroe High School
Conroe, TX

Meeting Active Physics for the First Time

Welcome! A Five-Minute Introduction

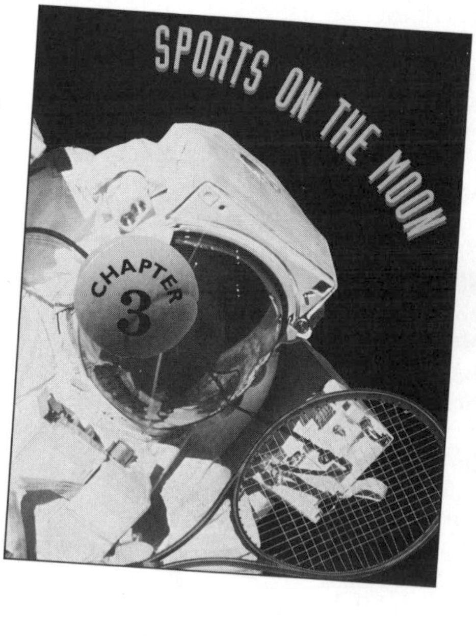

Active Physics is a different species of physics course. It has the mechanics, optics, and electricity you anticipate, but not where you expect to find them. In a traditional physics course, we teach forces in the fall, waves in the winter, and solenoids in the spring. In *Active Physics*, students are introduced to physics concepts on a need-to-know basis as they explore issues in Communication, Home, Medicine, Predictions, Sports, and Transportation.

Every chapter is independent of any other chapter. You can begin the year with any one of three chapters in any one of the six thematic units. As an example, let's start the year with Chapter 3 of the Sports unit.

On Day One, students are introduced to the chapter challenge. NASA, recognizing that residents of a future moon colony will need physical exercise, has commissioned our physics class to develop, adapt, or create a sport for the moon.

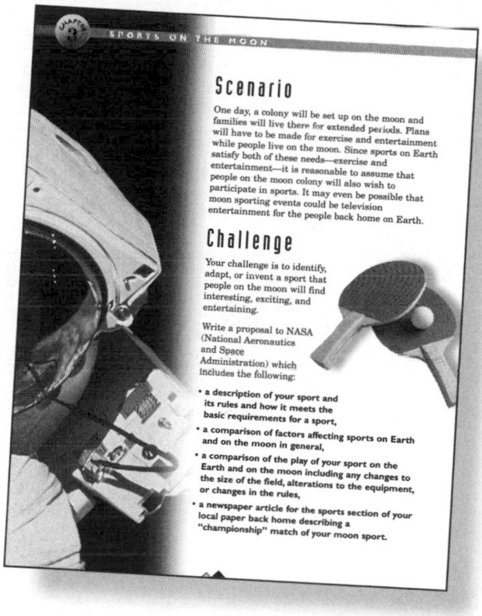

SPORTS ON THE MOON

Scenario

One day, a colony will be set up on the moon and families will live there for extended periods. Plans will have to be made for exercise and entertainment while people live on the moon. Since sports on Earth satisfy both of these needs—exercise and entertainment—it is reasonable to assume that people on the moon colony will also wish to participate in sports. It may even be possible that moon sporting events could be television entertainment for the people back home on Earth.

Challenge

Your challenge is to identify, adapt, or invent a sport that people on the moon will find interesting, exciting, and entertaining.

Write a proposal to NASA (National Aeronautics and Space Administration) which includes the following:

- **a description of your sport and its rules and how it meets the basic requirements for a sport,**
- **a comparison of factors affecting sports on Earth and on the moon in general,**
- **a comparison of the play of your sport on the Earth and on the moon including any changes to the size of the field, alterations to the equipment, or changes in the rules,**
- **a newspaper article for the sports section of your local paper back home describing a "championship" match of your moon sport.**

Our proposal to NASA will have to include the following:

a) a description of a sport and its rules;

b) a comparison of factors affecting sports on Earth and the moon in general;

c) a comparison of play of the sport on Earth and the moon including any changes to field, rules, or equipment;

d) a newspaper article for the people back 'home' describing a championship match of the moon sport.

How can students get started? How can students complete such a challenge without the requisite physics knowledge? Before the chapter activities begin, a discussion takes place about the criteria for success. The class discusses what is expected in an excellent proposal. How will this proposal be graded? For instance, the rubric for grading will describe whether "a comparison of factors affecting sports on Earth and the moon" implies two factors or four factors and whether an equation or graph or description should be a part of the comparison. Similarly, do the factors and newspaper article carry equal weight, or does one have a greater impact on the final grade? Students will have a sense of what is required for an excellent proposal before they begin. This will be revisited before work on the project begins.

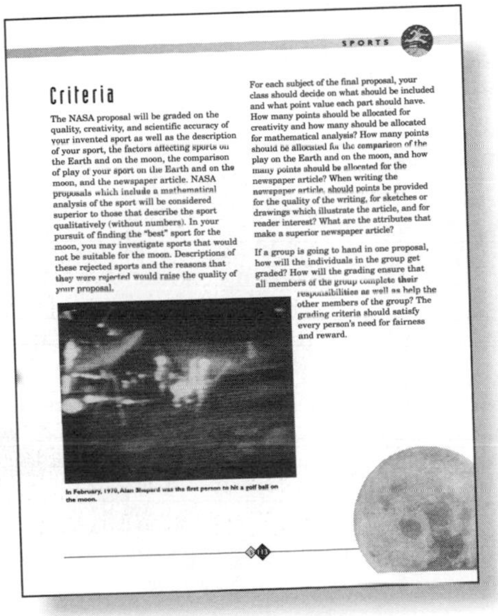

SPORTS

Criteria

The NASA proposal will be graded on the quality, creativity, and scientific accuracy of your invented sport as well as the description of your sport, the factors affecting sports on the Earth and on the moon, the comparison of play of your sport on the Earth and on the moon, and the newspaper article. NASA proposals which include a mathematical analysis of the sport will be considered superior to those that describe the sport qualitatively (without numbers). In your pursuit of finding the "best" sport for the moon, you may investigate sports that would not be suitable for the moon. Descriptions of these rejected sports and the reasons that they were rejected would raise the quality of your proposal.

For each subject of the final proposal, your class should decide on what should be included and what point value each part should have. How many points should be allocated for creativity and how many should be allocated for mathematical analysis? How many points should be allocated for the comparison of the play on the Earth and on the moon, and how many points should be allocated for the newspaper article? When writing the newspaper article, should points be provided for the quality of the writing, for sketches or drawings which illustrate the article, and for reader interest? What are the attributes that make a superior newspaper article?

If a group is going to hand in one proposal, how will the individuals in the group get graded? How will the grading ensure that all members of the group complete their responsibilities as well as help the other members of the group? The grading criteria should satisfy every person's need for fairness and reward.

In February, 1970, Alan Shepard was the first person to hit a golf ball on the moon.

113

Day Two begins with the first of nine activities. Each successive day begins with another activity. *Active Physics* is an activity-based curriculum. Let's look at Activity Seven: **Friction on the Moon**.

The activity begins by mentioning, "The Lunar Rover proved that there is enough frictional force on the moon to operate a passenger-carrying wheeled vehicle." The students are then asked, "How do frictional forces on Earth and the moon compare?"

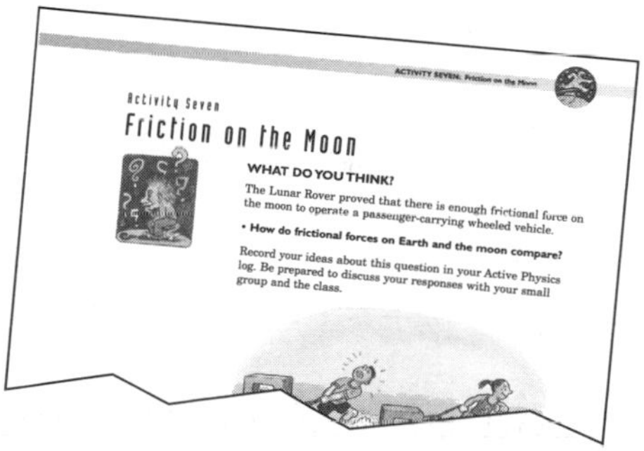

ACTIVITY SEVEN: Friction on the Moon

Activity Seven

Friction on the Moon

WHAT DO YOU THINK?

The Lunar Rover proved that there is enough frictional force on the moon to operate a passenger-carrying wheeled vehicle.

- **How do frictional forces on Earth and the moon compare?**

Record your ideas about this question in your Active Physics log. Be prepared to discuss your responses with your small group and the class.

This **What Do You Think?** question is intended to find out what students know about friction—to get into the 'friction part' of their brains. Formally, we say that this question is to elicit the student's prior understanding and is part of the constructivist approach. Students write a response for one minute and discuss for another two minutes. But we don't reach closure. The question opens the conversation.

Students then begin the **For You To Do** activity.

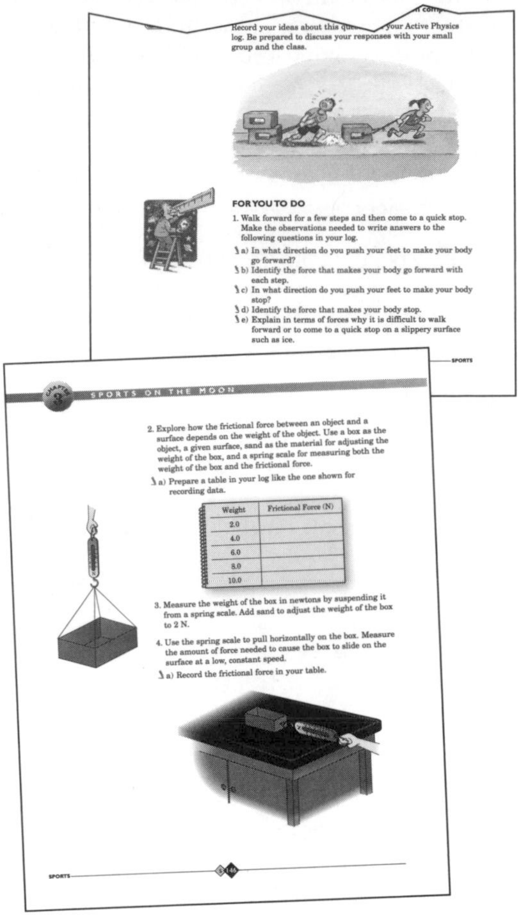
Record your ideas about this question in your Active Physics log. Be prepared to discuss your responses with your small group and the class.

FOR YOU TO DO

1. Walk forward for a few steps and then come to a quick stop. Make the observations needed to write answers to the following questions in your log.
   a) In what direction do you push your feet to make your body go forward?
   b) Identify the force that makes your body go forward with each step.
   c) In what direction do you push your feet to make your body stop?
   d) Identify the force that makes your body stop.
   e) Explain in terms of forces why it is difficult to walk forward or to come to a quick stop on a slippery surface such as ice.

SPORTS ON THE MOON

2. Explore how the frictional force between an object and a surface depends on the weight of the object. Use a box as the object, a given surface, sand as the material for adjusting the weight of the box, and a spring scale for measuring both the weight of the box and the frictional force.
   a) Prepare a table in your log like the one shown for recording data.

Weight	Frictional Force (N)
2.0	
4.0	
6.0	
8.0	
10.0	

3. Measure the weight of the box in newtons by suspending it from a spring scale. Add sand to adjust the weight of the box to 2 N.
4. Use the spring scale to pull horizontally on the box. Measure the amount of force needed to cause the box to slide on the surface at a low, constant speed.
   a) Record the frictional force in your table.

SPORTS 148

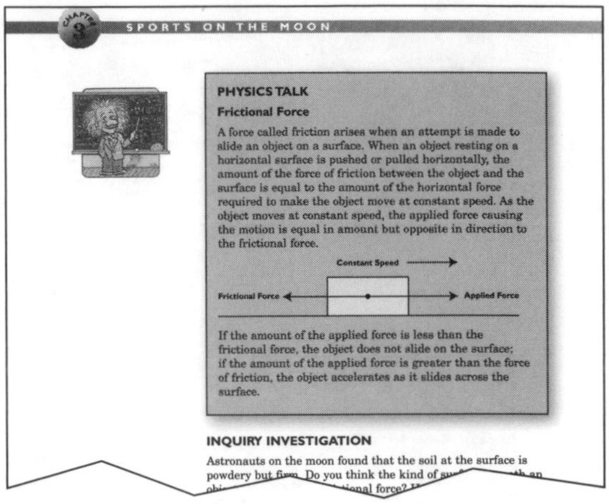
SPORTS ON THE MOON

PHYSICS TALK

Frictional Force

A force called friction arises when an attempt is made to slide an object on a surface. When an object resting on a horizontal surface is pushed or pulled horizontally, the amount of the force of friction between the object and the surface is equal to the amount of the horizontal force required to make the object move at constant speed. As the object moves at constant speed, the applied force causing the motion is equal in amount but opposite in direction to the frictional force.

If the amount of the applied force is less than the frictional force, the object does not slide on the surface; if the amount of the applied force is greater than the force of friction, the object accelerates as it slides across the surface.

INQUIRY INVESTIGATION

Astronauts on the moon found that the soil at the surface is powdery but firm. Do you think the kind of surface beneath an ...

An **Inquiry Investigation** is presented for specific students or classes who wish to go further independently. In this case, they can investigate the effect of friction of different surfaces.

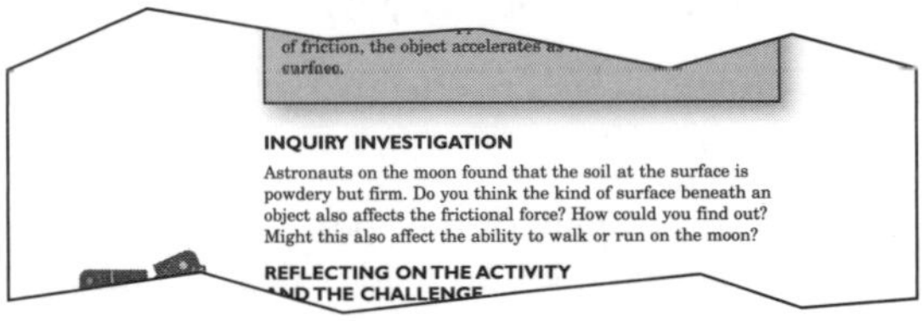
of friction, the object accelerates as it slides across the surface.

INQUIRY INVESTIGATION

Astronauts on the moon found that the soil at the surface is powdery but firm. Do you think the kind of surface beneath an object also affects the frictional force? How could you find out? Might this also affect the ability to walk or run on the moon?

REFLECTING ON THE ACTIVITY AND THE CHALLENGE

A **Reflecting On The Activity And The Challenge** relates the activity to the larger challenge of developing the moon sport.

In this activity, students weigh a box with a spring scale and measure the force required to pull it across a table at constant speed. By adding sand to the box, they take repeated measurements of weight and frictional force. A graph then shows them that the frictional force is directly proportional to the weight—more weight, more friction. An earlier activity convinced students that all objects weigh less on the moon. And so they can now conclude that friction must be less on the moon.

A **Physics Talk** summarizes the physics principle and includes equations where appropriate.

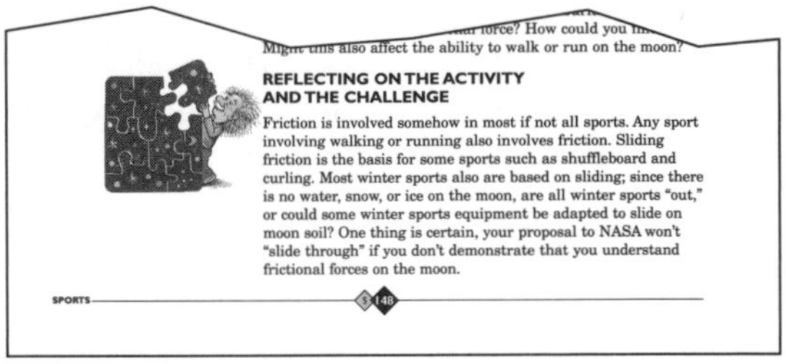
Might this also affect the ability to walk or run on the moon?

REFLECTING ON THE ACTIVITY AND THE CHALLENGE

Friction is involved somehow in most if not all sports. Any sport involving walking or running also involves friction. Sliding friction is the basis for some sports such as shuffleboard and curling. Most winter sports also are based on sliding; since there is no water, snow, or ice on the moon, are all winter sports "out," or could some winter sports equipment be adapted to slide on moon soil? One thing is certain, your proposal to NASA won't "slide through" if you don't demonstrate that you understand frictional forces on the moon.

SPORTS 148

"Friction is involved somehow in most if not all sports. . . One thing is certain, your proposal to NASA won't 'slide through' if you don't demonstrate that you understand frictional forces on the moon." Students have been given another piece of the jigsaw puzzle. How is the sport that they are developing going to be modified because of the decreased friction on the moon?

The activity concludes with a **Physics To Go** homework assignment.

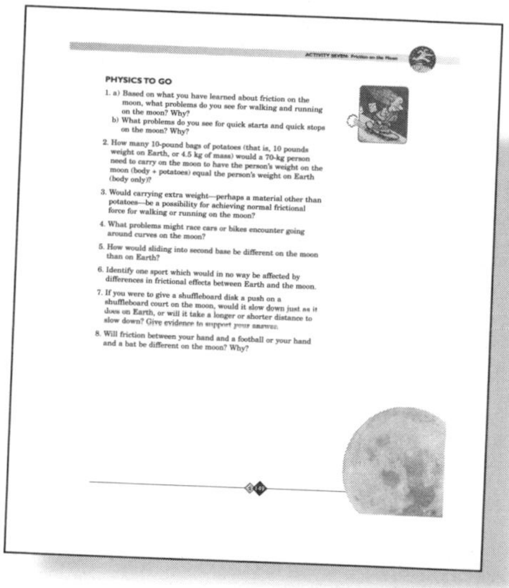
ACTIVITY SEVEN: Friction on the Moon

PHYSICS TO GO

1. a) Based on what you have learned about friction on the moon, what problems do you see for walking and running on the moon? Why?
   b) What problems do you see for quick starts and quick stops on the moon? Why?
2. How many 10-pound bags of potatoes (that is, 10 pounds weight on Earth, or 4.5 kg of mass) would a 70-kg person need to carry on the moon to have the person's weight on the moon (body + potatoes) equal the person's weight on Earth (body only)?
3. Would carrying extra weight—perhaps a material other than potatoes—be a possibility for achieving normal frictional force for walking or running on the moon?
4. What problems might race cars or bikes encounter going around curves on the moon?
5. How would sliding into second base be different on the moon than on Earth?
6. Identify one sport which would in no way be affected by differences in frictional effects between Earth and the moon.
7. If you were to give a shuffleboard disk a push on a shuffleboard court on the moon, would it slow down just as it does on Earth, or will it take a longer or shorter distance to slow down? Give evidence to support your answer.
8. Will friction between your hand and a football or your hand and a bat be different on the moon? Why?

The chapter concludes with a **Physics At Work** profile where students are introduced to someone whose job is related to the chapter challenge. In this chapter, astronaut Linda Godwin describes adapting to zero gravity during flight and space walks.

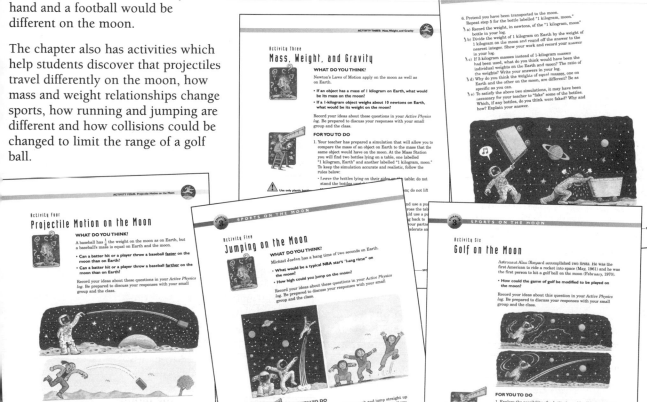

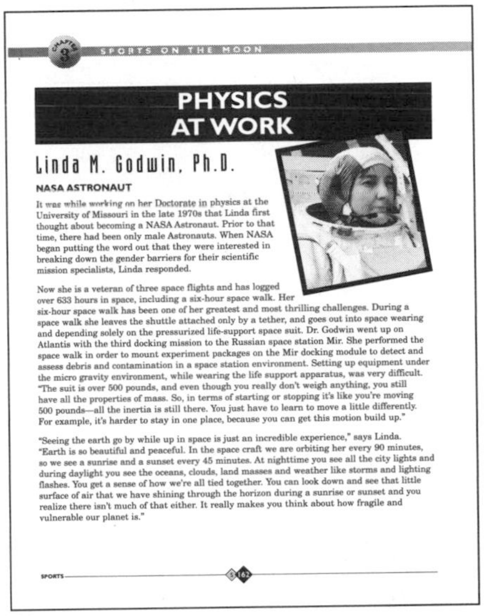
SPORTS ON THE MOON

PHYSICS AT WORK

Linda M. Godwin, Ph.D.

NASA ASTRONAUT

It was while working on her Doctorate in physics at the University of Missouri in the late 1970s that Linda first thought about becoming a NASA Astronaut. Prior to that time, there had been only male Astronauts. When NASA began putting the word out that they were interested in breaking down the gender barriers for their scientific mission specialists, Linda responded.

Now she is a veteran of three space flights and has logged over 633 hours in space, including a six-hour space walk. Her six-hour space walk has been one of her greatest and most thrilling challenges. During a space walk she leaves the shuttle attached only by a tether, and goes out into space wearing and depending solely on the pressurized life-support space suit. Dr. Godwin went up on Atlantis with the third docking mission to the Russian space station Mir. She performed the space walk in order to mount experiment packages on the Mir docking module to detect and assess debris and contamination in a space station environment. Setting up equipment under the micro gravity environment, while wearing the life support apparatus, was very difficult. "The suit is over 500 pounds, and even though you really don't weigh anything, you still have all the properties of mass. So, in terms of starting or stopping it's like you're moving 500 pounds—all the inertia is still there. You just have to learn to move a little differently. For example, it's harder to stay in one place, because you can get this motion build up."

"Seeing the earth go by while up in space is just an incredible experience," says Linda. "Earth is so beautiful and peaceful. In the space craft we are orbiting her every 90 minutes, so we see a sunrise and a sunset every 45 minutes. At nighttime you see all the city lights and during daylight you see the oceans, clouds, land masses and weather like storms and lighting flashes. You get a sense of how we're all tied together. You can look down and see that little surface of air that we have shining through the horizon during a sunrise or sunset and you realize there isn't much of that either. It really makes you think about how fragile and vulnerable our planet is."

SPORTS 162

Here students are asked about the specifics of the activity and required to explain how sliding into second base would be different on the moon; how shuffleboard play would be different on the moon; and whether the friction between your hand and a football would be different on the moon.

The chapter also has activities which help students discover that projectiles travel differently on the moon, how mass and weight relationships change sports, how running and jumping are different and how collisions could be changed to limit the range of a golf ball.

ACTIVITY THREE: Mass, Weight, and Gravity

Activity Three

Mass, Weight, and Gravity

WHAT DO YOU THINK?

Newton's Laws of Motion apply on the moon as well as on Earth.

- If an object has a mass of 1 kilogram on Earth, what would be its mass on the moon?
- If a 1-kilogram object weighs about 10 newtons on Earth, what would be its weight on the moon?

Record your ideas about these questions in your *Active Physics log*. Be prepared to discuss your responses with your small group and the class.

FOR YOU TO DO

1. Your teacher has prepared a simulation that will allow you to compare the mass of an object on Earth to the mass that the same object would have on the moon. At the Mass Station you will find two bottles lying on a table, one labelled "1 kilogram, Earth" and another labelled "1 kilogram, moon." To keep the simulation accurate and realistic, follow the rules below:

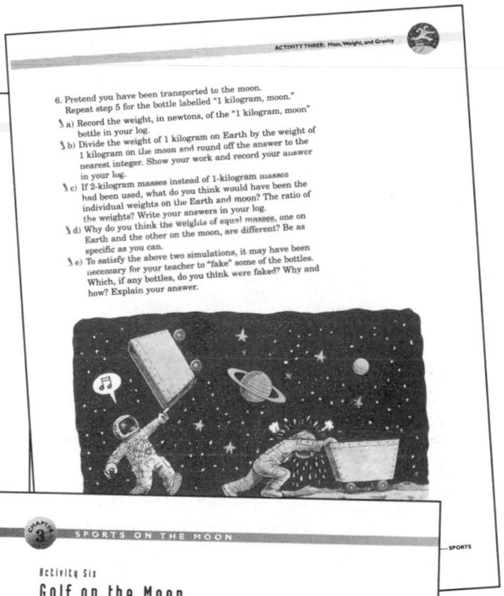
ACTIVITY THREE: Mass, Weight, and Gravity

6. Pretend you have been transported to the moon. Repeat step 5 for the bottle labelled "1 kilogram, moon."
   a) Record the weight, in newtons, of the "1 kilogram, moon" bottle in your log.
   b) Divide the weight of 1 kilogram on Earth by the weight of 1 kilogram on the moon and round off the answer to the nearest integer. Show your work and record your answer in your log.
   c) If 2-kilogram masses instead of 1-kilogram masses had been used, what do you think would have been the individual weights on the Earth and moon? The ratio of the weights? Write your answers in your log.
   d) Why do you think the weights of equal masses, one on Earth and the other on the moon, are different? Be as specific as you can.
   e) To satisfy the above two simulations, it may have been necessary for your teacher to "fake" some of the bottles. Which, if any bottles, do you think were faked? Why and how? Explain your answer.

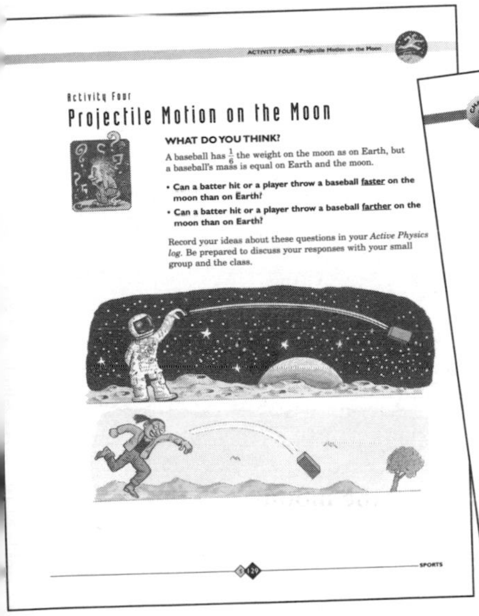
ACTIVITY FOUR: Projectile Motion on the Moon

Activity Four

Projectile Motion on the Moon

WHAT DO YOU THINK?

A baseball has $\frac{1}{6}$ the weight on the moon as on Earth, but a baseball's mass is equal on Earth and the moon.

- Can a batter hit or a player throw a baseball faster on the moon than on Earth?
- Can a batter hit or a player throw a baseball farther on the moon than on Earth?

Record your ideas about these questions in your *Active Physics log*. Be prepared to discuss your responses with your small group and the class.

SPORTS

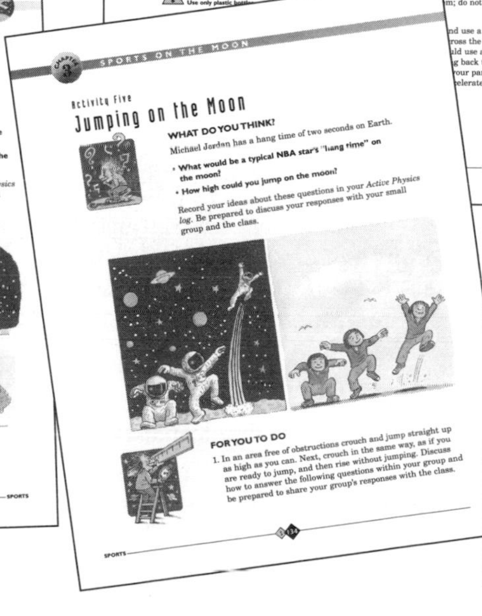
SPORTS ON THE MOON

Activity Five

Jumping on the Moon

WHAT DO YOU THINK?

Michael Jordan has a hang time of two seconds on Earth.

- What would be a typical NBA star's "hang time" on the moon?
- How high could you jump on the moon?

Record your ideas about these questions in your *Active Physics log*. Be prepared to discuss your responses with your small group and the class.

FOR YOU TO DO

1. In an area free of obstructions crouch and jump straight up as high as you can. Next, crouch in the same way, as if you are ready to jump, and then rise without jumping. Discuss how to answer the following questions within your group and be prepared to share your group's responses with the class.

SPORTS

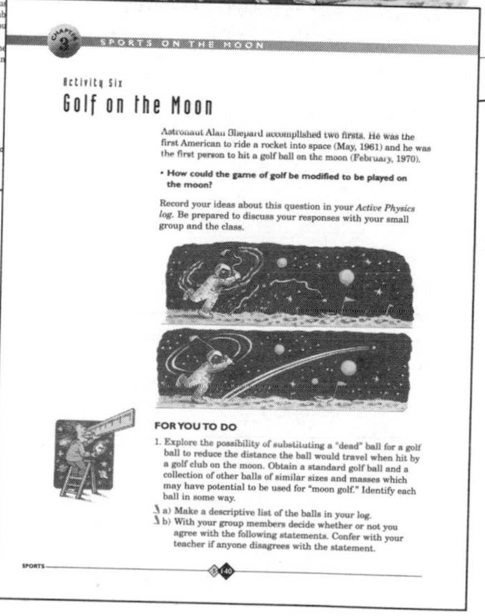
SPORTS ON THE MOON

Activity Six

Golf on the Moon

Astronaut Alan Shepard accomplished two firsts. He was the first American to ride a rocket into space (May, 1961) and he was the first person to hit a golf ball on the moon (February, 1970).

- How could the game of golf be modified to be played on the moon?

Record your ideas about this question in your *Active Physics log*. Be prepared to discuss your responses with your small group and the class.

FOR YOU TO DO

1. Explore the possibility of substituting a "dead" ball for a golf ball to reduce the distance the ball would travel when hit by a golf club on the moon. Obtain a standard golf ball and a collection of other balls of similar sizes and masses which may have potential to be used for "moon golf." Identify each ball in some way.
   a) Make a descriptive list of the balls in your log.
   b) With your group members decide whether or not you agree with the following statements. Confer with your teacher if anyone disagrees with the statement.

SPORTS

With the results of all of the activities before them, student teams now complete the challenge. They put the jigsaw pieces of friction, trajectories, collisions, running and jumping all together to construct their sport. Each team creates their own sport, reflecting the interests and creativity of the team members. The teams share their work with the rest of the class and the Sports chapter concludes.

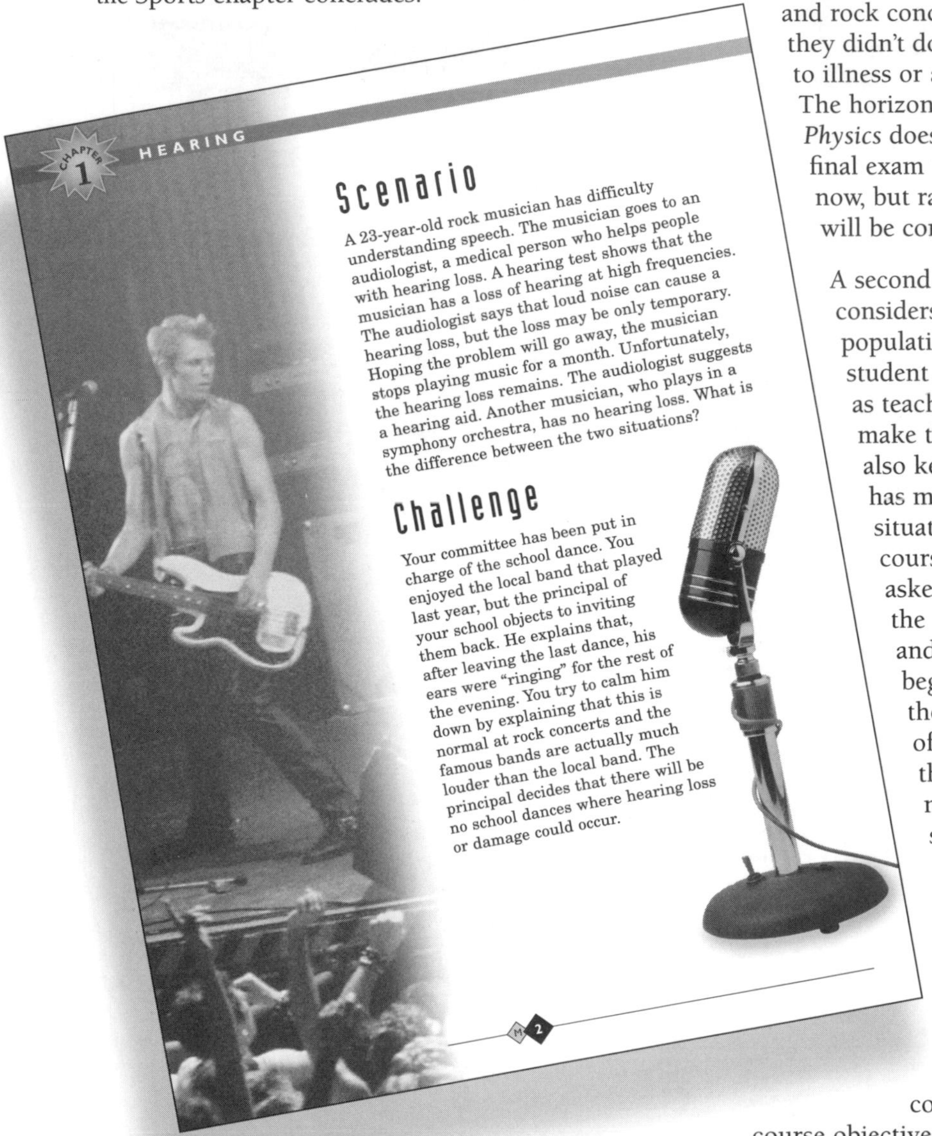
CHAPTER 1
HEARING
Scenario
A 23-year-old rock musician has difficulty understanding speech. The musician goes to an audiologist, a medical person who helps people with hearing loss. A hearing test shows that the musician has a loss of hearing at high frequencies. The audiologist says that loud noise can cause a hearing loss, but the loss may be only temporary. Hoping the problem will go away, the musician stops playing music for a month. Unfortunately, the hearing loss remains. The audiologist suggests a hearing aid. Another musician, who plays in a symphony orchestra, has no hearing loss. What is the difference between the two situations?
Challenge
Your committee has been put in charge of the school dance. You enjoyed the local band that played last year, but the principal of your school objects to inviting them back. He explains that, after leaving the last dance, his ears were "ringing" for the rest of the evening. You try to calm him down by explaining that this is normal at rock concerts and the famous bands are actually much louder than the local band. The principal decides that there will be no school dances where hearing loss or damage could occur.
M 2

One strength of *Active Physics* is the independence of the chapters. After finishing Sports, we begin anew. Let's choose Chapter 1 of Medicine as the next adventure. In this chapter, students are challenged to write a position paper to the school principal convincing him that a school dance can be held and guaranteeing that nobody's hearing will be damaged. It is for this purpose that students will learn about sound travel, decibels and frequency response, or human hearing. Or perhaps Chapter 2 of Transportation should be initiated. In this chapter, students are required to design and build an improved safety device for cars or bicycles. And it is in this context that students will learn about impulse, momentum, forces, and acceleration.

The beginning of a new chapter has two distinct advantages. For the students who did not do well on the Sports unit, they have a fresh start. Maybe they didn't do well because Sports didn't interest them and rock concerts or car collisions will. Or maybe they didn't do well because they missed school due to illness or a suspension. It's time to start over. The horizon for success is only four weeks. *Active Physics* does not ask students to worry about a final exam that will be given eight months from now, but rather to focus on one challenge that will be completed within a month.

A second advantage is apparent when one considers the transient nature of our school populations. In most courses, when that new student arrives in November, we do our best as teachers to greet the student and help them make the transition to the class. But we are also keenly aware of how much the student has missed and how difficult the learning situation really is. In an *Active Physics* course, that new student in November is asked to hang in for a week, get used to the class, work with the group over there and is reassured that we will soon be beginning a brand new chapter where they will be full participants irrespective of their late arrival. This removes one of the large hurdles which some students must face as they transfer programs, schools or communities.

Active Physics offers 18 chapters: six units with three chapters each. In a one-year physics or physical science course, students can be expected to complete 12 of the chapters at the most. This provides the teacher and students with a wide selection of content that meets local interests and course objectives.

Students in *Active Physics* never ask, "Why am I learning this?" Teachers of *Active Physics* never have to respond, "Because one day it will be useful to you." *Active Physics* is relevant physics. Students know that they have a challenge and they know that the activities will help them to be successful.

Please take a more careful, leisurely look at *Active Physics*. It's probably just what you and your students have been looking for.

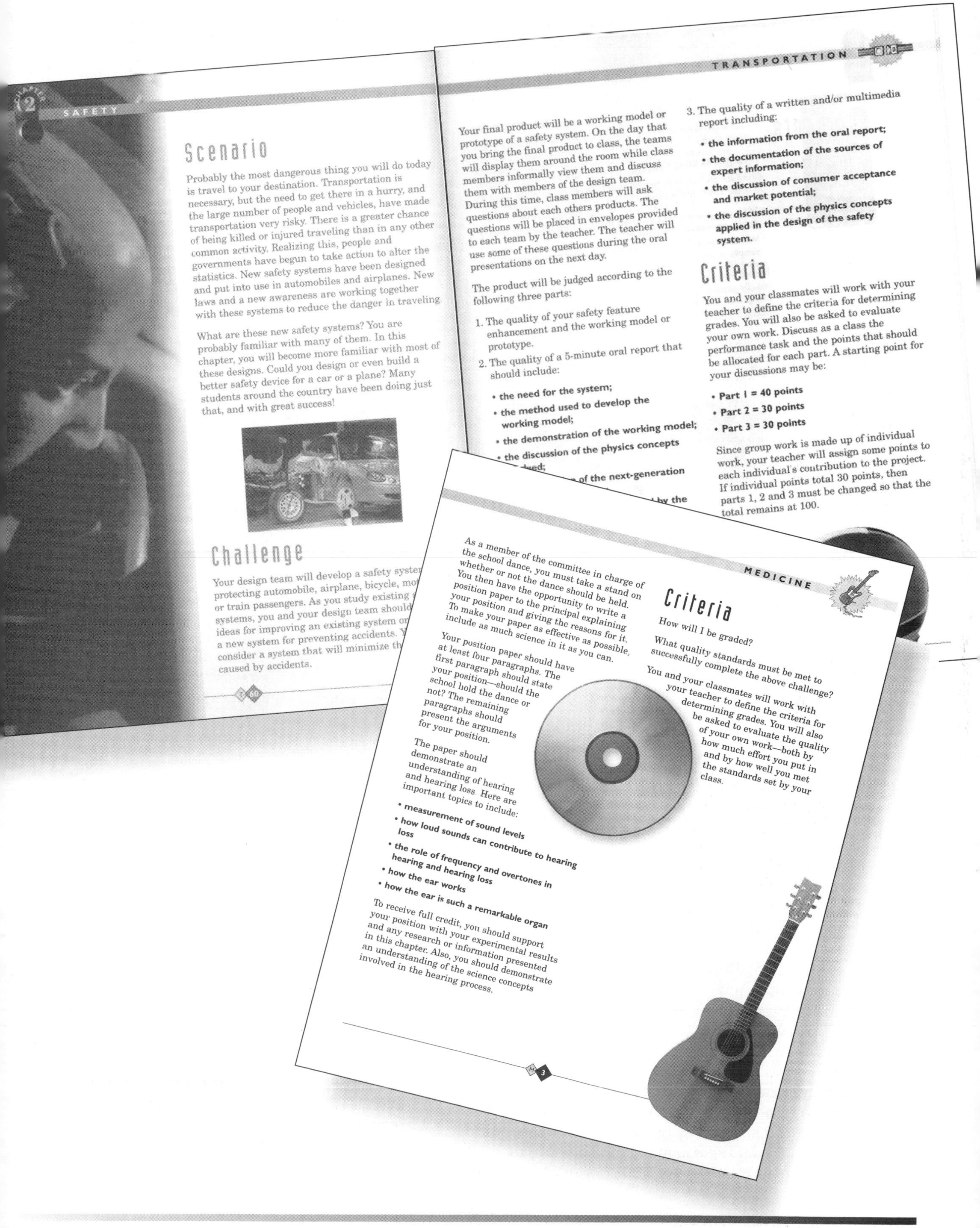

CHAPTER 2 SAFETY

Scenario

Probably the most dangerous thing you will do today is travel to your destination. Transportation is necessary, but the need to get there in a hurry, and the large number of people and vehicles, have made transportation very risky. There is a greater chance of being killed or injured traveling than in any other common activity. Realizing this, people and governments have begun to take action to alter the statistics. New safety systems have been designed and put into use in automobiles and airplanes. New laws and a new awareness are working together with these systems to reduce the danger in traveling.

What are these new safety systems? You are probably familiar with many of them. In this chapter, you will become more familiar with most of these designs. Could you design or even build a better safety device for a car or a plane? Many students around the country have been doing just that, and with great success!

Challenge

Your design team will develop a safety syste[m] protecting automobile, airplane, bicycle, mo[...] or train passengers. As you study existing [...] systems, you and your design team should [...] ideas for improving an existing system or [...] a new system for preventing accidents. [...] consider a system that will minimize th[...] caused by accidents.

T 60

TRANSPORTATION

Your final product will be a working model or prototype of a safety system. On the day that you bring the final product to class, the teams will display them around the room while class members informally view them and discuss them with members of the design team. During this time, class members will ask questions about each others products. The questions will be placed in envelopes provided to each team by the teacher. The teacher will use some of these questions during the oral presentations on the next day.

The product will be judged according to the following three parts:

1. The quality of your safety feature enhancement and the working model or prototype.
2. The quality of a 5-minute oral report that should include:
   - **the need for the system;**
   - **the method used to develop the working model;**
   - **the demonstration of the working model;**
   - **the discussion of the physics concepts [inv]olved;**
   - **[...] of the next-generation**
   - **[...] by the**
3. The quality of a written and/or multimedia report including:
   - **the information from the oral report;**
   - **the documentation of the sources of expert information;**
   - **the discussion of consumer acceptance and market potential;**
   - **the discussion of the physics concepts applied in the design of the safety system.**

Criteria

You and your classmates will work with your teacher to define the criteria for determining grades. You will also be asked to evaluate your own work. Discuss as a class the performance task and the points that should be allocated for each part. A starting point for your discussions may be:

- **Part 1 = 40 points**
- **Part 2 = 30 points**
- **Part 3 = 30 points**

Since group work is made up of individual work, your teacher will assign some points to each individual's contribution to the project. If individual points total 30 points, then parts 1, 2 and 3 must be changed so that the total remains at 100.

MEDICINE

As a member of the committee in charge of the school dance, you must take a stand on whether or not the dance should be held. You then have the opportunity to write a position paper to the principal explaining your position and giving the reasons for it. To make your paper as effective as possible, include as much science in it as you can.

Your position paper should have at least four paragraphs. The first paragraph should state your position—should the school hold the dance or not? The remaining paragraphs should present the arguments for your position.

The paper should demonstrate an understanding of hearing and hearing loss. Here are important topics to include:

- **measurement of sound levels**
- **how loud sounds can contribute to hearing loss**
- **the role of frequency and overtones in hearing and hearing loss**
- **how the ear works**
- **how the ear is such a remarkable organ**

To receive full credit, you should support your position with your experimental results and any research or information presented in this chapter. Also, you should demonstrate an understanding of the science concepts involved in the hearing process.

Criteria

How will I be graded?

What quality standards must be met to successfully complete the above challenge?

You and your classmates will work with your teacher to define the criteria for determining grades. You will also be asked to evaluate the quality of your own work—both by how much effort you put in and by how well you met the standards set by your class.

M 3

Features of Active Physics

1. Scenario

SPORTS ON THE MOON

Scenario

One day, a colony will be set up on the moon and families will live there for extended periods. Plans will have to be made for exercise and entertainment while people live on the moon. Since sports on Earth satisfy both of these needs—exercise and entertainment—it is reasonable to assume that people on the moon colony will also wish to participate in sports. It may even be possible that moon sporting events could be television entertainment for the people back home on Earth.

Challenge

Your challenge is to identify, adapt, or invent a sport that people on the moon will find interesting, exciting, and entertaining.

Write a proposal to NASA (National Aeronautics and Space Administration) which includes the following:

- **a description of your sport and its rules and how it meets the basic requirements for a sport,**
- **a comparison of factors affecting sports on Earth and on the moon in general,**
- **a comparison of the play of your sport on the Earth and on the moon including any changes to the size of the field, alterations to the equipment, or changes in the rules,**
- **a newspaper article for the sports section of your local paper back home describing a "championship" match of your moon sport.**

Each *Active Physics* chapter opens with an engaging scenario. Students from diverse backgrounds and localities have been interviewed in order to find situations which are not only realistic but meaningful to the high school population. The scenarios (only a paragraph or two in length) set the stage for the chapter challenge which immediately follows. Many teachers choose to read the scenario aloud to the class as a way of introducing the new chapter.

2. Challenge

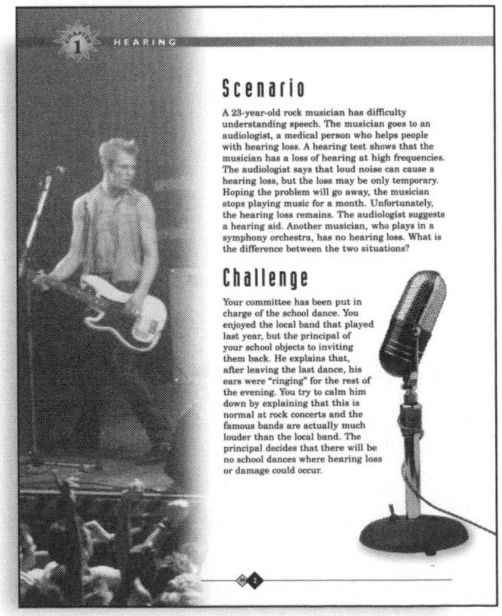
HEARING

Scenario

A 23-year-old rock musician has difficulty understanding speech. The musician goes to an audiologist, a medical person who helps people with hearing loss. A hearing test shows that the musician has a loss of hearing at high frequencies. The audiologist says that loud noise can cause a hearing loss, but the loss may be only temporary. Hoping the problem will go away, the musician stops playing music for a month. Unfortunately, the hearing loss remains. The audiologist suggests a hearing aid. Another musician, who plays in a symphony orchestra, has no hearing loss. What is the difference between the two situations?

Challenge

Your committee has been put in charge of the school dance. You enjoyed the local band that played last year, but the principal of your school objects to inviting them back. He explains that, after leaving the last dance, his ears were "ringing" for the rest of the evening. You try to calm him down by explaining that this is normal at rock concerts and the famous bands are actually much louder than the local band. The principal decides that there will be no school dances where hearing loss or damage could occur.

The chapter challenge is the heart and soul of *Active Physics*. It provides a purpose for all of the work that will follow. The challenges provide the rationale for learning. One of the common complaints teachers hear from students is, "Why am I learning this?" In *Active Physics*, no students raise this criticism. Similarly, no teacher has to answer, "Because one day it will be useful to you." The complaint is avoided because on Day One of the chapter students are presented with a challenge that, in essence, becomes their job for the next few weeks.

In Medicine, Chapter 1, students are challenged with a situation where the school principal is not going to permit a school dance because his ears were ringing after the last band performed. Students must write a position paper either agreeing with the principal or convincing him that nobody's hearing will be damaged if another dance is held. This is why the students then learn about decibels, frequencies and human response to sound.

In Transportation, Chapter 2, students are challenged to design and build an improved safety device for an automobile. The study of momentum, forces and Newton's Laws will be integral to their understanding of the required features in a safety device.

In Home, Chapter 2, students must create an appliance package that can be used in developing nations. The appliance package is limited by the wind generator available to the households. Students must also supply a rationale for how each suggested appliance will enhance the well-being of the family using it. This requires students to be able to differentiate between power and energy. It also provides a basis for students to reflect on quality of life issues in parts of the globe that they learn about in their social studies classes.

The beauty of the challenges lies in the variety of tasks and opportunities for students of different talents and skills to excel. Students who express themselves artistically will have an opportunity to shine in some challenges, while the student who can design and build may be the group leader in another challenge. Some challenges have a major component devoted to writing while others require oral or visual presentations. All challenges require the demonstration of solid physics understanding.

The challenges are not contrived situations for high school students. Professional engineers also design and build improved safety devices. Medical writers and illustrators design posters and pamphlets. The challenge in Chapter 3 of Sports requires students to create, invent, or adapt a sport that can be played on the moon. This challenge has been successfully completed by 9th grade high school students, 12th grade *Active Physics* students, and by NASA engineers. The expectation may be different for each of these audiences, but the challenge is consistent.

3. Criteria

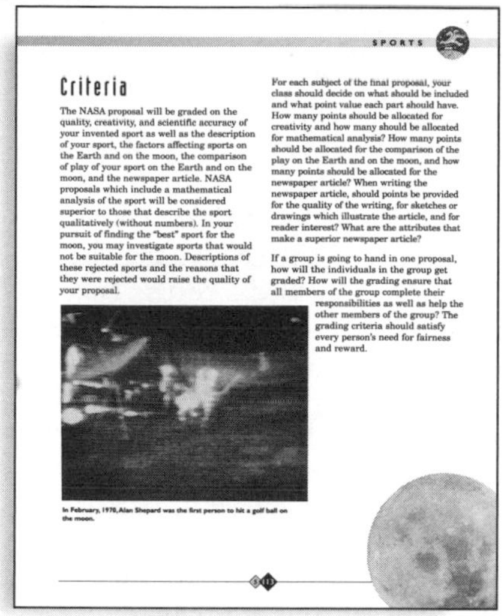

SPORTS

Criteria

The NASA proposal will be graded on the quality, creativity, and scientific accuracy of your invented sport as well as the description of your sport, the factors affecting sports on the Earth and on the moon, the comparison of play of your sport on the Earth and on the moon, and the newspaper article. NASA proposals which include a mathematical analysis of the sport will be considered superior to those that describe the sport qualitatively (without numbers). In your pursuit of finding the "best" sport for the moon, you may investigate sports that would not be suitable for the moon. Descriptions of these rejected sports and the reasons that they were rejected would raise the quality of your proposal.

For each subject of the final proposal, your class should decide on what should be included and what point value each part should have. How many points should be allocated for creativity and how many should be allocated for mathematical analysis? How many points should be allocated for the comparison of the play on the Earth and on the moon, and how many points should be allocated for the newspaper article? When writing the newspaper article, should points be provided for the quality of the writing, for sketches or drawings which illustrate the article, and for reader interest? What are the attributes that make a superior newspaper article?

If a group is going to hand in one proposal, how will the individuals in the group get graded? How will the grading ensure that all members of the group complete their responsibilities as well as help the other members of the group? The grading criteria should satisfy every person's need for fairness and reward.

In February, 1970, Alan Shepard was the first person to hit a golf ball on the moon.

S 113

In creating *Active Physics*, we had thought that the generation of the challenge was good enough. Upon reflection, we soon realized that criteria for success must also be included. When students agree to the matrix by which they will be measured, the research has shown that the students will perform better and achieve more. It makes sense. In the simplest situation of cleaning a lab room, the teacher may simply state, "Please clean up the lab." The results are often a minimal cleanup. If the teacher begins by asking, "What does a clean lab room look like?" and students and teacher jointly list the attributes of a clean lab room (i.e., no paper on the floor, all beakers put away, all materials on the back of the lab tables, all power supplies unplugged and all water removed), the students respond differently and the cleanup is better. When students are asked to include physics principles in an explanation, the students should know whether the expectation is for three physics principles or five.

The discussion of grading criteria and the creation of a grading rubric is a crucial ingredient for student success. *Active Physics* requires a class discussion, after the introduction of the challenge, about the grading criteria. How much is required? What does an "A" presentation look like? Should creativity be weighed more than delivery? The criteria can be visited again at the end of the chapter, but at this point it provides a clarity to the challenge and the expectation level that the students should set for themselves.

4. What Do You Think?

ACTIVITY FOUR: How Images Are Made: Converging Lenses

Activity Four

How Images Are Made: Converging Lenses

WHAT DO YOU THINK?

A successful movie can bring in over 100 million dollars.

- **How is the image of a movie projected onto a large screen from a small piece of film?**

Record your ideas about this question in your *Active Physics log*. Be prepared to discuss your responses with your small group and your class.

MEDICINE

During the past few years much has been written about a constructivist approach to learning. Videos of Harvard graduates, in caps and gowns, show that the students are not able to explain correctly why it is colder in the winter than it is in the summer. These students have previously answered these questions correctly in 4th grade, in Middle School, and then again in High School. How else would they have gotten into Harvard? We believe that they never internalized the logic and understanding of the seasons. One reason for this problem is that they were never confronted by what they did believe, and were never adequately shown why they should give up that belief system. Certainly, it is worth writing down a "book's perfect answer" on a test to secure a good grade, but to actually believe requires a more thorough examination of competing explanations.

The best way to ascertain a student's prior understanding is through extensive interviewing. Much of the research literature in this area includes the results of these interviews. In a classroom, this one-on-one dialogue is rarely possible. The **What Do You Think?** question introduces each activity in a way in which to elicit prior understandings. It gives students an opportunity to verbalize what they think about friction, or energy, or light, before they embark on an activity. The brief discussion of the range of answers brings the student a little closer in touch with that part of his/her brain which understands friction, energy, or light. The **What Do You Think?** question is not intended to produce a correct answer or a discussion of the features of the questions. It is not intended to bring closure. The activity which follows will provide that discussion as experimental results are analyzed. The **What Do You Think?** question should take no more than a few minutes of class time. It is the lead into the physics investigation. Students should be strongly encouraged to write their responses to the questions in their logs, to ensure that they have in fact addressed their prior conceptions. After students have discussed their responses in their small groups, activate a class discussion. Ask students to volunteer other students' answers which they found interesting. This may encourage students to exchange ideas without the fear of personally giving a "wrong" answer.

5. For You To Do

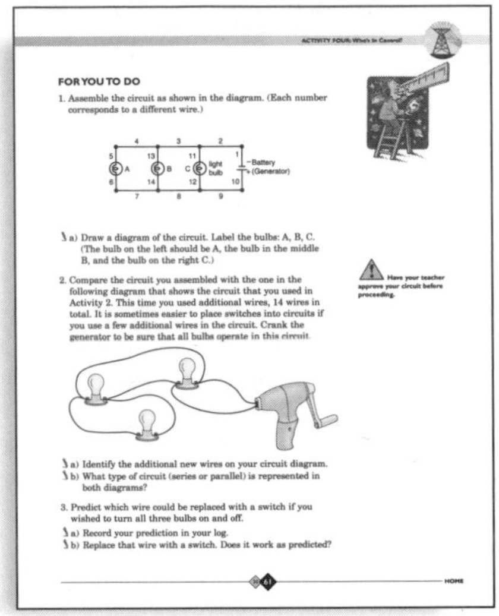
ACTIVITY FOUR: What's in Control?

FOR YOU TO DO

1. Assemble the circuit as shown in the diagram. (Each number corresponds to a different wire.)

a) Draw a diagram of the circuit. Label the bulbs: A, B, C. (The bulb on the left should be A, the bulb in the middle B, and the bulb on the right C.)

2. Compare the circuit you assembled with the one in the following diagram that shows the circuit that you used in Activity 2. This time you used additional wires, 14 wires in total. It is sometimes easier to place switches into circuits if you use a few additional wires in the circuit. Crank the generator to be sure that all bulbs operate in this circuit.

Have your teacher approve your circuit before proceeding.

a) Identify the additional new wires on your circuit diagram.
b) What type of circuit (series or parallel) is represented in both diagrams?

3. Predict which wire could be replaced with a switch if you wished to turn all three bulbs on and off.

a) Record your prediction in your log.
b) Replace that wire with a switch. Does it work as predicted?

61 HOME

Active Physics is a hands-on, minds-on curriculum. Students *do* physics; they do not *read* about doing physics. Each activity has instructions for each part of the investigation. The pencil icons are provided to remind students that data, hypotheses, or conclusions should be recorded in their log or laboratory manual.

Activities are the opportunity for students to garner the knowledge that they will need to complete the chapter challenge. Students will understand the physics principle involved because they have investigated it. In *Active Physics*, if a student is asked, "How do you know?" the response is, "Because I did an experiment!"

Recognizing that many students know how to read, but do not like reading, background information is provided within the context of the activity. Students have demonstrated that they will read when the information is required for them to continue with their exploration.

Occasionally, the activity will require the entire class to participate in a large, single demonstration simultaneously. The teacher, on other occasions, may decide that a specific activity is best done as a demonstration. This would be appropriate if there is limited equipment for that one activity, or the facilities are not available. Viewing demonstrations on an ongoing basis, though, is not what *Active Physics* is about.

There are specific **For You To Do** activities where computer spreadsheets, force transducers, or specific electronic equipment is required. Most of these activities have 'low-tech' alternatives provided in the Teacher's Edition. In the initial teaching of *Active Physics*, the low-tech alternative may be the only reasonable approach. As the course becomes a staple of the school offerings, it is hoped that funds can be set aside to improve the students' access to equipment.

Most of the **For You To Do** activities require between one and two class periods. With the present trend toward block scheduling, there are so many time structures that it is difficult to predict how *Active Physics* will best fit with your schedule. The other impact on time is the achievement and preparation level of the students. In a given activity, students may be required to complete a graph of their data. This is considered one small part of the activity. If the students have never been exposed to graphing, this could require a two-period lesson to teach the rudiments of graphing with suitable practice in interpretation. *Active Physics* is accessible to all students. The teacher is in the best position to make accommodations in time reflecting the needs of the students.

6. Physics Talk

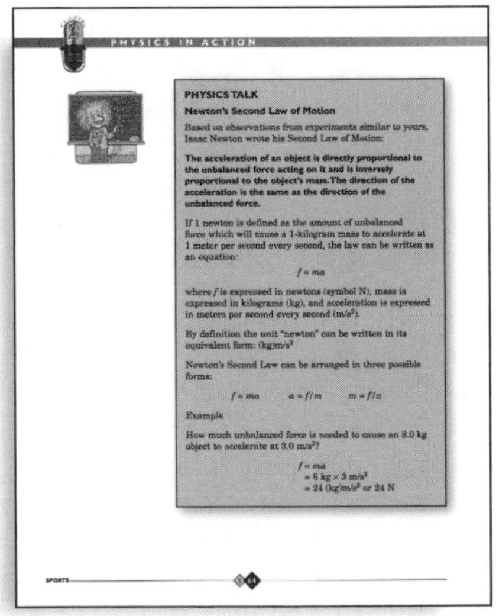
PHYSICS IN ACTION

PHYSICS TALK

Newton's Second Law of Motion

Based on observations from experiments similar to yours, Isaac Newton wrote his Second Law of Motion:

The acceleration of an object is directly proportional to the unbalanced force acting on it and is inversely proportional to the object's mass. The direction of the acceleration is the same as the direction of the unbalanced force.

If 1 newton is defined as the amount of unbalanced force which will cause a 1-kilogram mass to accelerate at 1 meter per second every second, the law can be written as an equation:

$$f = ma$$

where f is expressed in newtons (symbol N), mass is expressed in kilograms (kg), and acceleration is expressed in meters per second every second (m/s^2).

By definition the unit "newton" can be written in its equivalent form: (kg)m/s^2

Newton's Second Law can be arranged in three possible forms:

$$f = ma \qquad a = f/m \qquad m = f/a$$

Example

How much unbalanced force is needed to cause an 8.0 kg object to accelerate at 3.0 m/s^2?

$$f = ma$$
$$= 8 \text{ kg} \times 3 \text{ m/s}^2$$
$$= 24 \text{ (kg)m/s}^2 \text{ or } 24 \text{ N}$$

SPORTS 64

Equations are often the simplest, most straightforward, most concise, and clearest way of expressing physics principles. *Active Physics* limits the mathematics to the ninth grade curriculum. Students who have shied away from studying physics because of the mathematics prerequisites find that they are welcomed into *Active Physics*. **Physics Talk** is a means by which specific attention can be given to the mathematical equations. It also provides an opportunity to illustrate a problem solution or to derive a complex equation. For some students, there is a need to guide them through the algebraic manipulation which shows the equivalence of F=ma and a = F/m. Where appropriate, this manipulation is explicitly shown. Finally, sample problems required for the chapter challenge will also be in **Physics Talk**.

7. For You To Read

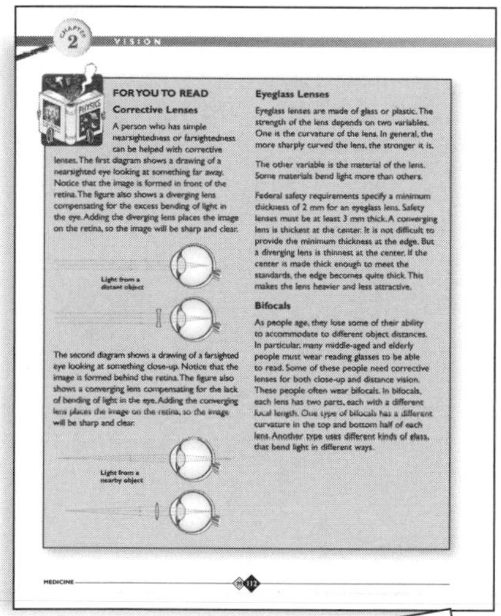

CHAPTER 2 VISION

FOR YOU TO READ

Corrective Lenses

A person who has simple nearsightedness or farsightedness can be helped with corrective lenses. The first diagram shows a drawing of a nearsighted eye looking at something far away. Notice that the image is formed in front of the retina. The figure also shows a diverging lens compensating for the excess bending of light in the eye. Adding the diverging lens places the image on the retina, so the image will be sharp and clear.

Light from a distant object

The second diagram shows a drawing of a farsighted eye looking at something close-up. Notice that the image is formed behind the retina. The figure also shows a converging lens compensating for the lack of bending of light in the eye. Adding the converging lens places the image on the retina, so the image will be sharp and clear.

Light from a nearby object

Eyeglass Lenses

Eyeglass lenses are made of glass or plastic. The strength of the lens depends on two variables. One is the curvature of the lens. In general, the more sharply curved the lens, the stronger it is.

The other variable is the material of the lens. Some materials bend light more than others.

Federal safety requirements specify a minimum thickness of 2 mm for an eyeglass lens. Safety lenses must be at least 3 mm thick. A converging lens is thickest at the center. It is not difficult to provide the minimum thickness at the edge. But a diverging lens is thinnest at the center. If the center is made thick enough to meet the standards, the edge becomes quite thick. This makes the lens heavier and less attractive.

Bifocals

As people age, they lose some of their ability to accommodate to different object distances. In particular, many middle-aged and elderly people must wear reading glasses to be able to read. Some of these people need corrective lenses for both close-up and distance vision. These people often wear bifocals. In bifocals, each lens has two parts, each with a different focal length. One type of bifocals has a different curvature in the top and bottom half of each lens. Another type uses different kinds of glass, that bend light in different ways.

MEDICINE M 112

ACTIVITY NINE: Tooth Tunes: The Inner Ear and Transducers

FOR YOU TO READ

Tooth Tunes

The apparatus you set up for this activity is called "tooth tunes."

Tooth tunes produce vibrations in the same way the speaker does. The diagram shows the path of these vibrations from the dowels to your inner ear and out again through vibrations of the eardrum.

[a] The tooth tunes has a coil of wire that vibrates when it is near the magnet.

[b] As the coil vibrates, it makes the dowel vibrate, too.

[c] These vibrations pass through your teeth and into your jaw and skull.

[d,e] These vibrations cause the tiny bones in the middle ear to vibrate. The oval window and the eardrum both vibrate. The vibrating inner ear lets you hear the music.

[f] The vibrating eardrum turns your ear into a speaker!

Conductive Hearing Loss

Tooth tunes show how sound is conducted from your teeth to the ossicles—the bones in your middle ear. These bones are surrounded by tissues in the middle ear.

As people age, the tissues surrounding the ossicles become less flexible. The ossicles' movement becomes restricted. They cannot transmit sound accurately from the eardrum to the oval window. This is called conductive hearing loss. The effect is something like pressing down on a stereo speaker while music is playing through it. The speaker can't vibrate freely, so the sound is distorted.

The Inner Ear and Neurosensory Hearing Loss

The inner ear is a transducer. A transducer changes energy from one form to another. You have already used transducers—you have used microphones, loudspeakers, oscilloscopes, and musical instruments. The inner ear is a transducer that changes sound energy (in the liquid in the inner ear) into electrical signals that travel on nerves to the brain.

The inner ear has two main parts:

1. three semicircular canals, which help control your sense of balance, and
2. the cochlea, which changes the sound to nerve impulses.

All are filled with liquid. They can be seen in the diagram on page M42. The cochlea is a small spiral about the size of the tip of your little finger.

MEDICINE M 55

The **For You To Read** inserts provide students with some reading at the ninth grade level. This section may be used to tie together concepts from the present activity or a set of activities. It may also be used to provide a glimpse into the history of the physics principle being investigated. Finally, **For You To Read** may provide background information which will help clarify the meaning of the physics principle investigated in **For You To Do**.

8. Reflecting On The Activity And The Challenge

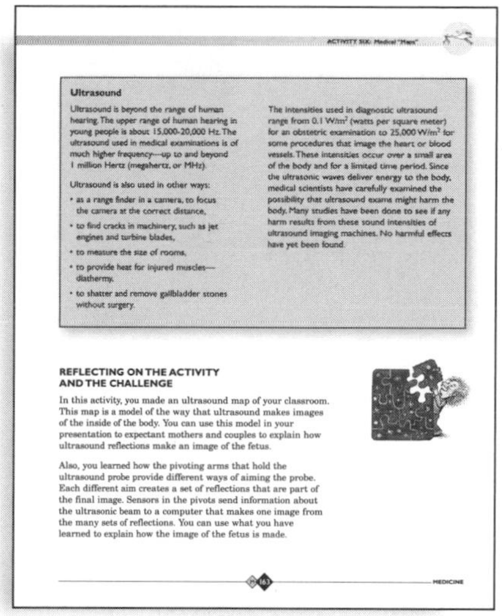

ACTIVITY SIX: Medical "Maps"

Ultrasound

Ultrasound is beyond the range of human hearing. The upper range of human hearing in young people is about 15,000-20,000 Hz. The ultrasound used in medical examinations is of much higher frequency—up to and beyond 1 million Hertz (megahertz, or MHz).

Ultrasound is also used in other ways:

- as a range finder in a camera, to focus the camera at the correct distance,
- to find cracks in machinery, such as jet engines and turbine blades,
- to measure the size of rooms,
- to provide heat for injured muscles—diathermy,
- to shatter and remove gallbladder stones without surgery.

The intensities used in diagnostic ultrasound range from 0.1 W/m^2 (watts per square meter) for an obstetric examination to 25,000 W/m^2 for some procedures that image the heart or blood vessels. These intensities occur over a small area of the body and for a limited time period. Since the ultrasonic waves deliver energy to the body, medical scientists have carefully examined the possibility that ultrasound exams might harm the body. Many studies have been done to see if any harm results from these sound intensities of ultrasound imaging machines. No harmful effects have yet been found.

REFLECTING ON THE ACTIVITY AND THE CHALLENGE

In this activity, you made an ultrasound map of your classroom. This map is a model of the way that ultrasound makes images of the inside of the body. You can use this model in your presentation to expectant mothers and couples to explain how ultrasound reflections make an image of the fetus.

Also, you learned how the pivoting arms that hold the ultrasound probe provide different ways of aiming the probe. Each different aim creates a set of reflections that are part of the final image. Sensors in the pivots send information about the ultrasonic beam to a computer that makes one image from the many sets of reflections. You can use what you have learned to explain how the image of the fetus is made.

M 163 MEDICINE

At the close of each activity, the student is often so involved with the completion of the single experiment that the larger context of the investigation is lost. **Reflecting On The Activity And The Challenge** is the opportunity for students to place the new insights and information into the context of the chapter and the chapter challenge. If the chapter challenge is considered a completed picture, each activity is a jigsaw piece. By completing enough of the **For You To Do** activities, the students will be able to fit the jigsaw pieces together and complete the challenge. This summary section ensures that the students do not forget about the larger context and continue their personal momentum toward completion of the challenge.

9. Physics To Go

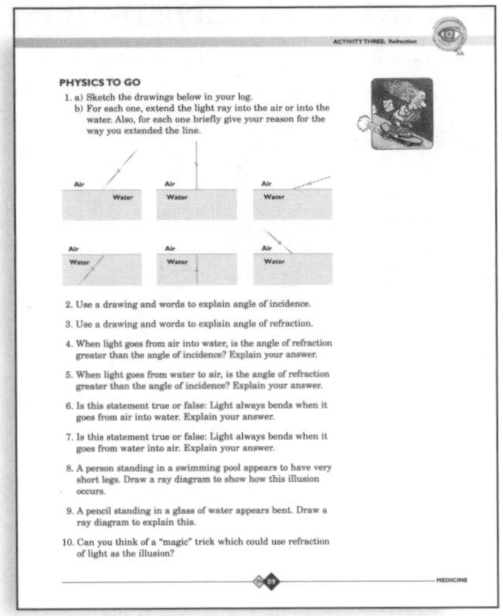
ACTIVITY THREE: Refraction

PHYSICS TO GO

1. a) Sketch the drawings below in your log.
   b) For each one, extend the light ray into the air or into the water. Also, for each one briefly give your reason for the way you extended the line.

2. Use a drawing and words to explain angle of incidence.
3. Use a drawing and words to explain angle of refraction.
4. When light goes from air into water, is the angle of refraction greater than the angle of incidence? Explain your answer.
5. When light goes from water to air, is the angle of refraction greater than the angle of incidence? Explain your answer.
6. Is this statement true or false: Light always bends when it goes from air into water. Explain your answer.
7. Is this statement true or false: Light always bends when it goes from water into air. Explain your answer.
8. A person standing in a swimming pool appears to have very short legs. Draw a ray diagram to show how this illusion occurs.
9. A pencil standing in a glass of water appears bent. Draw a ray diagram to explain this.
10. Can you think of a "magic" trick which could use refraction of light as the illusion?

M 89 MEDICINE

This section provides additional questions and problems that can be completed outside of class. Some of the problems are applications of the principles involved in the preceding activity. Others are replication of the work in the **For You To Do** activity. Still others provide an opportunity to transfer the results of the investigation to the context of the chapter challenge. **Physics To Go** provides a means by which students can be working on the larger chapter challenge in smaller chunks during the chapter.

10. Inquiry Investigation

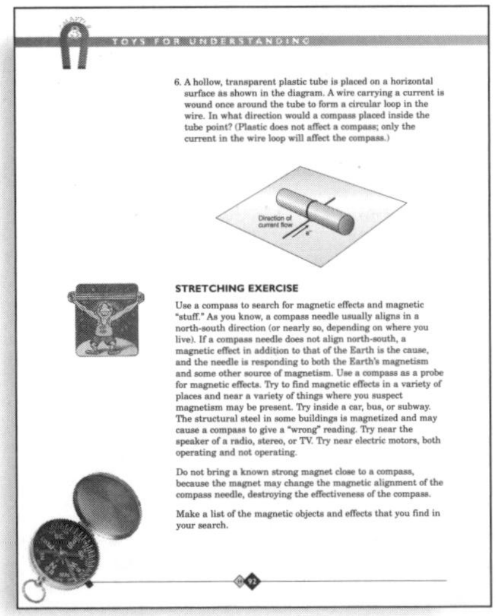
TOYS FOR UNDERSTANDING

6. A hollow, transparent plastic tube is placed on a horizontal surface as shown in the diagram. A wire carrying a current is wound once around the tube to form a circular loop in the wire. In what direction would a compass placed inside the tube point? (Plastic does not affect a compass; only the current in the wire loop will affect the compass.)

STRETCHING EXERCISE

Use a compass to search for magnetic effects and magnetic "stuff." As you know, a compass needle usually aligns in a north-south direction (or nearly so, depending on where you live). If a compass needle does not align north-south, a magnetic effect in addition to that of the Earth is the cause, and the needle is responding to both the Earth's magnetism and some other source of magnetism. Use a compass as a probe for magnetic effects. Try to find magnetic effects in a variety of places and near a variety of things where you suspect magnetism may be present. Try inside a car, bus, or subway. The structural steel in some buildings is magnetized and may cause a compass to give a "wrong" reading. Try near the speaker of a radio, stereo, or TV. Try near electric motors, both operating and not operating.

Do not bring a known strong magnet close to a compass, because the magnet may change the magnetic alignment of the compass needle, destroying the effectiveness of the compass.

Make a list of the magnetic objects and effects that you find in your search.

H 92

The outcome of good science instruction should be the ability of students to conceive of an experiment, design that experiment, complete the data collection, interpret the data and draw suitable conclusions based on the experiment. The nature of the daily immersion in activities in *Active Physics* often, by necessity, provides for detailed instructions in how to proceed. Inquiry is an opportunity to provide the right stimulus for students to try their hands at designing a specific experiment to answer a specific question. It affords students the chance to mirror the techniques and approaches that they have experienced in *Active Physics* and to expand the approach to secure new information. The Inquiry can be assigned as independent study or as a class extension to the lab.

11. Stretching Exercises

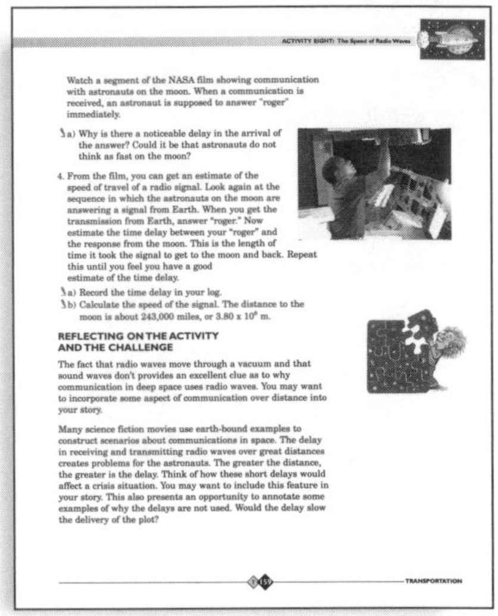
ACTIVITY EIGHT: The Speed of Radio Waves

Watch a segment of the NASA film showing communication with astronauts on the moon. When a communication is received, an astronaut is supposed to answer "roger" immediately.

a) Why is there a noticeable delay in the arrival of the answer? Could it be that astronauts do not think as fast on the moon?

4. From the film, you can get an estimate of the speed of travel of a radio signal. Look again at the sequence in which the astronauts on the moon are answering a signal from Earth. When you get the transmission from Earth, answer "roger." Now estimate the time delay between your "roger" and the response from the moon. This is the length of time it took the signal to get to the moon and back. Repeat this until you feel you have a good estimate of the time delay.
   a) Record the time delay in your log.
   b) Calculate the speed of the signal. The distance to the moon is about 243,000 miles, or 3.80×10^8 m.

REFLECTING ON THE ACTIVITY AND THE CHALLENGE

The fact that radio waves move through a vacuum and that sound waves don't provides an excellent clue as to why communication in deep space uses radio waves. You may want to incorporate some aspect of communication over distance into your story.

Many science fiction movies use earth-bound examples to construct scenarios about communications in space. The delay in receiving and transmitting radio waves over great distances creates problems for the astronauts. The greater the distance, the greater is the delay. Think of how these short delays would affect a crisis situation. You may want to include this feature in your story. This also presents an opportunity to annotate some examples of why the delays are not used. Would the delay slow the delivery of the plot?

T 159 TRANSPORTATION

Some students express additional interest in a specific topic or an extension to a topic. The **Stretching Exercises** provide an avenue in which to pursue that interest. **Stretching Exercises** often require additional readings or interviews. They may be given for extra credit to students who wish to attempt a more in-depth problem or a tougher exercise.

12. Chapter Assessment

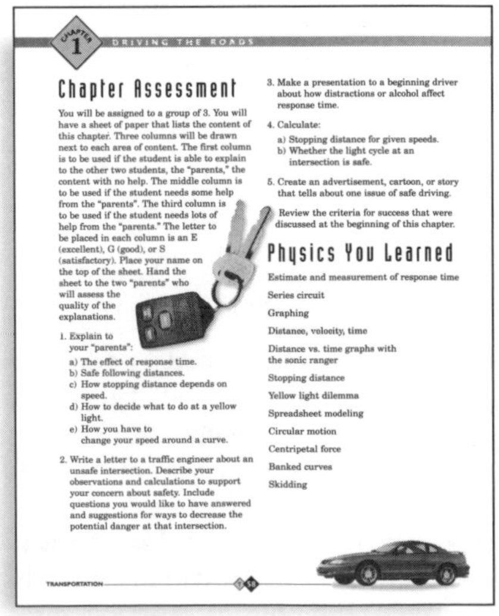
CHAPTER 1 DRIVING THE ROADS

Chapter Assessment

You will be assigned to a group of 3. You will have a sheet of paper that lists the content of this chapter. Three columns will be drawn next to each area of content. The first column is to be used if the student is able to explain to the other two students, the "parents," the content with no help. The middle column is to be used if the student needs some help from the "parents". The third column is to be used if the student needs lots of help from the "parents." The letter to be placed in each column is an E (excellent), G (good), or S (satisfactory). Place your name on the top of the sheet. Hand the sheet to the two "parents" who will assess the quality of the explanations.

1. Explain to your "parents":
   a) The effect of response time.
   b) Safe following distances.
   c) How stopping distance depends on speed.
   d) How to decide what to do at a yellow light.
   e) How you have to change your speed around a curve.
2. Write a letter to a traffic engineer about an unsafe intersection. Describe your observations and calculations to support your concern about safety. Include questions you would like to have answered and suggestions for ways to decrease the potential danger at that intersection.
3. Make a presentation to a beginning driver about how distractions or alcohol affect response time.
4. Calculate:
   a) Stopping distance for given speeds.
   b) Whether the light cycle at an intersection is safe.
5. Create an advertisement, cartoon, or story that tells about one issue of safe driving.

Review the criteria for success that were discussed at the beginning of this chapter.

Physics You Learned

Estimate and measurement of response time

Series circuit

Graphing

Distance, velocity, time

Distance vs. time graphs with the sonic ranger

Stopping distance

Yellow light dilemma

Spreadsheet modeling

Circular motion

Centripetal force

Banked curves

Skidding

TRANSPORTATION T 58

The **Chapter Assessment** is the return to the **Chapter Challenge and Criteria**. The students are ready to complete the challenge. They are able to view the challenge with a clarity that has emerged from the completion of the **For You To Do** activities of the chapter. Students are able to review the chapter as they discuss the synthesis of the information into the required context of the challenge. The students should have some class time to work together to complete the challenge and to present their project. In many physics courses, all students are expected to converge on the same solution. In *Active Physics*, each group is expected to have a unique solution. All solutions must have correct physics, but there is ample room for creativity on the students' part. This is one of the features that captures the imagination of students who have often previously chosen not to enroll in physics classes.

13. Physics You Learned

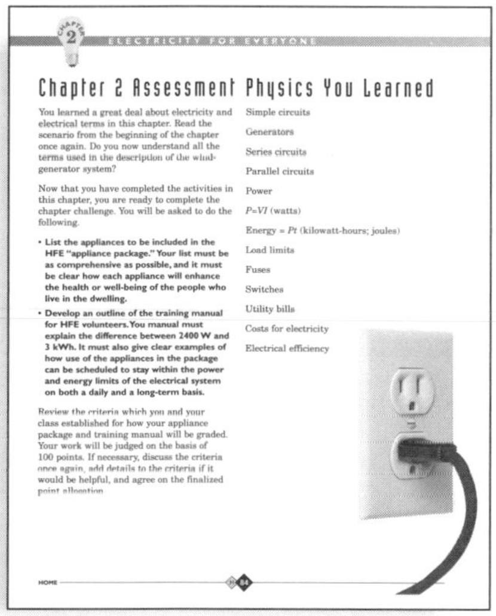

CHAPTER 2 ELECTRICITY FOR EVERYONE

Chapter 2 Assessment

You learned a great deal about electricity and electrical terms in this chapter. Read the scenario from the beginning of the chapter once again. Do you now understand all the terms used in the description of the wind-generator system?

Now that you have completed the activities in this chapter, you are ready to complete the chapter challenge. You will be asked to do the following.

- **List the appliances to be included in the HFE "appliance package." Your list must be as comprehensive as possible, and it must be clear how each appliance will enhance the health or well-being of the people who live in the dwelling.**
- **Develop an outline of the training manual for HFE volunteers. You manual must explain the difference between 2400 W and 3 kWh. It must also give clear examples of how use of the appliances in the package can be scheduled to stay within the power and energy limits of the electrical system on both a daily and a long-term basis.**

Review the criteria which you and your class established for how your appliance package and training manual will be graded. Your work will be judged on the basis of 100 points. If necessary, discuss the criteria once again, add details to the criteria if it would be helpful, and agree on the finalized point allocation.

Physics You Learned

Simple circuits

Generators

Series circuits

Parallel circuits

Power

$P=VI$ (watts)

Energy = Pt (kilowatt-hours; joules)

Load limits

Fuses

Switches

Utility bills

Costs for electricity

Electrical efficiency

HOME 84

This small section at the end of the chapter provides a list of physics concepts and equations which were studied in the context of the **For You To Do** activities. It provides students with a sense of accomplishment and serves as a quick review of all that was learned during the preceding weeks.

14. Physics At Work

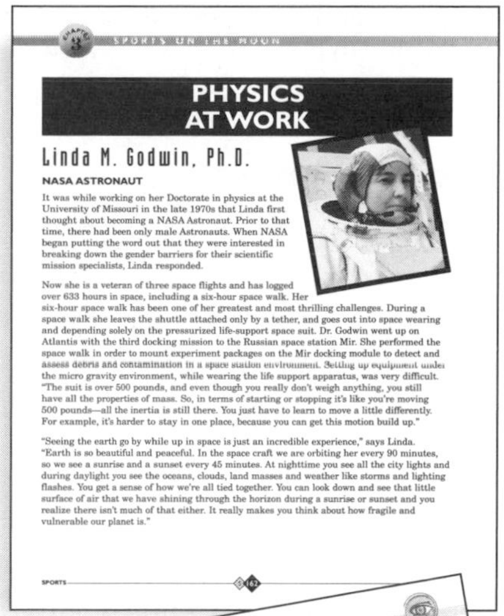

CHAPTER 3 SPORTS ON THE MOON

PHYSICS AT WORK

Linda M. Godwin, Ph.D.

NASA ASTRONAUT

It was while working on her Doctorate in physics at the University of Missouri in the late 1970s that Linda first thought about becoming a NASA Astronaut. Prior to that time, there had been only male Astronauts. When NASA began putting the word out that they were interested in breaking down the gender barriers for their scientific mission specialists, Linda responded.

Now she is a veteran of three space flights and has logged over 633 hours in space, including a six-hour space walk. Her six-hour space walk has been one of her greatest and most thrilling challenges. During a space walk she leaves the shuttle attached only by a tether, and goes out into space wearing and depending solely on the pressurized life-support space suit. Dr. Godwin went up on Atlantis with the third docking mission to the Russian space station Mir. She performed the space walk in order to mount experiment packages on the Mir docking module to detect and assess debris and contamination in a space station environment. Setting up equipment under the micro gravity environment, while wearing the life support apparatus, was very difficult. "The suit is over 500 pounds, and even though you really don't weigh anything, you still have all the properties of mass. So, in terms of starting or stopping it's like you're moving 500 pounds—all the inertia is still there. You just have to learn to move a little differently. For example, it's harder to stay in one place, because you can get this motion build up."

"Seeing the earth go by while up in space is just an incredible experience," says Linda. "Earth is so beautiful and peaceful. In the space craft we are orbiting her every 90 minutes, so we see a sunrise and a sunset every 45 minutes. At nighttime you see all the city lights and during daylight you see the oceans, clouds, land masses and weather like storms and lighting flashes. You get a sense of how we're all tied together. You can look down and see that little surface of air that we have shining through the horizon during a sunrise or sunset and you realize there isn't much of that either. It really makes you think about how fragile and vulnerable our planet is."

SPORTS 162

ACTIVITY NINE: Visual Activity

PHYSICS AT WORK

Rafael Ortiz, Jr.

GIVING THE GIFT OF SIGHT

Rafael grew up in Newark, New Jersey and always dreamed of being a football star. He wanted to play for the Dallas Cowboys, but the course of his life was to take a different, although deeply fulfilling, turn instead. When he was a young teenager, the man next door, an optician, opened an optical store. Rafael began hanging out there after school, doing his homework, and talking to his neighbor. The optician became Rafael's mentor. Rafael found himself helping out a lot in the store and after a while he began working there part time and during the summers. "It was this neighbor who first taught me the physics of optics."

After graduating high school Rafael continued in the optical field and went to work for an optometrist, the eye specialist who examines patients, diagnosing sight problems and prescribing corrective glasses. "Each person has a unique eye problem that has to be individually studied. It's never the same, and each person must be treated uniquely." Rafael found that he loved giving people the gift of sight.

He now knew he wanted to become an optician and began working towards that goal. He found the apprenticeship program at LensCrafters where he went on to get his license. Today he is the general manager for one of LensCrafters largest stores. "As general manager I oversee three departments: the retail store, the lab, and the optometrist department."

Rafael particularly loves to make glasses for the children who do not see clearly. For example, he tells this story: "Recently there was a little three-year-old girl for whom we made glasses. When I put them on her, she turned around to her mom and said, 'Mommy I can see you,' and then she touched her mom's face. It was very moving." Rafael considers himself very fortunate to be in a position to help people to see.

MEDICINE 127

This section highlights an individual whose work or hobby is illustrative of the **Chapter Challenge. Physics At Work** speaks to the authenticity of the **Chapter Challenges**. The profiles illustrate how knowledge of physics is important and valuable in different walks of life. The choice of profiles span the ethnic, racial, and gender diversity that we find in our nation.

Active Physics & National Science Education Standards

Active Physics was designed and developed to provide teachers with instructional strategies that model the following from *The Standards*:

Guide and Facilitate Learning

- Focus and support inquiries while interacting with students.
- Orchestrate discourse among students about scientific ideas.
- Challenge students to accept and share responsibility for their own learning.
- Recognize & respond to student diversity; encourage all to participate fully in science learning.
- Encourage and model the skills of scientific inquiry as well as the curiosity openness to new ideas and data and skepticism that characterize science.

Engage in ongoing assessment of their teaching and student learning

- Use multiple methods & systematically gather data about student understanding & ability.
- Analyze assessment data to guide teaching.
- Guide students in self-assessment.

Design and manage learning environments that provide students with time, space and resources needed for learning science

- Structure the time available so students are able to engage in extended investigations.
- Create a setting for student work that is flexible and supportive of science inquiry.
- Make available tools, materials, media, & technological resources accessible to students.
- Identify and use resources outside of school.

Develop communities of science learners that reflect the intellectual rigor of scientific attitudes and social values conducive to science learning

- Display and demand respect for diverse ideas, skills, & experiences of students.
- Enable students to have significant voice in decisions about content & context of work & require students to take responsibility for the learning of all members of the community.
- Nurture collaboration among students.
- Structure and facilitate ongoing formal and informal discussion based on shared understanding of rules.
- Model and emphasize the skills, attitudes and values of scientific inquiry.

Assessment Standards

- Features claimed to be measured are actually measured.
- Students have adequate opportunity to demonstrate their achievement and understanding.
- Assessment tasks are authentic and developmentally appropriate, set in familiar context, and engaging to students with different interests and experiences.
- Assesses student understanding as well as knowledge.
- Improve classroom practice and plan curricula.
- Develop self-directed learners.

Active Physics Addresses Key NSES Recommendations

Active Physics addresses the following science curriculum recommendations:

Scenario-Driven

In each thematic unit there are three chapters, each requiring approximately three to four weeks of class time. Each chapter begins with an engaging scenario or project assignment that challenges the students and sets the stage for the learning activities and chapter assessments to follow. Chapter contents and activities are selectively aimed at providing the students with the knowledge and skills needed to address the introductory challenge, thus providing a natural content filter in the "less is more" curriculum.

Flexibly Formatted

Units are designed to stand alone, so teachers have the flexibility of changing the sequence of presentation of the units, omitting the entire unit, or not finishing all of the chapters within a unit. Although intended to serve as a full-year physics course, the units of *Active Physics* could be adapted to spread across a four-year period in an integrated high school curriculum.

Multiple Exposure Curriculum

The thematic nature of the course requires students to continually revisit fundamental physics principles throughout the year, extending and deepening their understanding of these principles as they apply them in new contexts. This repeated exposure fosters the retention and transferability of learning, and promotes the development of critical thinking skills.

Constructivist Approach

Students are continually asked to explore how they think about certain situations. As they investigate new situations, they are challenged to either explain observed phenomena using an existing paradigm or to develop a more consistent one. This approach can be helpful in including situations to abandon previously held notions in favor of the more powerful ideas and explanations offered by scientists.

Authentic Assessment

For the culmination of each chapter, students are required to demonstrate the usefulness of their newly acquired knowledge by adequately meeting the challenge posed in the chapter introduction. Students are then evaluated on the degree to which they accomplish this performance task. The curriculum also includes other methods and instruments for authentic assessments as well as non-traditional procedures for evaluating and rewarding desirable behaviors and skills.

Cooperative Grouping Strategies

Use of cooperative groups is integral to the course as students work together in small groups to acquire the knowledge and information needed to address the series of challenges presented through the chapter scenarios. Ample teacher guidance is provided to assure that effective strategies are used in group formation, function, and evaluation.

Math Skills Development/Graphing Calculators and Computer Spreadsheets

The presentation and use of math in *Active Physics* varies substantially from traditional high school physics courses. Math, primarily algebraic expressions, equations, and graphs is approached as a way of representing ideas symbolically. Students begin to recognize the usefulness of math as an aid in exploring and understanding the world about them. Finally, since many of the students in the target audience are insecure about their math backgrounds, the course engages and provides instruction for the use of graphing calculators and computer spreadsheets to provide math assistance.

Minimal Reading Required

Because it is assumed that the target audience reads only what is absolutely necessary, the entire course is activity-driven. Reading passages are presented mainly within the context of the activities, and are written at the ninth grade level.

Use of Educational Technologies

Videos which capture students' attention explore a variety of the *Active Physics* topics. Opportunities are also provided for students to produce their own videos in order to record and analyze events. Computer software programs make use of various interfacing devices.

Problem Solving

For the curriculum to be both meaningful and relevant to the target population, problem solving related to technological applications and related issues is an essential component of the course. Problem solving ranges from simple numerical solutions where one result is expected, to more involved decision-making situations where multiple alternatives must be compared.

Challenging Learning Extensions

Throughout the text, a variety of **Stretching Exercises** are provided for more motivated students. These extensions range from more challenging design tasks, to enrichment readings, to intriguing and unusual problems. Many of the extensions take advantage of the frequent opportunities the curriculum provides for oral and written expression of student ideas.

Cooperative Learning

Benefits of Cooperative Learning

Cooperative learning requires you to organize and structure a lesson so that students work with other students to jointly accomplish a task. Group learning is an essential part of balanced methodology. It should be blended with whole-class instruction and individual study to meet a variety of learning styles and expectations as well as maintain a high level of student involvement.

Cooperative learning has been thoroughly researched and agreement has been reached on a number of results. Cooperative learning:

- promotes trust and risk-taking
- elevates self-esteem
- encourages acceptance of individual differences
- develops social skills
- permits a combination of a wide range of backgrounds and abilities
- provides an inviting atmosphere
- promotes a sense of community
- develops group and individual responsibility
- reduces the time on a task
- results in better attendance
- produces a positive effect on student achievement
- develops key employability skills

As with any learning approach, some students will benefit more than others from cooperative learning. Therefore, you may question as to what extent you should use cooperative learning strategies. It is important to involve the student in helping decide which type of learning approaches they prefer, and to what extent each is used in the classroom. When students have a say in their learning, they will accept to a greater extent any method which you choose to use.

Phases of Cooperative Learning Lessons

Organizational Pre-lesson Decisions

What academic and social objectives will be emphasized? In other words, what content and skills are to be learned and what interaction skills are to be emphasized or practiced?

What will be the group size? Or, what is the most appropriate group size to facilitate the achievement of the academic and social objectives? This will depend on the amount of individual involvement expected (small groups promote more individual involvement), the task (diverse thinking is promoted by larger groups), nature of the task or materials available and the time available (shorter time demands smaller groupings to promote involvement).

Who will make up the different groups? Teacher-selected groups usually have the best mix, but this can only happen after the teacher gets to know his/her students well enough to know who works well together. Heterogeneous groupings are most successful in that all can learn through active participation. The duration of the groups' existence may have some bearing on deciding the membership of groups.

How should the room be arranged? Practicing routines where students move into their groups quickly and quietly is an important aspect. Having students face-to-face is important. The teacher should still be able to move freely among the groups.

What Materials and/or Rewards Might be Prepared in Advance?

Setting the Lesson

Structure for Positive Interdependence: When students feel they need one another, they are more likely to work together--goal interdependence becomes important. Class interdependence can be promoted by setting class goals which all teams must achieve in order for class success.

Explanation of the Academic Task: Clear explanations and sometimes the use of models can help the students. An explanation of the relevance of the activity is importance. Checks for clear understanding can be done either before the groups form or after, but they are necessary for delimiting frustrations.

Explanation of Criteria for Success: Groups should know how their level of success will be determined.

Structure for Individual Accountability: The use of individual follow-up activities for tasks or social skills will provide for individual accountability.

Specification of Desired Social Behaviors: Definition and explanations of the importance of values of social skills will promote student practice and achievement of the different skills.

Monitoring/Intervening During Group Work

Through monitoring students' behaviors, intervention can be used more appropriately. Students can be involved in the monitoring by being "a team observer," but only when the students have a very clear understanding of the behavior being monitored.

Interventions to increase chances for success in completing the task or activity and for the teaching of collaborative skills should be used as necessary-- they should not be interruptions. This means that the facilitating teacher should be moving among the groups as much as possible. During interventions, the problem should be turned back to the students as often as possible, taking care not to frustrate them.

Evaluating the Content and Process of Cooperative Group Work

Assessment of the achievement of content objectives should be completed by both the teacher and the students. Students can go back to their groups after an assignment to review the aspects in which they experienced difficulties.

When assessing the accomplishment of social objectives, two aspects are important: how well things proceeded and where/how improvements might be attempted. Student involvement in this evaluation is a very basic aspect of successful cooperative learning programs.

Organizing and Monitoring Groups

An optimum size of group for most activities appears to be four; however, for some tasks, two may be more efficient. Heterogeneous groups organized by the teacher are usually the most sucessful. The teacher will need to decide what factors should be considered in forming the heterogeneous groups. Factors which can be considered are: academic achievement, cultural background, language proficiency, sex, age, learning style, and even personality type.

Level of academic achievement is probably the simplest and initially the best way to form groups. Sort the students on the basis of marks on a particular task or on previous year's achievement. Then choose a student from each quartile to form a group. Once formed, groups should be flexible. Continually monitor groups for compatability and make adjustments as required.

Students should develop an appreciation that it is a privilege to belong to a group. Remove from group work any student who is a poor participant or one who is repeatedly absent. These individuals can then be assigned the same tasks to be completed in the same time line as a group. You may also wish to place a ten percent reduction on all group work that is completed individually.

The chart on the next page presents some possible group structures and their functions.

What Does Cooperative Learning Look Like?

During a cooperative learning situation, students should be assigned a variety of roles related to the particular task at hand. Following is a list of possible roles that students may be given. It is important that students are given the opportunity of assuming a number of different roles over the course of a semester.

Leader:

Assigns roles for the group. Gets the group started and keeps the group on task.

Organizer:

Helps focus discussion and ensures that all members of the group contribute to the discussion. The organizer ensures that all of the equipment has been gathered and that the group completes all parts of the activity.

Recorder:

Provides written procedures when required, diagrams where appropriate and records data. The recorder must work closely with the organizer to ensure that all group members contribute.

Researcher:

Seeks written and electronic information to support the findings of the group. In addition, where appropriate, the researcher will develop and test prototypes. The researcher will also exchange information gathered among different groups.

Encourager:

Encourages all group members to participate. Values contributions and supports involvement.

Checker:

Checks that the group has answered all the questions and the group members agree upon and understand the answers.

Diverger:

Seeks alternative explanations and approaches. The task of the diverger is to keep the discussion open. "Are other explanations possible?"

Some Possible Group Structures and Their Functions*

Structure		Brief Description	Academic and Social Functions
Team Building	Round-robin	Each student in turn shares something with his/her teammates.	Expressing ideas and opinions, creating stories. Equal participation, getting acquainted with each other.
Class Building	Corners	Each student moves to a group in a corner or location as determined by the teacher through specified alternatives. Students discuss within groups, then listen to and paraphrase ideas from other groups.	Seeing alternative hypotheses, values, and problem solving approaches. Knowing and respecting differing points of view.
Mastery	Numbered heads together	The teacher asks a question, students consult within their groups to make sure that each member knows the answer. Then one student answers for the group in response to the number called out by the teacher.	Review, checking for knowledge comprehension, analysis, and divergent thinking. Tutoring.
	Color coded co-op cards	Students memorize facts using a flash card game or an adaption. The game is structured so that there is a maximum probability for success at each step, moving from short to long-term memory. Scoring is based on improvement.	Memorizing facts. Helping, praising.
	Pairs check	Students work in pairs within groups of four. Within pairs students alternate-one solves a problem while the other coaches. After every problem or so, the pair checks to see if they have the same answer as the other pair.	Practicing skills. Helping, praising.
Concept Development	Three-step interview	Students interview each other in pairs, first one way, then the other. Each student shares information learned during interviews with the group.	Sharing personal information such as hypotheses, views on an issue, or conclusions from a unit. Participation, involvement.
	Think-pair-share	Students think to themselves on a topic provided by the teacher; they pair up with another student to discuss it; and then share their thoughts with the class.	Generating and revising hypotheses, inductive and deductive reasoning, and application. Participation and involvement.
	Team word-webbing	Students write simultaneously on a piece of paper, drawing main concepts, supporting elements, and bridges representing the relation of concepts/ideas.	Analysis of concept into components, understanding multiple relations among ideas, and differentiating concepts. Role-taking.
Multifunctional	Roundtable	Each student in turn writes one answer as a paper and a pencil are passed around the group. With simultaneous roundtable, more than one pencil and paper are used.	Assessing print knowledge, practicing skills, recalling information, and creating designs. Team building, participation of all.
	Partners	Students work in pairs to create or master content. They consult with partners from other teams. Then they share their products or understandings with the other partner pair in their team.	Mastery and presentation of new material, concept development. Presentation and communication skills.
	Jigsaw	Each student from each team becomes an "expert" on one topic area by working with members from other teams assigned to the same topic area. On returning to their own teams, each one teaches the other members of the group and students are assessed on all aspects of the topic.	Acquisition and presentation of new material review and informed debate. Independence, status equalization.

* Adapted from Spencer Kagan (1990), "*The Structural Approach to Cooperative Learning,*" Educational Leadership, December 1989/January 1990.

Active Listener:

Repeats or paraphrases what has been said by the different members of the group.

Idea Giver:

Contributes ideas, information, and opinions.

Materials Manager:

Collects and distributes all necessary material for the group.

Observer:

Completes checklists for the group.

Questioner:

Seeks information, opinions, explanations, and justifications from other members of the group.

Reader:

Reads any textual material to the group.

Reporter:

Prepares and/or makes a report on behalf of the group.

Summarizer:

Summarizes the work, conclusions, or results of the group so that they can be presented coherently.

Timekeeper:

Keeps the group members focused on the task and keeps time.

Safety Manager:

Reponsible for ensuring that safety measures are being followed, and the equipment is clean prior to and at the end of the activity.

Group Assessment

Assessment should not end with a group mark. Students and their parents have a right to expect marks to reflect the students' individual contributions to the task. It is impossible for you as the instructor to continuously monitor and record the contribution of each individual student. Therefore, you will need to rely on the students in the group to assign individual marks as merited.

There are a number of ways that this can be accomplished. The group mark can be multiplied by the number of students in the group, and then the total mark can be divided among the students, as shown in the graphics that follow.

Activity:____________________

Group Mark: 8/10

Number in Group: 4

Total Marks: 32/40

Distribution of Marks

Student's Name	Mark	Signature
Ahmed	8/10	____________________
Jasmin	8/10	____________________
Mike	7/10	____________________
Tabitha	9/10	____________________

Another way to share group marks is to assign a factor to each student. The mark factors must total the number of students in the group. The group mark is then multiplied by this factor to arrive at each student's individual mark which best represents their contribution to the task, as shown below.

Activity:____________________

Group Mark: 8/10

Number in Group: 4

Mark Factors and Individual Marks

Student's Name	Mark Factor	Individual Mark	Signature
Ahmed	1.0	8/10	____________________
Jasmin	1.0	8/10	____________________
Mike	0.9	7.2/10	____________________
Tabitha	1.1	8.8/10	____________________
Total Mark Factor	4		

In any case, students must sign to show that they are in agreement with the way the individual marks were assigned.

You may also wish to provide students with an assessment rubric similar to the one shown which they can use to assess the manner in which the group worked together.

Assessment Rubric for Group Work: Individual Assessment of the Group

Individual's name: ____________________

Names of group members: ____________________

Name of activity :____________________

Circle the appropriate number: #1 is excellent, #2 is good, #3 is average, and #4 is poor.

1. The group worked cooperatively. Everyone assumed a role and carried it out.	1	2	3	4
2. Everyone contributed to the discussion. Everyone's opinion was valued.	1	2	3	4
3. Everyone assumed the roles assigned to them.	1	2	3	4
4. The group was organized. Materials were gathered, distributed, and collected.	1	2	3	4
5. Problems were addressed as a group.	1	2	3	4
6. All parts of the task were completed within the time assigned.	1	2	3	4
Comments:				

If you were to repeat the activity, what things would you change?

CHAPTER
1
DRIVING THE ROADS

TRANSPORTATION CHAPTER 1- DRIVING THE ROADS

National Science Education Standards

Chapter Summary

A newly licensed young driver asking to use the family car on a Friday night date establishes the scenario. Students are challenged to demonstrate to their parents that they know how to apply understanding of the laws of motion to safe driving. They can demonstrate this understanding with a convincing argument, a letter about an unsafe intersection, or a presentation about how distractions and alcohol affect response time that includes calculations of stopping distance.

To gain knowledge and understanding of physics principles necessary to meet this challenge, students work collaboratively on activities in which they apply concepts of potential and kinetic energy as they collect and analyze data collected in investigations of speed, acceleration, velocity, and friction. These experiences engage students in the following content identified in the *National Science Education Standards.*

Content Standards

Unifying Concepts

- Evidence, models and explanations
- Constancy, change and measurement
- Communicate and defend a scientific argument

Science as Inquiry

- Identify questions and concepts that guide scientific investigations
- Use technology and mathematics to improve investigations
- Formulate & revise scientific explanations & models using logic and evidence

Physical Science

- Motions and forces: Objects change their motion when a net force is applied
- Laws of Motion are used to calculate the effects of forces in motion

Key Physics Concepts and Skills

Activity Summaries	Physics Principles
Activity One: Response Time Using a response timer, students explore the time required for a driver to respond to a hazard. This activity introduces students to the process of beginning with their own ideas and predictions, then implementing an investigation that results in both qualitative and quantitative data.	• Series circuits • Switches • Response time
Activity Two: Speed and Following Distance Strobe, or multiple exposure photos of a moving vehicle are used to discuss speed and acceleration. Students then use a sonic ranger to measure how fast they walk and obtain a computer generated graph of their speed. Information about speed is then connected to response time with a discussion of tailgating.	• Average speed • Using data as basis for predictions • Speed, distance, and time relationships
Activity Three: Stopping Your Car Students use sloped tracks to investigate speed and distance a car travels before stopping. They then examine data on time and distance required to stop a vehicle moving at various speeds. This is connected to the total time required to respond to a hazard, apply force to the brake, and slow the motion of the vehicle to a complete stop.	• Acceleration • Average speed • Friction
Activity Four: Putting It All Together Distractions that slow response time – talking, loud music, and alcohol – are the focus of this activity in which students plan and conduct a scientific investigation to answer a question they posed themselves about braking distance, safe following distance, and speed. A computer simulation allows students to test their ideas.	• Acceleration • Instantaneous speed • Average speed
Activity Five: Intersections with a Yellow Light Using a spreadsheet model of an intersection, students explore how reaction time, speed, and stopping distance affect what they should do at a yellow light. This also introduces them to how transportation engineers use a computer simulation to model various factors affecting decisions about speed limits and traffic light cycles.	• Acceleration • Instantaneous speed
Activity Six: Yellow Light Dilemma... Students now have the opportunity to apply their understanding of response time, following distance, and braking distance to identify the stop, go, and dilemma zones at intersections when they see a yellow light.	• Acceleration • Velocity and speed • Inertia
Activity Seven: Driving on Curves Students perceptions and prior "learning" about the force needed to change the direction of a moving object are challenged in this activity. After performing investigations, they reflect on the discrepancy between their perceptions and observed results. Students then read for more information on how forces change the direction of motion.	• Gravity • Force • Circular motion
Activity Eight: Banking the Turns The concept that motion on a curve requires a centripetal force to keep the car "pushing" towards the curve is the focus of this activity. Predicting, observing, and describing the direction, relative speed, and the relationship of the radius and speed on a turntable enables students to develop and test their understanding of this concept about force.	• Gravity • Circular motion • Centripetal force
Activity Nine: Skids! Students apply what they now know about speed, reaction time, stopping a car, and handling a car on a turn to investigate what to do in a skid. They analyze observable results in terms of laws of motion. This activity concludes with students reading about cars with front wheel and rear wheel drive and horizontal motion of the projected object, and predict its trajectory.	• Friction • Gravity • Inertia

1

Equipment List For Chapter One

QTY	TO SERVE	ACTIVITY	ITEM	COMMENT
1	Class	5, 6	*Active Physics Transportation* Content Video	Segment: Intersection and Yellow light
1	Class	9	*Active Physics Transportation* Content Video	Segment: Skidding Cars
1	Class	5, 6	*Active Physics* Spreadsheet Template	File: Yellow Light
1	Group	3	Apparatus for measuring instantaneous speed	MBL or CBL with sonic ranger will serve
1	Group	1, 4	Battery holder for D-cell	Provision for connecting wires to battery
1	Group	5, 6	Computer with "Excel" spreadsheet software	Load file on each group's computer
4	Group	1, 4	Connecting wire, insulated	Preferably fitted with alligator clips
1	Group	1, 4	D-cell	
1	Group	8	Double stick tape or glue	May be needed to secure wedge to turntable
2	Group	1, 4	Knife switch	
1	Group	3. 9	Laboratory cart or toy car	
1	Group	1, 4	Light bulb & base, miniature screwbase	A "flashlight" bulb (such as No. 13) and base
1	Group	9	Locking device for wheels of cart	Such as tape or clips
1	Group	2	MBL or CBL with sonic ranger	May be done as a class demonstration
1	Group	3	Meter stick	
1	Class	1, 4	Response-time meter	The kind used in Driver Education classes.
1	Group	7	Rubber mat or sandpaper	To reduce friction on turntable surface
1	Group	1, 4	Ruler, 1 ft (30 cm)	
1	Individual	3	Sheet graph paper	
1	Group	3	Starting ramp for lab cart	Must provide range of speed for cart
2	Group	1, 4, 7	Stopwatch	
1	Group	7	String, about 0.5 m	
1	Group	7	Toy car, battery-operated	
1	Group	7, 8	Turntable, "Lazy Susan"-type	
1	Class	5, 6, 9	VCR and TV monitor	
1	Group	9	Wide ramp or tilted table	Wide enough for cart to "spin out"
1	Group	7, 8	Wood block, small	Size small compared to turntable diameter
1	Group	8	Wood wedge, approx. 20 degree angle	Sufficient size to support block on turntable

Organizer for Materials Available in Teacher's Edition

Activity in Student Text	Additional Material	Alternative / Optional Activities
ACTIVITY ONE: Response Time, p. T4	Assessment: Group Work, p. 24 Assessment: Scientific and Technological Thinking, p. 25	ACTIVITY One A: Response Time: High-Tech Alternative, pgs. 26-27
ACTIVITY TWO: Speed and Following Distance, p. T10	Assessment: Graphing Skills, p. 40	
ACTIVITY THREE: Stopping Your Car, p. T17		
ACTIVITY FOUR: Putting It All Together, p. T22		ACTIVITY Four A: Factors That Affect Response Time, pgs. 56-57
ACTIVITY FIVE: Intersections with a Yellow Light, p. T26	Data Tables for GO and STOP Zones, p. 66 Sample Spreadsheets for Yellow Light Model, p. 67 Assessment: Scientific Thinking, p. 70 Assessment: Driving Simulation, p. 71	
ACTIVITY SIX: Yellow Light Dilemma and Dangerous Intersections, p. T34	Dilemma Zone, p. 78	
ACTIVITY SEVEN: Driving on Curves, p. T40	Assessment: Scientific Thinking for Driving on Curves, p. 88 Centripetal Force, p. 91	ACTIVITY Seven A: Objects that Resist Moving and Resist Stopping, pgs. 89-90
ACTIVITY EIGHT: Banking the Turns, p. T46		
ACTIVITY NINE: Skids, p. T52		

1

CHAPTER 1 DRIVING THE ROADS

Scenario

Imagine your parents just bought a new car and your favorite rock group is in town. You ask to use the new car so that you can take some of your friends to the concert. What would your parents say? Would you have a conversation like the following?

"I don't care if it's your favorite rock group. You don't know enough about driving."

"But Dad, I've had my license two whole months!"

"All you did was memorize a bunch of facts to get your license."

"Yes, and now I know all about the law."

"Traffic laws, maybe. But what about natural laws—speed and stopping distance?"

"That's easy, the speed limits are all posted."

"I don't want you anywhere near the speed limit."

"Okay, now can I have the car?"

"No. You don't know about your response time and following distance. And what about curves; when should you slow down?"

"The yellow signs tell you what to do on the curves."

"You need to know more than that. What about a yellow light? What does it mean?"

"Step on it?"

"See what I mean, you're not ready to drive."

"It was a joke, Dad."

"Driving is no joke. What if you have an accident? What then? What if your friends distract you?"

"I don't plan on having an accident; besides, I'll always wear my seat belt."

"No one plans on an accident—that's why they're called accidents!"

"But Dad, I have my license."

"No buts."

"You just don't love me."

ACTIVE PHYSICS T 2

Chapter and Challenge Overview

Chapter 1 of *Transportation*, Driving the Roads, introduces students to the physics involved in the operation of an automobile. After completing the chapter the students should be on their way to being better informed drivers.

The Scenario presents a situation which may become familiar to many students. The students ask their parents to borrow a car. Their parents feel that they do not know enough about driving to be given the responsibility of operating a vehicle. One of the Challenges the students then encounter is to convince their parents that they have enough knowledge about the physics of driving to be permitted to use the car.

The chapter activities prepare the students to meet the challenge. They learn about speed, the measurements and calculations required. They study response time and the consequences of tailgating. The study of centripetal forces helps students explain how to drive safely on curved roads. An activity relating initial speed to stopping distance leads to an investigation of the factors that make an intersection with a yellow light safe. Students are then asked to write a letter to a traffic engineer to describe a potentially unsafe intersection.

To introduce the chapter you may wish to role-play the scene described in the scenario using students as parents and teenage drivers. Ask them how they would try to get the car from their parents and how their parents would try to avoid giving it to them. Explain how physics will help them convince their parents that they are safe drivers.

Read over the Challenge and the Criteria with the class to establish the rubric for assessing performance. Include in your grading criteria such factors as: the number of physics principles references, the number of physics terms used properly, clarity of expression, legality of advice, adherence to safety, and credulity.

As you review the Challenge assignments, reassure the students that while they may feel incompetent now, by the end of the chapter they will have the necessary skills and vocabulary to respond adequately.

As you begin *Active Physics*, be aware that the same physics concepts appear repeatedly in different contexts. It is not necessary for the students to achieve total understanding the first time that they encounter inertia, speed, or centripetal force.

Challenge

This chapter contains nine activities that provide experiences with the physics of motion and will help you better understand driving. After completing the activities, you will be challenged to do the following:

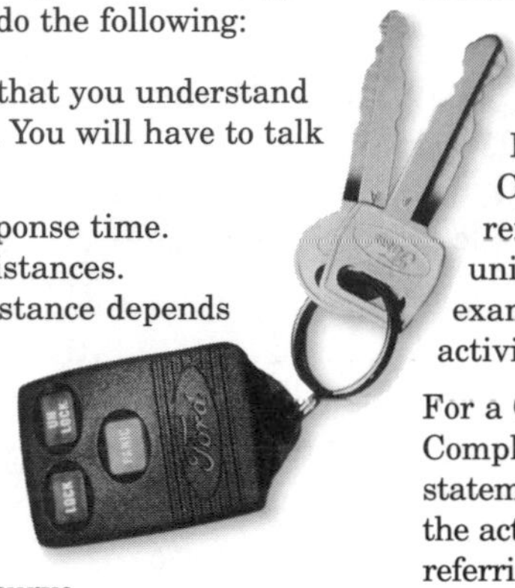

1. Convince a parent that you understand how to drive safely. You will have to talk about:
   a) The effect of response time.
   b) Safe following distances.
   c) How stopping distance depends on speed.
   d) How to decide what to do at a yellow light.
   e) How you have to change your speed around a curve.

2. Write a letter to a traffic engineer about an unsafe intersection. Describe your observations and calculations to support your concern about safety. Include questions you would like to have answered and suggestions for ways to decrease the potential danger at that intersection.

3. Make a presentation to a beginning driver about how distractions affect response time.

4. Calculate:
   a) Stopping distance for given speeds.
   b) Whether the light cycle at an intersection is safe.

5. Create an advertisement, cartoon, or story that tells about one issue of safe driving.

Criteria

How will I be graded? What quality standards will I have to meet to successfully complete each of the challenges? How many should I complete to receive an "A?"

Here is a possible rubric (criteria), for evaluating your success.

For a Grade of A
Completion of all 5 challenges, referencing all concepts presented in unit, with statements supported by clear examples and data collected from the activities.

For a Grade of B
Completion of 4 challenges, supporting all statements with clear examples and data from the activities OR completion of all 5 challenges, referring to concepts from unit, but without using collected data to support statements.

For a Grade of C
Completion of 3 challenges, using clear examples and data from the activities OR completion of 4 challenges, referring to concepts from the unit, but without using collected data to support statements.

For a Grade of D
Completion of 2 challenges, using clear examples and data from the activities OR completion of 3 or more challenges, without using collected data to support statements.

You and your classmates will work with your teacher to define the criteria for determining grades. You will also be asked to evaluate the quality of your own work—both how much effort you put in and how well you met the standards set by your class.

Assessment Rubric for Challenge: Driving the Roads

Convincing Parents That You Know How to Drive Safely. Together with the students prepare a score sheet listing the content of the chapter followed by three columns headed “No help,” “Some help,” and “Much help.” This will be used by the two “parents” in assessing the quality of the student's response during the role-play. Each student carries a sheet to the new group to again act as parent or potential driver.

The following shows a possible score sheet:

Content	**No Help** **E (excellent)**	**Some Help** **G (good)**	**Much Help** **S (satisfactory)**
the effect of response time			
what is a safe following distance?			
how stopping distance depends on speed			
how to decide what to do at a yellow light			
how you have to change your speed around a curve			

Assessment Rubric for Challenge: Letter to Traffic Engineer

Meets the standard of excellence. **5**	• Letter to traffic engineer clearly describes observations of a street corner, and includes visual evidence, either video, photographs, or diagrams. • Terms STOP Zone, GO Zone, and overlap or dilemma zone are fully explained and used correctly. • Letter shows complete calculations related to the intersection in question to support safety concerns. • Letter includes insightful questions which need to be answered by the engineer. • Letters suggests several alternative ways to decrease the danger of the intersection.
Approaches the standard of excellence. **4**	• Letter to traffic engineer clearly describes observations of a street corner, and but visual support evidence is not complete. • Terms STOP Zone, GO Zone, and overlap or dilemma zone are explained and used correctly. • Letter shows calculations to support safety concerns. • Letter includes questions which need to be answered by the engineer. • Letters suggests several alternative ways to decrease the danger of the intersection.
Meets an acceptable standard. **3**	• Letter to traffic engineer describes observations of a street corner. • Terms STOP Zone, GO Zone, and overlap or dilemma zone are explained and used correctly. • Letter attempts to support safety concerns with calculations. • Letter includes questions which need to be answered by the engineer. • Letters suggests a way to decrease the danger of the intersection.
Below acceptable standard and requires remedial help. **2**	• Letter to traffic engineer describes observations of a street corner. • Terms stop zone, go zone, and overlap or dilemma zone are mentioned, but sometimes used incorrectly. • Calculations are missing. • Letter includes erroneous questions for the engineer to answer. • Letters suggests a way to decrease the danger of the intersection, but is not correct.
Basic level that requires remedial help or demonstrates a lack of effort. **1**	• Letter to traffic engineer describes observations of a street corner. • Terms stop zone, go zone, and overlap or dilemma zone are not mentioned or always incorrectly used. • Calculations are missing. • Letter does not include questions for the engineer to answer. • Letter makes no attempt to suggest a way to decrease the danger of the intersection.

Maximum = 10 Points

For use with *Transportation*, Chapter 1

Assessment Rubric for Challenge: Scientific Language used in Conversation and in Letter

Meets the standard of excellence. **5**	• Scientific vocabulary is used consistently and precisely. • Sentence structure is consistently controlled. • Spelling, punctuation, and/or grammar are consistently used in an effective manner. • Scientific symbols for units of measurement are used appropriately in all cases. • Where appropriate, data is organized into tables or presented by graphs.
Approaches the standard of excellence. **4**	• Scientific vocabulary is used appropriately in most situations. • Sentence structure is usually consistently controlled. • Spelling, punctuation, and/or grammar are generally used in an effective manner. • Scientific symbols for units of measurement are used appropriately in most cases. • Where appropriate, most of the data is organized into tables or presented by graphs.
Meets an acceptable standard. **3**	• Some evidence that the student has used scientific vocabulary although usage is not consistent or precise. • Sentence structure is generally controlled. • Spelling, punctuation, and/or grammar do not impede the meaning. • Some scientific symbols for units of measurement are used. Generally, the usage is appropriate • Limited presentation of data by tables or graphs.
Below acceptable standard and requires remedial help. **2**	• Limited evidence that the student has used scientific vocabulary. Generally, the usage is not consistent or precise. • Sentence structure is poorly controlled. • Spelling, punctuation, and/or grammar impedes the meaning. • Some scientific symbols for units of measurement are used, but most often, the usage is inappropriate. • No presentation of data by tables or graphs.
Basic level that requires remedial help or demonstrates a lack of effort. **1**	• Limited evidence that the student has used scientific vocabulary and usage is not consistent or precise. • Sentence structure is poorly controlled. • Spelling, punctuation, and/or grammar impedes the meaning. • No attention to using scientific symbols for units of measurement. • No presentation of data by tables or graphs.

Maximum = 10 Points

For use with *Transportation*, Chapter 1

What is in the Physics InfoMall for Chapter 1?

The entire Chapter 1 of *Transportation* deals with the physics of automobiles. The Physics InfoMall CD-ROM has many good places to find additional information. An article that describes how physics relates to driving can be found in the *American Journal of Physics*, volume 10, issue 6 (pages 322-327), and is titled "The Physics of Automobile Driving." This journal can be found in the Articles and Abstract Attic. Click on American Journal of Physics, then click on volume 10, then click on the article "The Physics of Automobile Driving" listed under issue 6. Of course, you can search the InfoMall for other items, but many of the relevant items are listed in this Teacher's Edition with the most closely related activity.

NOTES

ACTIVITY ONE
Response Time

Background Information

Background information for most activities is provided for the interest and insight of the teacher only. It is not intended to be part of the classroom instruction.

Reaction time can be understood by grouping physiological processes into three categories: input of sensory information, coordination by the central nervous system, and the response by motor nerves and their effectors, muscles and/or glands. The simplest reaction pathway is that of a reflex arc. Sensory receptors identify environmental stimuli causing a sensory nerve cell to become excited. The sensory nerve transmits an electrochemical impulse to the spinal cord. Here an intermediary nerve cell transmits the sensory impulse to a motor nerve cell. The impulse is carried by the motor nerve cell to a muscle (or in some cases a gland). The contraction of the muscle signals the response. A knee-jerk response provides an excellent example of this simple nerve pathway. The impulse is carried between three nerve cells: sensory nerve, interneuron, and motor nerve cell, toward the muscle. Surprisingly, no integration is required by the brain. These reactions occur without thinking.

Reactions that require integration by the central nervous system, such as those that occur when driving, take considerably longer to occur. A moose running in front of a vehicle is identified by visual receptors within the eye. Sensory impulses are carried toward the brain by the optic nerve. Here the information is accumulated and the driver is made aware of the problem. Multiple nerve connections carry the impulses toward the motor area of the brain. A conscious decision is made to lift the foot from the accelerator peddle and push down on the brake. Because the sensory nerves are connected with motor nerves through a maze of circuits within the brain, the reaction time is much longer than that of a reflex arch. Each time an impulse passes between connecting nerve cells, the speed of transmission is slowed.

Conscious decisions, such as braking for a moose, depend upon a number of variables. The time it takes to catch sight of the moose may well be the largest variable. Any distraction or driver fatigue will increase reaction times. Most impulses travel at approximately 100 m/sec along a nerve cell, but the time required for the impulse to travel between two different nerve cells varies greatly. Transmitter chemicals diffuse between connecting nerve cells. Because diffusion takes much more time than the movement of an impulse along a nerve cell, the connections between nerve cells slows reaction time. Not surprisingly, the complexity of integration of sensory impulses by the brain to create a visual image and the number of nerve cells involved also affects response time. The greater the number of interconnecting nerves, the slower is the processing time. Moving images require greater time to process and interpret than still images.

To accurately determine response times, we must consider how the reaction is measured. The removal of the foot from the driver's pedal takes considerably more time than just pushing down on the brake. The distance the leg moves, the amount of muscle required, and the health of the muscle also affect reaction rates.

As people age reaction rates are said to decline. The buildup of pigmented Nissl Bodies with nerve cells, slows the transmission of nerve impulses. In addition, the production of transmitter chemicals, the things that allow impulses to travel between nerves, decreases with age. Older people also tend to have less healthy muscles, further increasing the time it takes to respond to a stimulus. But age is not the major factor when considering reaction rates. The alertness of the driver is far more important.

In this activity students are asked to wire a series circuit. A series circuit has all of the current from the battery traveling through every part of the circuit. If either switch is open, the current is not able to traverse the entire circuit. In the reaction time circuit, one switch begins in the closed position and the other in the open position. One student is able to complete the circuit by closing the switch and lighting the bulb. The other student will then turn the light off by opening the other switch.

The reaction time graph is created by using the equation for free fall motion

$d = 1/2at^2$

where
a is the acceleration due to gravity (9.8 m/s^2),
t is the elapsed time and
d is the distance fallen. Since all objects fall at the same rate, there is no need to be concerned with the mass of the ruler.

Solving the above equation for time:

$t = \sqrt{2d/a}$

allows us to compute the reaction tome for any given distance. The students will be introduced to this equation later in the course. To provide the equation with no evidence of constant acceleration would not help their understanding at this point. If, on the other hand, they have studied acceleration previously, you may use this equation to provide a reinforcement of this concept.

Active-ating the Physics InfoMall

This activity is primarily about reaction times. There are several good items from the InfoMall that relate to this. If you choose to search the InfoMall CD-ROM for this activity, choose "reaction time" rather than "response time," as the latter will find mostly items that describe mechanical or chemical systems rather than people. All of the items found for Activity One, and many for the following activities, were found searching for "reaction time" in all stores on the InfoMall at the same time (select stores to be searched using "compound search" and choose "select..." below "search in databases:").

The InfoMall has several methods for measuring a person's reaction time. The methods used in *Active Physics* can also be found on the InfoMall. Although not related to driving, the effect of reaction time in analyzing the Kennedy assassination can be found in the Articles and Abstracts Attic, *American Journal of Physics*, volume 44, issue 9, "A Physicist Examines the Kennedy Assassination Film."

Some good places to look for the effect on driving are the following:

For You To Do

Step 1: Testing the reaction time for the foot may be different than for the hand. This is discussed briefly in Articles and Abstracts Attic, *The Physics Teacher*, volume 8, issue 4, "Problems for Introductory Physics," problem 49. This can be found most easily by scrolling down to near the bottom of the article and then searching up, rather than down. Included are some questions to consider about the effect of reactions time on driving.

Step 2: The reaction time for visual stimuli can differ from the time for audible stimuli. This is discussed, along with methods for measuring the difference, in Articles and Abstracts Attic, *The Physics Teacher*, volume 28, issue 6, "Speed of Sound in a Parking Lot." Reaction time is discussed as a source for error in the measurement of the speed of sound for this particular activity, but the difference in audible versus visual stimuli is measured using a meter stick.

Steps 7 and 8: Alternate methods for measuring reaction times can also be found on the InfoMall.

A circuit using an oscilloscope can be found in the Demo and Lab Shop, *Laboratory Manual to Accompany Physics Including Human Applications*, by Fuller, Fuller, & Fuller, The Oscilloscope, Application I: Reaction Time Measurement. A graphic showing how the circuit should be set up is included.

Using a clock (if it uses a large sweep second hand and displays time in small increments) to measure reaction time is discussed in the Demo and Lab Shop, *Demonstration Handbook for Physics*, Mechanics, Kinematics, Reaction Time, and scroll down to Mb-1. Also, the use of a meter stick is discussed here, as it is in many other places.

Step 9: *Laboratory Manual to accompany Physics Including Human Applications*, by Fuller, Fuller, & Fuller; Human senses, Part III: reaction time. This shows how a meter stick can be used to measure reaction time.

Physics To Go

Methods mentioned in this activity include using a ruler or a dollar bill. These methods, including graphics are also discussed in the following places on the InfoMall:

Book Basement, *A Guidebook for Teaching Physics*, by Yurkewicz, Motion, topic IV: Uniform Acceleration. Activity #9 is about using a dollar bill, and Activity #10 is about using a meter stick.

The same methods are mentioned in the Demo and Lab Shop, *Physics Demonstrations and Experiments for High School*, Part II - Lab Experiments, #2 Using Acceleration of Gravity to Calculate Reaction Time," and uses a dollar bill and a meter stick.

The use of a dollar bill is also mentioned in Teacher Treasures, *Demonstration Guide for High School Physics*, and scroll down to "$ Bill & Reaction Time."

Planning for the Activity

Time Requirements

Allow about 40 minutes to construct the electrical circuit and complete steps 1 to 6. An additional 20 minutes to complete the remaining steps and record data may be required.

Materials needed

For each group:

- D-cell
- knife switch (2)
- flashlight bulb and socket
- connecting wire
- battery holder
- stopwatch (2)
- centimeter ruler

For the class:

- standard response-time meter, such as used in drivers' education classes

Advance Preparation and Setup

Search your school for a response timer formerly used in drivers' education. These units, about the size of an old movie projector, used to be quite common and included apparatus for testing peripheral vision and color blindness. It may well be in a closet somewhere in your building.

Should a response timer from a drivers' education class be unavailable, a usable circuit can be rigged if a clock measuring hundredths of a second is available. Set it up in series with its power source, a switch, and a normally closed foot switch. Response time is measured by having one student watch the clock, with a foot resting on the floor near the foot switch. When the student's partner starts the clock, the one being tested stops it by pressing the foot switch.

Teaching Notes

Active Physics uses a modified constructivist model. By confronting students' misconceptions and by having them do hands-on exploration of ideas, we seek to replace their misconceptions with correct perceptions of reality. In order to do this, a consistent scheme is integrated into the course activities to elicit the students' misconceptions early in any activity. Students' current mental models are sampled by one or more What Do You Think? questions. Students are not expected to know a "right" answer. These questions are supposed to elicit from students their beliefs regarding a very specific prediction or outcome, and students should commit to a written specific answer in their logs.

In Activity One the term "response time" is used instead of the more common "reaction time" to differentiate the behavior from the reflex reaction.

Discuss the response-time circuit. The circuit is not complicated, but will provide the students with the experience of wiring a circuit. This is an opportunity to point out the characteristics of a simple series circuit. Do not begin an extensive lesson on circuit theory unless the class is really excited by the topic. Let students follow the direction in the text, and answer the questions. The sophistication of the circuit can be improved with the use of specialized normally on and normally off switches, if available.

You may be tempted to skip building the circuit and get right into measuring response time accurately. Do not skip this step. The qualitative estimates before building the circuit and using the circuit provide the foundation for understanding the short time intervals measured next.

Encourage students to work cooperatively by assigning tasks prior to beginning the activity. The following tasks are designed for groups of four students:

- **Organizer:** helps focus discussion and ensures that all members of the group contribute to the discussion. The organizer ensures that all of the equipment has been gathered and that the group completes all parts of the activity.
- **Recorder:** provides written procedures when required, diagrams where appropriate and records data. The recorder must work closely with the organizer to ensure that all group members contribute.
- **Researcher:** seeks written and electronic information to support the findings of the group. In addition, where appropriate, the researcher will develop and test prototypes. The researcher will also exchange information gathered among different groups.
- **Diverger:** seeks alternative explanations and approaches. The task of the diverger is keep the discussion open. "Are other explanations possible?"

The technique using two stopwatches in step 8 can become a popular game. Count your stopwatches before the students leave.

Students often believe that age is the largest factor when determining response time. Many will indicate that because of their much faster response times, they are better equipped to travel at higher speeds than older people. Variations due to age increase response time by as little a 0.01 sec. The identification of sensory information has the greatest impact upon reaction time. Therefore, the alertness of the driver has the greatest impact upon stopping distances. The driver's experience may also play an important part in response time.

See the High Technology Alternative to Activity One: Response Time. The use of photogates and 0:00 sec timers will be required if you choose to do this alternative activity.

Activity Overview

This activity addresses questions of response time in its relation to the problem of bringing a car to rest.

Student Objectives

Students will:

- identify the parts of the process of stopping a car.
- measure reaction time.
- wire a series circuit.

ANSWERS FOR THE TEACHER ONLY

What Do You Think?

Response times will vary. The most important factor is speed, and distance is proportional to the square of the speed. The activity will provide a basis for this relationship. The identification of sensory information has the greatest impact on reaction time. Therefore, the alertness of the driver has the greatest impact on stopping distances. The driver's experience may also play an important part in response time. What Do You Think? is designed to provoke a discussion of the effects of listening to loud music on response time, as well as the distraction of talking or the effect of fatigue, alcohol, or drugs.

CHAPTER 1 DRIVING THE ROADS

Activity One

Response Time

WHAT DO YOU THINK?

Many deaths that occur on the highway are drivers and passengers in vehicles that did not cause the accident. The driver was not able to respond in time to avoid becoming a statistic.

- **How long would it take you to respond to an emergency?**

Record your ideas about these questions in your *Active Physics log*. Be prepared to discuss your responses with your small group and the class.

FOR YOU TO DO

1. To stop a car, you must move your foot from the gas pedal to the brake pedal. Try moving your right foot between imaginary pedals.

a) Estimate how long it takes to move your foot between the imaginary pedals. Record your estimate.

TRANSPORTATION T4

ANSWERS

For You To Do

1. a) A reasonable estimate would be about half a second.

2. The first step in stopping a car happens even before you move your foot to the brake. It takes time to see or hear something that tells you to move your foot. Test this by having a friend stand behind you and clap. When you hear the sound, move your foot between imaginary pedals.
   a) Estimate how long it took you to respond to the loud noise. Record your estimate.

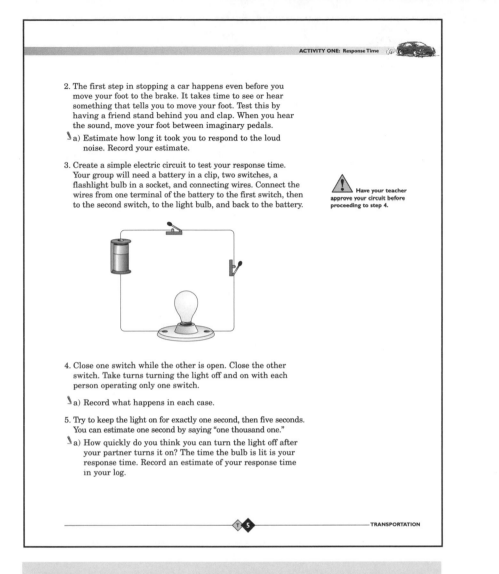

3. Create a simple electric circuit to test your response time. Your group will need a battery in a clip, two switches, a flashlight bulb in a socket, and connecting wires. Connect the wires from one terminal of the battery to the first switch, then to the second switch, to the light bulb, and back to the battery.

Have your teacher approve your circuit before proceeding to step 4.

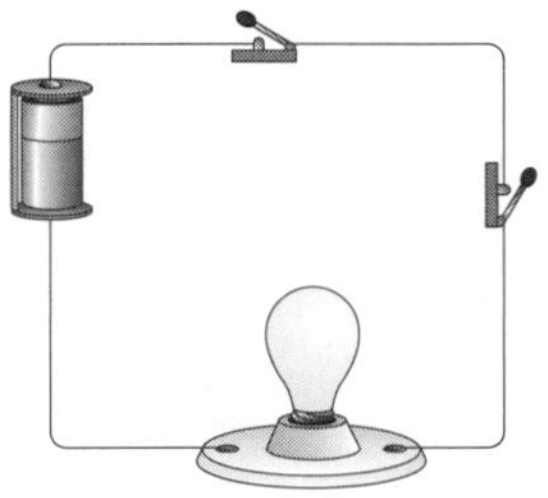

4. Close one switch while the other is open. Close the other switch. Take turns turning the light off and on with each person operating only one switch.
   a) Record what happens in each case.

5. Try to keep the light on for exactly one second, then five seconds. You can estimate one second by saying "one thousand one."
   a) How quickly do you think you can turn the light off after your partner turns it on? The time the bulb is lit is your response time. Record an estimate of your response time in your log.

ANSWERS

For You To Do *(continued)*

2. a) Estimates will vary. A reasonable estimate would be about half a second.

3. Students set up circuit.

4. a) The light bulb glows when both switches are closed.

5. a) Estimates will vary. Most students will be able to turn the light off in a quarter of a second or less. This is considerably less than the time it takes to move the foot from the gas pedal to the brake pedal.

ANSWERS

For You To Do
(continued)

6. a) If the light bulb were replaced by a clock, the accuracy of the measurement would be improved. Students should also note that it takes a lot longer to move your foot and press a pedal than it takes to move a finger that is already posed for action. Students might suggest replacing the switch with a foot pedal.

   b) By averaging the results of a number of trials, the accuracy can be improved.

7. a) Response times will vary. Response times will probably be between 0.5 s and 0.8 s.

8. a) Expect the response times using this method to be slower than for previous trials.

9. a) Expect the distances to vary. If students are anticipating the release by closing their fingers periodically, and their fingers are close enough together, results may be as low as 2 cm. Suggest students average a number of trials to obtain a more reasonable result.

   b) If interpreting the graph of distance vs. time for a body falling from rest: $d = 1/2gt^2$ is difficult for your students, they could use the formula: $t = 0.45\sqrt{d}$.

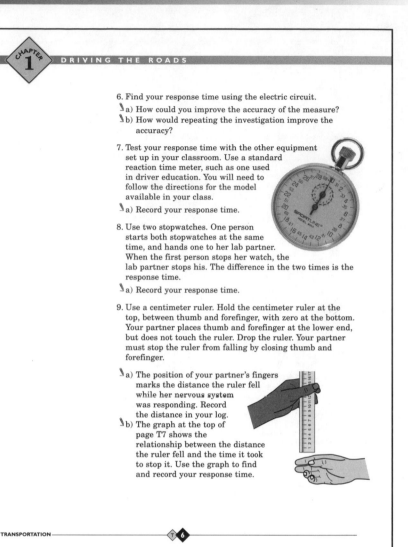

,045?

6. Find your response time using the electric circuit.
   a) How could you improve the accuracy of the measure?
   b) How would repeating the investigation improve the accuracy?

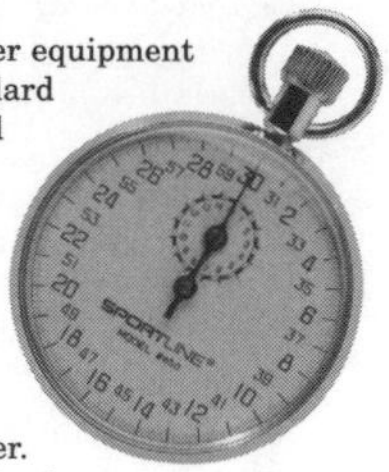

7. Test your response time with the other equipment set up in your classroom. Use a standard reaction time meter, such as one used in driver education. You will need to follow the directions for the model available in your class.
   a) Record your response time.

8. Use two stopwatches. One person starts both stopwatches at the same time, and hands one to her lab partner. When the first person stops her watch, the lab partner stops his. The difference in the two times is the response time.
   a) Record your response time.

9. Use a centimeter ruler. Hold the centimeter ruler at the top, between thumb and forefinger, with zero at the bottom. Your partner places thumb and forefinger at the lower end, but does not touch the ruler. Drop the ruler. Your partner must stop the ruler from falling by closing thumb and forefinger.
   a) The position of your partner's fingers marks the distance the ruler fell while her nervous system was responding. Record the distance in your log.
   b) The graph at the top of page T7 shows the relationship between the distance the ruler fell and the time it took to stop it. Use the graph to find and record your response time.

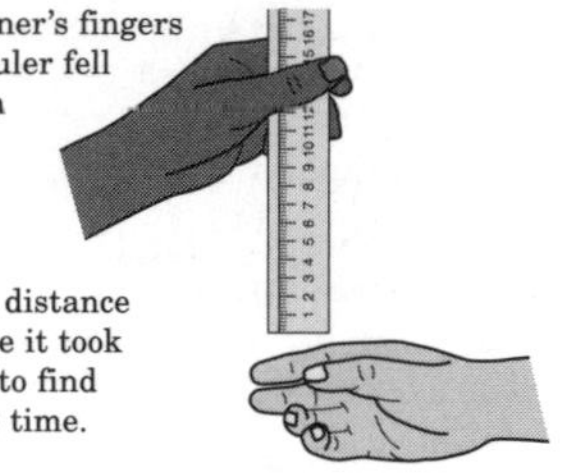

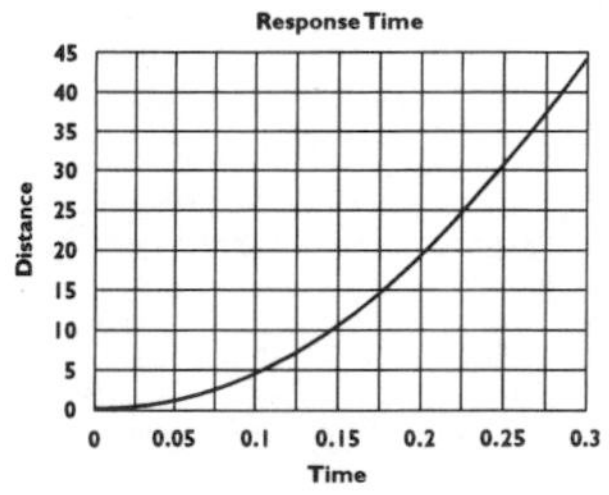

10. Compare the measures of your response obtained from each strategy.
   a) Explain why they were not all the same.
   b) What measure do you think best reports your response time? Why?

11. Compare the measures you obtained with those of other students.
   a) Record the results for the fastest, slowest, and average response times.
   b) Why do you think response times vary for people of the same age? Discuss this with your group and then record your answer.

REFLECTING ON THE ACTIVITY AND THE CHALLENGE

The amount of time a person requires before they can act has a direct impact on their driving. It takes time to notice a situation and more time to respond. A person who requires a second to respond to what they see or hear is more likely to have an accident than someone who responds in half a second. One part of your challenge is to explain the effect of response time on driving.

ANSWERS

For You To Do
(continued)

10.a) Students may suggest that some of the methods permit them to be ready and poised to respond better than others. Estimating the point on the ruler where the fingers are located may cause errors.

b) Students may suggest that the standard reaction timer used in drivers' education might be the most accurate. Accept any reasonable explanation.

11.a) Students compare classroom data.

b) Students answers will vary. Students may consider: physiological difference in nervous systems, the amount and health of the muscles being used, the alertness of the subject, the time of day the test was conducted, use of medications such as cough syrups.

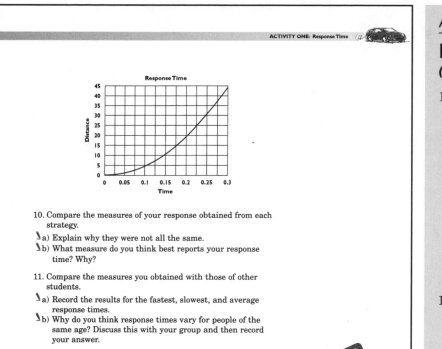

ANSWERS

Physics To Go

1. Encourage the students to continue the discussion of safe driving at home.
2. Students may find that response time for much older and very young family members may be slower. On the other hand, parents and siblings at home may be more motivated to produce excellent response times and therefore may be more alert than the subjects tested in class.
3. The length of a dollar bill is 15.7 cm. The free fall time is under 0.2 s, which makes it nearly impossible to catch the bill unless the hand is lowered or the release is anticipated. The grasping action with the thumb and forefinger is a much more familiar one than between the forefinger and middle finger. Refer the students to the graph, or provide them with a simple mathematical equation they can use to quantify their results.
4. The speed at which the race car driver is traveling requires a very quick response time. Although students will investigate the relationship between distance and time in the next activity, most will be able to answer this question from their previous experience. Encourage students to become aware of the distractions that the average driver faces, as well as the potential dangers. Compare the focused, alert race car driver encountering oil on the track, to a distracted student reacting to someone who has been pushed in front of the car "as a joke or dare."
5. Students should be assigned these questions routinely throughout the chapter. By answering this question, they have completed a part of their chapter challenge. Suggest that the students read the Reflecting on the Activity and the Challenge before they proceed with the answer. Answers will vary greatly. Some students who are familiar with video games may show "superhuman" responses.

CHAPTER 1 DRIVING THE ROADS

PHYSICS TO GO

1. Test the response time of some of your friends and family with the centimeter ruler. Bring in the results from at least three people of various ages.
2. How do the values you found in question 1 compare with those you obtained in class? What do you think explains the difference, if any?
3. Take a dollar bill and fold it in half lengthwise. Have someone try to catch the dollar bill between his or her *forefinger and middle* finger. Most people will fail this task.
   a) Explain why it is so difficult to catch the dollar bill.
   b) Repeat the dollar bill test, letting them catch it with their thumb and forefinger.
   c) Explain why catching it with thumb and forefinger may have been easier. Try to include numbers in your answer such as length of the dollar, time for dollar to fall, and average response time.
4. Does a race car driver need a better response time than someone driving around a school? Explain your answer, giving examples of the dangers each person encounters.
5. Apply what you learned from this activity to describe how knowing your own response time can help you be a safer driver. You will use this in meeting the challenge at the end of the chapter.

TRANSPORTATION T 8

STRETCHING EXERCISES

1. Build a device with a red light and a green light. If the red light turns on, you must press one button and measure the response time. If the green light turns on, you must press a second button and measure the response time. Have your teacher approve your design before proceeding. How do response times to this "decision" task compare with the response times measured earlier?

2. Use the graph on page T7 to construct a response-time ruler with the distance measurement converted to time. You can now read response times directly.

INQUIRY INVESTIGATION

Do you think some groups of people have better or worse response times than others? Consider groups such as basketball players, video game players, taxi drivers, or older adults. Plan and carry out an investigation to collect data that will help you find an answer. Include in your plan the number of subjects, how you will test them, and how you will organize and interpret the data collected.

ANSWERS

Stretching Exercises

1. This assignment may interest students who are enrolled in a technology program. It may be a way of getting a special reaction timer for use next year.

2. The students might want to mark a time scale on a strip of masking tape which could be affixed to a ruler or paint stirrer.

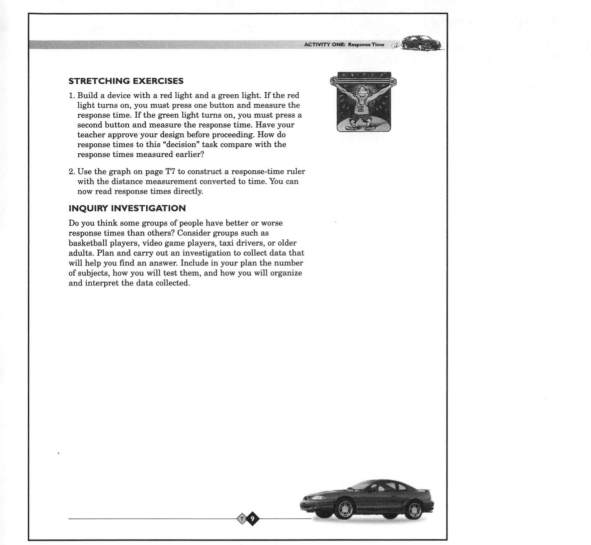

Assessment: Group Work

The following rubric can be used to access group work during the first six steps of the activity. Each member of the group can evaluate the manner in which the group worked to solve problems in the activity.

Maximum value = 12

1. Low level — indicates minimum effort or effectiveness.
2. Average — acceptable standard has been achieved, but the group could have worked more effectively if better organized.
3. Good — this rating indicates a superior effort. Although improvements might have been made, the group was on task all of the time and completed all parts of the activity.

Descriptor		Values	
1. The group worked cooperatively to design a circuit that would measure reaction times. Comments:	1	2	3
2. A plan was established before beginning and a light bulb was used to test the circuit. Comments:	1	2	3
3. The group was organized. Materials were collected and the problems were addressed by the entire group. Comments:	1	2	3
4. Data was collected and recorded in an organized fashion in data tables and in journals. Comments:	1	2	3

For use with *Transportation*, Chapter 1, ACTIVITY ONE: Response Time

Assessment: Scientific and Technological Thinking

Scientific and Technological Thinking can be assessed using the rubric below. Allow one mark for each check mark.

Maximum value = 10

Descriptor	Yes	No
1. A complete circuit is constructed.		
2. A light bulb is used to check for battery life and the functioning circuit.		
3. A switch is used to time reaction rates.		
4. Controls, such as the distance of the hand from the switch, are maintained throughout the experiment.		
5. Proper units are used to measure reaction times.		
6. A clock or timing device is integrated into the circuit to provide accuracy of measurement.		
7. Timing devices are tested and/or modified prior to collecting final data.		
8. Response time can be determined by using a distance vs time graph.		
9. Students can identify variables used in the experiment that would alter response time.		
10. Student is able to relate response times to the need for safe driving.		

Activity One A

Response Time: High-Tech Alternative

FOR YOU TO DO

1. Photogates can be used along with an electronic timer to determine reaction times. Hide the first photogate within a cardboard box, so that observation and reaction times can be accurately monitored. Use the setup below. The subject observes the timer clock for the "GO" signal.

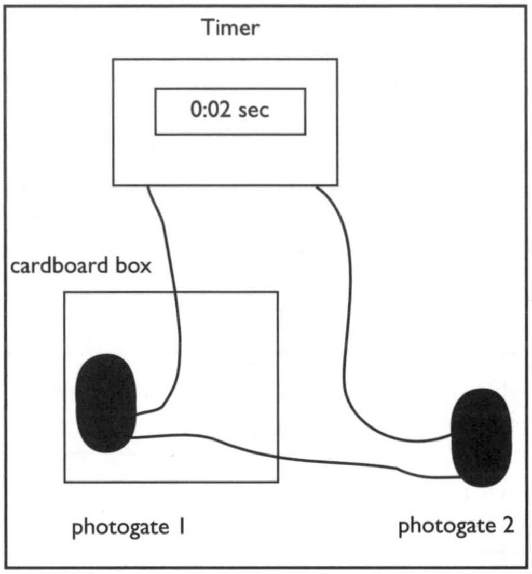

2. The tester moves his or her hand inside of the cardboard box and activates the first photocell.

3. The subject sees the clock begin to move and quickly moves his or her hand in front of the second photogate to stop the clock.

   a) Complete multiple trials and record your data. Calculate the mean time taken to stop the electronic timer.

   b) Explain why the mean time was determined.

   c) Repeat the procedure but this time use your non-dominant hand. Account for any differences in reaction rate.

   d) Why must the test subject's hand be held a specified distance from the timer?

   e) When braking, the right foot is moved from the gas to the brake. What advantage is gained from only using one foot to control both the accelerator pedal and the brake?

   f) A faster reaction time could be obtained by holding the left foot just millimeters above the brake pedal. As the left foot tramps on the brake, the right foot would leave the gas pedal. Explain why the practice of two-foot driving (using both the right and left foot) is discouraged.

For use with *Transportation*, Chapter 1, ACTIVITY ONE: Response Time

Activity One A

Response Time: High-Tech Alternative

Time Requirements

Approximately 40 minutes is required to complete the experiment.

Materials needed

- electrical clock (measuring 1/100 sec)
- 2 photogates

ANSWERS

For You To Do

3. a-b) Small variations can be expected. Sometimes the subject may anticipate when the experimenter was about to throw the switch. Other times small distractions may have increased the reaction time. By taking an average, variables that increase and decrease reaction times can be eliminated.

c) In general, the dominant hand responds faster. The more neural circuits are used, the faster is the response time.

d) The further the hand is from the photogate, the greater the time it takes to reach the photocell.

e) You can't accelerate and brake at the same time. Not only would this increase wear on the brakes, it would tend to throw the car into a spin. By using one foot, the problem of simultaneously braking and accelerating is eliminated.

f) Simultaneous pushing down on the gas pedal and the brake would increase the braking distance. Because the engine would be pulling or pushing the car forward, while the brakes are applied — the effectiveness of the braking system would be reduced. The car is not able to do both at the same time.

ACTIVITY TWO
Speed and Following Distance

Background Information

Kinematics is the study of motion. Every person will have experienced kinematics. From the moment we are able to crawl, we have a basic understanding of kinematics. As we grow and gain more experience, we are able to recognize objects as moving "fast" or "slow". We can make comparisons between the speed of a hare with the speed of a tortoise. In physics, we observe an object in motion, and then, using measurement and graphs, we are able to analyze the motion of that object.

To do this analysis, tools of measurement must be established which are appropriate for the object in motion and the speed at which it's moving. For example, a geologist who studies the movement of plates within the Earth's crust would measure the distances in inches (or cm) and the time in years or even thousands of years. When measuring the speed of an electron in a particle accelerator, we would use distances measured in meters or kilometers and times in millionths of seconds.

Understanding speed is critical in understanding motion and two tools used by scientists to achieve this understanding are mathematics, and graphical analysis. In this activity the students will be analyzing motion both mathematically and graphically.

A mathematical analysis is using the formula $v = d/t$.

Speed (symbol for speed is v) is the distance an object moves in a given time.

Average speed is the total distance traveled/total time. For example, you can travel from one city to the next in two hours, a total distance of 100 miles. Your average speed is (calculated mathematically)

v = total distance/total time

v = 100 miles/2 hours

v = 50 mph

However, if on the return trip you had a flat tire, and spent 30 minutes fixing your tire, the total time has now changed to 2.5 h and the average speed is now 100 miles/2.5 hours or 40 mph. Instantaneous speed, on the other hand, is the speed that you are traveling at a given moment. For example on the return trip, even though your average speed was 40 mph, your instantaneous speed at a given time may have been 65 mph. Instantaneous speed is the speed at which you happen to be traveling when you look down at your speedometer.

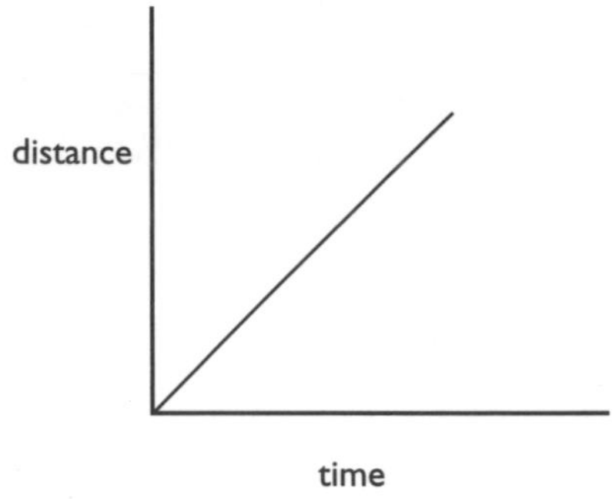

A graphical analysis of uniform motion (we will be using constant motion and uniform motion interchangeably) will involve collection of data, and then plotting that data onto a graph. Putting the information onto a distance-time graph will produce a straight line. (A straight line indicates uniform or constant motion.) The slope of that line $(\Delta d/\Delta t)$ will give us the speed. (Δd $(d_2 - d_1)$ = meters (m) (or miles) and Δt $(t_2 - t_1)$ = seconds (s) (or hours), therefore the unit for the slope is m/s (or mph).) For distance, d_2 usually represents the final distance. In most situations d_1 is the starting point and is most often indicated by zero. Similarly, Δt represents change in time, where t_2 is the final or end time and t_1 is the initial time.

Although the following is beyond the intent of the activity, some extension is presented here for the teacher.

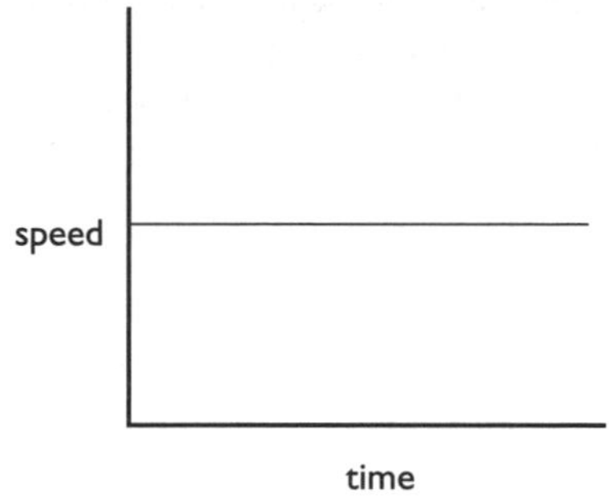

The speed-time graph of the same object can be obtained by taking the speed from the distance-time graph, at various times, and plotting them against time on a speed-time graph. The resulting line will be a horizontal straight line, which reinforces the concept of constant motion.

To find the distance an object travels while experiencing constant motion, we find the area under the graph. Area = length of side x the width of the side ($A = l \times w$). Therefore, $d = v \times t$.

Mathematically the formula $v = d/t$ will give the rearranged formula to solve for d as $d = v \times t$.

In later grades, students will move from the study of speed to the study of velocity. The concept is essentially the same, with the difference being speed is the only magnitude or how fast something is moving whereas velocity is the speed and the direction in which the object is moving.

Active-ating the Physics InfoMall

The effect of reaction time on following distance is discussed in Articles and Abstracts Attic, *The Physics Teacher,* volume 8, issue 4, "Problems for Introductory Physics," problem 49. This can be found most easily by scrolling down to near the bottom of the article and then searching up, rather than down. Included are some questions to consider about the effect of reactions time on driving.

Planning for the Activity

Time Requirements

During the class each group of students will require approximately 20 - 30 minutes to do the experiment and gather their data.

Materials needed

For each group:

- MBL or CBL with Sonic Ranger

Advance Preparation and Setup

Become familiar with the sonic rangers and the software that controls their output. Instructions come with the equipment, but you should use it yourself before putting it into the classroom. It will expedite the experiment if you are aware of the near and far limits of range. Prepare a list of the keystrokes required by your software to erase one graph and get ready to gather new data. Some programs ask several questions before recording data. You should know the best responses so that there will be little delay. Check as well on an appropriate sampling rate for your machine, since too much detail will cloud the issues at the moment. The sampling rate should be relatively slow.

In preparing for the class, set up the ranger and computer ready to go. Put masking tape on the floor to mark the range and perhaps another tape to indicate the lane so that students will stay "on track."

Teaching Notes

After the students have read and reacted to the What Do You Think? question, perhaps enhanced with a personal story about being tailgated by a poor driver, get right to the sonic rangers to perform the exercises. If you do not have access to separate computer setups for each group of students, do this as a demonstration using student volunteers.

Make sure the computer equipment is in a secure and stable environment.

Even if you have only one setup available, it is likely that most students will remain engaged by the activity. It can be presented as a human-sized video game where the challenge is to create the straightest line, the smoothest curve, the steepest slope, etc. One student can be asked to create a graph while the others look away, after which another student can describe the motion that caused the graph. There are many variations, including having students copy graphs created by other students.

While it is fairly easy to obtain good speed-time graphs using the sonic ranger, an uneven gait or even a baggy sweatshirt can produce some irregularity. Teach the students to focus on the general trends. Students may accidentally collect data or

1

construct graphs of displacement or acceleration instead of speed. You can use this error to your mutual advantage by asking them to explain what they see.

The graphs will quickly give students a secure understanding of the meaning of constant speed, and they can identify the different graphs almost at once. This provides preparation for algebraic analysis.

A common misconception held by students is that they go from zero to the speed they are walking or running instantly. In fact, there will always be some acceleration. Illustrate this with a set of data that has enough points to show that the first part of the graph is not straight.

Another common misconception of students that has been well documented is the confusion between distance and velocity. Look at the following pair of strobe pictures:

```
O     O     O     O     O
   X     X        X           X
```

Students may think that the X and O are traveling the same speed when they are aligned. They have the same speed when the distance between adjacent Xs is identical to the spacing between adjacent Os.

The sonic ranger has been shown to be extremely effective for students to gain an understanding of motion graphs. It is well worth the equipment investment.

The definition of velocity as the change in distance divided by the change in time can be written as an algebraic equation and can be solved for any of the variables.

$d = vt$

$v = d/t$

$t = d/v$

Some students deficient in algebra skills will need some help with this. You should emphasize the following points while students are learning this relationship:

The units of distance and time and velocity should always be presented with the numbers.

Any distance and any time can be used for velocity. (Cars move at miles/hour, km/h, or m/s; glaciers move at meters per year.)

To measure velocity, you need a ruler and a stopwatch.

Average velocity should be distinguished from initial velocity and final velocity. The average velocity for a trip does not give any indication of the initial and final velocity.

Before assigning the Physics To Go questions 4 to 7, work a few examples with the students. Some students will need help in manipulating the speed equation. You may wish to provide them with the equations required to calculate distance and time.

NOTES

1

Activity Overview

This activity should provide the student with a feel and definition for the notion of speed.

Student Objectives

Students will:

- define speed.
- identify constant and changing speeds.
- interpret distance-time and speed-time graphs.
- contrast average and instantaneous speeds.
- calculate the distance traveled at constant speed.

ANSWERS

What Do You Think?

The proper interval between your car and the vehicle in front is two seconds. (See the answer for Physics To Go, step 8 for more information.)

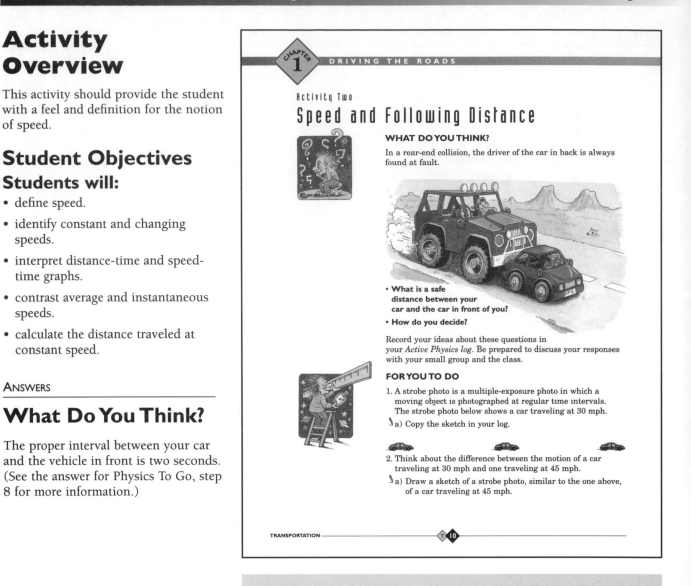

Activity Two

Speed and Following Distance

WHAT DO YOU THINK?

In a rear-end collision, the driver of the car in back is always found at fault.

- **What is a safe distance between your car and the car in front of you?**
- **How do you decide?**

Record your ideas about these questions in your *Active Physics log*. Be prepared to discuss your responses with your small group and the class.

FOR YOU TO DO

1. A strobe photo is a multiple-exposure photo in which a moving object is photographed at regular time intervals. The strobe photo below shows a car traveling at 30 mph.
   a) Copy the sketch in your log.

2. Think about the difference between the motion of a car traveling at 30 mph and one traveling at 45 mph.
   a) Draw a sketch of a strobe photo, similar to the one above, of a car traveling at 45 mph.

ANSWERS

For You To Do

1. a) If the students do not feel comfortable sketching cars, suggest that they use O or X symbols instead. Check to see that the students understand that the spaces between the cars are even.

2. a) The sketch should show the cars with larger, even gaps between them.

   b) The marks are a greater distance apart.

   c) The cars should be twice the distance apart as they were for 30 mph.

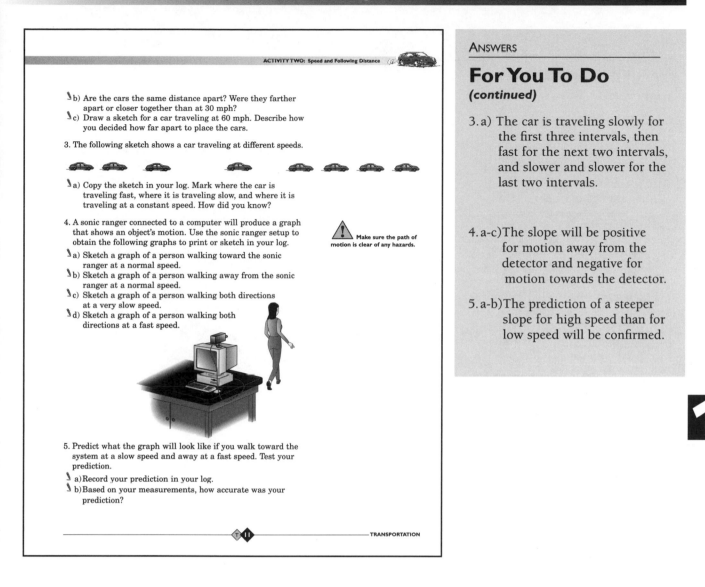

b) Are the cars the same distance apart? Were they farther apart or closer together than at 30 mph?

c) Draw a sketch for a car traveling at 60 mph. Describe how you decided how far apart to place the cars.

3. The following sketch shows a car traveling at different speeds.

a) Copy the sketch in your log. Mark where the car is traveling fast, where it is traveling slow, and where it is traveling at a constant speed. How did you know?

4. A sonic ranger connected to a computer will produce a graph that shows an object's motion. Use the sonic ranger setup to obtain the following graphs to print or sketch in your log.

Make sure the path of motion is clear of any hazards.

a) Sketch a graph of a person walking toward the sonic ranger at a normal speed.

b) Sketch a graph of a person walking away from the sonic ranger at a normal speed.

c) Sketch a graph of a person walking both directions at a very slow speed.

d) Sketch a graph of a person walking both directions at a fast speed.

5. Predict what the graph will look like if you walk toward the system at a slow speed and away at a fast speed. Test your prediction.

a) Record your prediction in your log.

b) Based on your measurements, how accurate was your prediction?

ANSWERS

For You To Do

(continued)

3. a) The car is traveling slowly for the first three intervals, then fast for the next two intervals, and slower and slower for the last two intervals.

4. a-c) The slope will be positive for motion away from the detector and negative for motion towards the detector.

5. a-b) The prediction of a steeper slope for high speed than for low speed will be confirmed.

1

ANSWERS

For You To Do

(continued)

6. a) For motion away from the sonic ranger, the total distance will be the maximum y-value of the graph. For motion towards the ranger the final y-value must be subtracted from the starting y-value.

   b) The total time is measured on the x-axis for the points corresponding to those for distance.

   c) Students divide the value they obtained in 6. a) by the one in 6. b) to obtain their average speed. Check that the units used are m/s.

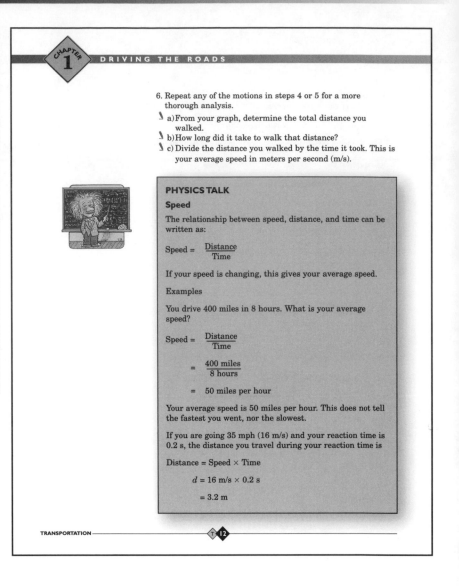

6. Repeat any of the motions in steps 4 or 5 for a more thorough analysis.
   a) From your graph, determine the total distance you walked.
   b) How long did it take to walk that distance?
   c) Divide the distance you walked by the time it took. This is your average speed in meters per second (m/s).

PHYSICS TALK

Speed

The relationship between speed, distance, and time can be written as:

$$\text{Speed} = \frac{\text{Distance}}{\text{Time}}$$

If your speed is changing, this gives your average speed.

Examples

You drive 400 miles in 8 hours. What is your average speed?

$$\text{Speed} = \frac{\text{Distance}}{\text{Time}} = \frac{400 \text{ miles}}{8 \text{ hours}} = 50 \text{ miles per hour}$$

Your average speed is 50 miles per hour. This does not tell the fastest you went, nor the slowest.

If you are going 35 mph (16 m/s) and your reaction time is 0.2 s, the distance you travel during your reaction time is

Distance = Speed × Time

$$d = 16 \text{ m/s} \times 0.2 \text{ s} = 3.2 \text{ m}$$

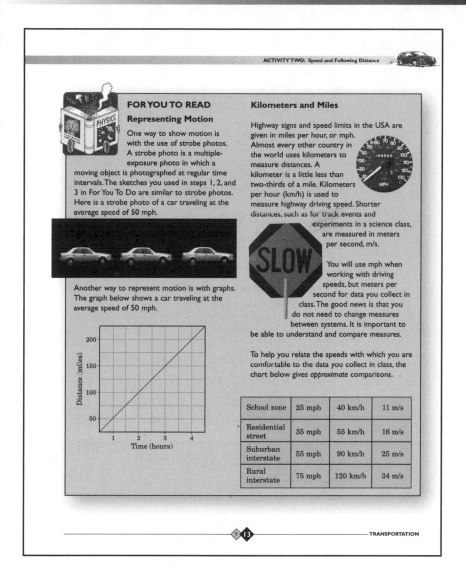

FOR YOU TO READ

Representing Motion

One way to show motion is with the use of strobe photos. A strobe photo is a multiple-exposure photo in which a moving object is photographed at regular time intervals. The sketches you used in steps 1, 2, and 3 in For You To Do are similar to strobe photos. Here is a strobe photo of a car traveling at the average speed of 50 mph.

Another way to represent motion is with graphs. The graph below shows a car traveling at the average speed of 50 mph.

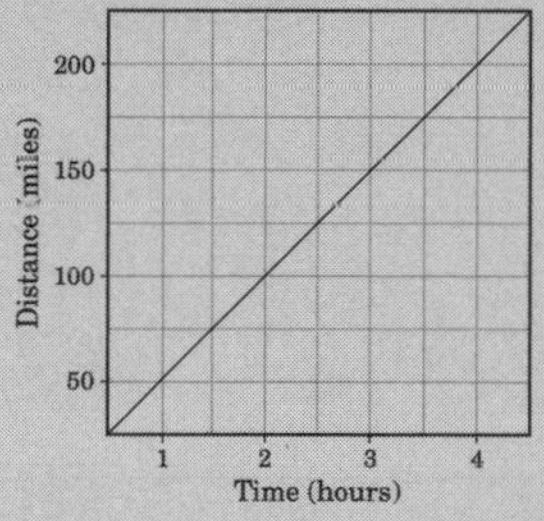

Kilometers and Miles

Highway signs and speed limits in the USA are given in miles per hour, or mph. Almost every other country in the world uses kilometers to measure distances. A kilometer is a little less than two-thirds of a mile. Kilometers per hour (km/h) is used to measure highway driving speed. Shorter distances, such as for track events and experiments in a science class, are measured in meters per second, m/s.

You will use mph when working with driving speeds, but meters per second for data you collect in class. The good news is that you do not need to change measures between systems. It is important to be able to understand and compare measures.

To help you relate the speeds with which you are comfortable to the data you collect in class, the chart below gives *approximate* comparisons.

School zone	25 mph	40 km/h	11 m/s
Residential street	35 mph	55 km/h	16 m/s
Suburban interstate	55 mph	90 km/h	25 m/s
Rural interstate	75 mph	120 km/h	34 m/s

ANSWERS

Physics To Go

1. a) The car is moving at a constant speed every three seconds.
   b) The car speeds up, slows down, speeds up, and then slows again.

REFLECTING ON THE ACTIVITY AND THE CHALLENGE

You know that response time has a direct impact on your driving and the possibility of being involved in a car accident. In this activity you observed what happens to the car while the driver responds before applying the brake. The car continues moving. The slower a person's response time, the greater the distance the car moves before stopping.

You now know how reaction time and speed affect the distance to stop. You should be able to make a good argument about tailgating as part of the chapter challenge.

PHYSICS TO GO

1. Describe the motion of each car moving to the right. The strobe pictures were taken every 3 s (seconds).

a)
b)

2. Sketch strobe pictures of the following.
   a) A car starting at rest and reaching a final constant speed.
   b) A car traveling at a constant speed then coming to a stop.

3. For each graph below, describe the motion of the car:

a) b) c) d)

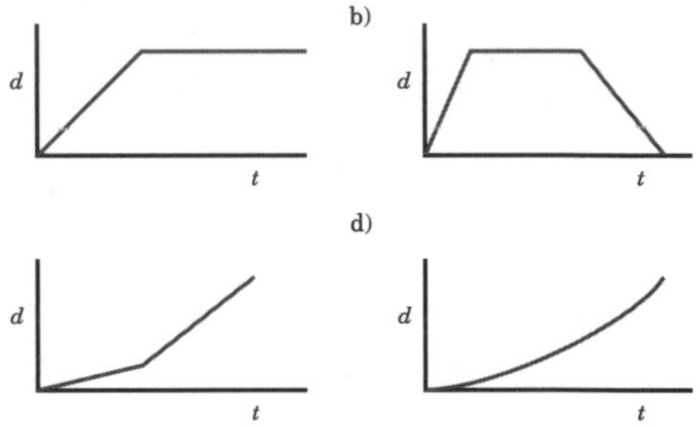

2. a) Answers will vary, but there should be a measurable increase in the distance of the first few sketches, and then the same distance while the car travels at a constant speed.

   E.g.: Δ Δ Δ Δ Δ Δ Δ Δ Δ Δ

   b) The reverse of the above situation, moving at a constant speed then slowing down.

   E.g.: Δ Δ Δ Δ Δ Δ Δ Δ ΔΔ

3. a) A car travels at a constant speed, and then stops.
   b) A car travels at a rapid, constant speed, stops, and then returns at a slower constant speed.
   c) A car travels at a slow constant speed, and then increases to travel at a faster constant speed.
   d) A car accelerates as it travels.

   Note: If students have difficulty interpreting this graph, suggest they return to the question after completing the next activity.

4. A race car driver travels at 110 m/s (that's almost 250 mph) for 20 s. How far has the driver traveled?

5. A salesperson drove the 215 miles from New York City to Washington, DC, in $4\frac{1}{2}$ hours.
   a) What was her average speed?
   b) How fast was she going when she passed through Baltimore?

6. If you planned to bike to a park that was 5 miles away, what average speed would you have to keep up to arrive in 2 hours?

7. Use your average response time from Activity 1 to answer the following:
   a) How far does your car travel in meters during your response time if you are moving at 55 mph (25 m/s)?
   b) How far does your car travel during your response time if you are moving at 35 mph (16 m/s)? How does the distance compare with the distance at 55 mph?
   c) Suppose you are very tired and your response time is doubled. How far would you travel at 55 mph during your response time?

8. According to traffic experts, the proper following distance you should leave between your car and the vehicle in front of you is two seconds. As the vehicle in front of you passes a fixed point, say to yourself "one thousand one, one thousand two." Your car should reach the point as you complete the phrase. How can the experts be sure? Isn't two seconds a measure of time? Will two seconds be safe on the interstate highway?

9. You calculated the distance your car would move during your response time. Use that information to determine a safe following distance at:
   a) 25 mph
   b) 55 mph
   c) 75 mph

ANSWERS

Physics To Go
(continued)

4. Using the formula $v = d/t$, therefore;
   $d = vt$, then;
   $d = 110\text{m/s} \times 20\text{ s}$
   $d = 2200\text{ m}$ or 2.2 km
   The driver traveled 2200 m, or 2.2 km

5. a) $v = d/t$ $v = 215\text{ miles}/4.5\text{ hours}$
   $v = 48\text{ mph}$ Her average speed was about 48 mph.
   b) This question cannot be answered with the data provided. We do not know her instantaneous speed at any one time. We can only assume that she was *probably* doing about 48 mph.

6. $v = d/t$ $v = 5\text{ miles}/2\text{ hours}$
   $v = 2.5\text{ mph}$ You would need to keep up an average speed of 2.5 mph.

7. a) At 55 mph, the car will be moving at about 25 m/s, therefore to find the distance,
   $v = d/t$, then $d = vt$
   $d = 25\text{ m/s} \times$ response time (response times will vary according to student)
   For example, for a response time of 0.8 s: $d = vt$
   $d = 25\text{ m/s} \times 0.8\text{ s}$ $d = 20\text{ m}$
   b) Assume a response time of 0.8 s.At 40 mph, the car will be moving at about 19 m/s, therefore to find the distance,
   $v = d/t$, then $d = vt$
   $d = 19\text{ m/s} \times 0.8\text{ s}$ $d = 15\text{ m}$
   A greater speed produces a greater stopping distance with the same reaction time.
   c) You will travel double the distance.

8. Since distance traveled is directly proportional to time for constant speed, the two-second rule should work at any speed, and the distance can be described by the travel time. The premise for this rule is that the two cars have similar braking ability. The lead vehicle does not "stop on a dime." The two-second distance is not an adequate stopping distance, it is meant to cover the driver's response time and the time that the lead car has slowed before the driver's car begins to slow. Exceptions can be made for poor road, tire, or brake conditions.

9. a) 30 mph b) 45 mph c) 75 mph

ANSWERS

Physics To Go

(continued)

10. Students answers will vary. Tailgating increases the potential hazards of driving. During the time from when you see the brake light of the lead car flash on until you hit the brake and begin to slow, your car is still traveling at top speed while the lead car has been slowing down from the time the light first flashed. If the two cars have equivalent braking ability, there had better be an extra distance equal to the product of your speed and response time between the two cars. Since safe driving means minimizing risks, following distances must be commensurate with speed and response time, in addition to road conditions.

    Student answers could also indicate that road conditions will increase the stopping time, physical conditions of the driver will increase the response time, distractions in and outside the car will increase the response time, etc. Also the condition of the car in front, which is not in the control of the person tailgating, must be taken into consideration as an intangible. This could be that the car in front has faulty tail lights, or brakes that are very good, or that the driver in front is slowing down using the engine (gearing down) rather than brakes.

10. Apply what you learned in this activity to write a convincing argument that describes why following a car too closely (tailgating) is dangerous. Include the factors you would use to decide how close counts as "tailgating."

STRETCHING EXERCISES

Measure a distance of about 100 m. You can use a football field or get a long tape or trundle wheel to measure a similar distance. You also need a watch capable of measuring seconds. Determine your average speed traveling that distance for each of the following:

a) a slow walk
b) a fast walk
c) running
d) on a bicycle
e) a method of your choice

NOTES

Assessment: Graphing Skills

The following assessment rubric provides insight into the attainment of graphing skills and monitors communication by way of mathematical expression. Place a check mark (√) in the appropriate box. Two check marks will be required for one point. A sample conversion scale is provided below the chart.

Descriptor	Yes	No
Analysis and Communication • data is recorded in an organized data table • manipulated and responding variables identified in data table • appropriate units are recorded for distance (meters), time (seconds) and speed (m/sec) • multiple trials are used and averages are calculated • average speed (v) is calculated from formula d/t • distance or time can be calculated from $v = d/t$ • distance can be calculated by pacing • student is able to explain why increasing the speed will require greater distance between cars to allow for reaction time		
Graphing Skills • graph has a title • the x-axis and y-axis are clearly labeled • units of measurement are provided for distance and time • manipulated variable (time) is plotted along the x-axis • responding variable (distance) is plotted along the y-axis • x-axis and y-axis are drawn to proper scale • student is able to plot distance/time coordinates • a best fit line is used to connect coordinates for a line graph • distance and time relationships taken from the sonic ranger can be interpreted from computer-generated graph • distance traveled can be determined from graphs where a constant velocity is provided • time of travel can be determined from graphs where a constant velocity is provided • average speed can be determined from distance/time graph by calculating the slope of the line		

Conversion

20 check marks = 10 points

18 + check marks = 9 points

16+ check marks = 8 points, etc.

For use with *Transportation*, Chapter 1, ACTIVITY TWO: Speed and Following Distance

NOTES

1

ACTIVITY THREE
Stopping Your Car

Background Information

Students will continue the car-stopping activity by analyzing the problem of "slowing down" the car. The physics of stopping a car involves reaction time while moving with constant or uniform motion (motion which has no change in speed) and then while braking; changing speed or non-uniform motion (motion in which there is a change in speed).

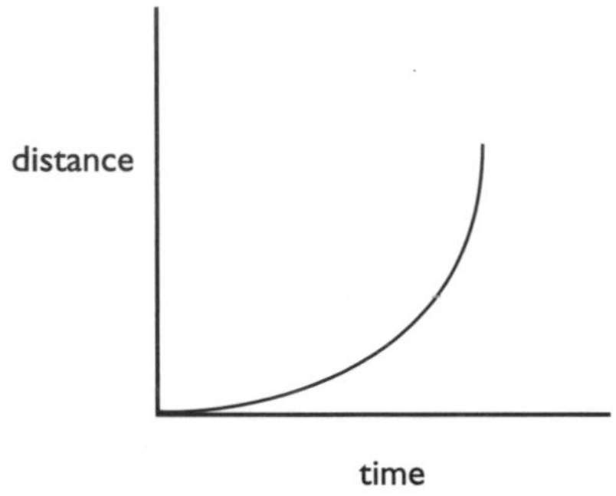

If students plot data distance versus time, for non-uniform motion, they get a parabola. Unfortunately, reading and making predictions from a parabola is very difficult. Students would require calculus to make sense of such a graph. Changing speed or acceleration is the change in the speed of an object in a given time period. Acceleration (symbol is *a*)is $a = \Delta v/\Delta t$. The Δv represents change in velocity and is measured by recording velocity at two different periods. The initial velocity is often indicated as v_1 and final velocity as v_2. In this activity the students will be solving for the distance required to stop, while traveling at different velocities.

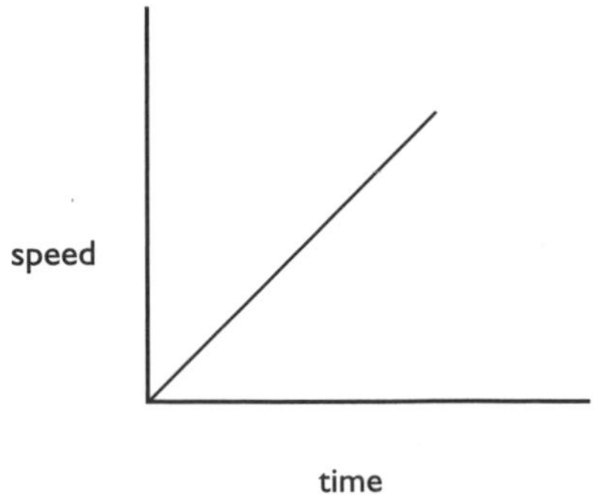

By plotting speed versus time, the result is a straight line with the slope of that line indicating acceleration.

Slope = $\Delta v/\Delta t$.

The units, for v are m/s and for t are s.

Therefore,
$a = \Delta v/\Delta t$,

a = m/s/s or a = m/s^2.

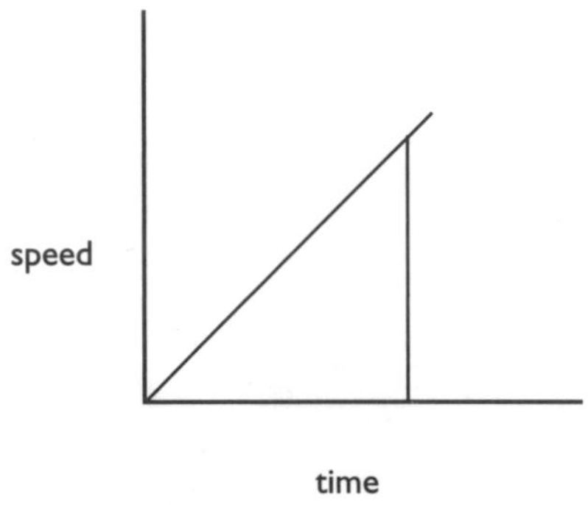

However, when we are looking at stopping distances, it is usually in some context where the distance is important. Example: knowing the distance a plane requires when it lands is important when building a runway. So too is knowing how far you will continue to go while you are stopping a car. Therefore, we need to look at the distance that is required when a car is slowing down. From our speed-time graph, if we find the area under the graph, we will find the distance.

The area under the graph above is Area = 1/2 b x h. Using the units from the graph, we get an expression $d = vt/^2$. However, since we do not know the time, we must go back to our original equation of acceleration, $a = v/t$ and rearrange to solve for t. Therefore, $t = v/a$.

Now, combine $d = vt/^2$ and $t = v/a$, and we get $d = v_2/2^a$. This gives us an expression where the distance an object travels is proportional to the square of its speed. Therefore, when we double the speed the object is traveling, we can see that the distance traveled is quadrupled.

EXAMPLE:

If an object is traveling at 3 m/s and with an acceleration of 2 m/s_2, what would be the distance traveled?

Use the formula $d = v_2/2^a$.

$d = v^2 /2^a$

$d = (3\text{m/s})^2 / 2 \times 2 \text{ m/s}^2$

$d = 9\text{m}^2/\text{s}^2 / 4 \text{ m/s}^2$

$d = 2.25$ m

Now suppose you double the speed to 6 m/s.

$d = (6 \text{ m/s})^2 / 2 \times 2 \text{ m/s}^2$

$d = 36 \text{ m}^2/\text{s}^2 / 4 \text{ m/s}^2$

$d = 9$ m

The data supplied to the student is an average speed, and average stopping distance chart. It is based on a standard acceleration rate on dry pavement, with normal driving conditions, and normal (or average) brake wear, and tire wear. Students will have to be made aware of this, in order to fully appreciate the stopping distance.

The kinematics relationship which relates stopping distance and speed is

$v^2 = 2ad$

In this activity, we expect students to recognize that v^2 is proportional to distance.

This can best be understood by looking at changes in the stopping distance as it relates to changes in the initial velocity. If the velocity doubles, the stopping distance quadruples. If the velocity triples, the stopping distance is nine times as great. If the velocity quadruples, the stopping distance is sixteen times longer. Similarly, if the velocity is halved, the stopping distance is quartered.

The equation can be derived from the definition of velocity and acceleration.

$a = \Delta v/\Delta t = v_f - v_i /t$

$v_f = at + v_i$

Since $v_f = 0$

$v_i = -at$

$v_i^2 = a^2t^2$

$v_i^2 = (1/2at^2)2a$

$v_i^2 = 2ad$

As an enrichment activity, the students can run the same experiment, but on different surfaces. They could then draw analogies to stopping on different road surfaces and how they would drive under those circumstances. An example might be to have the cart run on sandpaper, wet floor, dirt surface, etc.

Active-ating the Physics InfoMall

An excellent discussion of driving cars is included in the Textbook Trove, *Physics: The Excitement of Discovery*, Chapter 2: Motion, by Margaret Stautberg Greenwood. Included in this discussion is a section on stopping distances of cars, with a table of typical stopping distances for various speeds. This may helpful in other activities in *Transportation* as well. The Demo & Lab shop also has several good references, with some decent graphics. For example, "A Potpourri of Physics Teaching Ideas" contains such topics as "Kinematics and the Driver," "Automobile Stopping Distances," and "Driving Safety," all in the Mechanics section.

Planning for the Activity

Time Requirements

In order for the students to run 10 good trials, after proper instruction, they would need at least one class of about 45 minutes. (If there is only one set of equipment for the entire class, then allow the appropriate amount of time accordingly.) Allow for one more class to plot the data and analyze the graph.

Materials needed

For each student:

- graph paper

For each lab group (or for the class):

- laboratory cart
- starting ramp
- apparatus for measuring instantaneous speed
- meter stick

Advance Preparation and Setup

Determine whichever speed-measuring equipment will be used.

If a photogate or a sonic ranger is not available you may use a camcorder and monitor, VCR with stop forward advance and monitor that shows a clear

1

picture of each frozen frame. Practice using the camcorder if you are not familiar with it. Be ready to advise students on how to use the freeze frame advance capability of the tape player or camcorder. Secure a suitable scale behind the path of the car so that its position is easily observed on the screen.

A single photogate can be used if the associated software will measure the eclipsed time. Don't forget to measure the part of the car or an attached flag that blocks the light.

Should no method be available to measure the speed at the bottom of the ramp, measure the time of descent from rest to the bottom of the ramp. Calculate the average speed on the ramp and double it to get the speed at the bottom. While this method avoids much apparatus, it requires the students to trust and understand the mathematics. They are more likely to trust the technology that gives a direct measurement.

Be sure that the transition from the ramp to the floor is smooth.

Teaching Notes

There may be some confusion as to just when the speed is to be measured and why. Make sure your students understand that their problem is to find out how far the cart travels on the level surface. The speed we need is its maximum value which is just as the cart begins to travel horizontally. The purpose of the adjustable ramp is simply to provide a variable series of initial speeds.

Depending on the mathematical sophistication of your students, you may decide to point out that the graph of stopping distance vs. speed is parabolic, showing that the distance depends on the square of the speed. Otherwise, stick to discussing how doubling the speed will quadruple the required stopping distance.

The students may not have a good sense of distances in meters. Convert distances to car-lengths, city blocks, or even street light spacing if it helps the students visualize the distance.

As the students will be working with delicate equipment, be sure to remind them to treat the equipment carefully.

Acceleration is a difficult abstract concept for the students to pick up. Most students cannot understand the m/s/s, and prefer to simply memorize the formulae associated with acceleration. This will get them through a junior level physics class, however, it will not get them into senior level or university level courses. Try to bring the students to understand as with speed and velocity there is a change in the distance per unit time, acceleration is simply a change in velocity per unit time.

After completing the activity, you may wish to discuss situations in which engineers must allow for appropriate stopping times and distances. At a grade-level railroad crossing, how long must the warning bell sound? How long does it take for the gate to lower? How long before the train reaches the intersection? This situation could be handled as a separate class day, an extra assignment, or an excursion.

Activity Three

Stopping Your Car

WHAT DO YOU THINK?

In 1995, only 14% of speed-related traffic deaths happened on interstate highways. Imagine you are driving at the speed limit, and you suddenly see a moose crossing the road ahead of you.

- **Will you be able to stop in time to avoid hitting the moose?**
- **What are all the factors that determine how soon you will be able to stop the car?**

Record your ideas about these questions in your *Active Physics log*. Be prepared to discuss your responses with your small group and the class.

Activity Overview

This activity addresses the distance traveled during uniform braking acceleration as a function of the initial speed.

Student Objectives

Students will:

- relate stopping distance to initial speed.
- determine stopping distance from response time and braking distance.
- examine accelerated motion.

ANSWERS FOR THE TEACHERS ONLY

What Do You Think?

The most important factor in determining if you will stop in time is speed. The distance required to stop is proportional to the square of the speed.

After posing the What Do You Think? question, create a master list and allow the students to argue as they try to justify their factors and try to dismiss others. The few students who have taken a course in driving may know that the most important factor is speed, and that distance is proportional to the square of the speed. The activity will provide a basis for this relationship.

1

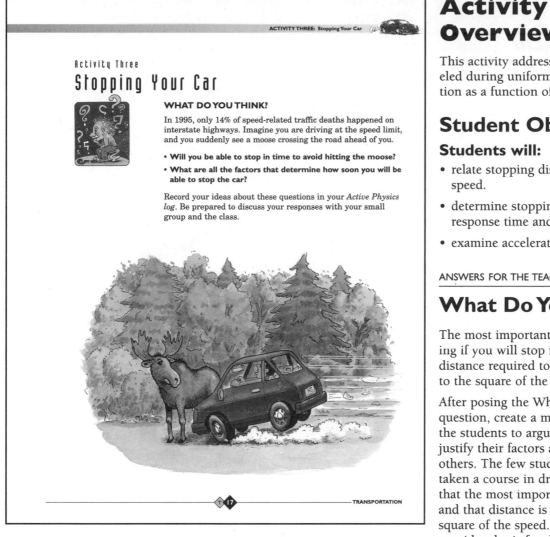

ANSWERS

For You To Do

1.- 3. Student activity.

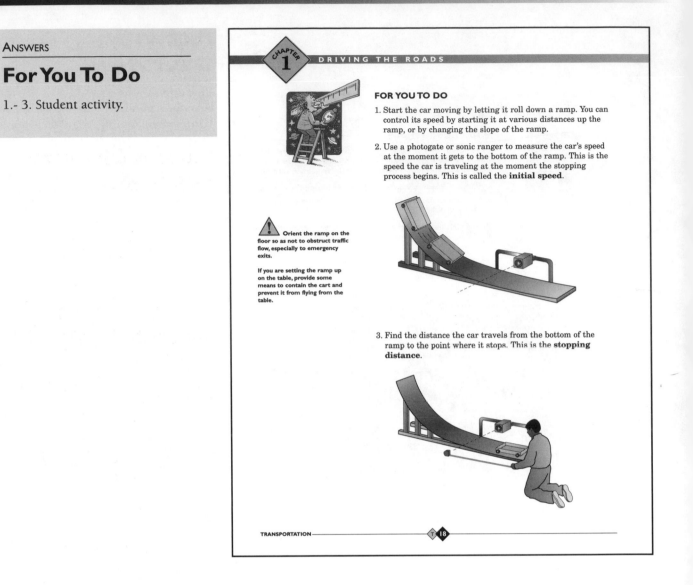

Orient the ramp on the floor so as not to obstruct traffic flow, especially to emergency exits.

If you are setting the ramp up on the table, provide some means to contain the cart and prevent it from flying from the table.

FOR YOU TO DO

1. Start the car moving by letting it roll down a ramp. You can control its speed by starting it at various distances up the ramp, or by changing the slope of the ramp.
2. Use a photogate or sonic ranger to measure the car's speed at the moment it gets to the bottom of the ramp. This is the speed the car is traveling at the moment the stopping process begins. This is called the **initial speed**.

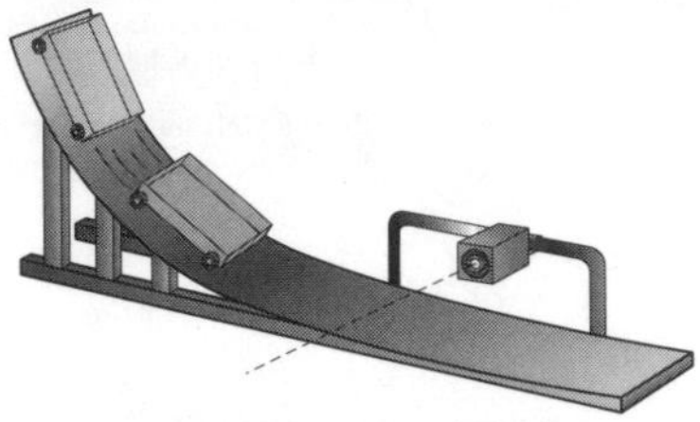

3. Find the distance the car travels from the bottom of the ramp to the point where it stops. This is the **stopping distance**.

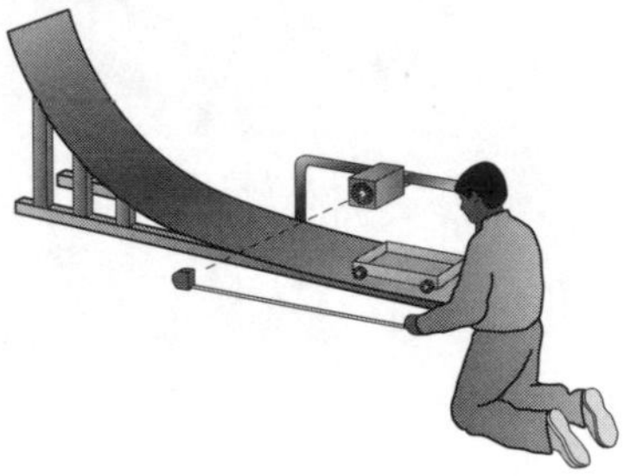

4. Do at least 10 trials with the car going at different speeds and measure the corresponding stopping distances.
   a) Record your data in a chart like the one below.

Initial Speed (m/s)	Distance Traveled (m)

5. One way to display data is on a graph. In this activity you are interested in seeing how the stopping distance relates to the initial speed. Place the initial speed on the horizontal axis and the stopping distance on the vertical axis.
   a) Plot a graph of your data in your log.
   b) How does the stopping distance change with initial speed?
   c) What kind of relationship does your graph show?

6. Select two values of speed from your graph, with one value just double the other. When the speed of the car doubles, what happens to the stopping distance?
   a) What is the effect of doubling speed on distance traveled during response time? (Refer to Activity 2)
   b) What is the effect of doubling speed on distance traveled during stopping?

7. Compare two stopping distances for which the second speed is three times as fast.
   a) What is the effect of tripling the speed on the distance traveled during stopping?
   b) Predict how going four times as fast will affect stopping distance.

Answers

For You To Do
(continued)

4. a) Students copy the chart from the text and record their data.

5. a) Students graph data in log.
   b) As you increase the speed the stopping distance increases much faster.
   c) The graph will be a parabola, concave upward.

6. a) The students should recognize that the response distance is proportional to the speed, therefore, the distance should double with the speed doubling.
   b) The stopping distance appears to quadruple while the speed only doubles.

7. a) Increasing the speed three times gives a stopping distance about nine times as great.
   b) Because this is a quadratic relationship, the stopping distance will be 16 times as great. The actual relationship, as explained in Background Information for the Teacher is $d = v^2/2a$.

ANSWERS

Physics To Go

1. Initial speed Stopping distance graph.

   The graph should be a parabola. Emphasize to students the need for a curved line of best fit. See below.

2. As the speeds increase, the stopping distances increase at a much greater rate.

REFLECTING ON THE ACTIVITY AND THE CHALLENGE

Safe driving requires the ability to stop safely. Some people think that if you double your speed, the car will require double the stopping distance. You now know that it will take more than double the stopping distance it is closer to four times the stopping distance!

You should be able to explain the importance of stopping distance as it relates to speed. You should understand why slowing down is so helpful in terms of stopping distance and what will happen to the required stopping distance if you decrease your speed by one half.

PHYSICS TO GO

1. A student measured the stopping distance of her car and recorded the data in the chart below. Plot the data on a graph and describe the relationship that exists between initial speed and stopping distance.

Initial Speed	Stopping Distance
5 m/s	4 m
10 m/s	15 m
15 m/s	35 m
20 m/s	62 m
25 m/s	98 m
30 m/s	140 m

2. Below are the stopping distances in relation to speed graphs for two cars. Compare qualitatively the stopping distances when each car is going at a slow speed and then again at a higher speed. Which car is safer? Why?

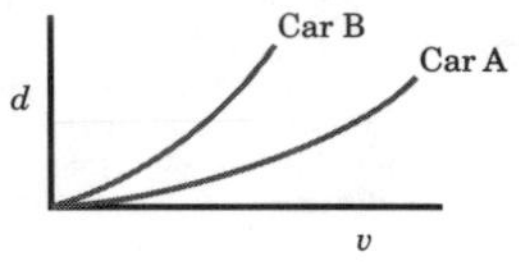

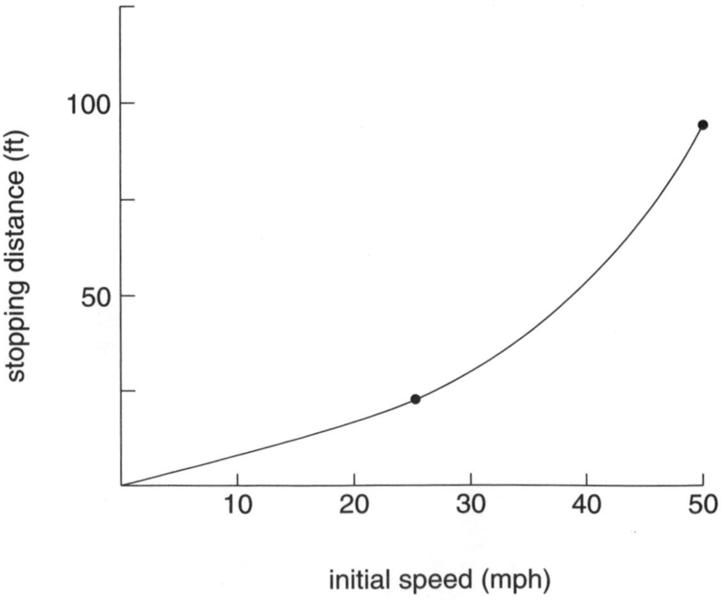

3. A car is able to stop in 20 m when traveling at 30 mph. How much distance will it require to stop when traveling at:
   a) 15 mph? (half of 30 mph)
   b) 60 mph? (twice 30 mph)
   c) 45 mph? (three times 15 mph)
   d) 75 mph? (five times 15 mph)
4. A car traveling at 10 m/s requires a stopping distance of 30 m. If the driver requires 0.9 s response time, what additional distance will the car travel before stopping?
5. Consult the information for the 1998 Corvette Convertible found on page T56 of this book. This shows the stopping distance from *Road & Track* magazine. How far would you expect this car to travel until coming to rest when brakes are applied at a speed of 30 mph?
6. Use the information on page T55. Find the braking distances for 50 mph and 25 mph. Create a graph using the different braking distances. Plot the speeds on the horizontal axis and the stopping distances on the vertical axis.
7. Does the braking information on page T55 include the driver's response time? Who should let the consumer know about this—the information sheet or a driver training manual?
8. Apply what you learned from this activity to write a statement explaining the factors that affect stopping distance. What do you now know about stopping that will make you a safer driver?

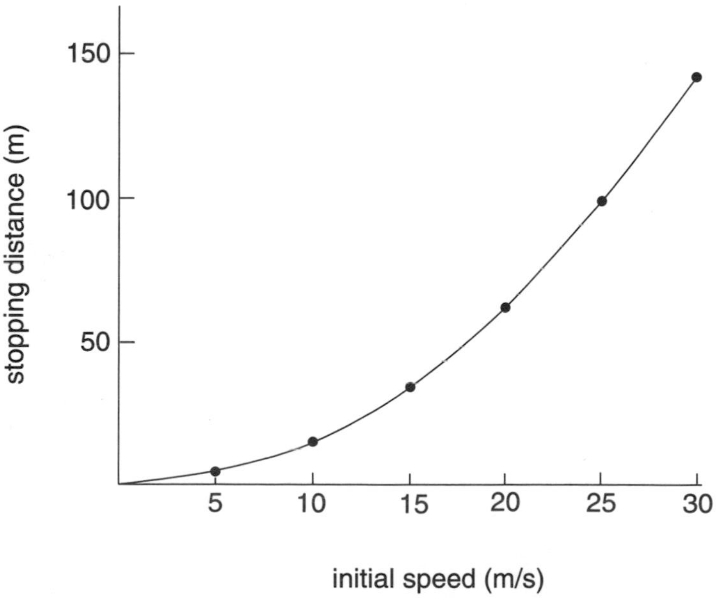

ANSWERS

Physics To Go
(continued)

3. a) The students should recognize that the stopping distance for half the speed will be 1/4 of the distance. Therefore, the stopping distance for 15 mph will be 5 m.

   b) 60 mph is double the 30 mph, therefore it will be 4x the 4x 20=80 stopping distance or ~~100 m~~. 80m

   c) 45 mph is three times the speed of 15 mph therefore 9 times the stopping distance at 15 mph or 45 m.

   d) 75 mph is 5 times the speed of 15 mph therefore 5^2 or 25 x 20= times the stopping distance or 125 m.

4. This is a question referring to adding the stopping distance to the response distance to get a complete picture of stopping distances. Therefore, we use constant or uniform motion formula
   $v = d/t$ to solve for d
   $d = vt$
   $d = 10$ m/s x 0.9 s
   $d = 9$ m
   Therefore, the car will travel an additional 9 m before coming to a complete stop.

5. At 30 mph, half of 60 mph, the stopping distance will be 1/4 of 118 ft., or about 30 ft.

6. The stopping distance for 50 mph is about 94 ft. The stopping distance for 25 mph is about 23 ft. The shape of the graph should be a parabola.

7. The driver's response time is not included on the data sheet. As to who should supply this information is the student's opinion - answers will vary. Look for sound arguments that can be shared with the class.

8. Answers will vary. Expect some of the following:
   - speed of travel
   - road conditions
   - brake condition
   - response times
   - tire condition
   - weather conditions

1

ACTIVITY FOUR
Putting It All Together

Background Information

Refer to Background Information for Activity One, regarding reaction time.

Active-ating the Physics InfoMall

Drinking and other safety issues are discussed in "The Science of Traffic Safety," by Leonard Evans, found in *The Physics Teacher*, volume 26, issue 7. Following this article is a list of references that you may also find useful in teaching traffic safety.

Planning for the Activity

Time Requirements

For the inquiry investigation, the students will need approximately 40 minutes to organize their investigation, and prepare the materials and procedures. This activity could be done on their own time, with a class to allow the students to share their investigations.

For the computer simulation, time will vary with the number of computers, and the number of trials the students attempt. Allow at least two 40 minute classes, with an option of another class for different variables.

Materials needed

Students may wish to use some of the following materials.

For each lab group:

- D-cell
- battery holder
- knife switch (2)
- flashlight bulb and socket
- connecting wire (4)
- stopwatch (2)
- centimeter ruler

For the class:

- standard response-time meter, such as used in drivers' education classes

Advance Preparation and Setup

If students are completing this investigation in the classroom, obtain each lab group's list of equipment, and check to make sure all equipment required is available. If students are completing this investigation outside the classroom, then probably using a ruler to measure response time might be advisable. We suggest that the students look after their own "equipment" for the "distractions."

Teaching Notes

The What Do You Think? question is designed to provoke a discussion of the effects of listening to loud music on response time, as well as the distraction of talking or the effect of fatigue, alcohol, or drugs.

Be sure to review all the students' procedures before they begin their investigations.

Students may still think that the only time that is needed is the time to slow down once their foot is on the brake. Emphasize that the time it takes to react to a yellow light or to red brakes lights of the car in front, can be significant, when traveling at high speeds. This is why on some freeways, or high-speed city streets, there are warning lights well ahead of the intersection to warn drivers that the light is about to change and to get ready to stop.

You may wish to use the Activity Four A, Factors that Affect Response Time found in the Program Resources.

NOTES

1

Activity Overview

In this inquiry investigation, students design an experiment to test for the effect of various distractions on response time.

Student Objectives

Students will:

- review the processes required to stop a car.
- determine a variable which affects response time.
- design an experiment to measure response time.
- conduct an experiment to measure response time.

ANSWERS FOR THE TEACHER ONLY

What Do You Think?

When response time is slowed, the driver requires more time and a longer distance to stop safely. Driver response time may be improved by being well rested, avoiding such distractions as playing loud music or engaging in conversation, and by refraining from drinking alcohol or taking medications or other drugs that effect response time.

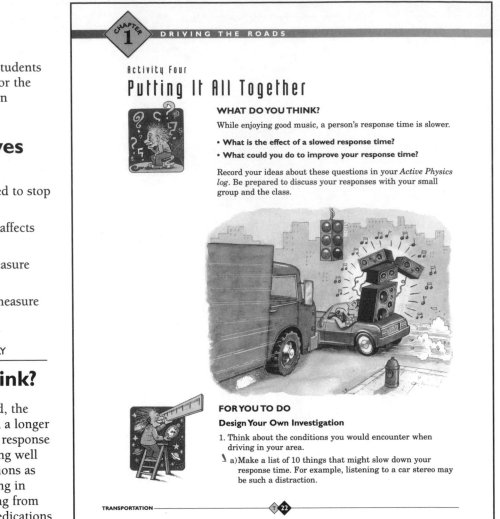

CHAPTER 1 DRIVING THE ROADS

Activity Four

Putting It All Together

WHAT DO YOU THINK?

While enjoying good music, a person's response time is slower.

- **What is the effect of a slowed response time?**
- **What could you do to improve your response time?**

Record your ideas about these questions in your *Active Physics log*. Be prepared to discuss your responses with your small group and the class.

FOR YOU TO DO

Design Your Own Investigation

1. Think about the conditions you would encounter when driving in your area.

   a) Make a list of 10 things that might slow down your response time. For example, listening to a car stereo may be such a distraction.

TRANSPORTATION T 22

ANSWERS

For You To Do

1. a) Students' responses will vary. Some might include being in a bad mood, being on your first date, driving dad's restored '57 Chevy for the first time, bad weather, good weather, driving by a beach on a hot day, driving by a burger joint when you're hungry, late for work or school, smoking, drinking, talking on your cellular phone, talking with your friends, cruisin'.

   b) Answers will vary. Perhaps one of the above distractions, may have possibly caused them to have an accident, or close to an accident.

2. In this activity you will investigate the effect of distractions on response time. As a conclusion, you will relate your results to safe driving.
   a) Choose one of the things that you listed in step 1 to investigate. Record it in your log in the form of a question.

3. Follow your teacher's guidelines for using time, space, and materials as you carry out the investigation and prepare your report and conclusions.
   a) Make a list of materials you will need, the procedure you will use, and how you will organize and report the data that you collect.
   b) After your teacher has approved your procedure, carry out your investigation.

REFLECTING ON THE ACTIVITY AND THE CHALLENGE

Teenagers often have a very good response time. You now know that drinking, listening to loud music, and even eating french fries while you drive can slow down your response time.

Based on this activity, you may have new ideas about other activities or behaviors that could slow your response time. Write these in your log.

PHYSICS TO GO

1. Write a paragraph about the factors that you must consider when calculating the distance a car travels, from the instant you see danger to finally stopping the car.
2. Many driver education manuals describe stopping in the following way: IDENTIFY the problem; PREDICT what may happen; DECIDE what to do; and EXECUTE your decision. Does this description exaggerate the process of stopping?
3. One of your friends tells you, "I always tailgate. I never get into an accident because I pay attention and I'm quick!" What can you say to your friend to convince him that this is not smart driving?

ANSWERS

For You To Do
(continued)

2. a) Students' activity and response. For example: Does bad weather cause a decrease in your response time?
3. a) Students will list the materials they need to investigate their identified problem. The students will identify and develop their own procedure for investigating their problem. They will also organize and report the data they collect.
   b) Students' investigation.

1

ANSWERS

Physics To Go

1. Answers will vary. Some responses may include condition of road, condition of tires, physical condition of student, weather, impairment of some kind, distracted by something in or out of car.
2. Answers will vary. Expect answers which will include the physics of stopping up to now. Their answers should include when you identify there is a problem, (someone with brake lights on), predict what may happen. Is this person stopping because they are turning or because a cat ran out in front of them? Are they hard braking or soft braking? What are the road conditions? Can I stop in time? Do I have an "out"? Once you have identified, predicted, you can decide what to do based on this information. Then execute. As a young driver, there is sometimes not enough experience for a driver to do all of these things after the situation has taken place. An experienced driver will have already established some kind of prediction and decision on what to do should a situation arise. Therefore, as was stated earlier in Activity One, just because a person is young and has fast response times, doesn't mean he or she will make the right choice in a given situation.
3. Answers will vary. See the previous answer.

ANSWERS

Physics To Go

(continued)

4. Answers will vary. People who are under the influence will not be able to make fast decisions because of reduced response time or be able to make good judgments. Therefore, they may think they are okay to drink and drive, when in fact they are impaired. One other problem may be that some people think that they are invincible, and that they won't get caught. These people can often be young people, as they tend to think that they can do things based on superior response times.

5. Answers will vary. People who are under the influence will not be able to make fast decisions or be able to make good decisions when required. This will inevitably get them into trouble such as accidents.

6. Answers will vary. Students will probably use the arguments that the car phone will be a distraction and will cause an increase in the response time. This information could be used to help their parents understand that the student has a much better understanding of their knowledge of driving. Emphasis should still be on the years of experience of driving that is needed to become a good driver. The old catch 22 - you need experience to become a good driver, and the only way to become a good driver is through driving experience.

4. Alcohol-related crashes and injuries cost society $46 billion each year in lost income, medical bills, property damage, and other costs. Knowing this, why do you think people still drive after drinking?

5. Why do you think it is against the law to drive while under the influence of alcohol?

6. Apply what you learned from this activity to explain to your parents why it is not safe to drive while talking on a car phone. How could you use this information to improve your argument for the opening challenge?

STRETCHING EXERCISES

Driving Simulation

It is often stated that when following a car on a highway, you should allow a minimum of one car length of space for each 10 mph of speed.

- Would you do this?
- How far behind a car do you usually follow?
- If the driver in front of you suddenly braked, at that distance would you have enough room to stop?
- Do you think that having one car length of space for each 10 mph is enough?

Ask your teacher for the **Driving Simulation** computer game so you can test that theory. In the game, two cars are cruising at the same steady speed on a two-lane road. You are driving the second car. Suddenly you see the brake lights on the lead car. Your response time determines your fate. When driving, you are usually preoccupied and don't expect the car in front of you to stop. Therefore, this game is designed to take your mind off the lead car.

Note: Do not try to anticipate or ready yourself for braking. The idea is to get an accurate measure of your braking response time, not to beat the clock.

Directions

1. Open the spreadsheet DRIVESIM.XLS. Click on the "start" button for the simulation to begin.

2. When you see the red stoplight, quickly move the mouse to the brake button and click. Your response time will be displayed.

3. Read the manufacturer's recommendations for the stopping distance of a car at 55 mph. The lead car will stop in this distance. Your car will stop in this distance plus the distance you traveled before you reacted to the brake lights. That extra distance can be calculated from this equation:

   extra distance = speed × response time.

4. If you are closer to the lead car than this extra distance, you will have an accident. To find out the necessary distance, follow these steps:

   Click on the tab at the bottom of the spreadsheet labeled "Calculations."

   Measure the length of an average car or use the manufacturer's specifications. Enter that number in the box labeled "Car Lengths."

   Enter recommended trailing distance in "Car Lengths."

   Calculate your extra braking distance.

   Enter your speed in mph and your response time in the boxes.

5. Compare your extra distance with the recommended following distance. Will this following distance cause an accident?

6. Discuss the safety of the original distance assumption about allowing one car length for every 10 mph.

Note: To enter a number on the spreadsheet, click in the box, type the number (do not include units or commas) and press <Enter>. If you get the message "Locked cells cannot be changed" it means that you did not click in the proper box. Try again.

T 25

Activity Four A

Factors that Affect Response Time

FOR YOU TO DO

1. Repeat the ruler drop experiment described on pages T6 and T7, but prior to catching the ruler clench your hand into a fist and release it at a rate of once per second for 30 seconds. Use as much exertion as possible in making a fist.

   a) Record the distance for five trials before making a fist. Find the average response distance. Use the graph on T7 to find the average response time.

   b) Record the distance for five trials after making a fist. Find the average response distance. Use the graph on T7 to find the average response time.

   c) How does muscle fatigue affect your response time?

   d) Provide examples of how a driver might experience fatigue?

   e) What technological improvements to automobiles would help reduce fatigue?

2. Fill an 800 mL beaker with a mixture of cold water and ice. Immerse your catching hand in the cold water for approximately 20 seconds or as long as you feel possible. Repeat the procedure to determine response time.

   a) Record the response distance for five trials after immersing your hand in cold water. Find the average response distance. Use the graph on T7 to find the average response time.

   b) How does cold temperature affect your response time?

   c) Hypothesize about why cold temperatures change response time.

   d) Provide example of how a driver might react to cold temperatures.

   e) Hypothesize about how high temperatures might affect reaction time.

   f) Suggest a way in which you might go about testing the hypothesis.

For use with *Transportation*, Chapter 2, ACTIVITY FOUR: Putting it All Together

Activity Four A

Factors that Affect Response Time

Time Requirements

Approximately 40 minutes is required to complete the experiment.

Materials needed

- large container
- ice/water
- rulercar is not able to do both at the same time.

ANSWERS

For You To Do

1. a-b) Student data.

   c) Fatigued muscles respond at a much slower rate.

   d) Many different examples can be provided. A few samples are: length of time the person drives, bright headlights from oncoming cars, loud music, warm temperatures, and repetitive scenery.

   e) Tinted glass to reduce glare, comfortable seats, adjustable seats, and climate control.

2. a) Student data.

   b) Response rates increase; reactions slow.

   c) Cold temperature reduces blood flow to muscles, which in turn decreases the delivery of oxygen and nutrients to muscle cells.

   d) Many different examples are possible. Shivering is one example.

   e) High temperatures cause blood vessels to dilate. This lowers blood pressure and slows the delivery of oxygen to the brain, making the subject sleepy. Accept any reasonable hypothesis.

   f) Place subject in a warm setting and test their alertness by timing reaction times reduced. The car is not able to do both at the same time.

1

ACTIVITY FIVE
Intersections with a Yellow Light

Background Information

While you are driving at a constant speed, you need a certain length of time to react to a stimulus (such as the neighbor's cat running on the road), interpret the stimulus (I never did like that cat), then tell your muscles to perform an action (put on the brakes). During the time it takes to react to a green-to-yellow light change, your car will continue to move with the original speed. It will cover a distance ($d = v \times t$). This distance will be added to the distance that is required to stop once the brakes are applied ($d = v^2 /2a$.) (Because the acceleration rate is not known for each vehicle, there will be an arbitrary rate chosen to reflect an average. It is usually based on an average car, with good brakes, on clean, dry pavement.) The total distance, then, is the distance that is required to come to a stop, after the stimulus (the cat) is presented [total $d = (v \times t) + (v^2/2a)$].

Computing the GO Zone

Determining the GO Zone is an application of the equation:

distance = velocity x time

While the yellow light is illuminated, the car must be able to go through the intersection. The total distance traveled is the distance from the intersection, plus the width of the intersection.

GO Zone + width = velocity x yellow light time

$GZ + w = vT_y$

$GZ = vT_y - w$

The GO Zone actually includes a range of possible distances. If car A goes through the intersection, as shown,

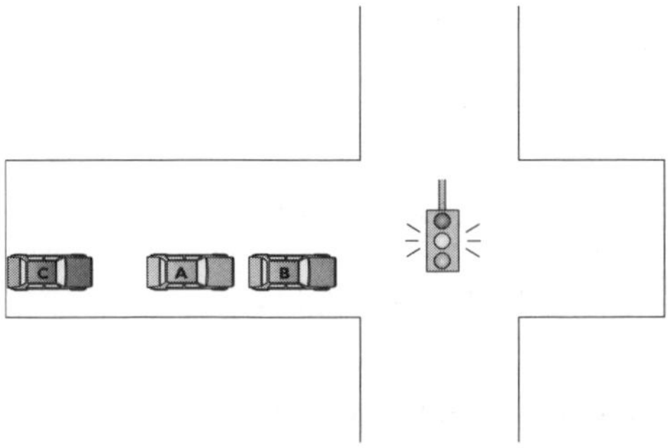

then any car closer than car A can also make it through the intersection. The correct equation for the GO Zone is

$GZ \leq vT_y - w$

It can be shown in a sketch with a shaded area.

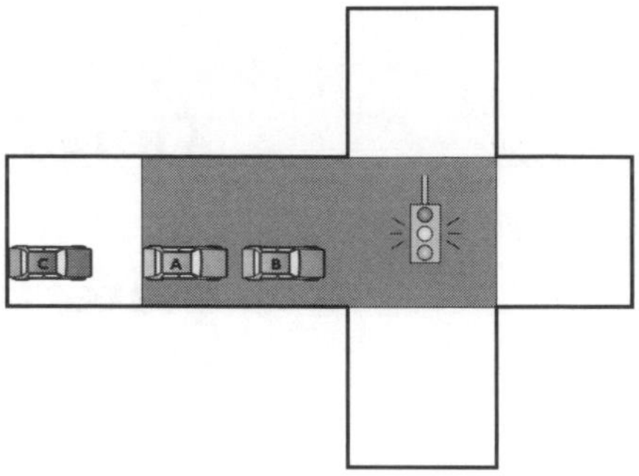

Computing the STOP Zone

Determining the STOP Zone requires one to realize that the total stopping distance is the sum of the coasting distance (the distance you travel during the response time) and the braking distance. Both of these factors were investigated in Activity Three. The coasting distance is an application once again of the equation:

distance = velocity x time

In this case, time is the response time.

$d = vT_r$

The braking distance is an application of the kinematics equation which relates velocity, acceleration, and distance.

velocity squared = 2 x acceleration x distance

$v_2 = 2ad$

STOP Zone = velocity x response time +
velocity squared/2 x deceleration rate

$SZ = vT_r + v^2/2a$

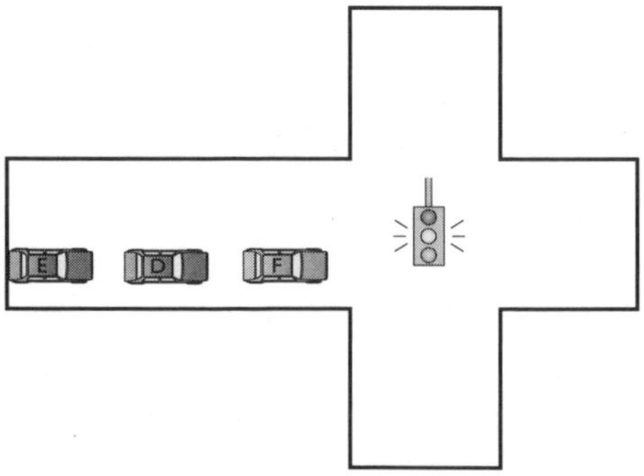

The STOP Zone actually includes a range of possible distances. If car B is able to stop before the intersection, as shown below, then any car further than car *D* can also stop before the intersection. The correct equation for the STOP Zone is

$SZ \geq vT_r + v^2/2a$

It can be shown in a sketch with a shaded area.

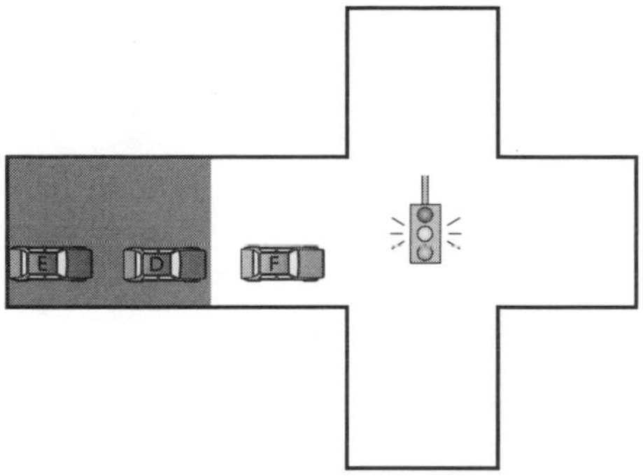

Active-ating the Physics InfoMall

Yellow lights and traffic are also discussed on the InfoMall. For example, "A Potpourri of Physics Teaching Ideas" (found in the Demo & Lab shop) has "To stop or not to stop—kinematics and the yellow light." Articles from major journals also discuss stoplights and the Dilemma Zone. See, for example, *The Physics Teacher,* volume 25, issue number 1, "The Spotlight Dilemma Revisited", which also contains a reference to an article that is not on the InfoMall: J. Fred Watts, *The Physics Teacher*, volume 19, 114 (1981), a discussion of stoplight kinematics. This is another strength of the InfoMall; even when the article or book is not on the CD-ROM, there may be a reference to it that could lead you to a wealth of additional information. Another resource on the InfoMall is found in the Utilities Closet. A search of the index for the *American Journal of Physics* uncovers The Stop-Light Dilemma, by Howard S. Seifert, United Technology Corporation and Stanford University; *Am. J. Phys.*, Vol. 30, No. 3, March 1962 Pages 216-218. This is enough information to easily locate the article at any library which carries this journal.

Planning for the Activity

Time Requirements

Time will vary with the number of computers, and the number of trials the students attempt. Allow at least two 40-minute classes.

Materials needed

For the class:

- *Active Physics Transportation* content video (Segment: Intersection and Yellow Light)
- VCR and TV monitor

For each lab group:

- computer with Excel spreadsheet software
- *Active Physics* Spreadsheet Template (File: Yellow Light)

Advance Preparation and Setup

Preview the video and note the cars that should have stopped for the yellow light and those that did not need to stop.

Input the spreadsheet model into your spreadsheet software. Test your spreadsheet by changing the yellow light time and see if your samples match those in the text. If you are using a local area network, simply download each spreadsheet to the work stations that the student groups will be using. Otherwise make a computer disk for each work station. You need to make sure that specific jobs are assigned to each student in the group and rotate the jobs periodically. If the groups need to share or compare information, assign a communicator to represent each group.

If you are using a low-tech alternative to this activity, you will need to copy a set of spreadsheets for each group of students.

Teaching Notes

After students have answered the What Do You Think? question, discuss the decision that a driver has to make when approaching an intersection as the yellow light comes on. Ask students to explain their understanding of the GO and STOP Zones.

Allow the students to view the video twice, permitting time to discuss which cars they felt should have stopped for the yellow light and which cars they felt did not need to stop. Have them record their responses to the questions before viewing the video a second time.

You may wish to work through the first few examples with the entire class, so you can be sure that the students understand the concept of the STOP and GO Zones.

If you should take your students to an intersection, it is important to review the safety rules regarding intersections. If you are going to be measuring the intersection, the students should use traffic safety jackets, available at your local police or highway department.

Students will still think that the only time that is needed is the time to slow down once their foot is on the brake. Emphasize that the time it takes to react to a yellow light can be significant, when traveling at high speeds. This is why on some freeways, or high-speed city streets, there are warning lights well ahead of the intersection to warn drivers that the light is about to change and to get ready to stop.

Introduce the students to the spreadsheet model using the systems diagram with the five inputs and two outputs, on page T29. Discuss how the computer model is like a "black box" and that the challenge is to figure out what is inside the box. In this example, the black box is a mathematical model that consists of physics equations. Encourage students to understand what is going on while the computer does the mathematical work.

In this investigation students will determine which inputs affect which outputs. That is, which independent variable affects which dependent variables.

Students may need some help in learning how to translate spreadsheet equations into physics equations. You may also wish to refer them to the Physics To Go questions, where the equations are given.

If your class does not have access to computers or spreadsheet programs, you can have the students complete the activity using printouts from the spreadsheets. Included in this guide are five sets of spreadsheets. In each set, one variable is changed five times. The students can look at the five spreadsheets in a single set, determine which variable has changed, and record the changes in the GO Zone and STOP Zone as if they were manipulating the spreadsheets themselves. These spreadsheet sets can be copied for classroom use. Each spreadsheet set can be rotated among student groups to save on copying costs. As an alternative, the spreadsheet set can be displayed on the overhead. This turns the activity into a teacher-centered demonstration and is not as beneficial to the students.

NOTES

1

Activity Overview

This activity combines the reaction time (constant speed) and time required to stop after the brake has been applied (acceleration or changing speed) in the situation of a yellow traffic light.

Student Objectives

Students will:

- identify the variables that can be used to model the yellow light problem.
- use equations to represent the GO and STOP Zones at a traffic light.

ANSWERS FOR THE TEACHER ONLY

What Do You Think?

The time it takes to react to a yellow light can be significant when traveling at high speeds. If all traffic lights stayed yellow the same amount of time, drivers might be better able to judge when they must stop and when they need not stop.

CHAPTER 1 DRIVING THE ROADS

Activity Five

Intersections with a Yellow Light

WHAT DO YOU THINK?

Some traffic lights stay yellow for 3 seconds. Others stay yellow for 6 seconds.

- **If all traffic lights stayed yellow the same amount of time, how would this affect drivers' decisions at intersections?**

Take a few minutes to write your ideas in your log. Discuss your response with your small group and see if you agree or disagree. Be prepared to discuss your responses with your small group and the class.

FOR YOU TO DO

1. Watch the video of an intersection, carefully noting what happens when the light turns yellow.
   a) Are there cars that you think should have stopped?
   b) Were there cars that stopped, but you think should have continued through the intersection?

TRANSPORTATION T 26

ANSWERS

For You To Do

1. a-b) Student observations and response.

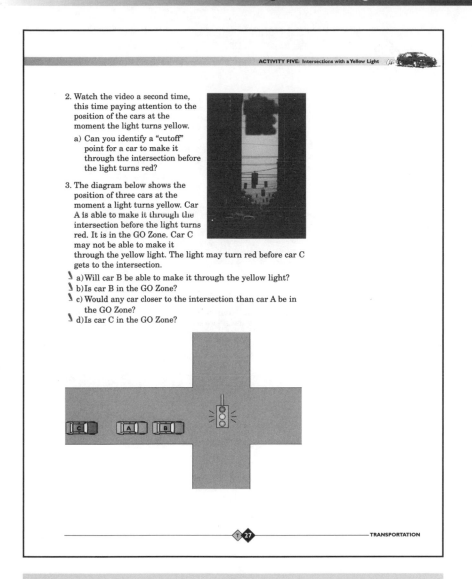

2. Watch the video a second time, this time paying attention to the position of the cars at the moment the light turns yellow.
   a) Can you identify a "cutoff" point for a car to make it through the intersection before the light turns red?

3. The diagram below shows the position of three cars at the moment a light turns yellow. Car A is able to make it through the intersection before the light turns red. It is in the GO Zone. Car C may not be able to make it through the yellow light. The light may turn red before car C gets to the intersection.
   a) Will car B be able to make it through the yellow light?
   b) Is car B in the GO Zone?
   c) Would any car closer to the intersection than car A be in the GO Zone?
   d) Is car C in the GO Zone?

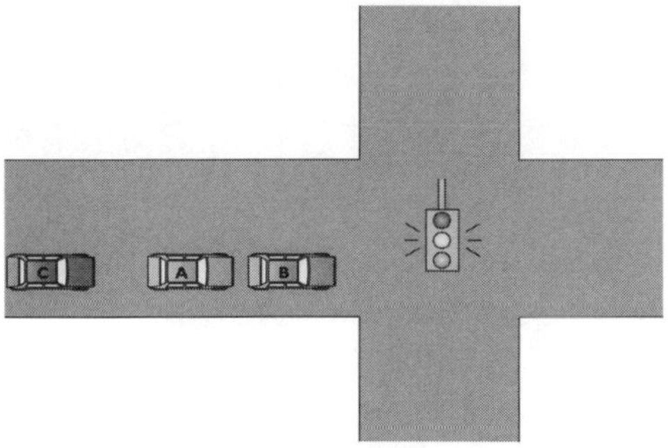

Answers

For You To Do *(continued)*

2. a) Student observations and response.

3. a) Yes
   b) Yes
   c) Yes
   d) Not sure. It could be, but we can't tell from the data provided. It probably is not.

ANSWERS

For You To Do

(continued)

4. a) Yes. It is farther away from the intersection than car D, and if car D can stop, so should car E.

   b) Not sure. It could be but we can't tell from the data provided. It appears to be too close to the intersection to stop safely.

   c) Student sketch, below.

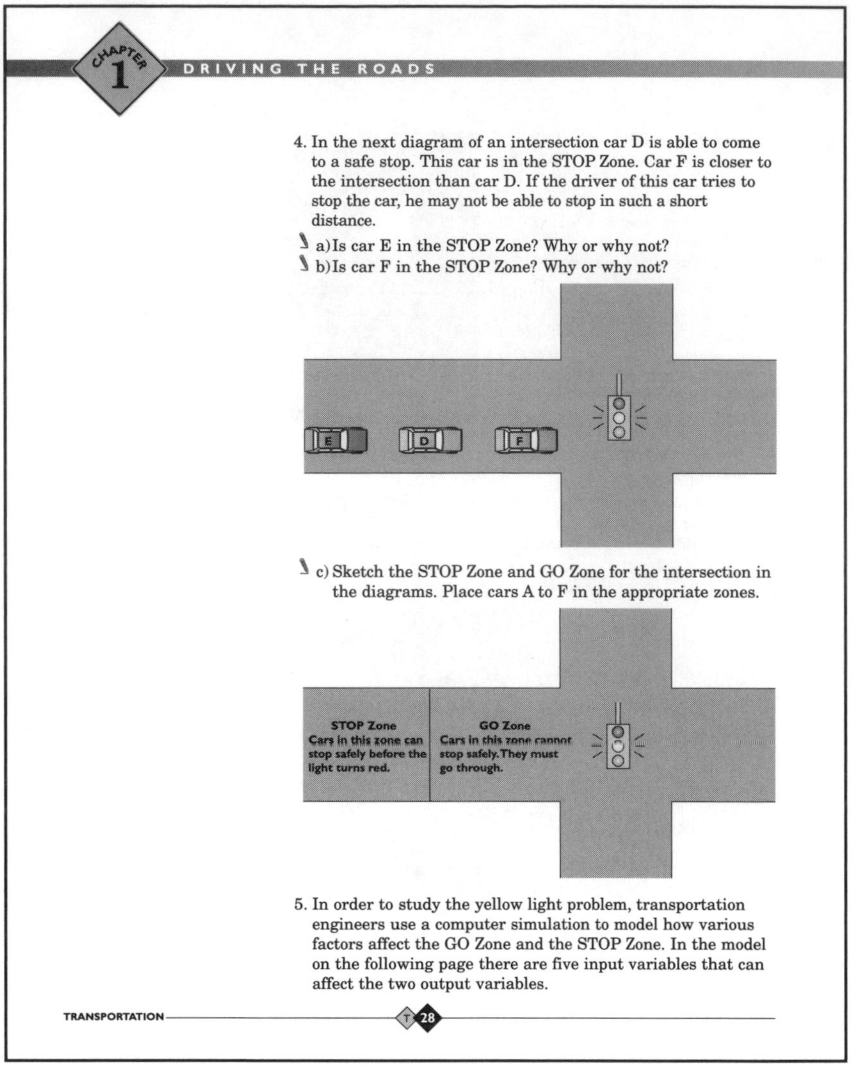

CHAPTER 1 DRIVING THE ROADS

4. In the next diagram of an intersection car D is able to come to a safe stop. This car is in the STOP Zone. Car F is closer to the intersection than car D. If the driver of this car tries to stop the car, he may not be able to stop in such a short distance.

   a) Is car E in the STOP Zone? Why or why not?

   b) Is car F in the STOP Zone? Why or why not?

E
D
F

   c) Sketch the STOP Zone and GO Zone for the intersection in the diagrams. Place cars A to F in the appropriate zones.

STOP Zone
Cars in this zone can stop safely before the light turns red.
GO Zone
Cars in this zone cannot stop safely. They must go through.

5. In order to study the yellow light problem, transportation engineers use a computer simulation to model how various factors affect the GO Zone and the STOP Zone. In the model on the following page there are five input variables that can affect the two output variables.

TRANSPORTATION T 28

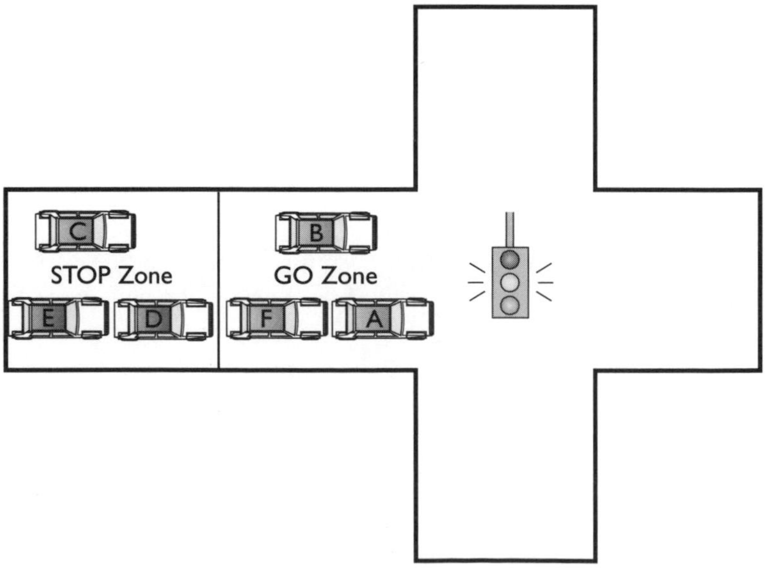

C
STOP Zone
E
D
B
GO Zone
F
A

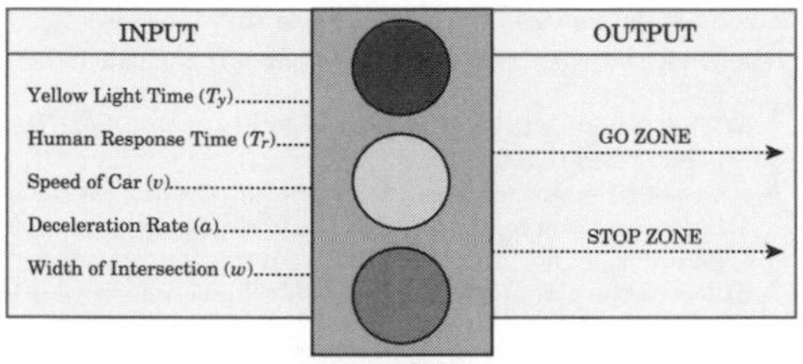

Yellow Light Model

a) List the five variables shown in the model.

b) You will first study how the variables affect the GO Zone. Copy the chart below in your log.

Variable	Change		Predicted Effect of Change on GO Zone	Actual Effect of Change on GO Zone
T_y	Yellow Light Time	increase T_y		
		decrease T_y		
T_r	Response Time	increase T_r		
		decrease T_r		
v	Speed Limit	increase v		
		decrease v		
a	Deceleration Rate	increase a		
		decrease a		
w	Width of Intersection	increase w		
		decrease w		

c) Predict how increasing or decreasing each variable affects the size of the GO Zone. Remember to consider one variable at a time; the other four variables will stay constant. For example, if the time the light is yellow increases from 3 s to 3.5 s, how will the boundaries and size of the GO Zone change? Will the zone increase or decrease? Record your predictions.

Answers

For You To Do

(continued)

5. a) Yellow light time, human response time, speed of car, deceleration rate, width of intersection

   b) Students copy chart. You may wish to provide them with a copy available at the end of this activity in the Teacher's Edition.

   c) Student predictions will vary.

ANSWERS

For You To Do

(continued)

6. a) 53 meters

   b) The GO Zone increases to 63 meters.

c-d) Student response.

7. a) Student responses.

   b) See chart on previous page.

8. a) vty - w
   (speed of car x yellow light time) - width of intersection

   b) Students should understand that by increasing the light time, there is more time to get through the yellow light safely. If there is more time, then at the same speed, you can cover a greater distance. Thus, the GO Zone increases. By increasing the speed, you can cover a greater distance in a shorter time, therefore the GO Zone increases. The wider the intersection, the greater the distance that needs to be covered, therefore the GO Zone is smaller.

   c) You are neither responding to the yellow light, nor are you slowing down when you consider the GO Zone.

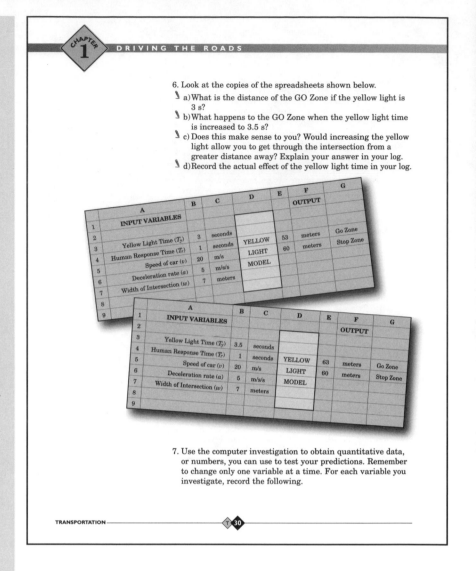

CHAPTER 1 DRIVING THE ROADS

6. Look at the copies of the spreadsheets shown below.
   a) What is the distance of the GO Zone if the yellow light is 3 s?
   b) What happens to the GO Zone when the yellow light time is increased to 3.5 s?
   c) Does this make sense to you? Would increasing the yellow light allow you to get through the intersection from a greater distance away? Explain your answer in your log.
   d) Record the actual effect of the yellow light time in your log.

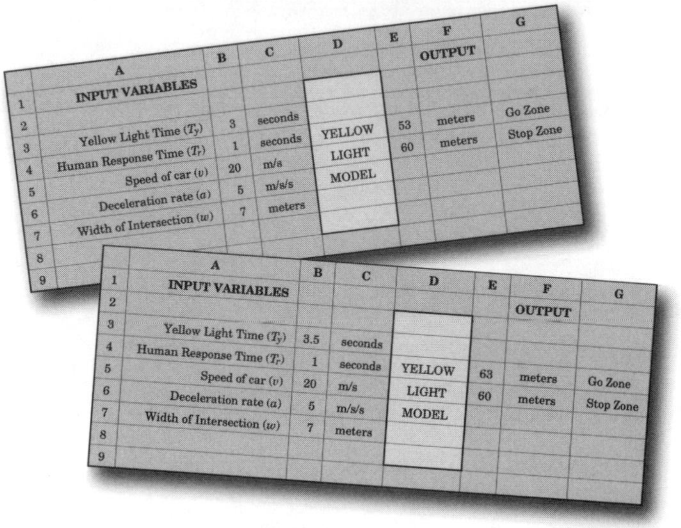

7. Use the computer investigation to obtain quantitative data, or numbers, you can use to test your predictions. Remember to change only one variable at a time. For each variable you investigate, record the following.

TRANSPORTATION T 30

Variable		Change	Predicted Effect of Change on GO Zone	Actual Effect of Change on GO Zone
T_y	Yellow Light Time	increase decrease	student response	increase decrease
T_r	Response Time	increase decrease	student response	no change no change
v	Speed Limit	increase decrease	student response	increase decrease
a	Deceleration Rate	increase decrease	student response	no change no change
w	Width of Intersection	increase decrease	student response	decrease increase

a) Did the effect of the change of the variable make sense to you? Explain.

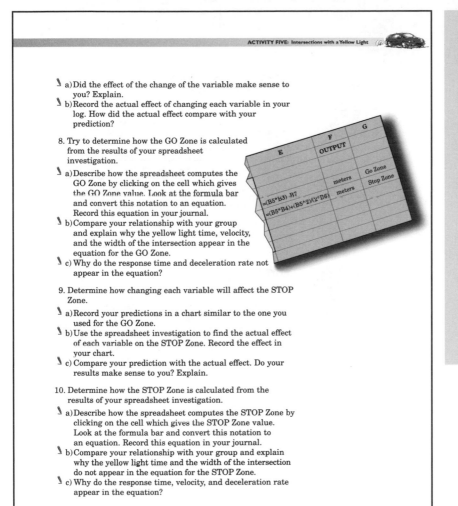

b) Record the actual effect of changing each variable in your log. How did the actual effect compare with your prediction?

8. Try to determine how the GO Zone is calculated from the results of your spreadsheet investigation.

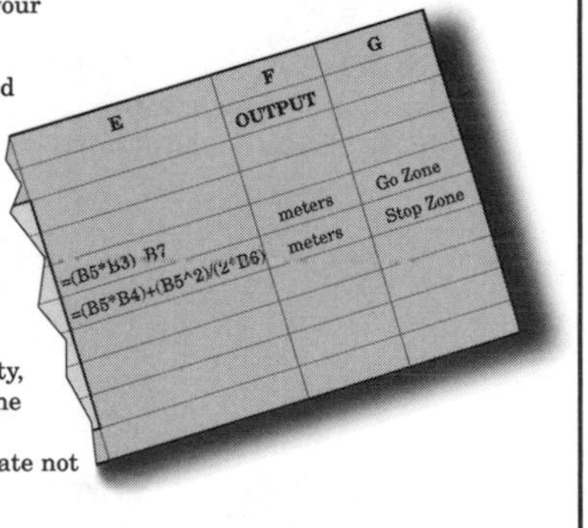

a) Describe how the spreadsheet computes the GO Zone by clicking on the cell which gives the GO Zone value. Look at the formula bar and convert this notation to an equation. Record this equation in your journal.

b) Compare your relationship with your group and explain why the yellow light time, velocity, and the width of the intersection appear in the equation for the GO Zone.

c) Why do the response time and deceleration rate not appear in the equation?

9. Determine how changing each variable will affect the STOP Zone.

a) Record your predictions in a chart similar to the one you used for the GO Zone.

b) Use the spreadsheet investigation to find the actual effect of each variable on the STOP Zone. Record the effect in your chart.

c) Compare your prediction with the actual effect. Do your results make sense to you? Explain.

10. Determine how the STOP Zone is calculated from the results of your spreadsheet investigation.

a) Describe how the spreadsheet computes the STOP Zone by clicking on the cell which gives the STOP Zone value. Look at the formula bar and convert this notation to an equation. Record this equation in your journal.

b) Compare your relationship with your group and explain why the yellow light time and the width of the intersection do not appear in the equation for the STOP Zone.

c) Why do the response time, velocity, and deceleration rate appear in the equation?

Yellow Light Time	Actual Effect
increase decrease	no change no change
Response Time	**Actual Effect**
increase decrease	increase decrease
Speed Limit	**Actual Effect**
increase decrease	increase decrease
Deceleration Rate	**Actual Effect**
increase decrease	decrease increase
Width of Intersection	**Actual Effect**
increase decrease	no change no change

ANSWERS

For You To Do

(continued)

9. a-c)

See chart below.
(speed of car x response time) + (speed x speed) / (2 x deceleration)

10. a) $vt_r + v^2/2a$

b) The length of time the light stays yellow does not affect the distance in which you can stop. Also, the width of the intersection has no effect on the distance required to stop.

c) The driver is reacting to a stimulus (yellow light) and then is decelerating.

Answers

Physics To Go

1. a) $GZ = vt_y - w$

   $GZ = (15 \text{ m/s})(4.0 \text{ s}) - 15 \text{ m}$

   $GZ = 45 \text{ m}$

   b) $SZ = vt_r + v^2/2d$

   $SZ = (15 \text{ m/s})(1.0 \text{ s})$

   $+ (15\text{m/s})2/(2 \times 5 \text{ m/s}2)$

   $SZ = 37.5 \text{ m}$

   c) Student sketch. Check that the students include the correct units in the sketch. See sample.

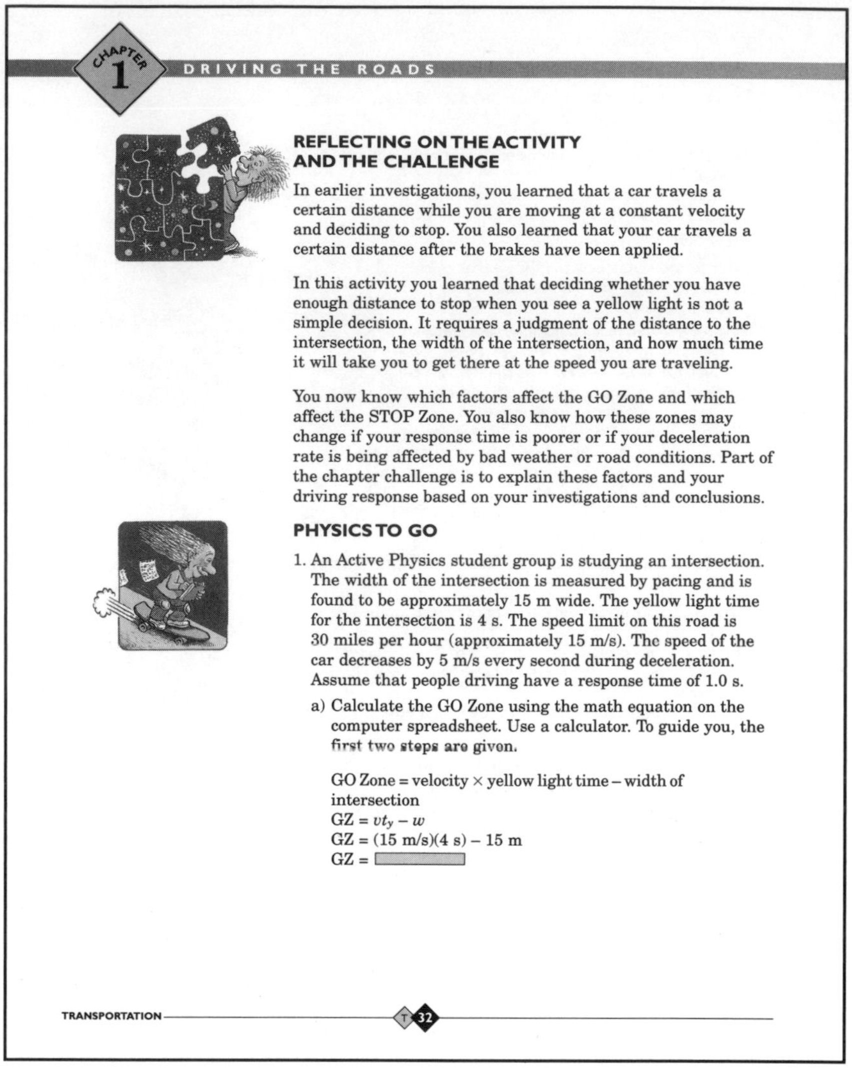

CHAPTER 1 DRIVING THE ROADS

REFLECTING ON THE ACTIVITY AND THE CHALLENGE

In earlier investigations, you learned that a car travels a certain distance while you are moving at a constant velocity and deciding to stop. You also learned that your car travels a certain distance after the brakes have been applied.

In this activity you learned that deciding whether you have enough distance to stop when you see a yellow light is not a simple decision. It requires a judgment of the distance to the intersection, the width of the intersection, and how much time it will take you to get there at the speed you are traveling.

You now know which factors affect the GO Zone and which affect the STOP Zone. You also know how these zones may change if your response time is poorer or if your deceleration rate is being affected by bad weather or road conditions. Part of the chapter challenge is to explain these factors and your driving response based on your investigations and conclusions.

PHYSICS TO GO

1. An Active Physics student group is studying an intersection. The width of the intersection is measured by pacing and is found to be approximately 15 m wide. The yellow light time for the intersection is 4 s. The speed limit on this road is 30 miles per hour (approximately 15 m/s). The speed of the car decreases by 5 m/s every second during deceleration. Assume that people driving have a response time of 1.0 s.

   a) Calculate the GO Zone using the math equation on the computer spreadsheet. Use a calculator. To guide you, the first two steps are given.

   GO Zone = velocity × yellow light time – width of intersection

   $GZ = vt_y - w$

   $GZ = (15 \text{ m/s})(4 \text{ s}) - 15 \text{ m}$

   GZ = ▭

TRANSPORTATION T 32

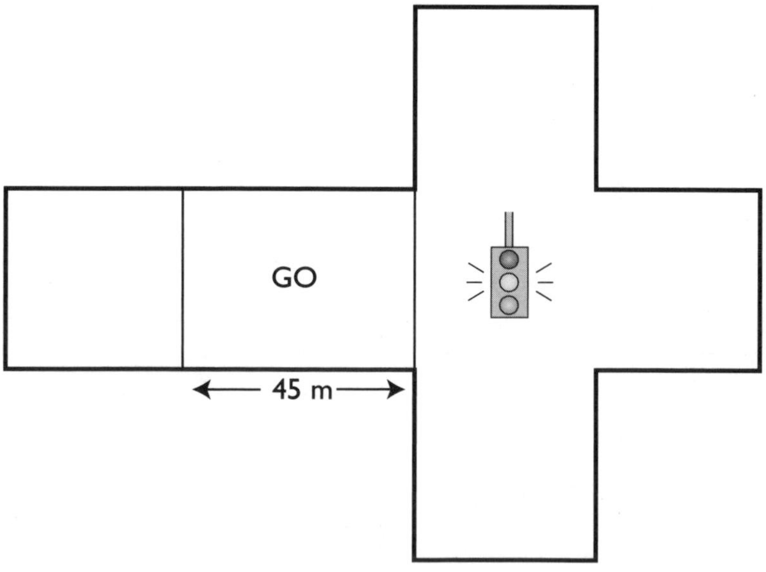

b) Calculate the STOP Zone using the math equation on the computer spreadsheet. Use a calculator to help you.

STOP Zone = velocity × response time + velocity²/2 × deceleration rate
$SZ = vt + v^2/2a$
SZ = ▭

c) Make a sketch of the intersection and label both the GO Zone and the STOP Zone. Include the dimensions of the intersection and each zone.

2. A person is listening to loud music while driving. Explain why the increase in response time caused by the music does not affect the GO Zone. Explain how it affects the STOP Zone.

3. A car has worn tires and bad brakes. How will this affect the GO Zone and the STOP Zone at a yellow light?

4. Some people disregard the 40 mph speed limit (20 m/s) and travel at 60 mph (30 m/s) on the road described in question 1. Calculate STOP and GO Zones at this speed. Write several sentences and sketch the intersection to inform these drivers of the danger of driving at 60 mph if the light turned yellow.

5. How would a decrease in the speed limit to 20 mph (about 10 m/s) affect the STOP and GO Zones in question 1? Use the spreadsheet or calculator to calculate both, then sketch the intersection, marking both zones.

6. Go out near your school and take measurements at an intersection that has a traffic light. Use the spreadsheet program or a calculator to calculate the STOP and GO Zones, then make a scale drawing of the intersection that includes both zones.

Excercise extreme caution. Follow the safety procedures outlined by your teacher. It is recommended that this activity be carried out with co-operation of the local Police Department.

7. Do you think it would be a good idea to paint lines at all intersections showing the boundaries of the STOP and GO Zones? Why or why not?

ANSWERS

Physics To Go

(continued)

2. The GO Zone is the area in which you can pass safely through the intersection, therefore there is no reaction time necessary. The STOP Zone is the distance traveled while reacting to a stimulus plus the distance required to stop. Therefore, the stop distance is affected by the response time, which can be affected by the music.

3. Worn tires and bad brakes will have no effect on the GO Zone, as there is no stopping distance needed at that point. However, the STOP Zone will be affected as the worn tires and bad brakes will increase the braking distance, thus increasing the stop zone.

4. Some people disregard the 30 mph speed limit (15 m/s) and travel at 60 mph (30 m/s) on the road described in question 1. Calculate STOP and GO Zones at this speed. Write several sentences and sketch the intersection to inform these drivers of the danger of driving at 60 mph if the light turned yellow.

GO zone = *vty - w*
= 30 m/s x 4.0 s - 15 m
= 105 m

STOP zone = *vtr + v2/2a*
= 30 m/s x 1.0 s + (30m/s)2 / 2 x 5 m/s2
= 120 m

5. GO zone = *vty - w*
= 10 m/s x 4.0 s - 15 m
= 25 m

STOP zone = *vtr + v2/2a*
= 10 m/s x 1.0 s + (10m/s)2 / 2 x 5 m/s2
= 20 m

6. Students use local data.

7. Student responses will vary. Accept any reasonable explanation, but be sure that the students also include in their arguments a discussion of road conditions, driver response, brake and tire wear.

1

Assessment: Scientific Thinking

The following assessment criteria may be used to evaluate the students' scientific thinking.

Place a check mark (√) in the appropriate column. Allow 1 point for each check.
Point total = 8.

Learner outcome demonstrated	**Yes**	**No**
• Student is able to identify 5 driving variables and identify those that affect the GO ZONE.		
• Student is able to determine which physics concepts are used in the GO ZONE.		
• Student is able to describe how the spreadsheet computes the GO ZONE.		
• Student identifies and is able to use an equation for the GO ZONE.		
• Student is able to identify 5 variables that affect the STOP ZONE.		
• Student is able to determine which physics concepts are used in the STOP ZONE.		
• Student is able to describe how the spreadsheet computes the STOP ZONE.		
• Student identifies and is able to use an equation for the STOP ZONE.		

For use with *Transportation*, Chapter 1, ACTIVITY FIVE: Intersections with a Yellow Light

Assessment: Driving Simulation

Place a check mark (√) in the appropriate column. Allow 1 point for each check.
Point total = 8.

Learner outcome demonstrated	**Yes**	**No**
• Student relates his or her driving pattern to tailgating data.		
• Student is able to use simulation to determine his or her reaction time.		
• Spreadsheet is used to determine extra braking distance by: 1. Measuring and entering the length of the average car. 2. Entering the recommended trailing distance. 3. Entering speed in mph. 4. Entering student's individual reaction time.		
• Student is able to compare his or her extra braking distance, calculated in the spreadsheet, with the recommended braking distance.		
• Student is able to explain the discrepancy between the recommended stopping distance of one car length for every 10 mph to that obtained by the spreadsheet calculations.		
• Student is able to calculate the GO ZONE using math equations on the computer spreadsheet.		
• Student is able to calculate the STOP ZONE using math equations on the computer spreadsheet.		
• Student makes a sketch of the intersection and labels both STOP and GO ZONES.		

1

For use with *Transportation*, Chapter 1, ACTIVITY FIVE: Intersections with a Yellow Light

ACTIVITY SIX
Yellow Light Dilemma and Dangerous Intersections

Background Information

Using information from Activity Five, this activity examines the problems that may be encountered while approaching an intersection, and what will happen when the input variables are changed. The GO Zone (where it is safe to continue when the light changes), and the STOP Zone (where it is safe to stop) are easily understood. The dilemma zone, however, introduces the area or region where the driver must make a more difficult decision as to stop or go. The five input variables must be examined separately.

The sample data below give a good representation of the dilemma zone increasing as the speed of the vehicle increases. This zone is too dangerous to stop (not enough room to stop) and too dangerous to go through—when the light changes to red, there is a good possibility you will either be in the intersection or approaching it at the high speed you were initially driving.

Sample Data

Ty (s)	w (m)	*v*(m/s)	*T r* (s)	*a* (m/s^2)	GO Zone (m)	STOP Zone (m)	Dil Zone (m)
3	15	9	1	3.7	12	20	8
3	15	13	1	3.7	24	36	12
3	15	18	1	3.7	39	62	23
3	15	22	1	3.7	51	87	36
3	15	27	1	3.7	66	125	59
3	15	31	1	3.7	78	160	82

The intersection will be unsafe if the GO Zone is smaller than the STOP Zone. The overlap zone provides a buffer, an area where it is safe to either go or stop. Since there is always some latitude in the way people drive, it is important to provide this overlap zone.

The physics of the GO Zone and the STOP Zone can probably be made clearer if we were to graph both functions. In the graph shown, the distances for the corresponding GO Zone and STOP Zone are displayed as a function of velocity.

The GO Zone is a linear graph ($GZ = vTy - w$). Its *y*-intercept changes with the width of the intersection and its slope changes with the yellow light time. Either change can alter the overlap and dilemma zones.

The STOP Zone is a parabola ($SZ = vTr + v2/2a$). Its shape can be altered by varying the response time or the deceleration rate. The change in the shape or position of the parabola can alter the overlap and dilemma zones.

Even though any of the variables can eliminate a dilemma zone, it is fairly obvious that a change is the width of an intersection would be an expensive approach. Changing human response time or assuming that people will be more alert is hardly a worthwhile strategy. Likewise, the deceleration rate of cars is so dependent on individual cars and drivers that this is also a poor strategy. This leaves us with lengthening yellow light time (which can be adjusted easily) or lowering the speed limit.

Active-ating the Physics InfoMall

See the Infomall listings for Activity Five.

Planning for the Activity

Time Requirements

Allow one class period (40 to 60 minutes) to go over some of the different combinations of input variables. If time is available, allow another class period for students to input many different combinations.

Materials needed

For each lab group:

- computer with Excel spreadsheet software

For the class:

- *Active Physics* Spreadsheet Template (File: Yellow Light)

Advance Preparation and Setup

Input the spreadsheet model into your spreadsheet software. Test your spreadsheet by changing the yellow light time and see if your samples match those in the text. If you are using a local area network, simply download each spreadsheet to the work stations that the student groups will be using. Otherwise make a computer disk for each work station. You need to make sure that specific jobs are assigned to each student in the group and rotate the jobs periodically. If the groups need to share or compare information, assign a communicator to represent each group.

Teaching Notes

This activity is a continuation of the previous activity. Before you begin, be sure that students understand the GO Zone and the STOP Zone. For You To Do, steps 1 to 4 serve partly as a review as well as an introduction to the overlap or dilemma zones.

You may want to give students specific scenarios to help them integrate this simulation into real life. For example, all the input variables will be the same, but if the road is wet, the deceleration rate will increase, increasing the stopping distance. Another is to change the reaction time, with distractions, (driving by a swimming pool on a hot day) or various physiological inhibitors (drugs, alcohol, fatigue, bad moods). If you give them a few examples, they will then be able to continue with their own examples.

Emphasize to the students that it is not as simple as changing variables one at a time and that the actual process of stopping is complicated. Often all the variables may be changing and adding to the distance required to stop. Reemphasize that the distance required to stop after the brakes are applied is proportional to the square of the speed ($d = v^2/2a$).

For groups that work faster, challenge them to modify the program to reflect For You To Do step 9. Figuring out how to incorporate the length of the car should not be too difficult. Basically, the car length is going to decrease the GO Zone.

Activity Overview

In this activity students apply the yellow light model that they learned about in Activity Five, to intersections that have dilemma zones. This activity allows the students to manipulate the variables to see how the dilemma zone changes, and to extrapolate the possible consequences.

Student Objectives

Students will:

- understand what an overlap zone is at a traffic light.

ANSWERS FOR THE TEACHER ONLY

What Do You Think?

See Background Information.

Activity Six

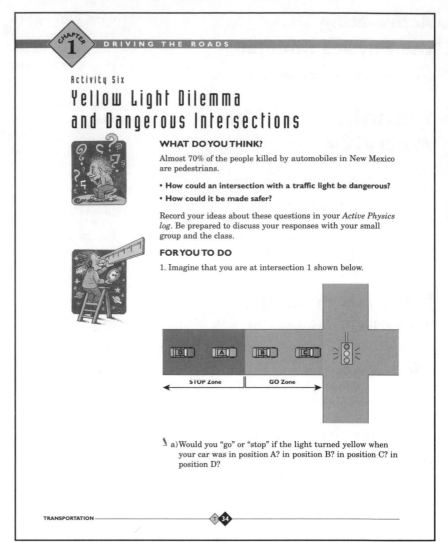

Yellow Light Dilemma and Dangerous Intersections

WHAT DO YOU THINK?

Almost 70% of the people killed by automobiles in New Mexico are pedestrians.

- **How could an intersection with a traffic light be dangerous?**
- **How could it be made safer?**

Record your ideas about these questions in your *Active Physics log*. Be prepared to discuss your responses with your small group and the class.

FOR YOU TO DO

1. Imagine that you are at intersection 1 shown below.

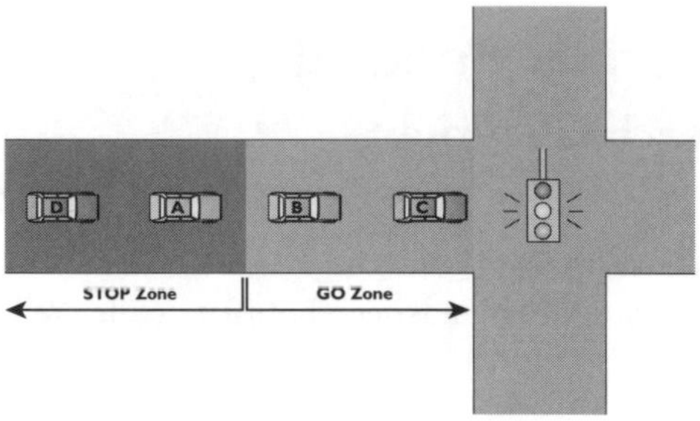

a) Would you "go" or "stop" if the light turned yellow when your car was in position A? in position B? in position C? in position D?

ANSWERS

For You To Do

1. a) in position A? Stop

in position B? Go

in position C? Go

in position D? Stop

2. Imagine that you are at intersection 2 shown below.

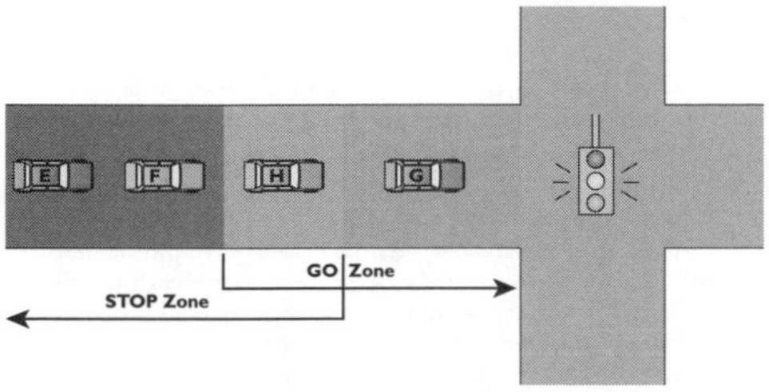

a) Would you "go" or "stop" if the light turned yellow when your car was in position E? in position F? in position G? in position H?

3. Imagine you are at intersection 3 shown below.

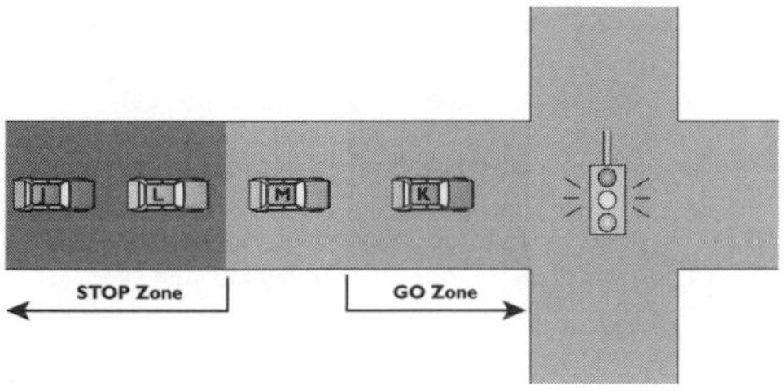

a) Would you "go" or "stop" if the light turned yellow when your car was in position J? in position K? in position L? in position M?

Answers

For You To Do *(continued)*

2. a)	in position E?	Stop
	in position F?	Stop
	in position G?	Go
	in position H?	Stop or go
3. a)	in position J?	Stop
	in position K?	Go
	in position L?	Stop
	in position M?	You cannot stop or go safely.

1

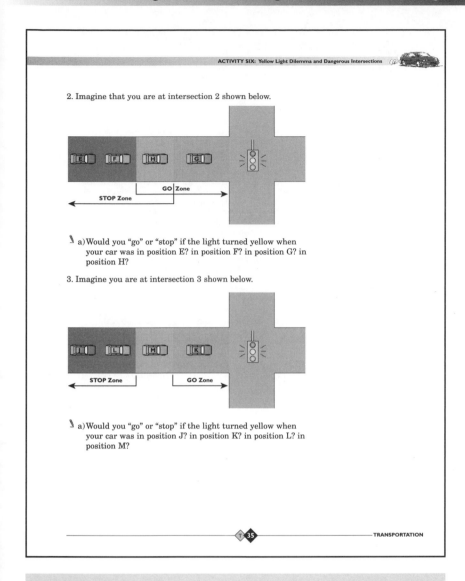

ANSWERS

For You To Do

(continued)

4. a) In intersection 2 the GO Zone and the STOP Zone overlap. In intersection 3, there is a gap between the two zones.

   b) Stop or go. Both choices are safe, because the car is in both the STOP and GO Zones.

   c) Stop or go. Neither choice is safe because the car is in neither the STOP nor GO Zone.

   d) Intersection 2 has an overlap zone, and intersection 3 has a dilemma zone.

5. a) The spreadsheet calculates the difference between the GO and STOP Zones.

   b) No

   c) Both the GO Zone and the STOP Zone increase. There is a Dilemma Zone.

   d) The GO Zone becomes 27 m and the STOP Zone is 22 m. There is an Overlap Zone of 5 m.

4. Compare the GO Zone and the STOP Zone for intersections 1, 2, and 3.
   a) How are the intersections different?
   b) In intersection 2, if the light turned yellow when you were in the overlap between the GO Zone and the STOP Zone, what are your choices? Which choice(s) would be safe?
   c) In intersection 3, if the light turned yellow when you were in the space between the STOP Zone and the GO Zone, what are your choices? Which choice(s) would be safe?
   d) When both choices are safe, the space between the GO and STOP Zones is called the Overlap Zone. When neither choice is clearly safe, it is called the Dilemma Zone. Intersections with a Dilemma Zone are not safe. Which intersection has an Overlap Zone and which has a Dilemma Zone?

5. Use a computer spreadsheet program, very similar to the one you used in Activity 5. There is an additional OUTPUT that tells you whether the intersection is safe and has an Overlap Zone or is unsafe and has a Dilemma Zone. Use the spreadsheet to determine ways in which an unsafe intersection can be made into a safe intersection and vice versa.
   a) How does the spreadsheet figure out whether the intersection is safe? What is the relationship between the GO Zone and the STOP Zone at an unsafe intersection?

	A	B	C	D	E	F	G
1	INPUT VARIABLES					OUTPUT	
2							
3	Yellow Light Time (T_Y)	3.7	seconds				
4	Human Response Time (T_T)	1.2	seconds	YELLOW	64	meters	Go Zone
5	Speed of Car (v)	20	m/s	LIGHT	64	meters	Stop Zone
6	Deceleration Rate (a)	5	m/s/s	MODEL	0	meters	Overlap Zone
7	Width of Intersection (w)	10	meters				Safe
8							
9							
10							
11	Yellow Light Time (T_Y)	3.7	seconds				
12	Human Response Time (T_T)	1.2	seconds	YELLOW	101	meters	Go Zone
13	Speed of Car (v)	30	m/s	LIGHT	126	meters	Stop Zone
14	Deceleration Rate (a)	5	m/s/s	MODEL	-25	meters	Dilemma Zone
15	Width of Intersection (w)	10	meters				UNSAFE
16							

b) Use the sample spreadsheet shown. Is there an Overlap or Dilemma Zone at 20 m/s?

c) What happens to the GO Zone and the STOP Zone when the speed is increased to 30 m/s? Is there still an Overlap or Dilemma Zone?

d) Now lower the speed to 10 m/s (20 mph). Is the intersection now safer? Why or why not?

6. Continue your exploration by resetting the speed to its original value of 20 m/s. Adjust the yellow light time and determine its effect on the Dilemma and Overlap Zones.

a) Record the results of this investigation in your log.

7. What effect do human response time, deceleration rate, and width of the intersection have on the safety of the intersection? Conduct investigations with your spreadsheet.

a) Record the results in your log.

8. More than one variable change can eliminate a Dilemma Zone and replace it with an Overlap Zone.

a) Of the five variables, explain the ease or difficulty in changing each one to make the intersection safer. For example, why might you suggest changing the yellow light time rather than changing the width of the intersection?

9. The Yellow Light Problem is based on a simple model and only provides approximate calculations. It does not include other factors such as whether the road is flat or the length of your car.

a) How does the length of the car affect the model? Which outputs are affected by the length of your car?

ANSWERS

For You To Do
(continued)

6. a) Students record their observations.

7. a) Students response to data from spreadsheet. Students need to see that increasing the GO Zone to at least the STOP Zone will eliminate the dilemma zone. Therefore, decreasing width, decreasing response time, and increasing acceleration rate will make the intersection safer, by eliminating the dilemma zone.

8. a) Human response time is hard to change. The width of the intersection is very difficult to change as it involves rebuilding the road. The speed limit on the road could be changed, but it is difficult to enforce at all intersections. The deceleration rate of vehicles is very difficult to change as every different vehicle has a different rate, as well as the rate changes depending on the weather, road surface, temperature of tires and road, hills, etc. The easiest variable to change would be the yellow light time. This may involve only changing a timer or at a central location reprogramming a computer program.

9. a) The length of the car is affected by the width of the intersection as it takes a longer period of time to clear the intersection. Therefore, the output which is affected would be the GO Zone.

1

ANSWERS

Physics To Go

1. Using the formulae $vt_y - w$ = GO Zone and $vt_r + v^2/2a$ = STOP Zone, students can find the dilemma zones for each intersection.

   a) GZ $= vt_y - w$
   $= 48$ m
   $= 20$ m/s x 3.0 s - 12 m
   SZ $= vt_r + v^2/2a$
   $= (20$ m/s$)(1.2$ s$) +$

   $(20 m/s)^2/2 \times 7 m/s^2$

   $= 52.6$ m
   Similarly, the rest of the values can be put into a chart, below:

(A safe intersection is when there is a negative dilemma zone, in other words, the GO Zone — the STOP Zone is a positive value.)

CHAPTER 1 DRIVING THE ROADS

REFLECTING ON THE ACTIVITY AND THE CHALLENGE

It appears from this activity that a traffic engineer has to be sure that an intersection has an overlap zone and not a dilemma zone. As you now know, any intersection can be made safer by slowing the speed limit or by lengthening the yellow light time. Occasionally a light is mounted at the intersection and its time is not adjusted but left at the manufacturer's default value. Accidents are more likely to occur at such an intersection because it may have a dilemma zone. Part of your chapter challenge is to write a letter to a traffic engineer about an unsafe intersection. If you complete question 5 in the Physics to Go, you have already completed this part of your challenge.

PHYSICS TO GO

1. Compute the GO Zones and STOP Zones for each intersection. Also determine if each intersection is safe and describe how you know.

   a) Yellow light time 3.0 s
   Response time 1.2 s
   Speed of car 20 m/s
   Deceleration rate 7 m/s/s
   Width of intersection 12 m

   b) Yellow light time 4.0 s
   Response time 1.2 s
   Speed of car 20 m/s
   Deceleration rate 7 m/s/s
   Width of intersection 8 m

   c) Yellow light time 3.0 s
   Response time 1.0 s
   Speed of car 20 m/s
   Deceleration rate 7 m/s/s
   Width of intersection 12 m

   d) Yellow light time 3.0s
   Response time 1.8 s
   Speed of car 20 m/s
   Deceleration rate 7 m/s/s
   Width of intersection 12 m

Intersection	STOP Zone (m)	GO Zone (m)	Dilemma Zone (m)	Safe (Y or N)
a)	52.6	48	-4.6	N
b)	52.6	72	+19.4	Y
c)	48.6	48	-0.6	Too close
d)	64.6	48	-16.6	N
e)	34.1	40.5	+6.4	Y

e) Yellow light time 3.5 s
   Response time 1.2 s
   Speed of car 15 m/s
   Deceleration rate 7 m/s/s
   Width of intersection 12 m

2. Another name for the Dilemma Zone could be the "You're in Big Trouble Zone." Can you think of a catchier phrase or name that will help you explain to your friends the problems in this unsafe zone?

3. The stopping distance of a car approaching a yellow light depends on response time and speed. Write a paragraph in your *Active Physics log* that applies all of this information to making a wise decision when in the Dilemma Zone.

4. Now that you know how the length of the yellow light time and other factors affect the safety of a traffic intersection, you are ready to study an actual intersection.

   a) Choose a traffic intersection in your community and measure the yellow light time and the width of the intersection.

   b) Draw a sketch of the intersection and include the GO Zone and the STOP Zone.

   c) Assume that human response time is 1.0 s and the deceleration rate is 5 m/s every second. Run the spreadsheet program with this data and find the STOP and GO Zones. You may also use a calculator and the appropriate equations.

   d) From your data, does a dilemma zone or an overlap zone exist? Is the intersection safe?

5. Assume that you have found a dangerous Dilemma Zone in a nearby intersection. As a good citizen, you would like to inform the Chamber of Commerce that the intersection is unsafe and that changing it will prevent some accidents and damage to property and people. You realize that the people at the Chamber of Commerce may not know about Go Zones and Stop Zones. You also know that you have a better chance of action if you are able to state the problem and suggest a solution.

   a) Prepare an outline of the information that should be included in the letter.

   b) Write the letter.

Observe the intersection from a safe distance. Follow all safety precautions set out by your teacher.

ANSWERS

Physics To Go

(continued)

2. Student response will vary. (There is a popular song called *Highway to the Danger Zone.*)

3. Student responses will vary. Students should conclude that when approaching an intersection it would be advisable to be doing no more than the speed limit, and perhaps slow down slightly, and also to be extra careful. For example, do not use this time to adjust the car radio.

4. This question requires local data. The students may find that the intersections are for the most part safe.

5. Here is a good opportunity for the students to show their understanding of physics in explaining how to make the intersection safer. In their letter, elements of what increases the dilemma zone (increased response time, decreased deceleration, decreased yellow light time) should be clearly articulated in the explanation. The dilemma zone is determined by subtracting the GO Zone from the STOP Zone, so anything that increases the GO Zone, and decreases the STOP Zone will make the intersection safer.

1

ACTIVITY SEVEN
Driving on Curves

Background Information

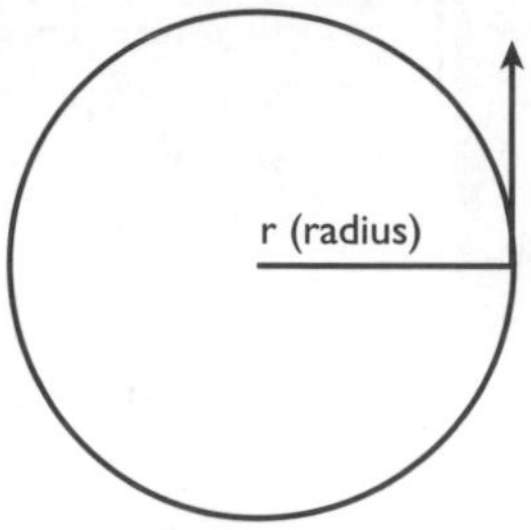

Sir Isaac Newton did more than anyone else to unravel the mysteries of motion. Born on Christmas Day in 1642, this English physicist organized his observations into scientific laws that helped predict motion. Newton noticed objects set in motion would continue to move until a force acted upon them. A ball rolling down a ramp would continue to move forever if friction did not eventually slow the ball. A surface, like sandpaper, with great friction would slow the ball faster than a surface with low friction. Newton's first law of motion is often called the Law of Inertia. Newton's First Law of Motion states that an object in motion or at rest will remain in motion or at rest unless acted upon by an outside, unbalanced force. Therefore, an object moving in a straight path must have an outside unbalanced force acting on it to change its velocity (speed) or its path. Any change in the velocity must involve an acceleration ($a = \Delta v/\Delta t$). The change in velocity can be a change in speed, or a change in direction, as is the case for objects moving in a circular path.

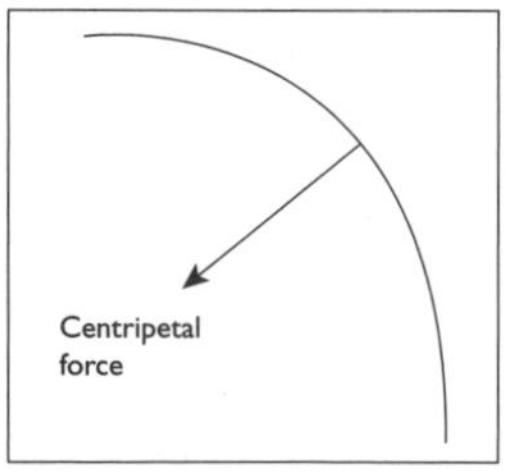

In order for an object to stay in a circular path there must be a force acting on the object to keep it from moving in a straight line (Newton's first law). This force is the centripetal force (Fc) which always acts toward the center of the circle. ($Fc = mac$).

For a ball on the end of a string to stay in a circular path, it must have a force acting on the ball to keep it from going in a straight line. This is supplied by the force you apply to the string from the center of the circle (sometimes called tension).

Previously, when we wanted to find the speed of an object, we used the formula $v = d/t$.

However, since the object is traveling in a circular path, we need to find the speed while it is traveling in a circle. Using the same formula, $v = d/t$, where the distance is the circumference, $2\pi r$ and the time is the period of one complete rotation (called the period - T) the speed of an object is $v = 2\pi r/T$.

To find the period, when you know the frequency, $T = 1/f$.

Example:

A turntable is revolving at 10 rotations per second, the time (period) for one revolution is

$T = 1/f$

$T = 1/10$

$T = 0.1$ s

Active-ating the Physics InfoMall

Curved motion is a topic found throughout physics. The InfoMall has an abundance of information on this. For example, in the Book Basement is D. Kutliroff's Teaching High School Physics, which has an entire chapter entitled "Curved Motion."

Planning for the Activity

Time Requirements

The approximate time for this activity will be 30 minutes. Extra time will be required to perform more tests with the block on the lazy Susan, investigating different surfaces

Materials needed

For each lab group:

- toy car (battery-operated)
- string (about 0.5 m)
- lazy Susan turntable
- small block of wood

- stopwatch
- rubber mat (or sandpaper)

Advance Preparation and Setup

You might wish to tape a card to the outer edge of the lazy Susan to help the students in counting the revolutions per minute.

Teaching Notes

After a brief discussion of the What Do You Think? question, start by asking students to complete step 1 of For You To Do. Be sure each student commits to a choice. Before moving on to step 2, challenge their answers with a demonstration: attempt to push a toy car into a circular path. Ask the students why it cannot move in a circle after it has left your hand. Then let them go ahead to try step 2. Discuss the direction of the force that keeps the car in its circular path.

There are many misconceptions regarding centripetal motion. The most common misconception is that when an object (such as a rubber stopper on a string) is traveling in a circular path and the string is cut, students will describe the motion of the rubber stopper as traveling either straight away from the center (continuing along the radius), or that it will continue to travel in the circular path. The actual path will be the tangent to the circle.

Another misconception is the idea of a centrifugal force, as a force which causes your body to move to the outside of the car as it rounds the curve. Help the students to understand that the movement towards the outside of a car is inertia (the tendency to travel in a straight line) and it is the centripetal force that is forcing them to the inside of the circle, supplied by the car door.

To help students understand inertia, you may wish to do Activity Seven A as a demonstration, or ask students to complete the activity at home.

Note that the term "traction" is used in step 3, but is not clearly defined at first. Allow the idea of useful friction to emerge.

Point out that the relative motion of the turntable is similar to the motion of a car on a stationary surface. The assigned task is to find a relationship between the radius of curvature of the path and the highest speed at which static friction can keep the block on the surface. The rubber mat brings out the importance of the surface in defining the traction.

In step 8, the block is placed at different radii from the center. Check that the students are aware that the speeds for the different radii are different, even though the lazy Susan's rotational frequency is the same. Most students recognize the concept, but don't always carry the idea into the analysis. They are to compare maximum speeds at different radii.

Students should be aware that objects at the end of strings can be dangerous if "flung" with exuberance.

Activity Overview

In this activity, the students will identify and test the nature of a centripetal force.

Student Objectives

Students will:

- recognize the need for a centripetal force when rounding a curve.
- predict the effect of an inadequate centripetal force.
- relate speed to centripetal force.

ANSWERS FOR THE TEACHER ONLY

What Do You Think?

To give students a feel for curved motion, see *The Physics Teacher*, volume 21, issue 3, "People Demos." Toward the end is a section on circular motion. Along the way, you may find other demos you wish to use for other topics.

Activity Seven

Driving on Curves

WHAT DO YOU THINK?

You are driving along a road at the posted speed limit of 40 mph (20 m/s). A road sign warns that you are approaching a curve and tells you to slow down to 20 mph (10 m/s).

- **Why are they telling you to slow down?**
- **How do they know how much you should slow down?**

Record your ideas about these questions in your *Active Physics log*. Be prepared to discuss your responses with your small group and the class.

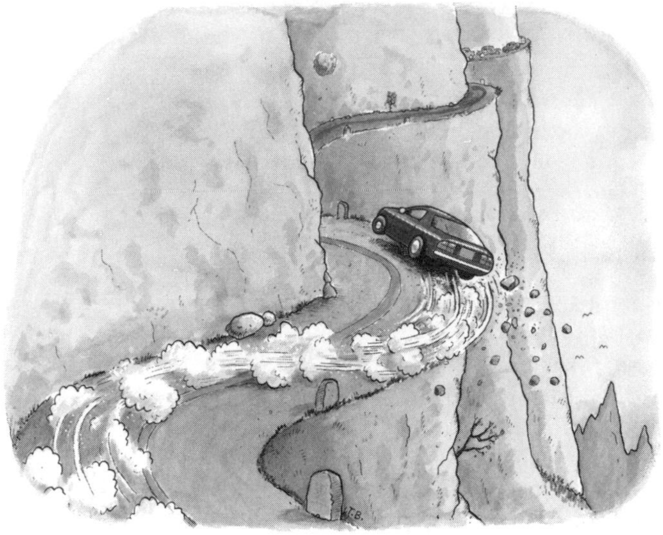

FOR YOU TO DO

1. Driving around a curve produces some special problems. Physics lets you model some of these problems. Imagine that you have a toy car at the end of a string, and it is moving in a circle. If you let go of the string, which way will the car go? The figure below gives you several choices.
   a) Choose in which direction you think the car will go.

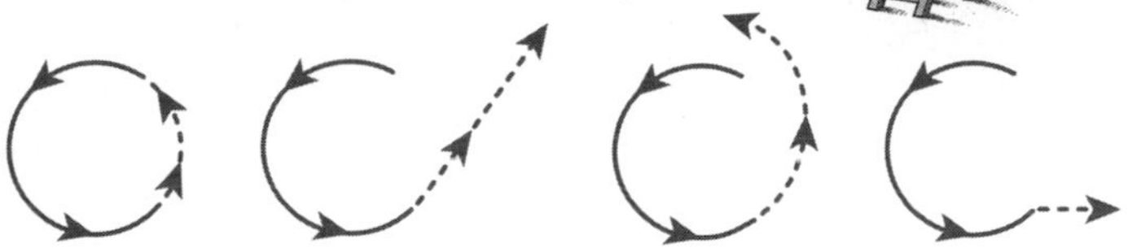

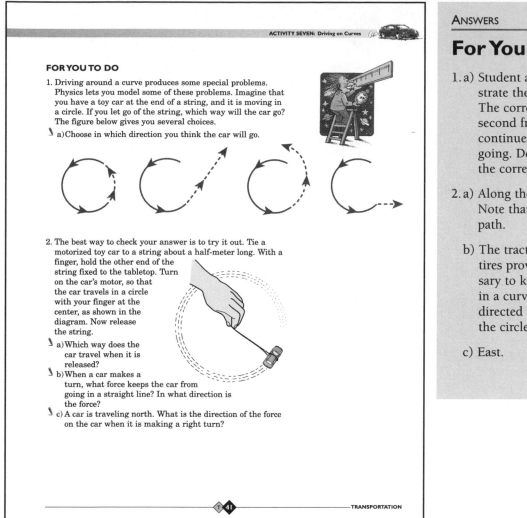

2. The best way to check your answer is to try it out. Tie a motorized toy car to a string about a half-meter long. With a finger, hold the other end of the string fixed to the tabletop. Turn on the car's motor, so that the car travels in a circle with your finger at the center, as shown in the diagram. Now release the string.

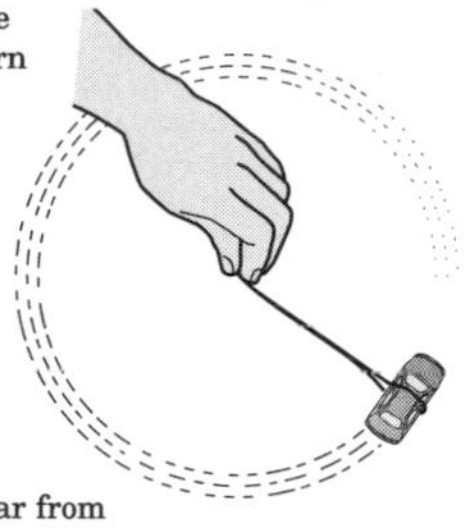

   a) Which way does the car travel when it is released?
   b) When a car makes a turn, what force keeps the car from going in a straight line? In what direction is the force?
   c) A car is traveling north. What is the direction of the force on the car when it is making a right turn?

Answers

For You To Do

1. a) Student answers will demonstrate their misconceptions. The correct answer is the second from the left, the car continues in the way it was going. Do not expect or offer the correct answer.

2. a) Along the tangent to the circle. Note that it is not a radial path.

   b) The traction of the road on the tires provides the force necessary to keep the car traveling in a curved path. The force is directed towards the center of the circle.

   c) East.

1

ANSWERS

For You To Do

(continued)

4\. a) The speed can be determined by measuring the time required for ten revolutions (e.g.: 5 seconds for ten revolutions or 10 revs per 5 seconds or reduced to 2 rev per s).

a) Revolutions per minute (rpm) or frequency, is the number of revs per second x 60 s, Therefore using above example, the frequency is 120 rpms.

b) Students observe when the block slides off.

c) Time for one revolution or period is equal to 1/frequency. Therefore, from the example above, period = 1/2 revs per second or 0.5 second.

5\. a) Students record their measurements.

3\. To look at the factors that determine whether a car will stay on the road as it goes around a curve, you will do a second investigation. You will need a "lazy Susan" that you can turn, and a block of wood. Place a block of wood near the outer edge of the lazy Susan. Spin the lazy Susan. As it spins, the block is held in place by friction. This is not really the same as the traction that holds a car on the road, but it is similar.

4\. Gradually increase the rotational speed of the lazy Susan until the block just begins to slide off. Now practice until you find the fastest speed where the block will stay in place. Determine the speed by measuring the time required for 10 revolutions.

a) Record the number of revolutions per minute made by the lazy Susan when the friction is strong enough to keep the block going in a circle.

b) How fast (revolutions per minute) is the lazy Susan turning when friction can no longer hold the block in place?

c) How much time goes by during one revolution?

5\. To find out how fast the block was going, you will need one other piece of information: the distance of the block from the center of the lazy Susan. Measure this in centimeters.

a) Record your measurement.

6\. To calculate the speed of an object you can divide the distance traveled by the time.

$$\text{Speed} = \frac{\text{distance}}{\text{time}}$$

When an object moves in a circle, the distance traveled in one revolution is the circumference of the circle.

Circumference = $2 \times \pi \times$ radius of circle

a) What was the speed of the block when it stayed on the lazy Susan? slid off the lazy Susan?

Note: You may not be able to find the exact speed where the block leaves the lazy Susan. You can find a speed where the block stays in place and a speed where the block is not able to stay on the lazy Susan. You can call the first of these a "safe speed" and the second an "unsafe speed." Any speed lower than the "safe speed" will also be safe. Any speed higher than the "unsafe speed" will also be unsafe.

7. Place a rubber mat or some sandpaper between the block and the lazy Susan. Repeat the entire investigation.
   a) Record all the necessary data.
   b) Calculate the greatest speed at which the block can stay on the rubber mat.
   c) How does the surface affect the maximum speed?

8. In addition to the speed and the road surface, you also need to look at the curvature of the road. Investigate this question by placing the block at various distances from the center of the lazy Susan.
   a) What happens to the maximum speed as the radius of the path increases?
   b) At each distance, find the maximum stable speed of the block.

REFLECTING ON THE ACTIVITY AND THE CHALLENGE

In this activity you learned that friction between the road and the tires helps keep the car on the road when it goes around a curve. More friction allows you to move faster and still stay on the road.

A tight turn requires more friction or a slower speed than a wider turn. Since you cannot change the friction on the road, a slower speed will keep the car on the road.

The challenge requires you to explain how driving around a curve may require a different speed than the normal speed limit. You may also want to explain what happens if the road conditions change, if your tires are in bad shape, or how the tightness of the turn also requires extra attention and a lower speed.

Answers

For You To Do
(continued)

6. a) The speed when it stayed on should be slower than the speed when slid off.

7. a) Student data.
   b) Use $v = 2\pi r/t$
   c) The greater the force of friction, supplied by the sandpaper or rubber mat, the greater the speed of the turntable before the block flies off.

8. a) As you increase the radius of the path, the maximum speed will also increase.
   b) Students record their observations and measurements.

ANSWERS

Physics To Go

1. $v = d/t$, where $d = 2\pi r$,
therefore, d = 2 x π x 6 400 000m
using, π = 3.14
d = 40 192 000 m
and t = 24 h x 60 min/h x 60 s/min
t = 86 400 s.
then, v = 40 192 000 m/86 400 s
v = 465 m/s or approximately 1000 mph
$v = d/t$, where $d = 2\pi r$,
therefore, d = 2 x π x 6 400 km
d = 40 192 km
and t = 24 h
then, v = 40 192 km /24 h
v = 1675 km/h

If students do not feel comfortable or lack competence manipulating numbers, accept answers in km/h only.

2. The earth travels in a circular motion around the sun. The radius of the earth's motion is about 1.5 ¥ 10^{-8} km. What is the speed of the earth around the sun? Compute the speed in m/s and in km/h.

PHYSICS TO GO

1. A person at the equator travels once around the circumference of the earth in 24 hours. The radius of the earth is 6,400 km. How fast is the person going? Compute the speed in m/s and in km/h (one kilometer is equal to 1,000 m).
2. Earth travels in a circular motion around the sun. The radius of the Earth's motion is about 1.5×10^8 km. What is the speed of the Earth around the sun? Compute the speed in m/s and in km/h.
3. A fan turns at a rate of 60 revolutions per second. If the tip of the blade is 15 cm from the center, how fast is the tip moving?
4. Friction can hold a car on the road when it is traveling at 20 m/s and the radius of the turn is 15 m. What happens if
   a) the turn is tighter?
   b) the road surface gets slippery?
   c) both the turn is tighter and the road is more slippery?

5. Think about other examples in which objects travel in curved paths, such as the clothes in a spin-dryer, or the moon traveling around the earth. For each example, tell what produces the force that is constantly pushing the object toward the center of the curve.

$v = d/t$, where $d = 2\pi r$,
therefore, $d = 2 \times \pi \times 1.5 \times 10^{11}$ m
using, π = 3.14
$d = 9.42 \times 10^{11}$
and t = 365 days x 24 h/day x 60 min/h x 60 s/min
t = 31,536,000 s.
then, $v = 9.42 \times 10^{11}$ m/31,536,000 s
v = 29,850 m/s
v = 30,000 m/s or approximately 60,000 mph
$v = d/t$, where $d = 2\pi r$
therefore, $d = 2 \times \pi \times 1.5 \times 10^{8}$ km
$d = 9.42 \times 10^{8}$ km
and t = 365 days x 24 h/day
t = 8760 h
then, $v = 9.42 \times 10^{8}$ km/ 8760 h
v = 107 500 km/h
v = 110 000 km/h

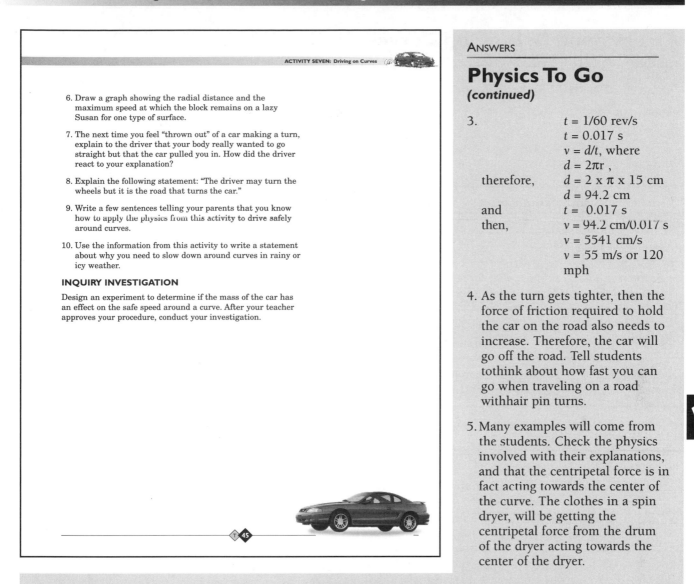

6. Draw a graph showing the radial distance and the maximum speed at which the block remains on a lazy Susan for one type of surface.

7. The next time you feel "thrown out" of a car making a turn, explain to the driver that your body really wanted to go straight but that the car pulled you in. How did the driver react to your explanation?

8. Explain the following statement: "The driver may turn the wheels but it is the road that turns the car."

9. Write a few sentences telling your parents that you know how to apply the physics from this activity to drive safely around curves.

10. Use the information from this activity to write a statement about why you need to slow down around curves in rainy or icy weather.

INQUIRY INVESTIGATION

Design an experiment to determine if the mass of the car has an effect on the safe speed around a curve. After your teacher approves your procedure, conduct your investigation.

ANSWERS

Physics To Go

(continued)

3.
t = 1/60 rev/s
t = 0.017 s
$v = d/t$, where
$d = 2\pi r$,
therefore, d = 2 x π x 15 cm
d = 94.2 cm
and t = 0.017 s
then, v = 94.2 cm/0.017 s
v = 5541 cm/s
v = 55 m/s or 120 mph

4. As the turn gets tighter, then the force of friction required to hold the car on the road also needs to increase. Therefore, the car will go off the road. Tell students tothink about how fast you can go when traveling on a road withhair pin turns.

5. Many examples will come from the students. Check the physics involved with their explanations, and that the centripetal force is in fact acting towards the center of the curve. The clothes in a spin dryer, will be getting the centripetal force from the drum of the dryer acting towards the center of the dryer.

6. The graph should show that the radius is directly proportional to the velocity squared. This relationship should be a straight line. If the radius is plotted against only the velocity, then there will still be an increasing relationship - as the radius increases the velocity increases.

7. Look for correct physics in the student's analysis of the driver's comments. A passenger is not thrown radially outward, but continues along a straight inertial path.

8. If there were no friction, the car would continue in a straight line even if the driver turned the steering wheel. It is the friction of the road on the tire that causes the car to turn.

9. Answers will vary. Expect that the students will relay information about how the increase of radius will allow you to go faster. The increase of friction on the road will also allow you to increase the speed you can go. Check for proper scientific vocabulary and physics to explain the centripetal forces in action.

10. Answers will vary. Friction is needed to supply the centripetal force to keep the car traveling in a straight path or to allow it to move in a curved path. Without friction (the outside unbalanced force) the inertia of the object will keep it traveling in a straight line.

Assessment: Driving on Curves

The following criteria may be used to assess scientific thinking.

Place a check mark (√) in the appropriate column.

Point total = 12.

Learner outcome demonstrated	Yes	No
• Student identifies that a car moves tangential to the arc when the string is released.		
• Student is able to explain what force keeps the car from moving in a straight line when it makes a turn.		
• Student is able to identify the direction of the force applied to a car while it is turning.		
• Student is able to determine the amount of time that has elapsed during one revolution of a turntable.		
• Student is able to determine how fast a turntable can spin while holding a block in place.		
• Student is able to explain how the friction between the wooden block and turntable affects the movement of the block on the spinning turntable.		
• Student is able to explain how the radius of spin (position of block) affects the movement of the block on the spinning turntable.		
• Student is able to calculate how fast the block was moving at each distance from the center of the turntable when it slid off the turntable.		
• Student is able to calculate the maximum speed at which the block can stay on the rubber mat.		
• Student is able to explain why the maximum speed on the block decreases as the radius of the path for rotation increases.		
• Student is able to construct a graph relating radial distance and maximum speed at which the block remains on the turntable for one type of surface.		
• Student can explain why the passengers and driver tend to keep moving in a straight line while the car is turning.		

Activity Seven A

Objects that Resist Movement and Resist Stopping

FOR YOU TO DO

1. Place a playing card under a coin so that half the card hangs over the table. Now pull the card very slowly.

a) Describe what happens.

2. Repeat the procedure, but this time pull the playing card out very quickly. A short, quick, jerking motion should be used.

a) Describe what happens.

b) Explain your results.

3. Place a hard-boiled egg in a saucer and spin the egg. Once it is spinning, place your index finger on top of it and bring it to a stop.

4. Repeat the same procedure with a raw egg.

a) Which egg was more difficult to stop?

b) Provide an explanation for your observations.

Activity Seven A

Objects that Resist Movement and Resist Stopping

Background

Everything has inertia, making it reluctant to move or reluctant to stop moving. Inertia is often described as a resistance to motion. A body at rest has a tendency to remain at rest. The law of inertia also indicates that once an object is in motion, it has a tendency to keep moving.

Time Requirements

Approximately 10 minutes is required to complete the activity.

Materials Needed

- playing card
- coin
- table top (without table cloth)
- saucer
- raw egg
- hard-boiled egg (6 min.)

ANSWERS

For You To Do

1. a) The coin falls. The coin sticks to the card.

2. a) The card moves, but the coin doesn't.

   b) By pulling very quickly the force moving the card is much greater than the force of friction holding the coin to the card. The important part of the demonstration deals with inertia. The card moves because it has little mass. The coin, by contrast, is much heavier and has more inertia, which resists movement. The card is light so it moves quickly when given a quick tug. The heavier coin stays right where it is.

3. a) The raw egg resisted stopping more than the hard-boiled egg.

   b) The raw egg contains a yolk that floats inside a slippery white liquid. When heated the egg white and the yolk coagulate forming a single firm structure. Inertia makes the yolk spin rather slowly when the egg shell is spun. However, when the shell is stopped the yolk continues to spin. If you practice you might be able to get the egg to stop, and then release your finger only to see it revolve again.

Centripetal Force

According to Newton's First Law of Motion (Inertia), an object in motion will continue in motion unless acted upon by an outside unbalanced force (a push or a pull). Therefore, an object that is moving at a constant speed in a circle must have a force acting on that object, in order to keep on turning. That force is the centripetal force.

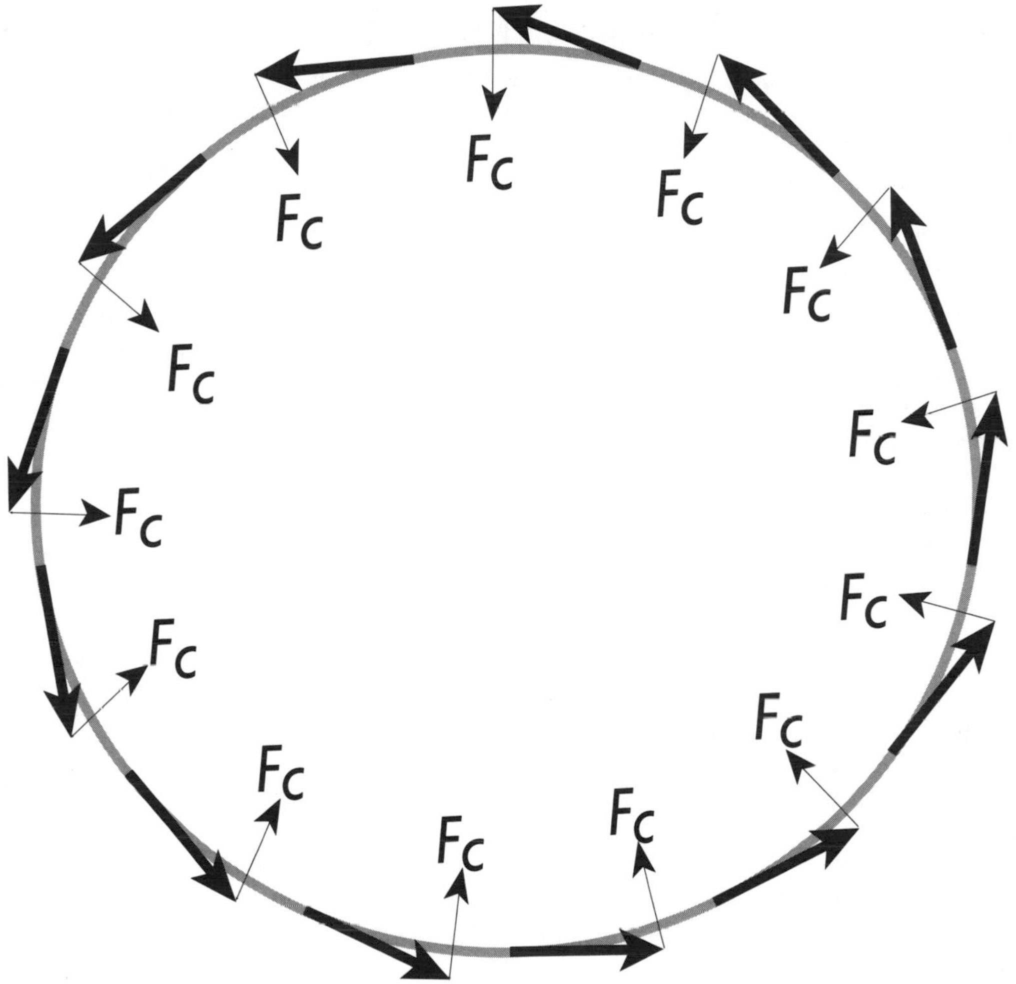

The centripetal force is that force directed toward the center of the circular path. That force is supplied by the tension in the string on a flying ball, the friction between the tires and the road of a turning vehicle, gravity as the space shuttle orbits the earth.

ACTIVITY EIGHT
Banking the Turns

Background Information

Symbols

F_c = centripetal force

m = mass (kg)

F_f = force of friction (N)

F_N = normal force (N) (weight)

F_g = force of gravity(N)

Any object traveling in a circular path will be affected by the centripetal force acting inwards. As with the block of wood on the turntable, friction supplies the centripetal force on a car moving in a curved path.

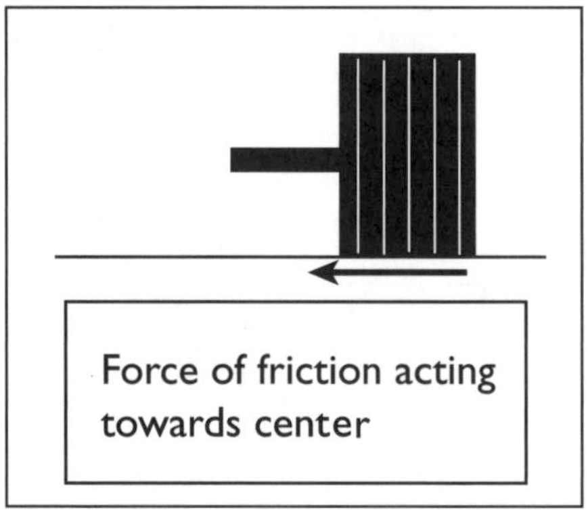

The friction between the tires and the road keep the car moving in a circular path. When you ask students what keeps a car moving in a circular path, most will say the front tires turning. When asking them if turning the front tires will keep the car moving on a curve if there is ice, students will probably say traction (another term for friction) is needed. Therefore, introduce friction as the centripetal force which acts towards the center of the circle of the turning vehicle.

(Although the following is beyond the intent of the activity, some extension is presented here for the teacher.)

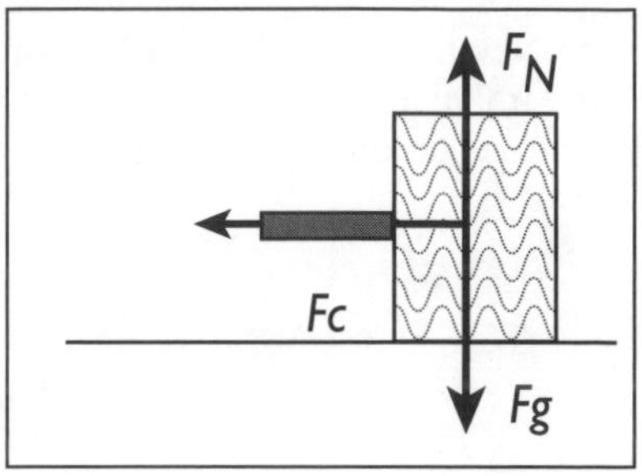

On a flat surface, the frictional force supplies all of the force needed to keep the car moving in a curved path. In the diagram, *Fc* is the centripetal force, which on a flat surface is the frictional force. The frictional force is proportional to the normal force (*FN*), and on a flat surface, the normal force is equal to the gravitational force.

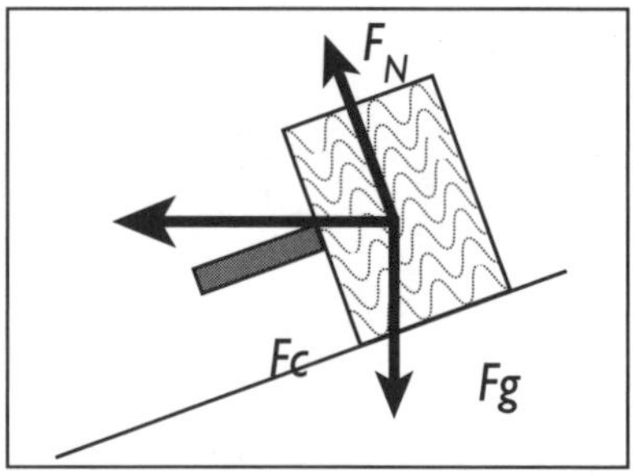

On a banked surface the normal force gets smaller (as the angle increases), and, therefore, the frictional force gets smaller. As the frictional force gets smaller, there must be another force that, when added to the horizontal component of the frictional force, keeps the car on the road.

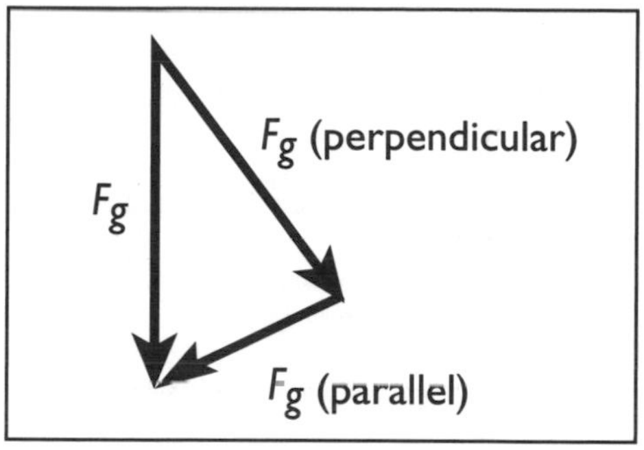

We can find this force by vector analysis. The horizontal component of the normal force and the horizontal component of the friction both contribute to the centripetal force.

Active-ating the Physics InfoMall

The article "Analysis of Running on Banked and Unbanked Curves," by Van E. Neie can be found in *The Physics Teacher*, volume 19, issue 5. This article gives a detailed description of the physics involved in banked turns. Arons's book (*A Guide to Introductory Physics Teaching,* mentioned in Activity Seven) also discusses banked versus unbanked turns.

Planning for the Activity

Time Requirements

This activity will take approximately the same time as Activity Seven (30 minutes). Additional time will be required if you choose to complete the Stretching Exercise.

Materials needed

For each lab group:

- lazy Susan turntable
- small block of wood
- wooden wedge, approx. 20 degree angle
- stopwatch
- rubber mat (or double stick tape, or glue)

Advance Preparation and Setup

The wooden wedge should be attached to the lazy Susan so that it slants down towards the center of rotation. If it is not heavy enough to ride on the lazy Susan, use a piece of rubber mat underneath, or hot glue the wedge to the lazy Susan.

Teaching Notes

Review last night's Physics To Go questions with an emphasis on the source of the centripetal force, emphasizing its direction. Follow up on yesterday's class by discussing what happens when there is not enough friction to cause a car to turn a corner. Get students' answers to the What Do You Think? questions. It is unlikely that they will see at once that banking causes gravity to provide a centripetal force. Leave the question open pending investigation. Move right into the lazy Susan activity.

1

Activity Overview

This activity extends the concept of centripetal force to banked curves.

Student Objectives

Students will:

- investigate the effectiveness of banked curves.
- identify the source of the centripetal force on a banked curve.
- compare the centripetal force produced by banking with that resulting from friction.

ANSWERS FOR THE TEACHER ONLY

What Do You Think?

Banking causes gravity to push automobiles to the center of the curve (centripetal force) so that they stay on the road.

CHAPTER 1 DRIVING THE ROADS

Activity Eight

Banking the Turns

WHAT DO YOU THINK?

On a race track, the curves are banked—the outer edge of the road is higher than the inner edge.

- **Why do you think the road is banked?**
- **Why is the outer edge of the road higher?**

Record your ideas about these questions in your *Active Physics log*. Be prepared to discuss your responses with your small group and the class.

TRANSPORTATION T46

FOR YOU TO DO

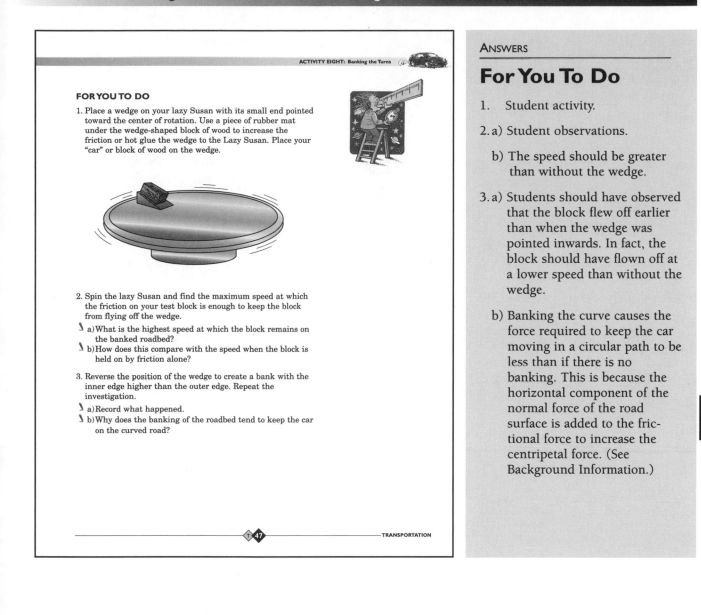

1. Place a wedge on your lazy Susan with its small end pointed toward the center of rotation. Use a piece of rubber mat under the wedge-shaped block of wood to increase the friction or hot glue the wedge to the Lazy Susan. Place your "car" or block of wood on the wedge.

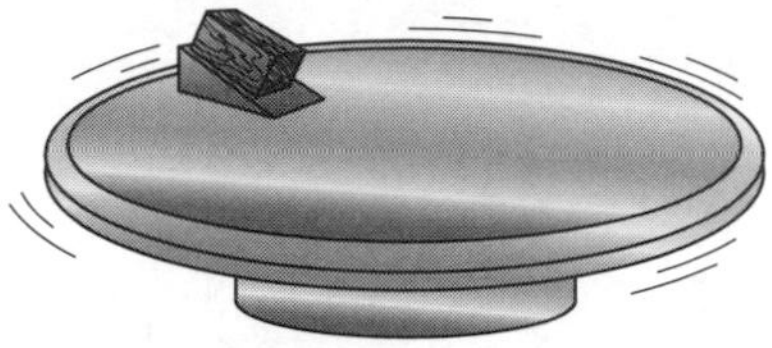

2. Spin the lazy Susan and find the maximum speed at which the friction on your test block is enough to keep the block from flying off the wedge.
   a) What is the highest speed at which the block remains on the banked roadbed?
   b) How does this compare with the speed when the block is held on by friction alone?

3. Reverse the position of the wedge to create a bank with the inner edge higher than the outer edge. Repeat the investigation.
   a) Record what happened.
   b) Why does the banking of the roadbed tend to keep the car on the curved road?

ANSWERS

For You To Do

1. Student activity.

2. a) Student observations.

   b) The speed should be greater than without the wedge.

3. a) Students should have observed that the block flew off earlier than when the wedge was pointed inwards. In fact, the block should have flown off at a lower speed than without the wedge.

   b) Banking the curve causes the force required to keep the car moving in a circular path to be less than if there is no banking. This is because the horizontal component of the normal force of the road surface is added to the frictional force to increase the centripetal force. (See Background Information.)

CHAPTER 1 DRIVING THE ROADS

FOR YOU TO READ

Centripetal Force

As you saw with the toy car and the string, an object will travel in a straight line unless a force changes its direction. This is called The Law of Inertia, or NEWTON'S FIRST LAW: unless a force acts, an object will travel in a straight line at constant speed.

If something is traveling in a circular path, a force must act on it constantly, pulling it toward the center of the circle. Any force acting in this direction is called a centripetal force. You can see part of the word "center" in the word "centripetal." A centripetal force is always toward the center. For the toy car tied to a string, the centripetal force was supplied by the string. With the block on the turntable, the centripetal force is provided by the friction between the block and the turntable.

Why does banking the road provide more centripetal force? When a car is on a flat road, the road pushes up so that the car does not sink into the ground. When a car is on a banked road, the road surface keeps the car from sinking but also pushes toward the center of the curve. This push toward the center is a centripetal force.

If the car is going slow, this may be enough to keep it on the road. Let's say that the car needs a force of 20 N to keep it moving in a circle. The friction of a flat road surface must supply the entire 20 N. If the road is banked so that the road surface pushes the car toward the center, then the road surface may supply 15 N of the required 20 N of force. The friction of the road must supply only 5 N, giving the necessary total of 20 N.

A newton is a force unit, just like a meter is a length unit. One newton is approximately 1/4 lb. Yes, pounds also can be used to measure force. At McDonald's you could order a Newton Burger!

Centripetal Acceleration

Acceleration is the rate of change of velocity. This means that any change of speed or direction is an acceleration. There are three kinds of acceleration, each produced by a force:

A force applied in the direction of motion makes the object go faster.

A force applied against the direction of motion makes it go slower.

A force applied perpendicular to the direction of motion changes the direction without changing its speed. If a force acts continuously in a direction perpendicular to velocity, the object travels in a circle. The force, and the resulting acceleration, are then said to be centripetal.

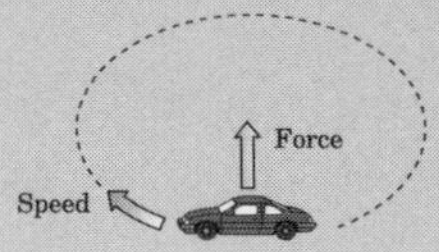

REFLECTING ON THE ACTIVITY AND THE CHALLENGE

A banked turn helps to keep a car on the road when it goes around the curve. With a correctly banked curve, the road surface provides some of the centripetal force needed to make the turn. This means that if the road were to get slippery or icy, the banking of the road may provide the centripetal force to keep you from going off the road.

Explaining to your parents about banked roads is one part of the chapter challenge. You have performed experiments that can be used to illustrate your understanding of this road assist.

PHYSICS TO GO

1. Have you ever heard anyone brag about going around curves at speeds higher than the posted speed limit? How could they cheat the need for a large centripetal force? Is it by moving across lanes on the curve? Why is this not safe?
2. Why are indoor running tracks usually banked? Why are outdoor running tracks usually not banked?
3. a) How do runners turn fast corners on flat tracks?
   b) Where does a runner get centripetal force on a flat track?
4. Sometimes a road is banked the wrong way. Describe how a bank could be "the wrong way."
5. What happens if the road surface is banked so that road surface pushes you away from the center of the circle?
6. If there is a road in your neighborhood that is banked the wrong way, there are probably more traffic accidents there than at other locations. Explain why banking the road "the wrong way" makes driving more difficult.

ANSWERS

Physics To Go

1. Drivers will often disregard reduced speed warnings. They must then compensate by increasing the turning radius if they are to round the curve at a speed greater than that calculated to be safe. They cut across several lanes, begin on the outside lane, move toward the inside, and then back to the outside. In some cases the result might even be a straight line. On some winding roads with little traffic, drivers can be observed using both lanes to avoid having to slow down and steer excessively. Point out that curves in the road often have reduced friction also because leaves, water, and sand tend to gather there.

2. Larger centripetal forces are required for small radius turns. Outdoor tracks have large curves; runners do not require the assistance of gravity as a centripetal force. This and the next question are dealt with extensively in *Sports*. Save an extended discussion for then.

3. a-b) Runners lean inward on turns to increase the traction between their running shoes and the track. It is similar to banking a turn.

4. If the road surface is pushing you away, then the speed at which you are driving must decrease to be able to stay on the road. Inertia of your car will have it going in a straight path. The friction on the road provides the force necessary to move it in a curved path. If the bank is the wrong way, then the normal force of the road surface is working against you. In order to compensate for a wrong bank, the speed of the car must be decreased.

5. The bank could be the "wrong way" if the inner part of the curve was higher than the outer part of the curve. This produces a situation similar to placing the block on the wedge with the thick part of the wedge towards the middle.

6. If the road is banked the wrong way, then gravity is working against you, by "pushing" you away from the center of the circle. This practice dates back to the times of slow traffic speeds, and roads were crowned so that water would run off the road. For the outer lane of the road, gravity provides a force that pulls the car to the outside of the intended path. A larger frictional force is required to compensate for gravity and provide the centripetal force. Therefore, the safe speed is substantially slower.

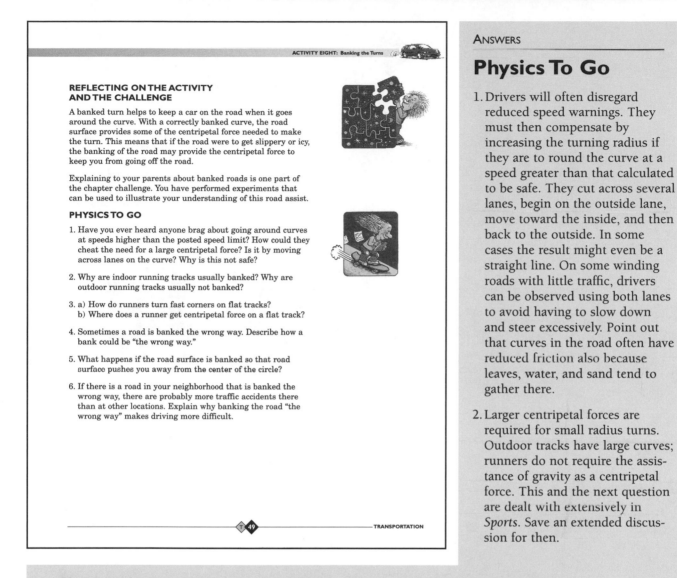

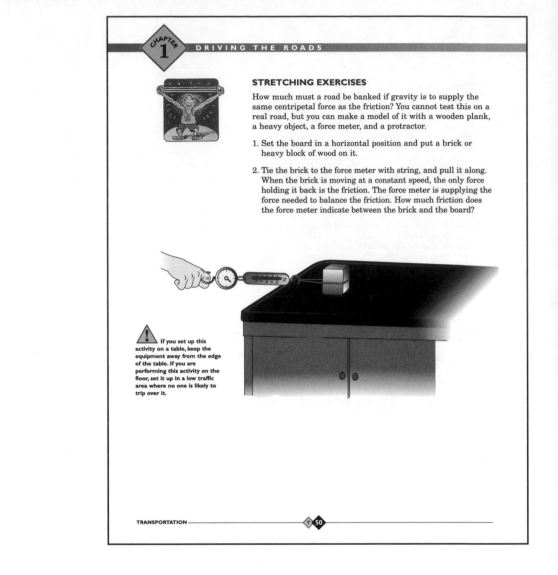

STRETCHING EXERCISES

How much must a road be banked if gravity is to supply the same centripetal force as the friction? You cannot test this on a real road, but you can make a model of it with a wooden plank, a heavy object, a force meter, and a protractor.

1. Set the board in a horizontal position and put a brick or heavy block of wood on it.

2. Tie the brick to the force meter with string, and pull it along. When the brick is moving at a constant speed, the only force holding it back is the friction. The force meter is supplying the force needed to balance the friction. How much friction does the force meter indicate between the brick and the board?

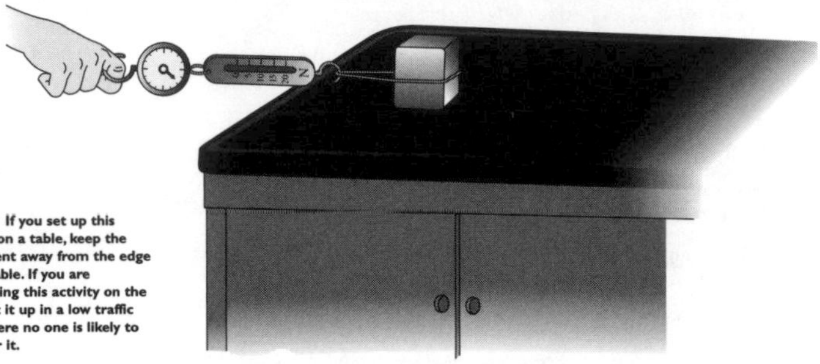

If you set up this activity on a table, keep the equipment away from the edge of the table. If you are performing this activity on the floor, set it up in a low traffic area where no one is likely to trip over it.

3. Tilt the board by putting something under one end of it. In this position, the brick will have a tendency to slide downhill, due to the gravity. If you now pull it uphill at a constant speed, the force you exert is acting against both friction and the downhill pull of gravity. The force meter will now show the combined downhill forces of friction and gravity.

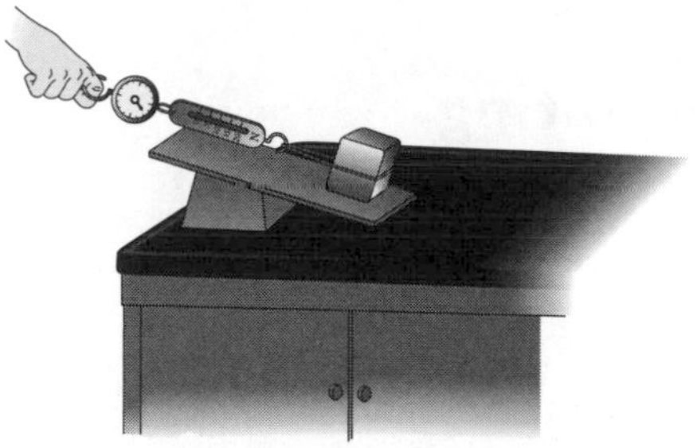

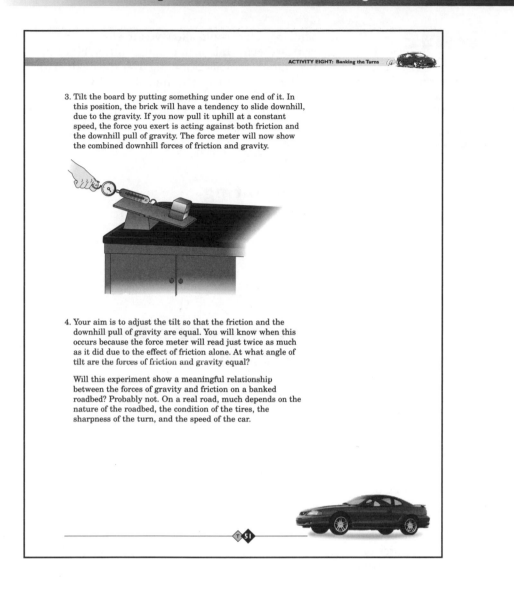

4. Your aim is to adjust the tilt so that the friction and the downhill pull of gravity are equal. You will know when this occurs because the force meter will read just twice as much as it did due to the effect of friction alone. At what angle of tilt are the forces of friction and gravity equal?

   Will this experiment show a meaningful relationship between the forces of gravity and friction on a banked roadbed? Probably not. On a real road, much depends on the nature of the roadbed, the condition of the tires, the sharpness of the turn, and the speed of the car.

ACTIVITY NINE
Skids!

Background Information

Symbols

v = speed

d = distance

t = time

a = acceleration

F = force (N)

m = mass (kg)

F_f = force of friction (N)

μ = coefficient of friction

F_N = normal force (N)

Skidding on a road is simply a loss of friction. The coefficient of friction is greater for static friction (friction of an object at rest) than for sliding or kinetic (object moving) friction. Using the formula for friction, $F_f = \mu F_N$, where F_f is force of friction, μ is the coefficient of friction, and F_N is the normal force (on a flat surface F_N is the same as force of gravity or the weight of the vehicle), force of friction is proportional to the normal force or the weight of the vehicle.

Given that you have the same surface, and that the weight of the vehicle does not change significantly (ignoring the amount of rubber left on the road), the only thing that can change or affect the force of friction is the coefficient of friction. As was mentioned above, the coefficient for sliding friction is less than that of static friction. Static friction is the friction between the tires and the road when they are touching and not sliding. Sliding friction is when the tires are moving at a different speed than the relative speed of the road underneath the tires. Therefore, to get maximum friction (or traction), it is necessary to not have the tires moving relative to the road.

This is the theory behind ABS brakes. If you slam on your brakes without ABS, then your car will start to skid, and the car will be out of control. Without ABS brakes, you could manually "pump" the brakes, or use threshold braking to prevent the wheels from skidding. This would allow you to slow your vehicle down while maintaining control, because the tires are moving or rolling over the road (static friction) rather than skidding (sliding friction). ABS brakes when applied under skid conditions, will do the "pumping" of the brakes for you. The action of "pumping" the brakes keeps the tires rolling, causing static friction which has the higher coefficient of friction.

Active-ating the Physics InfoMall

Nothing pertaining directly to this topic was found on the InfoMall. However, this topic may be discussed briefly by many of the references cited previously in this chapter.

Planning for the Activity

Time Requirements

Allow students approximately 10 minutes to do each of the four parts of the activity and record their observations.

Materials needed

For each lab group:

- lab cart or toy car
- locking device for wheels or cart (tape or clips)
- wide ramp or tilted table

For the class:

- *Active Physics Transportation* Content Video (Segment: Skidding Car Demonstrations)
- VCR and TV monitor

Advance Preparation and Setup

Check that the wheels on the toy cars can be frozen as described in the text. Four-wheeled dynamics carts are fine, but the ramp used must be wide enough for the cart to spin out. If the laboratory tables are moveable, tilt them slightly by elevating one end to form a ramp. Pushing the cars does not always have the same effect as releasing the cars on the ramp because of the nature of the push.

Teaching Notes

Members of the class will have some great stories about skid situations that they have been in or heard about. The stories make an exciting beginning. The key points are that a loss of friction causes a skid and that the path is a straight-line inertial path. The details of friction are difficult to explain. The exercises are not meant to lead students to precise comparisons of rolling, static, and sliding friction, rather to provide discrepant events that will provoke discussion.

Some students may see skidding as an increase in traction, and not a decrease in traction. This may come from watching vehicles in movies accelerate where the cars are skidding all over the place, while accelerating. Some will see the skidding of tires as traction, causing them to stop. Help the students understand that there must be friction between the tires and the road in order for anything to move or to stop.

Activity Overview

This activity endeavors to make the students better drivers by explaining the physics of skidding.

Student Objectives

Students will:

- identify a skid as a loss of friction.
- recognize a skid as an inertial effect.
- compare different kinds of skids.
- describe the procedure for ending a skid.
- compare front and rear-wheel drive cars.

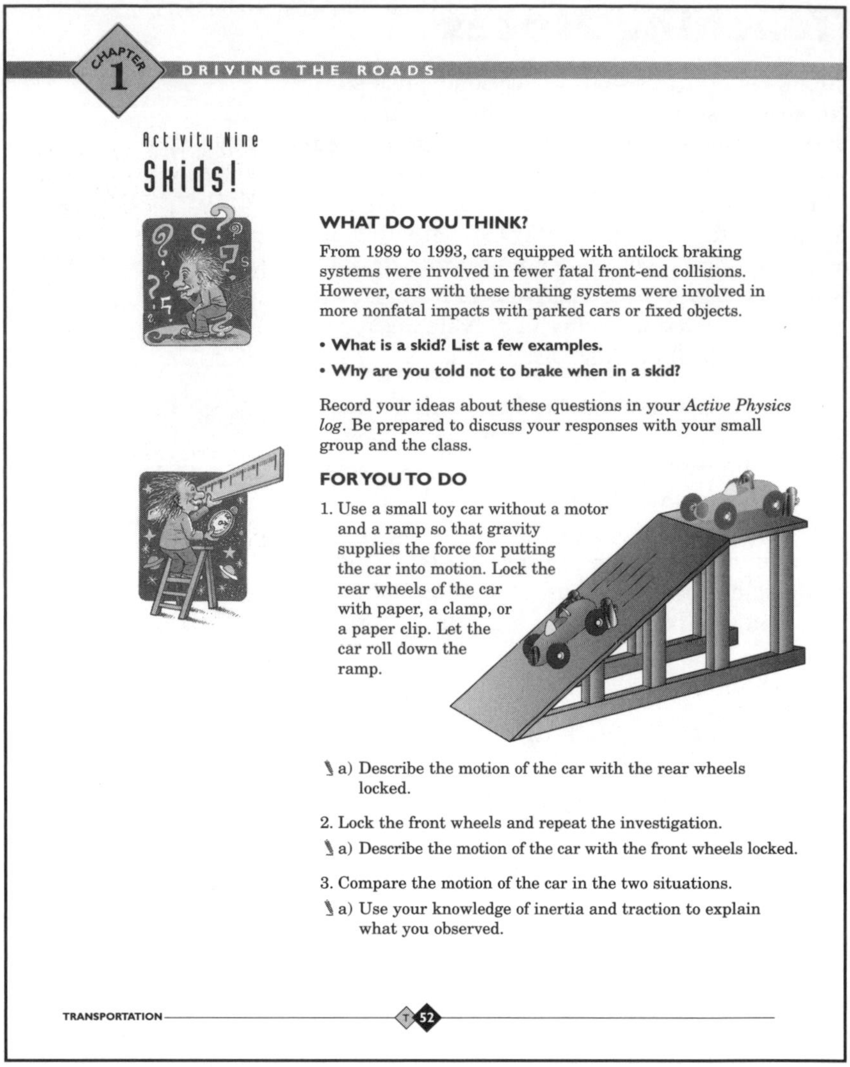
CHAPTER 1 DRIVING THE ROADS

Activity Nine

Skids!

WHAT DO YOU THINK?

From 1989 to 1993, cars equipped with antilock braking systems were involved in fewer fatal front-end collisions. However, cars with these braking systems were involved in more nonfatal impacts with parked cars or fixed objects.

- **What is a skid? List a few examples.**
- **Why are you told not to brake when in a skid?**

Record your ideas about these questions in your *Active Physics log*. Be prepared to discuss your responses with your small group and the class.

FOR YOU TO DO

1. Use a small toy car without a motor and a ramp so that gravity supplies the force for putting the car into motion. Lock the rear wheels of the car with paper, a clamp, or a paper clip. Let the car roll down the ramp.

a) Describe the motion of the car with the rear wheels locked.

2. Lock the front wheels and repeat the investigation.

a) Describe the motion of the car with the front wheels locked.

3. Compare the motion of the car in the two situations.

a) Use your knowledge of inertia and traction to explain what you observed.

TRANSPORTATION T 52

ANSWERS FOR THE TEACHER ONLY

What Do You Think?

Skidding on a road is simply a loss of friction. To get maximum friction (or traction), it is necessary to not have the tires moving relative to the road. This causes static friction, which is greater than sliding friction. If you slam on your brakes without ABS, you will start to skid out of control.

ANSWERS

For You To Do

1.-3.a).When the rear wheels lock, they suffer a loss of traction and may slide along the ramp faster than the front wheels, causing the car to spin. With the front wheels locked, they will have little or no traction, but because the rear wheels are rolling, there is greater friction or traction and the car will travel in a straight path. With the rear wheels locked, there is a greater net force acting on the rear of the car than the front of the car. Therefore, the inertia of the rear will change, resulting in a loss of control.

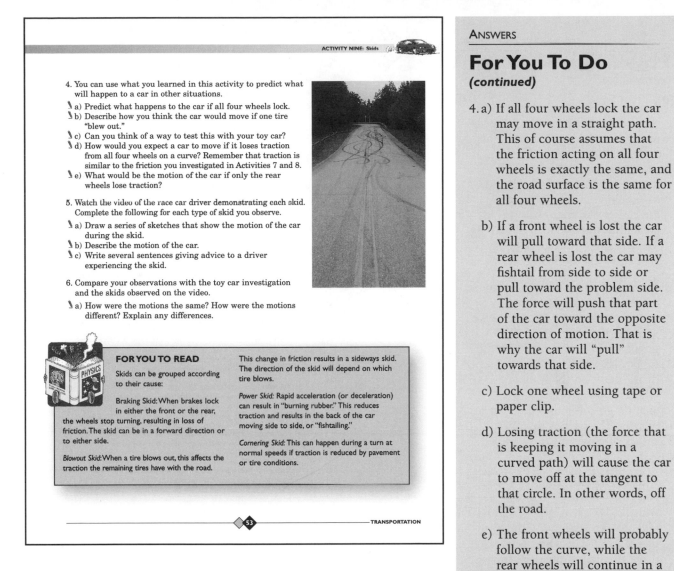

4. You can use what you learned in this activity to predict what will happen to a car in other situations.
   a) Predict what happens to the car if all four wheels lock.
   b) Describe how you think the car would move if one tire "blew out."
   c) Can you think of a way to test this with your toy car?
   d) How would you expect a car to move if it loses traction from all four wheels on a curve? Remember that traction is similar to the friction you investigated in Activities 7 and 8.
   e) What would be the motion of the car if only the rear wheels lose traction?

5. Watch the video of the race car driver demonstrating each skid. Complete the following for each type of skid you observe.
   a) Draw a series of sketches that show the motion of the car during the skid.
   b) Describe the motion of the car.
   c) Write several sentences giving advice to a driver experiencing the skid.

6. Compare your observations with the toy car investigation and the skids observed on the video.
   a) How were the motions the same? How were the motions different? Explain any differences.

FOR YOU TO READ

Skids can be grouped according to their cause:

Braking Skid: When brakes lock in either the front or the rear, the wheels stop turning, resulting in loss of friction. The skid can be in a forward direction or to either side.

Blowout Skid: When a tire blows out, this affects the traction the remaining tires have with the road. This change in friction results in a sideways skid. The direction of the skid will depend on which tire blows.

Power Skid: Rapid acceleration (or deceleration) can result in "burning rubber." This reduces traction and results in the back of the car moving side to side, or "fishtailing."

Cornering Skid: This can happen during a turn at normal speeds if traction is reduced by pavement or tire conditions.

ANSWERS

For You To Do
(continued)

4. a) If all four wheels lock the car may move in a straight path. This of course assumes that the friction acting on all four wheels is exactly the same, and the road surface is the same for all four wheels.

   b) If a front wheel is lost the car will pull toward that side. If a rear wheel is lost the car may fishtail from side to side or pull toward the problem side. The force will push that part of the car toward the opposite direction of motion. That is why the car will "pull" towards that side.

   c) Lock one wheel using tape or paper clip.

   d) Losing traction (the force that is keeping it moving in a curved path) will cause the car to move off at the tangent to that circle. In other words, off the road.

   e) The front wheels will probably follow the curve, while the rear wheels will continue in a straight line tangent to the circle. The common term for that is spinout.

5. a) Diagram by students after watching the video.

   b) Students' answers.

   c) Answers will vary. Some advice might be: turn into the skid in a rear wheel drive car; don't put on your brakes when skidding; drive more slowly when encountering surfaces with less friction

6. a) Students' answers.

ANSWERS

Physics To Go
(continued)

1. A front-wheel drive car is pulled by the front wheels. The center of mass follows along behind. If any sideways torque are created by the rear wheels, they are self-correcting. In a rear-wheel drive car, the driver must be sure that the center of mass is being pushed in the intended direction with no sideways torque being created by the front wheels.

2. In the Ford Contour the weight on the front wheels is much greater than on the back wheels and therefore the center of gravity is further forward. In the Chevrolet Corvette the weight distribution on the front and rear wheels is fairly even, with a slightly greater mass on the front wheels. This means that the center of mass is further back.

3. The Ford Contour is a front-wheel drive car, and the Chevrolet Corvette is a rear-wheel drive car. Students should take into consideration the qualities of front-wheel and rear-wheel drive cars talked about in this activity.

4. Students' answers will vary. Look for sound arguments based on the physics discussed in this chapter. The students may look for cosmetic or performance kind of things. Try to encourage safety oriented features.

5. Answers will vary.

6. Answers will vary.

7. Students' answers will vary. Answers should include that the most important thing is prevention. However, accidents happen and surprises can happen on roads. If you lose control on a curve, and it is rear-wheel skid, with rear-wheel drive, you need to turn into the direction of the skid and slow down. Do not apply brakes as it will only cause all the wheels to lock and lose traction. With a rear-wheel skid and front-wheel drive, you can accelerate to bring the car into line. If it is a front-wheel skid on a front-wheel drive, you need to slow down without applying brakes. The best way to teach this would be to go to a closed track, but the next best thing would be to observe training films of drivers or have a driving πinstructor come into the class.

CHAPTER 1 DRIVING THE ROADS

REFLECTING ON THE ACTIVITY AND THE CHALLENGE

Loss of traction, which is called skidding, happens when the tires stop rolling and begin to slide. There are different causes for skids, but all affect the motion of the car.

The chapter challenge does not require you to explain skids. You will not be asked to discuss why a front-wheel-drive car may be more stable than a rear-wheel-drive car. However, this information can increase your understanding of the physics of driving and help you become a better driver.

PHYSICS TO GO

1. Is a front-wheel-drive car more stable than a rear-wheel-drive car? Why or why not?
2. Consult the specification sheets for the Ford SVT Contour and the Chevrolet Corvette Convertible found on pages T55 and T56. Look for the weight distribution figures under the heading "General Data." Which of the two cars has its center of mass further forward? Why does this make a difference?
3. Look under "Chassis and Body" to find out which are the drive wheels. How would the drive wheel affect the behavior of the two cars under different conditions?
4. Select one of the main headings in the specification sheets for the two cars, and compare that feature in the two cars. Write a paragraph explaining why you would prefer one of the cars if that were the only consideration.
5. You can find safety facts and specifications for most cars and trucks by logging on to the National Highway Traffic Safety Administration's web page at http://www.nhtsa.dot.gov. What information can you use to find out which cars are the safest?
6. Use what you have learned about skids to convince your parents that you understand the physics of driving.
7. Combine your new understanding of skids with what you learned about going around curves to explain to a new driver how to react if he or she loses control of the car on a curve.

TRANSPORTATION T54

1998 Ford SVT CONTOUR

MANUFACTURER

Ford Motor Company
P.O Box 490
Dearborn, Mich. 48121

PRICE

List price.......................... $22,900
Price as tested..................... $23,635

Price as tested includes std equip. (dual airbags, air cond, 16-in. alloy wheels and 205/55ZR-16 tires, leather interior, AM/FM stereo/cassette; pwr windows, seats, door locks & mirrors; dest charge), pwr sunroof ($595), CD player ($140).

0–60 mph .... 7.2 sec
0–¼ mi .... 15.4 sec
Top speed............ est 143 mph
Skidpad 0.83g
Slalom .... 61.9 mph
Brake rating............ excellent

TEST CONDITIONS

Temperature .... 70° F
Wind .... calm
Elevation .... 1010 ft

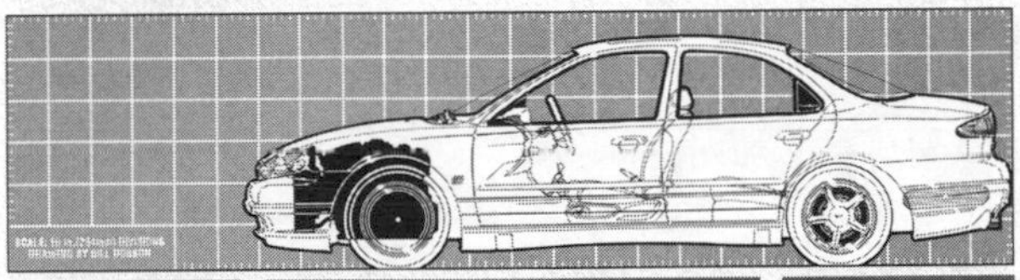

ENGINE

Type... aluminum block and heads, **V-6**
Valvetrain .... dohc 4 valve/cyl
Displacement..... 155 cu in./2544 cc
Bore x stroke........ 3.24 x 3.11 in./ 82.4 x 79.0 mm
Compression ratio 10.0:1
Horsepower (SAE)........ **195 bhp @ 6625 rpm**
Bhp/liter.................... 76.7
Torque........ **165 lb-ft @ 5625 rpm**
Maximum engine speed .... 6750 rpm
Fuel injection.... elect. sequential port
Fuel..... prem unleaded, 91 pump oct

CHASSIS & BODY

Layout ...... **front engine/front drive**
Body/frame .... unit steel
Brakes
Front .... **10.9-in. vented discs**
Rear.......... **9.9-in. vented discs**
Assist type........... vacuum; ABS
Total swept area .... 366 sq in.
Swept area/ton.......... 230 sq in.
Wheels .... cast alloy, **16 x 6½**
Tires .... Goodyear Eagle GS-C, **P205/55ZR-16**
Steering... **rack & pinion,** power assist
Overall ratio 14.5:1
Turns, lock to lock 2.7
Turning circle .... 38.4 ft
Suspension
Front .... **MacPherson struts,** lower A-arms, coil springs, tube shocks, anti-roll bar
Rear...... **struts,** trailing links, dual lower lateral links, coil springs, tube shocks, anti-roll bar

DRIVETRAIN

Transmission .... **5-sp manual**

Gear	Ratio	Overall ratio	(Rpm) Mph
1st	3.42:1	13.89:1	(6750) 34
2nd	2.14:1	8.69:1	(6750) 55
3rd	1.45:1	5.89:1	(6750) 81
4th	1.03:1	4.18:1	(6750) 114
5th	0.77:1	3.13:1	est (6310) 143

Final drive ratio........................ 4.06:1
Engine rpm @ 60 mph in 5th.............. 2650

GENERAL DATA

Curb weight.............. **3055 lb**
Test weight............... 3180 lb
Weight dist (with driver), f/r, % 63/37
Wheelbase............... 106.5 in.
Track, f/r .... 59.2 in./58.5 in.
Length.................. **183.9 in.**
Width .... **69.1 in.**
Height.................. **54.5 in.**
Ground clearance........... 8.2 in.
Trunk space......... 18.0 + 7.0 cu ft

MAINTENANCE

Oil/filter change 5000 mi/5000mi
Tuneup .... 100,000 mi
Basic warranty ..... 36 mo/36,000 mi

ACCOMMODATIONS

Seating capacity **5**
Head room, f/r...... 39.0 in./35.0 in.
Seat width, f/r ... 2 x 20.5 in./50.0 in.
Front-seat leg room .... 43.0 in.
Rear-seat knee room .... 25.0 in.
Seatback adjustment......... 85 deg
Seat travel .... 8.5 in.

INTERIOR NOISE

Idle in neutral.............. 54 dBA
Maximum in 1st gear .... 78 dBA
Constant 50 mph .... 66 dBA
70 mph .... 71 dBA

INSTRUMENTATION

160-mph speedometer, 8000-rpm tach, coolant temp, fuel level

Test Notes...

■ Around the skidpad, the SVT Contour moderately understeers, though its cornering attitude is quite responsive to lifting the throttle. Indeed, it reacts even more strongly to light brake taps.

■ Through the slalom, the SVT Contour is again highly responsive to throttle and impressively placeable. Body roll is considerable, but it doesn't slow the Contour's reflexes.

■ Although it offers no more torque than the V-6-powered Contour SE, and most of its extra power is near redline, the SVT's 195-bhp engine sounds wonderful and is extremely flexible.

ACCELERATION

Time to speed	Seconds
0–30 mph	2.5
0–40 mph	3.8
0–50 mph	5.2
0–60 mph	7.2
0–70 mph	9.3
0–80 mph	11.6
0–90 mph	14.8
0–100 mph	18.8
Time to distance	
0–100 ft	3.3
0–500 ft	8.4
0–1320 ft (¼ mi):	15.4 @ 91.5 mph

FUEL ECONOMY

Normal driving............ 20.0 mpg
EPA city/highway .... 20/29 mpg
Cruise range............ 270 miles
Fuel capacity .... 14.5 gal.

BRAKING

Minimum stopping distance
From 60 mph .... 135 ft
From 80 mph .... 228 ft
Control................. excellent
Pedal effort for 0.5g stop .... na
Fade, effort after six 0.5g stops from 60 mph .... na
Brake feel............... excellent
Overall brake rating......... excellent

HANDLING

Lateral accel (200-ft skidpad) ... 0.83g
Balance...... moderate understeer
Speed thru 700-ft slalom.... 61.9 mph
Balance .... mild understeer
Lateral seat support........ very good

Subjective ratings consist of excellent, very good, good, average, poor; na means information is not available.

JULY 1997 93

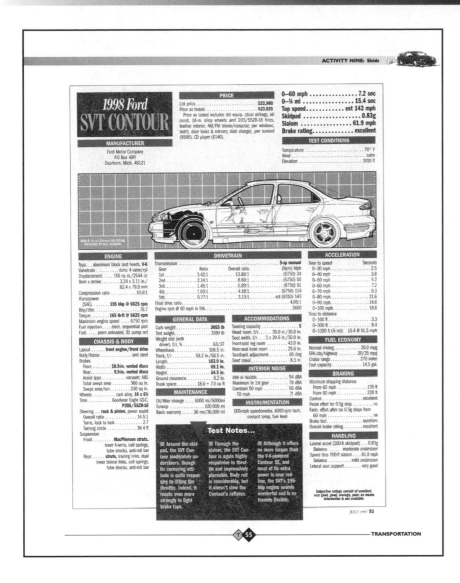

1998 Chevrolet CORVETTE CONVERTIBLE

MANUFACTURER

Chevrolet Motor Division
30007 Van Dyke Road
Warren, Mich. 48090

PRICE

List price	est $44,990
Price as tested	est $54,554

Price as tested includes std equip. (dual airbags, cruise control, ABS, traction control, security system, removable roof panel, AM/FM stereo/cassette, pwr windows & mirrors), magnesium wheels (est $3000), F45 Real-Time Damping Suspension (est $1700), Preferred Equip. Pkg 1 (includes central locking and dual temp control) est $1330, leather pwr adj sport seats (est $1200), CD player/changer (est $395), luxury tax (est $1374), dest charge (est $565).

0–60 mph	**5.2 sec**
0–¼ mi	**13.8 sec**
Top speed	**est 165 mph**
Skidpad	**na**
Slalom	**62.5 mph**
Brake rating	**excellent**

TEST CONDITIONS

Temperature	86° F
Wind	calm
Elevation	est 700 ft

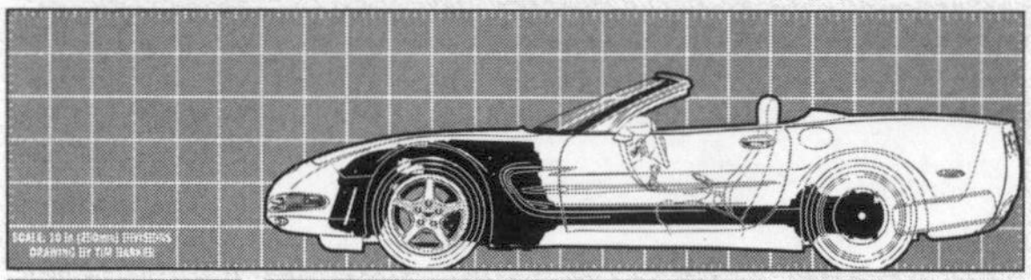

ENGINE

Type	aluminum block and heads, **V-8**
Valvetrain	ohv 2 valve/cyl
Displacement	346 cu in./5666 cc
Bore x stroke	3.90 x 3.62 in./ 99.0 x 92.0 mm
Compression ratio	10.1:1
Horsepower (SAE)	**345 bhp @ 5600 rpm**
Bhp/liter	60.9
Torque	**350 lb-ft @ 4400 rpm**
Maximum engine speed	6000 rpm
Fuel injection	elect. sequential port
Fuel	prem unleaded, 91 pump oct

CHASSIS & BODY

Layout	**front engine/rear drive**
Body/frame	fiberglass/ steel unit frame
Brakes	
Front	**12.8-in. vented discs**
Rear	**12.0-in. vented discs**
Assist type	vacuum; ABS
Total swept area	433 sq in.
Swept area/ton	257 sq in.
Wheels	cast magnesium; **17 x 8½ f, 18 x 9½ r**
Tires	Goodyear Eagle F1: **P245/45ZR-17 f, P275/40ZR-18 r**
Steering	**rack & pinion,** variable power assist
Overall ratio	16.1:1
Turns, lock to lock	2.7
Turning circle	38.5 ft
Suspension	
Front	**upper & lower A-arms,** transverse composite monoleaf spring, tube shocks, anti-roll bar
Rear	**upper & lower A-arms,** toe links, transverse composite monoleaf spring, tube shocks, anti-roll bar

DRIVETRAIN

Transmission .... **6-sp manual**

Gear	Ratio	Overall ratio	(Rpm) Mph
1st	2.66:1	9.10:1	(6000) 52
2nd	1.78:1	6.09:1	(6000) 77
3rd	1.30:1	4.45:1	(6000) 105
4th	1.00:1	3.42:1	(6000) 137
5th	0.74:1	2.53:1	est (5365) 165
6th	0:50:1	1.71:1	est (3625) 165

Final drive ratio	3.42:1
Engine rpm @ 60 mph in 6th	1320

GENERAL DATA

Curb weight	**est 3240 lb**
Test weight	est 3380 lb
Weight dist (with driver), f/r, %	51/49
Wheelbase	104.5 in.
Track, f/r	62.0 in./62.0 in.
Length	**179.7 in.**
Width	**73.6 in.**
Height	**47.7 in.**
Ground clearance	3.7 in.
Trunk space	13.5 cu ft (top up)/ 10.8 cu ft (top down)

MAINTENANCE

Oil/filter change	7500 mi/7500 mi
Tuneup	100,000 mi
Basic warranty	36 mo/36,000 mi

ACCOMMODATIONS

Seating capacity	**2**
Head room	36.5 in.
Seat width	2 x 18.0 in.
Leg room	43.5 in.
Seatback adjustment	45 deg
Seat travel	8.0 in.

INTERIOR NOISE

Idle in neutral	61 dBA
Maximum in 1st gear	78 dBA
Constant 50 mph	73 dBA
70 mph	76 dBA

INSTRUMENTATION

200-mph speedometer, 7500-rpm tach, coolant temp, fuel level, volts, oil press.

ACCELERATION

Time to speed	Seconds
0–30 mph	2.0
0–40 mph	2.9
0–50 mph	4.2
0–60 mph	5.2
0–70 mph	6.6
0–80 mph	8.7
0–90 mph	10.9
0–100 mph	13.3
Time to distance	
0–100 ft	3.0
0–500 ft	7.5
0–1320 ft (¼ mi): 13.8 @ 102.1 mph	

FUEL ECONOMY

Normal driving	est 18.5 mpg
EPA city/highway	18/28 mpg
Cruise range	est 335 miles
Fuel capacity	19.1 gal.

BRAKING

Minimum stopping distance	
From 60 mph	118 ft
From 80 mph	209 ft
Control	excellent
Pedal effort for 0.5g stop	na
Fade, effort after six 0.5g stops from 60 mph	na
Brake feel	excellent
Overall brake rating	excellent

HANDLING

Lateral accel (200-ft skidpad)	na
Balance	na
Speed thru 700-ft slalom	62.5 mph
Balance	moderate understeer
Lateral seat support	excellent

Test Notes...

■ Through the slalom, the convertible's P275/40ZR-18 rear tires helped make quick work of the cones. Even near the limit of rear adhesion, a quick burst of the throttle settles the tail back in line.

■ Quick acceleration times in the Vette require the right combination of engine rpm and clutch modulation. Dropping the clutch at 3000 rpm gave just enough wheelspin to produce the best run of the day.

■ At cruising speeds, the convertible is predictably noisier than the coupe. Especially noticeable is the thumping of the big rear tires on the road, heard through the open cargo area behind the seats.

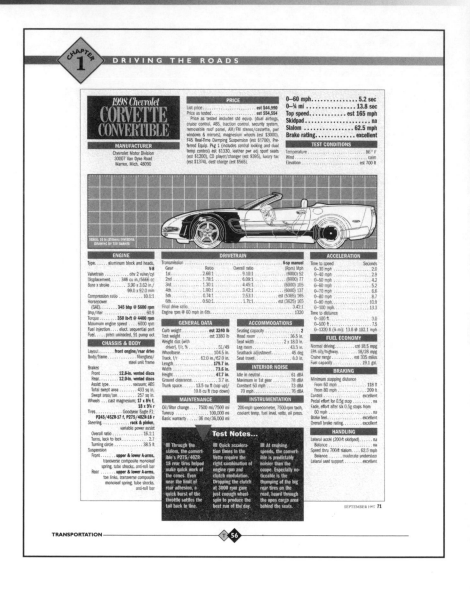

PHYSICS AT WORK

Sara Senske*

RACE CAR DRIVING IS HER PASSION

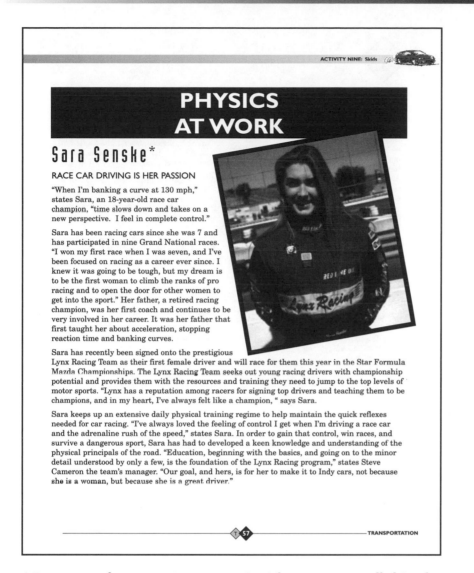

"When I'm banking a curve at 130 mph," states Sara, an 18-year-old race car champion, "time slows down and takes on a new perspective. I feel in complete control."

Sara has been racing cars since she was 7 and has participated in nine Grand National races. "I won my first race when I was seven, and I've been focused on racing as a career ever since. I knew it was going to be tough, but my dream is to be the first woman to climb the ranks of pro racing and to open the door for other women to get into the sport." Her father, a retired racing champion, was her first coach and continues to be very involved in her career. It was her father that first taught her about acceleration, stopping reaction time and banking curves.

Sara has recently been signed onto the prestigious Lynx Racing Team as their first female driver and will race for them this year in the Star Formula Mazda Championships. The Lynx Racing Team seeks out young racing drivers with championship potential and provides them with the resources and training they need to jump to the top levels of motor sports. "Lynx has a reputation among racers for signing top drivers and teaching them to be champions, and in my heart, I've always felt like a champion, " says Sara.

Sara keeps up an extensive daily physical training regime to help maintain the quick reflexes needed for car racing. "I've always loved the feeling of control I get when I'm driving a race car and the adrenaline rush of the speed," states Sara. In order to gain that control, win races, and survive a dangerous sport, Sara has had to developed a keen knowledge and understanding of the physical principals of the road. "Education, beginning with the basics, and going on to the minor detail understood by only a few, is the foundation of the Lynx Racing program," states Steve Cameron the team's manager. "Our goal, and hers, is for her to make it to Indy cars, not because she is a woman, but because she is a great driver."

* Due to an unfortunate printing error, Sara's last name was spelled Senske instead of Penske. She is the daughter of Hall of Fame driver Roger Penske.

1

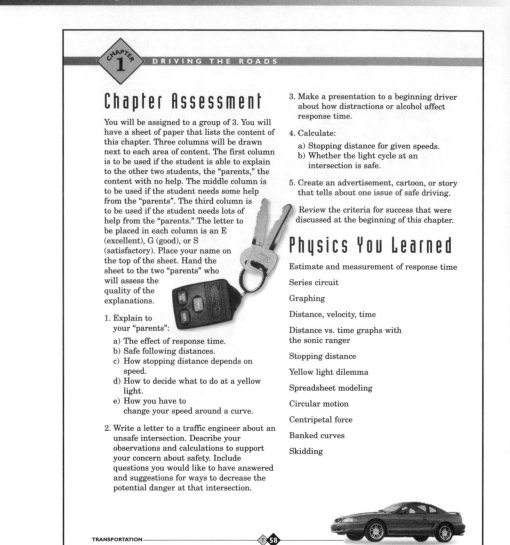

CHAPTER 1 DRIVING THE ROADS

Chapter Assessment

You will be assigned to a group of 3. You will have a sheet of paper that lists the content of this chapter. Three columns will be drawn next to each area of content. The first column is to be used if the student is able to explain to the other two students, the "parents," the content with no help. The middle column is to be used if the student needs some help from the "parents". The third column is to be used if the student needs lots of help from the "parents." The letter to be placed in each column is an E (excellent), G (good), or S (satisfactory). Place your name on the top of the sheet. Hand the sheet to the two "parents" who will assess the quality of the explanations.

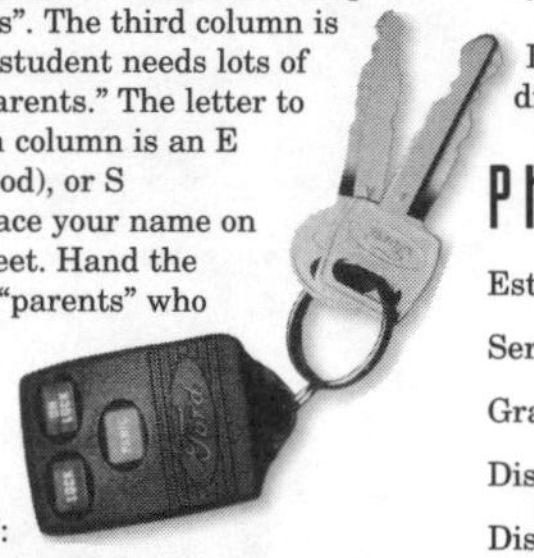

1. Explain to your "parents":
   a) The effect of response time.
   b) Safe following distances.
   c) How stopping distance depends on speed.
   d) How to decide what to do at a yellow light.
   e) How you have to change your speed around a curve.
2. Write a letter to a traffic engineer about an unsafe intersection. Describe your observations and calculations to support your concern about safety. Include questions you would like to have answered and suggestions for ways to decrease the potential danger at that intersection.
3. Make a presentation to a beginning driver about how distractions or alcohol affect response time.
4. Calculate:
   a) Stopping distance for given speeds.
   b) Whether the light cycle at an intersection is safe.
5. Create an advertisement, cartoon, or story that tells about one issue of safe driving.

Review the criteria for success that were discussed at the beginning of this chapter.

Physics You Learned

Estimate and measurement of response time

Series circuit

Graphing

Distance, velocity, time

Distance vs. time graphs with the sonic ranger

Stopping distance

Yellow light dilemma

Spreadsheet modeling

Circular motion

Centripetal force

Banked curves

Skidding

NOTES

Alternative Chapter Assessment Test

Part A: Multiple Choice

Choose the best answer and place on your answer sheet.

1. Reaction time is

   a) dependent on your state of mind
   b) dependent on your attentiveness to the road
   c) dependent on your activity in the car
   d) all of these

2. While you are reading a map in the car, it will ______________ your reaction time.

   a) increase
   b) decrease
   c) not affect

3. Which of the following may affect your reaction time?

   a) driving under the influence of prescription drugs
   b) driving under the influence of alcohol
   c) driving with your girlfriend or boyfriend
   d) any of the above

4. Tailgating is dangerous, because

   a) it decreases the time you have to react to the driver ahead of you
   b) it will increase your driving speed and decrease reaction time
   c) you will not be able to see the lights at the next intersection
   d) all of the above

5. While you are reacting to a yellow light, your car's speed is

   a) increasing
   b) decreasing
   c) not changing
   d) dependent on the road conditions

Use the following information to answer questions 6 - 9.

Your group has measured and collected the following data from an intersection.
the width of the intersection is w =16 m;
the yellow light time is Ty = 4.5 seconds;
the speed limit on the road is v = 35 mph (18 m/s);
the response time is Tr = 1.0 s.
the deceleration rate is a = 5.0 m/s/s

6. The GO Zone for the above intersection is

a) 35 m
b) 65 m
c) 81 m
d) 158 m

7. The STOP Zone for the above intersection is

a) 158 m
b) 50 m
c) 35 m
d) 16 m

8. How long is the Dilemma Zone?

a) -16 m
b) 0 m
c) +16 m
d) -77 m

9. If the car approaches a yellow light, and the driver had to make a decision to stop or go, which of the following would he/she need to take into consideration in order to be safe

a) the driver is being tailgated
b) the road is wet and slippery
c) the car is old
d) any of these

10. What causes the block to fly off a record player as it spins?

a) centripetal force
b) centripetal acceleration
c) centrifugal force
d) inertia

11. Choose which picture best represents the direction of the object as it flies off the turntable.

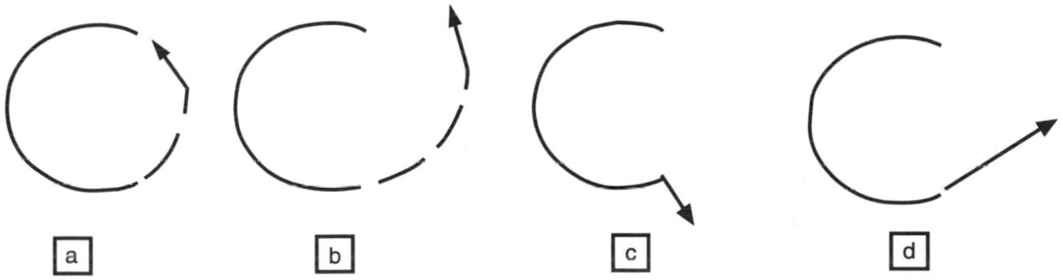

Use the following information to answer questions 12 - 16.

A block is placed on a turntable spinning at 10 revolutions per second. The block is 5 cm from the center of the turntable.

12. What is the time of one revolution?

a) 10 s
b) 1 s
c) 0.1 s
d) 2 s

13. What is the distance the block will travel in one revolution?

a) 5 cm
b) 10 cm
c) 6.28 cm
d) 31.4 cm

14. What is the speed of the block?

a) 1 cm/s
b) 314 cm/s
c) 31.4 cm/s
d) 3.14 cm/s

15. What force is needed to keep the block from flying off the turntable?

a) gravitational force
b) centripetal force
c) centrifugal force
d) inertial force

16. When engineers design roads with banked curves, which force are they using to help keep the car on the road?

a) gravitational force
b) centripetal force
c) centrifugal force
d) inertial force

17. If you are going faster than the posted speed limit for a left-hand corner, you risk an accident because

a) the bank in the corner is too great and the car will slide into oncoming traffic
b) the bank is not steep enough for the speed, and you will drift down into oncoming traffic
c) centrifugal force will cause the car to fly off the curve into the ditch
d) inertia will cause the car to fly off into the ditch

18. As you move a block closer to the middle of a turntable, the force required to keep it on the turntable

a) increases due to the greater mass of the block
b) increases due to its proximity to the center
c) decreases due to the decreased speed
d) decreases due to its proximity to the center

19. Skidding is really

a) a loss in the force of gravity
b) an increase in the force of friction
c) a decrease in the force of friction
d) an increase in the force of gravity

20. While you are stopping and you start to skid, it is called a

a) braking skid
b) blowout skid
c) power skid
d) cornering skid

21. If you were to start skidding as one wheel was turning independently from the other wheel, it is called a

a) braking skid
b) blowout skid
c) power skid
d) cornering skid

Part B: Matching

Match the words or phrases on the left with the matching word or phrase on the right.

__ 1. average speed	A. area to slow and stop when approaching a yellow light
__ 2. reaction time	B. term used when describing something using numbers
__ 3. DWI	C. the change in direction when moving in a circle
__ 4. qualitative	D. loss of friction while moving
__ 5. quantitative	E. total distance divided by the total time
__ 6. dilemma zone	F. the force needed to keep an object moving in a circle
__ 7. STOP zone	G. area in which to decide to stop or proceed when approaching a yellow light
__ 8. friction	H. Newton's First Law of Motion
__ 9. centripetal force	I. drunk driving
__ 10. inertia	J. time to move foot to brake
__ 11. centripetal acceleration	K. traction
__ 12. skidding	L. term used to describe without using numbers

Part C: Written Response

Write the answers in complete sentences in the space provided.

1. Describe some of the influences which can affect your driving skills by increasing your response time.

   A: Answers will vary. Any intoxicant, alcohol, drugs, etc., will increase your reaction time. Other distractions, can increase your reaction time because you do not see the initial stimulus, due to talking to someone in the car, on the cell phone, changing CDs, etc. Tailgating causes accidents, because you do not leave enough space between you and the driver in front. Therefore, the distance you travel while reacting to the brake lights of the driver in front is usually enough to collide with him. Positive influences can be a good driver as a mentor, and a role model. Taking driver education and defensive driving courses will also increase your driving skills.

2. Tailgating can be dangerous. Explain the physics involved in the dangerous act of tailgating.

   A: As above. Tailgating does not leave enough space to allow for the distance you travel while reacting to the stimulus.

3. While traveling on a highway the distance between you and the car in front of you must be greater than if you are traveling in the city. Explain why.

   A: Since you are traveling at a greater speed on the highway, the distance you travel increases, ($d = v \times t$), even though you are leaving enough time in between you and the car in front.

4. Describe which intersection below is the safest, and why.

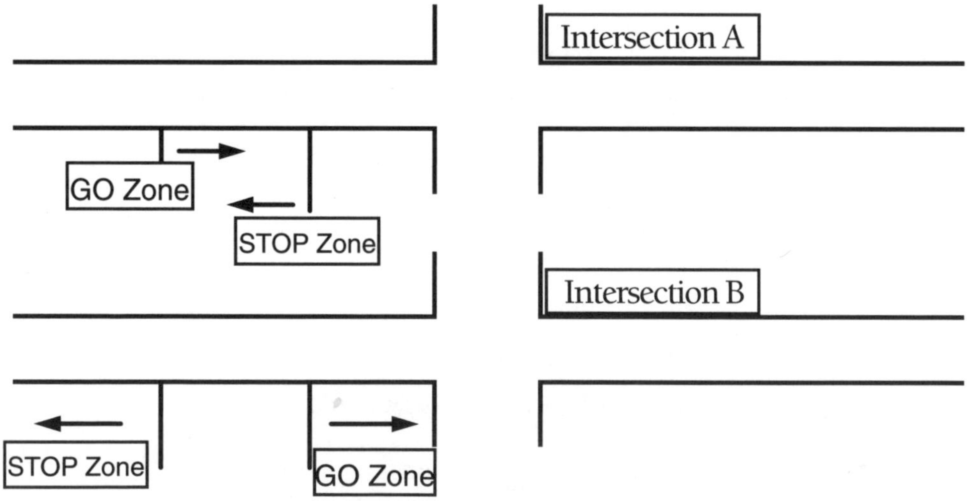

5. What are the five variables you need to take into consideration in order to have safe STOP, and GO zones?

   A: Yellow light time, speed, reaction time, width of intersection, deceleration rate.

6. You measured and collected the following data from an intersection.

the width of the intersection is $w = 20$ m;
the yellow light time is $Ty = 5.5$ seconds;
the speed limit on the road is $v = 40$ mph (20 m/s);
response time is $Tr = 1.0$ s.
deceleration rate is $a = 5.0$ m/s/s

Using the following equations (learned in the computer program)
Equations: $(v \times Ty) - w =$ GO Zone
$(Tr \times v) + (v2/2a) =$ STOP Zone

calculate the:
a) GO zone
b) STOP zone
c) sketch a picture of the intersection

A: a) 90 m
b) 60 m
c) student sketch

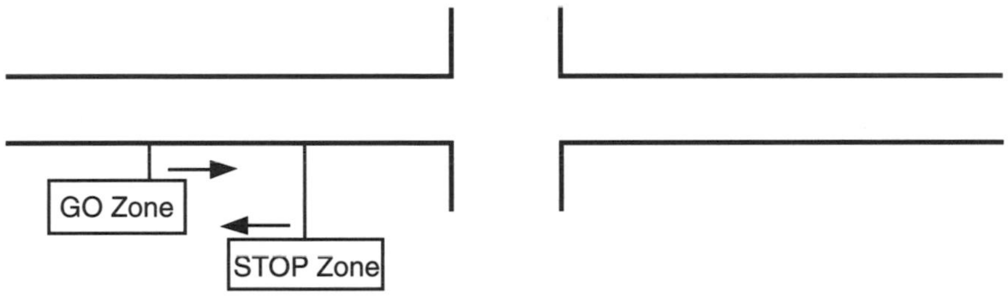

7. Describe three effects of acceleration.

A: An object's speed increases in the direction of motion; an object's speed decreases in the direction of motion; centripetal acceleration, causing an object's direction to change.

8. Define centripetal acceleration and centripetal force.

A: Centripetal acceleration is the change in direction of an object while continuing at the same speed. Centripetal force is the force which directed inward, changes the direction of the object to keep the object traveling in a curved path.

9. Explain why front-wheel drive is more stable than rear-wheel drive.

A: The center of mass is behind the power in a front-wheel drive, therefore the car will self correct any force acting sideways to the back of the car. In rear-wheel drive, the center of mass is ahead of the power, or being pushed. Therefore, the sideways forces can cause the car to loose control. (It is easier to pull a rope, than it is to push it!)

Alternative Chapter Assessment Answers

Multiple Choice:

1. d
2. a
3. d
4. a
5. c
6. b
7. b
8. a
9. d
10. d
11. d
12. c
13. d
14. b
15. b
16. a
17. d
18. b
19. c
20. a
21. b

Matching:

1. e
2. j
3. i
4. l
5. b
6. g
7. a
8. k
9. f
10. h
11. c
12. d

NOTES

1

NOTES

NOTES

NOTES

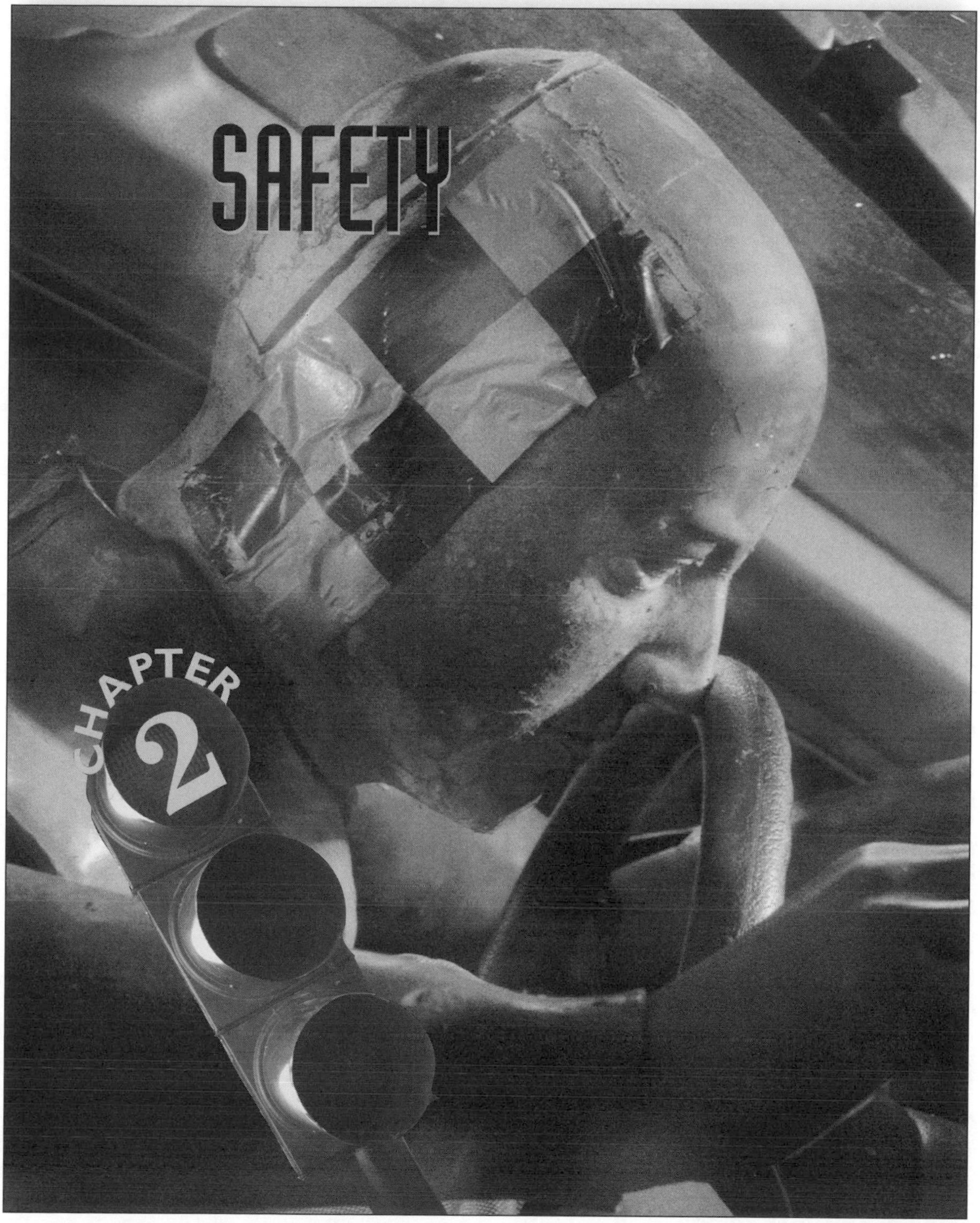

2

Transportation Chapter 2- Safety
National Science Education Standards

Chapter Challenge

Dangers inherent in travel provide the context for this chapter. Students are challenged to design or build a safety device, or system, for protecting automobile, airplane, bicycle, motorcycle, or train passengers. New laws, increased awareness, and improved safety systems are explored as students work on this challenge. They are also encouraged to design improvements to existing systems and to find ways to minimize harm caused by accidents.

Chapter Summary

To meet this challenge, students engage in collaborative activities that explore motions and forces and the principles of design technology. These experiences engage students in the following content from the *National Science Education Standards.*

Content Standards

Unifying Concepts

- Systems, order & organization
- Evidence, models and explanations
- Constancy, change, and measurement

Science as Inquiry

- Identify questions and concepts that guide scientific investigations
- Use technology and mathematics to improve investigations
- Formulate & revise scientific explanations & models using logic and evidence
- Communicate and defend a scientific argument

History and Nature of Science

- Nature of scientific knowledge

Physical Science

- Motions and forces

Science in Personal and Social Perspectives

- Personal and community health
- Natural and human-induced hazards

Science and Technology

- Understandings about science and technology
- Ability to apply technology

Key Physics Concepts and Skills

Activity Summaries	Physics Principles
Activity One: Accidents Following an investigation crashing cars against barriers, students use advertisements and consumer reports to learn about safety devices on automobiles. Each is analyzed to determine the type of collision-related injuries it prevents, and to identify if the device could in fact increase injuries in a unique setting.	• Physical properties of matter • Effect of forces on motion
Activity Two: Life (and Death) before Seat Belts Using a lump of clay on a motion cart to represent a person in a car, students explore "objects in motion stay in motion." They then relate this to actual automobile collisions.	• Acceleration • Inertia
Activity Three: Life (and Fewer Deaths) after Seat Belts Students focus on the design and materials used in seat belt construction as they study force and pressure. They investigate how increasing surface area decreases the pressure exerted. They relate this to the challenge by finding ways to increase the area of impact in a collision.	• Inertia • Newton's Laws of Motion • Force and pressure • Newton as a unit of measure
Activity Four: Why Air Bags? A model of an airbag is used in an investigation of what happens on impact when objects of different mass are dropped from different heights. They observe the amount of damage in each case and relate this to the concept of "impulse" and how spreading out the time of the impulse reduces damage.	• Inertia • Force and pressure • Impulse
Activity Five: The Rear End Collision Students investigate the effect of rear-end collisions on passengers by using a model of the neck muscles and bones of the vertebral column. They then read to learn more about Newton's Second Law of Motion and consider how they can apply this information in designing a safety device that prevents movement of the head in a collision.	• Collisions • Newton's Second Law of Motion • Momentum
Activity Six: The Bungee Jump (Computer Analysis) Students apply their understanding of momentum and impulse as they use a force probe to investigate the changes in force on a bungee jumper. This enables them to further investigate how increasing stopping distance decreases chance of injury by spreading the force out over time.	• Inertia • Force and pressure • Impulse as a function of time • Momentum
Activity Seven: Automatic Triggering Devices In this inquiry investigation, students design a device that will trigger an air bag to inflate. These simulations allows them to apply concepts of inertia and impulse as they test ideas that help them address the chapter challenge.	• Inertia • Force and pressure • Impulse
Activity Eight: Cushioning Collisions (Computer Analysis) Using a force probe, students investigate the effectiveness of different types of systems designed to minimize the impact of collisions. The systems include sand canisters around bridge supports and padded car interiors. This investigation provides an opportunity to develop deeper understanding of the concepts of acceleration, velocity, and momentum.	• Inertia • Impulse • Momentum • Change in Momentum • Conservation of Momentum
Activity Nine: Safety in the Air Analyzing and interpreting exit seating instructions enables students to revisit issues raised in the chapter challenge from a different perspective. These activities also require them to consider size and strength required to open an airplane's emergency exit door.	• Force and pressure • Transportation

2

Equipment List For Chapter Two

QTY	TO SERVE	ACTIVITY	ITEM	COMMENT
1	Class	3	*Active Physics Transportation* Content Video	Segment: Crash Dummy
1	Class	9	*Active Physics Transportation* Content Video	Segment: Safety in Air
1	Group	5, 6, 8	Balance	Measure masses of 2x4 piece, doll, toy car
1	Group	7	Battery holder for D-cell	Provision for connecting wires to battery
1	Group	1	Brochures describing auto safety features	Minimum of 3 kinds of autos
1	Group	4	Camcorder on tripod	Ticker-tape timer may serve as low-tech substitute
1	Group	2, 7	Concrete block or similar barrier	To stop moving lab cart
1	Group	7	D-cell	
1	Group	6	Doll, small	
1	Group	5	Duct tape, 4" to 6" length	Neck of model passenger
1	Group	6	Elastic cord, approx 50 cm length	
1	Group	4	Heavy coconut-like object	
1	Group	4	Inflatable beach ball	Substitute: Plastic garbage bag
2	Group	2, 3, 5, 6	Laboratory cart	Only one cart needed for Activities 2, 3, 6
1	Group	4	Landing surface materials of 3 hardnesses	Such as bare, carpeted and foam-covered floor
1	Group	7	Light bulb and base, miniature screwbase	A "flashlight" bulb (such as No. 13) and base
1	Group	6, 8	MBL or CBL with force probe	
1	Group	8	MBL or CBL with Sonic Ranger	
1	Group	5	Meter stick	
1	Group	2, 3	Modeling clay, baseball-size piece	
1	Group	3	Ribbon or tape, various widths	Approx. 25 cm length of each width
1	Group	6	Ringstand and supports for probe, doll	
1	Group	5	Spring scale, 0-10 Newton range	
1	Group	2, 3, 5, 7, 8	Starting ramp	
1	Group	6	String, approx. 50 cm length	
1	Group	8	Tape or rubber bands	For attaching cushions to toy car
1	Group	8	Toy car	
1	Group	8	Variety of cushioning materials	To form "bumpers" for toy car
1	Class	3, 9	VCR and TV monitor	
1	Group	4	VCR having single-frame advance mode	
1	Group	4	Video monitor	
1	Group	3	Wire, approx. 25 cm length	
1	Group	5	Wood piece, 1"x2"x2"	Head of model passenger
1	Group	5	Wood piece, 1"x3"x10"	Torso of model passenger
1	Group	5	Wood piece, 2x4, approx 1 ft long	A scrap piece of 2x4 will serve

Organizer for Materials Available in Teacher's Edition

Activity in Student Text	Additional Material	Alternative / Optional Activities
ACTIVITY ONE Accidents p. T62	Assessment: Participation in Discussion, p. 139	
ACTIVITY TWO Life (and Death) before Seat Belts p. T67		Activity Two A: Dropping a Clay Ball to Investigate Inertia, pgs. 149-150 Activity Two B: Low-Tech Alternative, p. 151
ACTIVITY THREE Life (and Fewer Deaths) after Seat Belts p. T73	Assessment, p. 162	
ACTIVITY FOUR Why Air Bags? p. T79	Assessment, p. 172	
ACTIVITY FIVE The Rear End Collision p. T84		
ACTIVITY SIX The Bungee Jump (Computer Analysis) p. T89		Activity Six A: Effects of Mass on Bungee Jumping (Low-Tech), pgs. 189-190
ACTIVITY SEVEN Automatic Triggering Devices p. T93	Assessments for Activity Seven and for Scientific and Technological Thinking, p. 197	
ACTIVITY EIGHT Cushioning Collisions (Computer Analysis) p. T95		
ACTIVITY NINE Safety in the Air p. T100		

2

Scenario

Probably the most dangerous thing you will do today is travel to your destination. Transportation is necessary, but the need to get there in a hurry, and the large number of people and vehicles, have made transportation very risky. There is a greater chance of being killed or injured traveling than in any other common activity. Realizing this, people and governments have begun to take action to alter the statistics. New safety systems have been designed and put into use in automobiles and airplanes. New laws and a new awareness are working together with these systems to reduce the danger in traveling.

What are these new safety systems? You are probably familiar with many of them. In this chapter, you will become more familiar with most of these designs. Could you design or even build a better safety device for a car or a plane? Many students around the country have been doing just that, and with great success!

Challenge

Your design team will develop a safety system for protecting automobile, airplane, bicycle, motorcycle, or train passengers. As you study existing safety systems, you and your design team should be listing ideas for improving an existing system or designing a new system for preventing accidents. You may also consider a system that will minimize the harm caused by accidents.

T 60

Chapter and Challenge Overview

Divide the class into design teams consisting of three or four students. As there is a diversity of skills required - design, construction, writing, speaking, etc. – all students should be involved in the process. You may want to allow some time early in the week for group meetings for the purpose of brainstorming as well as an opportunity for you to check on the progress of the teams.

Encourage broad thinking. The projects do not have to be limited to the vehicle, but can include the roadway, traffic control, etc. Students may use their experiences with skateboarding, cycling, in-line skating or other athletic pursuits to help them get started.

Explain the two-day presentation format. On the first day a poster session is conducted during which students informally explain their projects to classmates and answer their questions. Meanwhile, the students are writing down questions about the projects, and placing them into envelopes, provided by you for each project. The formal presentations the next day may be quite brief, since most students will have seen the projects the day before. After a few sentences addressing the points listed in the student text, randomly draw a student question from the appropriate envelope for the team to answer. Use as many as time might allow.

Scoring the project might be based on assigning credit for each of the items listed in the student text with, perhaps, greater emphasis on how the physics concepts are utilized and explained. Discuss with the students the relative credit weighting of the project. Use as a starting point, the criteria mentioned in the student text, with the total points being 100. An example might be Part 1 --30, Part 2 -- 20, Part 3 -- 20, with a teacher assigned (or peer assessment) of 30 points, adding to a total of 100.

The intention in this exercise is to motivate students into learning about the safety of various modes of transportation. As they develop their project, while studying this chapter, they should be revising and changing their safety system.

Your final product will be a working model or prototype of a safety system. On the day that you bring the final product to class, the teams will display them around the room while class members informally view them and discuss them with members of the design team. During this time, class members will ask questions about each others products. The questions will be placed in envelopes provided to each team by the teacher. The teacher will use some of these questions during the oral presentations on the next day.

The product will be judged according to the following three parts:

1. The quality of your safety feature enhancement and the working model or prototype.
2. The quality of a 5-minute oral report that should include:
   - **the need for the system;**
   - **the method used to develop the working model;**
   - **the demonstration of the working model;**
   - **the discussion of the physics concepts involved;**
   - **the description of the next-generation version of the system;**
   - **the answers to questions posed by the class.**
3. The quality of a written and/or multimedia report including:
   - **the information from the oral report;**
   - **the documentation of the sources of expert information;**
   - **the discussion of consumer acceptance and market potential;**
   - **the discussion of the physics concepts applied in the design of the safety system.**

Criteria

You and your classmates will work with your teacher to define the criteria for determining grades. You will also be asked to evaluate your own work. Discuss as a class the performance task and the points that should be allocated for each part. A starting point for your discussions may be:

- **Part 1 = 40 points**
- **Part 2 = 30 points**
- **Part 3 = 30 points**

Since group work is made up of individual work, your teacher will assign some points to each individual's contribution to the project. If individual points total 30 points, then parts 1, 2 and 3 must be changed so that the total remains at 100.

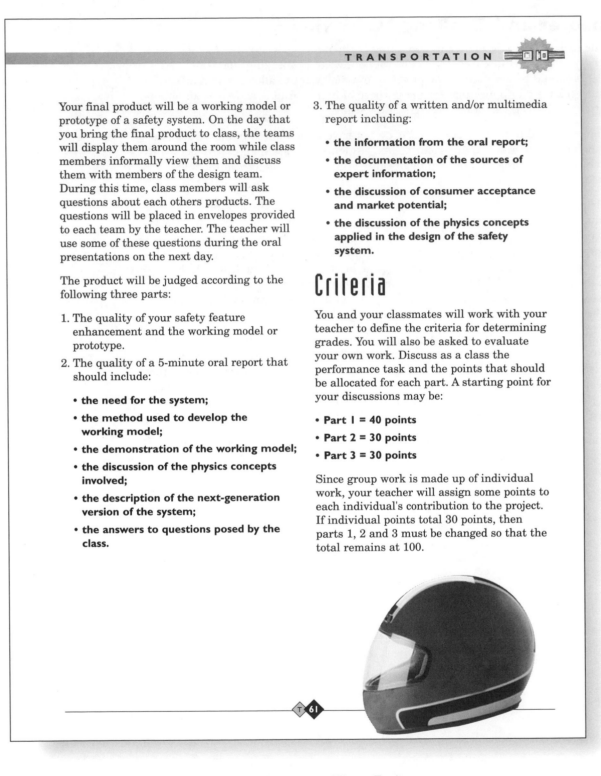

Assessment Rubric for Challenge: Group Work in Designing Safety Feature Content

Total = 9 marks

1. Low level – indicates minimum effort or effectiveness.
2. Average – acceptable standard has been achieved, but the group could have worked more effectively if better organized.
3. Good – this rating indicates a superior effort. Although improvements might have been made, the group was on task all of the time and completed all parts of the activity.

Descriptor	Values		
1. The group worked cooperatively to design a safety feature. Comments:	1	2	3
2. The group was organized. Materials were collected and the problems were addressed by the entire group. Comments:	1	2	3
3. Data was collected and recorded in an organized fashion in data tables in their logs. Comments:	1	2	3

2

For use with *Transportation*, Chapter 2

Assessment Rubric for Challenge: Safety Feature and Working Model

Descriptor	5	4	3	2	1
Skills Required for Working Model/Prototype					
understands the need to control variables					
has run at least three trials with safety feature					
demonstrates or explains why there is a need for several trials					
has rebuilt or modified safety feature as necessary					
uses appropriate materials in the construction of the safety feature					
care and attention has been given in assembling the working model					
working model functions appropriately during demonstration					
group has worked efficiently as a team in assembling the model					
Oral Report					
understands and explains the need for the system					
describes the method used to develop the working model					
demonstrates the working model					
discusses the physics concepts illustrated by the safety feature					
describes the next generation of the system					
answers questions posed by the class					
Written and/or Multimedia Report					
contains the points included in the oral report					
spelling, punctuation, grammar, and sentence structure are correctly used					
science vocabulary and symbols are used correctly					
documents sources of expert information					
discusses consumer acceptance and marketing potential					
data is presented in tables and graphs as appropriate					

For use with *Transportation*, Chapter 2

What is in the Physics InfoMall for Chapter 2?

Chapter 2 of Transportation deals with the physics of safety systems in automobiles, airplanes, and bicycles. The Physics InfoMall CD-ROM contains an enormous amount of material related to the physics of many phenomena, and safety is one of them. At first, it seems like a good idea to see what the InfoMall has to say about "safety systems." So the first thing you may want to do is perform a search on the entire CD-ROM for "safety system*" (the asterisk is a wild character asking the search engine to look for any words that share the same beginning, such as "system", "systems", or even "systematic"). The only result from this search that is relevant to our needs is "The science of traffic safety," by Leonard Evans, and found in *The Physics Teacher*, volume 26, issue 7. Early in this article, Evans states "No one who lives in a motorized society can fail to be concerned about the enormous human cost of traffic crashes; as many young males are killed in traffic crashes as by all other causes combined. The United States Department of Transportation maintains a file containing information on all fatal traffic crashes in the United States since 1975. This data file now documents over half a million fatalities, and of course, injuries are enormously more numerous. Recent research, discussed below, should demonstrate that the study of phenomena related to traffic safety presents problems of intellectual challenge similar in character and difficulty to those encountered in physics. Traffic safety means the safety of the overall traffic system, as distinct from more specific properties of individual components, such as laboratory crash tests of vehicles." This passage lends support to the Scenario described at the beginning of this chapter. Following this article is a list of references that you may also find useful in teaching traffic safety. While this article is specific to traffic safety, it is a great beginning to this chapter.

ACTIVITY ONE
Accidents

Background Information

Most of the physics involved with this chapter on Safety, involves an understanding of Inertia and Momentum.

Symbols

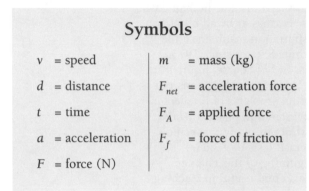

v = speed	m = mass (kg)
d = distance	F_{net} = acceleration force
t = time	F_A = applied force
a = acceleration	F_f = force of friction
F = force (N)	

Newton's First Law of Motion states (Inertia) that an object in motion or at rest will remain in motion or at rest unless acted upon by an outside unbalanced force. An object at rest staying at rest is fairly obvious for students to understand. Even understanding that an object in motion remaining in motion should be easily understood once an understanding that friction is acting on things on Earth in one form or another.

Therefore, an object in motion, say an automobile, will continue in motion. However, students will observe that the automobile slows down (decelerates). Enter into a discussion on what slows the automobile. Friction (in the engine, axles, wheels, transmission, and tires on the road) is the outside unbalanced force acting on the automobile which stops it from moving at a constant speed. Therefore in order to keep it moving at a constant speed, you must be applying a force to it.
F_{net} (the accelerating force)
= F_A (the force applied by the engine) +
F_f (force of friction always acting opposite to the direction of motion).

$$F_{net} = F_A + F_f$$

When there is no acceleration (therefore, constant motion), there is no net force. This means that the force applied is the same as the force of friction; only opposite in direction. As long as the force applied and the force of friction are the same magnitude but opposite in direction, the object will continue to move at a constant speed.

Safety, then is a discussion on how inertia affects the movement of a body in an automobile. While the automobile is moving, everything and everyone in the automobile are moving at the same speed as the automobile. When the automobile stops, everything that is attached to the automobile (bumper, seats, steering wheel, etc.) are stopping or experiencing the deceleration as well. However, anything not attached to the automobile, (people, dogs, tape cases, hockey sticks, etc.) will continue to move according to Newton's First Law. In this chapter, we will be doing an analysis of the inertia of the objects inside a vehicle and how to prevent injury.

Active-ating the Physics InfoMall

The articles mentioned above are good for this activity. One of the safety devices mentioned in this activity is the air bag. A quick search for "air bags" found several interesting hits, including "Resource letter PE-1: Physics and the environment, *American Journal of Physics*, vol. 42, 267-273 (1974).

Planning for the Activity

Time Requirements

This activity is centered primarily on reading and answering the questions in For You To Do. After the students have answered the questions, there should be a class discussion, to investigate the understanding students have now about accidents and to help the students to open their minds to the seriousness of accidents. As the majority of students are entering the most dangerous time of their lives, in terms of learning to drive, and being involved in accidents, the discussion should be serious. Allow more time if a film and a discussion are added to the lesson.

Materials needed

For each group:

- set of brochures describing safety features of cars (3 minimum)

Teaching Notes

If students have a tough time with the discussion from What Do You Think? you may try using brainstorming on these activities. See Assessment for a possible rubric for this activity.

While discussing accidents, be aware that some students may have already been in a serious accident, or know of someone close to them, who has been injured or killed in an accident. Be sensitive to the student who sits quietly and doesn't want to participate in the discussion.

Activity Overview

This activity centers around the students own experiences with safety in transportation. The students will be exploring their own ideas, misconceptions and evaluating quantitatively their ideas in the "test".

Student Objectives

Students will:

- evaluate their own understandings of safety.
- evaluate the safety features on selected vehicles.
- compare and contrast the safety features on selected vehicles.
- identify safety features in selected vehicles.
- identify safety features required for other modes of transportation (in-line skates, skate boards, cycling, etc.)

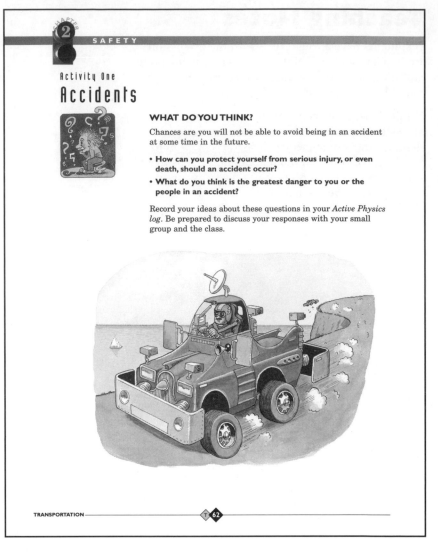

CHAPTER 2 SAFETY

Activity One

Accidents

WHAT DO YOU THINK?

Chances are you will not be able to avoid being in an accident at some time in the future.

- **How can you protect yourself from serious injury, or even death, should an accident occur?**
- **What do you think is the greatest danger to you or the people in an accident?**

Record your ideas about these questions in your *Active Physics log*. Be prepared to discuss your responses with your small group and the class.

TRANSPORTATION T 62

ANSWERS FOR THE TEACHER ONLY

What Do You Think?

Students answers will vary. Most students will come up with the obvious – seat belts, air bags, roll cages, etc. However, some students may come up with ideas, which will convey their misconceptions of accidents, such as, bend over, and get into a ball, hang on to the dash board.

Again, students will relay the most obvious, flying through the windshield, automobile rolling over you if you get thrown out, etc.; be prepared for answers such as being burned in the automobile, the automobile explodes on impact; look for sensible answers, that will steer the students toward an understanding of the physics, i.e., inertia, forces, momentum, without having to talk about the details of the "physics". Some of the answers which students may not think of might include: other people in the automobile flying around during the collision, being knocked unconscious as you enter a lake or slough, objects not tied or secured flying around inside the automobile.

Try not to limit the discussion to only cars and trucks. Expand if appropriate to motorcycles, snowmobiles, motorized tricycles and quads. Also, if it is brought up by the students, a discussion about the safety of bicycles could develop.

FOR YOU TO DO

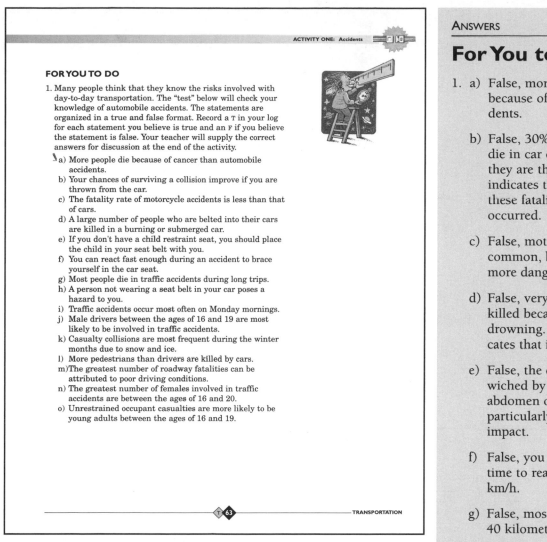

1. Many people think that they know the risks involved with day-to-day transportation. The "test" below will check your knowledge of automobile accidents. The statements are organized in a true and false format. Record a T in your log for each statement you believe is true and an F if you believe the statement is false. Your teacher will supply the correct answers for discussion at the end of the activity.
   a) More people die because of cancer than automobile accidents.
   b) Your chances of surviving a collision improve if you are thrown from the car.
   c) The fatality rate of motorcycle accidents is less than that of cars.
   d) A large number of people who are belted into their cars are killed in a burning or submerged car.
   e) If you don't have a child restraint seat, you should place the child in your seat belt with you.
   f) You can react fast enough during an accident to brace yourself in the car seat.
   g) Most people die in traffic accidents during long trips.
   h) A person not wearing a seat belt in your car poses a hazard to you.
   i) Traffic accidents occur most often on Monday mornings.
   j) Male drivers between the ages of 16 and 19 are most likely to be involved in traffic accidents.
   k) Casualty collisions are most frequent during the winter months due to snow and ice.
   l) More pedestrians than drivers are killed by cars.
   m) The greatest number of roadway fatalities can be attributed to poor driving conditions.
   n) The greatest number of females involved in traffic accidents are between the ages of 16 and 20.
   o) Unrestrained occupant casualties are more likely to be young adults between the ages of 16 and 19.

ANSWERS

For You to Do

1. a) False, more people die because of automobile accidents.

   b) False, 30% of the people who die in car crashes die because they are thrown. One report indicates that at least 50% of these fatalities need not have occurred.

   c) False, motorcycles are less common, but they are much more dangerous.

   d) False, very few people are killed because of burning or drowning. One study indicates that it is less than 0.1%.

   e) False, the child can be sandwiched by your mass. The abdomen of small children is particularly vulnerable to impact.

   f) False, you don't have enough time to react even at 50 km/h.

   g) False, most people die within 40 kilometers of home.

   h) True, the person becomes a projectile once the car stops.

   i) False, most traffic accidents occur on Friday afternoon or evening traffic.

   j) True, that accounts for the higher insurance rates.

   k) False, the months May, June, and August have the greatest number of casualty collisions.

   l) False, pedestrians only account for 6.1% of traffic fatalities.

   m) False, more accidents take place when road conditions are dry.

   n) True, young female drivers, like their male counterparts, are responsible for the greatest number of accidents. Inexperience may be the major contributing factor.

   o) True.

CHAPTER 2 SAFETY

2. Calculate your score. Give yourself two points for a correct answer, and subtract one point for an incorrect answer. You might want to match your score against the descriptors given below.

   21 to 30 points: Expert Analyst

   14 to 20 points: Assistant Analyst

   9 to 13 points: Novice Analyst

   8 points and below: Myth Believer

   a) Record your score in your log. Were you surprised about the extent of your knowledge? Some of the reasons behind these facts will be better understood as you travel through this chapter.

Obtain permission from the cars' owners before proceeding.

3. Survey at least three different cars for safety features. The list on the next page will allow you to evaluate the safety features of each of the cars. Place a check mark in the appropriate square.

   Number 1 indicates very poor or nonexistent, 2 is minimum standard, 3 is average, 4 is good, and 5 is very good.

   For example, when rating air bags: a car with no air bags could be given a 1 rating, a car with only a driver-side air bag a 2, a car with driver and passenger side air bags a 3, a car with slow release driver and passenger-side air bags a 4, and a car which includes side-door air bags to the previous list a 5. You may add additional safety features not identified in the chart. Many additional features can be added!

   a) Copy and complete the table in your log.

   b) Which car would you evaluate as being safest?

ANSWERS

For You to Do *(continued)*

2. a) Students scores will vary. A short discussion can follow with the expectation that the students will be able to better understand the physics of the accidents after the next few chapters.

3. a) Students should be able to come up with at least five more safety features. These might include side impact beams in doors, shoulder belts for all outboard seats, laminated windshield glass, ABS brakes, tempered shatterproof glass, etc.

   b) Students answers will vary. Look for reasonable arguments for their evaluation. They should include factors such as speed, forces on the body, analysis of the effect on the body from different kinds of collisions.

Car Tested: Make and Model ____	Year ____				
Safety Feature	Rating				
Padded front seats	1	2	3	4	5
Padded roof frame	1	2	3	4	5
Head rests	1	2	3	4	5
Knee protection	1	2	3	4	5
Anti-daze rear-view mirror that brakes on impact	1	2	3	4	5
Child proof safety locks on rear doors	1	2	3	4	5
Padded console	1	2	3	4	5
Padded sun visor	1	2	3	4	5
Padded doors and arm rests	1	2	3	4	5
Steering wheel with padded rim and hub	1	2	3	4	5
Padded gear level					
Padded door pillars					
Air bags					

REFLECTING ON THE ACTIVITY AND CHALLENGE

Serious injuries in an automobile accident have many causes. If there are no restraints or safety devices in a vehicle, or if the vehicle is not constructed to absorb any of the energy of the collision, even a minor collision can cause serious injury. Until the early 1960's, automobile design and construction did not even consider passenger safety. The general belief was that a heavy car was a safe car. While there is some truth to that statement, today's lighter cars are far safer than the "tanks" of the past.

The safety survey may have provided ideas for constructing a prototype of a safety system used for transportation. If it has, write down ideas in your log that have been generated from this activity.

ANSWERS

Physics To Go

1. Looking at the chart from page 65, these are possible answers-
   - Padded front seats F, R
   - Padded roof frame T
   - Head rests F, R
   - Knee protection F, S
   - Anti-daze rear-view mirror F, S
   - Child-proof safety locks
   - Padded console F, R, S, T
   - Padded sun visor F, S, T
   - Padded doors and arm rests S
   - Steering wheel-padded F
   - Padded gear level F, S
   - Padded door pillars S, T
   - Air bags F, S, T

2. Safety features for cycling could be: padded handle bars, better brakes, padded seat and top bar, lots of lighting, and reflectors, safety flags for better visibility, safety training, like defensive driving, helmet, padding for knees, hands and elbows and shoulders.

3. Many of the same for bikes, but emphasis on padding and helmets.

4. As above, with an emphasis on padding again.

5. Students answers will vary. Look for a thorough evaluation, using the previous list, and emphasize to the students that the discussion with the owner of the vehicle is as important as the evaluation.

PHYSICS TO GO

1. Review and list all the safety features found in today's new cars. As you compile your list, write next to each safety feature one or more of the following designations:

   F: effective in a front-end collision.

   R: effective in a rear-end collision.

   S: effective in a collision where the car is struck on the side.

   T: effective when the car rolls over or turns over onto its roof.

2. Make a list of safety features that could be used for cycling.
3. Make a list of safety features that could be used for in-line skating.
4. Make a list of safety features that could be used for skate boarding.
5. Ask family members or friends if you may evaluate their car. Discuss and explain your evaluation to the car owners. Record your evaluation and their response in your log.

STRETCHING EXERCISES

1. Read a consumer report on car safety. Are any cars on the road particularly unsafe?
2. Collect brochures from various automobile dealers. What new safety features are presented in the brochures? How much of the advertising is devoted to safety?

ANSWERS

Stretching Exercises

1. There may be many cars on the road that have elements which are unsafe. Have the students evaluate which ones constitute true safety breaches, and which are more along cosmetic lines. For example, electronic fuel filters which may ignite, or dashboards which spontaneously start on fire, or brakes which fail would constitute major safety hazards. Radios which fail or brakes that squeal when stopping, or cars that prematurely rust, are more cosmetic, and don't constitute a safety hazard.

2. Students answers will vary. Students will likely come up with the observation that a great deal of advertising has to do with driver safety.

Assessment: Participation in Discussion

The following is an assessment rubric, designed for informal feedback to the students on their discussions related to their personal experiences with safety in a vehicle. While they are discussing this, the students may want to brainstorm on some of the safety features with which they are familiar.

Descriptor	most of the time	some of the time	almost never	comments
shows interest				
stays on task				
asks questions related to topic				
listens to other students' ideas				
shows cooperation in group brainstorming				
provides leadership in group activity				
demonstrates tolerance of others' viewpoints				

2

For use with *Transportation*, Chapter 2, ACTIVITY ONE: Accidents

ACTIVITY TWO
Life (and Death) before Seat Belts

Background Information

Newton's First Law of Motion (Inertia) gives us an understanding of constant motion (or rest). Therefore, when an object such as a car is stopping, there is a change in velocity (previously introduced as speed). In other words there is an acceleration. Analyzing a collision involves examining the changes in velocity of a car. The crumple zone refers to the stopping distance as the car is pushed in, while stopping. Cars designed today are built with crumple zones. This is to increase the distance a car takes to stop, therefore reducing the acceleration and ultimately the force being applied to your body.

Increasing the crumple zone will affect the acceleration of the people inside the car, initially using the average velocity ($v_{ave} = d/t$). Average velocity is the sum of the two velocities divided by 2

$v_{ave} = (v_1 + v_2)/2.$

$v_{ave} = (40 \text{ m/s} + 0 \text{ m/s})/2$

$v_{ave} = 20 \text{ m/s}$

Find the time required to stop (crumple zone of the vehicle),

$t = d/ v_{ave}$

$t = 0.50 \text{ s}/20 \text{ m/s}$

$t = 0.025 \text{ s}$

and substitute t into the equation for acceleration

$a = \Delta v/\Delta t$

$a = 40 \text{ m/s} / 0.025 \text{ s}$

$a = 1600 \text{ m/s}^2$

This is clearly enough to rip out the aorta.

Another way to emphasize the impact of this force, is that a 10 m/s^2 acceleration is roughly equivalent to holding 1 kg (2.2 pounds) mass (you need 10 N of force to lift 1 kg of mass). Therefore, if we look at the above acceleration, you could picture a 160 kg (352 pound) person being held up by the aorta...ouch that would hurt!

This model should help students realize that the external safety devices we use help, but there is not very much we can do to improve on the safety devices that are built into our own bodies.

Factors which may enter into the discussion, regarding race car drivers traveling at 200 mph, may be the fact that most race car drivers are in very good physical shape, and are generally younger.

One other way to help the students understand that the internal organs undergo acceleration, is how they feel while driving in a car over a hilly road. The feeling often expressed is that of your stomach rising and falling at the crests and valleys.

In the FYTD activity, the students will be releasing the carts at different heights on the ramp. If the carts experience an almost frictionless surface, the speed at which the cart hits the barrier can be determined using the height from which the cart is released.

Conservation of Energy Theory (First Law of Thermodynamics) states that energy can be neither created nor destroyed, only transferred from one form to another. Therefore, the energy at the top of the ramp (gravitational energy) $E_p = mgh$ (where m is the mass of the cart and clay, g is gravity (9.81 m/s2) and h is the height from which the cart is released) will be the same as the kinetic energy ($E_k = 1/2\ mv2$ where m is the mass, v is the velocity) at the bottom.

$E_p = E_k$

$mgh = 1/2mv_2$

masses cancel out

$gh = 1/2v_2$

$v = \sqrt{2gh}$

For example: the cart is released at a height of 0.50 m. Therefore the speed of the cart as it reaches the bottom of the ramp would be

$v = \sqrt{2gh}$

$v = \sqrt{2 \text{ x } 9.81 \text{ m/s}^2 \text{ x } 0.50 \text{ m}}$

$v = 3.1 \text{ m/s}$

Active-ating the Physics InfoMall

The title of this activity leads naturally to a search for "seat belt*". The very first result from this search is from *The Fascination of Physics*, in the Textbook Trove, which says "Automobile accidents involve two collisions. The first occurs when the automobile strikes an object, such as a telephone pole. The pole provides the force needed to change the car's momentum, eventually bringing it to rest. A second collision, which occurs shortly after the first, involves the passengers. If they are not in some way attached to the car, the passengers do not experience the force exerted by the telephone pole. The car may stop, but the passengers continue moving forward at a constant velocity. According to Newton's First Law, their forward motion will continue until they experience a force. Unfortunately, this force is usually exerted by the dashboard or windshield, and serious injuries result." This can be compared to the For You To Read passage, which goes a little further by looking at three collisions. You should do this search and read the results.

The second hit from this search is the epilogue to *The Fascination of Physics*, and mentions that "The benefits of not using seat belts are the saving of a few second in buckling and unbuckling, a slight increase in the freedom of movement inside a car, and some psychological or emotional benefits that are difficult to define. The benefits and the belief that the probability of an accident is small convince most people to sit on top of their seat belts." This applies directly to question 2 of the Stretching Exercise.

A little further down the list from this "seat belt*" search is an article that you might not otherwise find - "The car, the soft drink can, and the brick wall," from *The Physics Teacher*, vol. 13, (1975). This article was written by a co-PI for the InfoMall. It describes an experiment very similar to this activity, but with some variations.

A big concept in this activity is the concept of force. Students' understanding of this concept has been studied extensively. An InfoMall search using "force" AND "misconception*" in only the Articles and Abstracts Attic produced many great references. The first such hit is the article containing the Force Concept Inventory. The second is "Common sense concepts about motion," *American Journal of Physics*, vol. 53, issue 11, 1985 in which it is mentioned that "(a) On the pretest (post-test), 47% (20%) of the students showed, at least once, a belief that under no net force, an object slows down. However, only 1% (0%) maintained that belief across similar tasks. (b) About 66% (54%) of the students held, at least once, the belief that under a constant force an object moves at constant speed. However, only 2% (1%) held that belief consistently." More results are reported in this article.

The third hit in this search is "Physics that textbook writers usually get wrong," in *The Physics Teacher*, vol. 30, issue 7, 1992. This article is good reading for any introductory physics teacher. The list of hits from this search is long. In fact, it had to be limited to just the Articles and Abstracts Attic to prevent the "Too many hits" warning. If you search the rest of the CD-ROM, you will find many other great hits, such as this quote from Chapter 3 of Arons' *A Guide to Introductory Physics Teaching: Elementary Dynamics*: "In the study of physics, the Law of Inertia and the concept of force have, historically, been two of the most formidable stumbling blocks for students, and, as of the present time, more cognitive research has been done in this area than in any other."

Speed is one of the first concepts introduced in introductory physics. It is also one that causes students problems. If you search the InfoMall for "student difficult*" OR "student understand*" you will find several articles that deal with research into how students learn fundamental concepts in physics. Some of these are "Investigation of student understanding of the concept of velocity in one dimension," *American Journal of Physics*, vol. 48, issue 12 (see "Diagnosis and remediation of an alternative conception of velocity using a microcomputer program," *American Journal of Physics*, vol. 53, issue 7 for a discussion of this); "Research and computer-based instruction: Opportunity for interaction," *American Journal of Physics*, vol. 58, issue 5 (if you look at other articles in this volume, you will find "Learning motion concepts using real-time microcomputer-based laboratory tools," *American Journal of Physics*, vol. 58, issue 9); and more.

These last two articles make specific mention of the use of computers in teaching physics. This is a trend that is gaining strength and shows great promise. Look for more such articles in journals that are newer than the CD-ROM. As a starting point, you can always look in the annual indices of the physics journals and look under the names of the authors of the articles mentioned above.

Note that Physics To Go step 1 mentions curved motion. This topic was discussed in Chapter 1 of this book, where we found that you can give students a feel for curved motion with *The Physics Teacher*, volume 21, issue 3, "People Demos." Curved motion often brings up "centrifugal force," which is discussed in *Physics Education* (in the Articles and Abstracts Attic), issue 3, "Centrifugal force: fact or fiction," by Michael D. Savage and Julian S. Williams. See also Robert P. Bauman, "What is centrifugal force?," *The Physics Teacher*, vol. 18, number 7. Another good reference for centripetal and centrifugal forces is Arnold Arons' book (found in the Book Basement) *A Guide to Introductory Physics Teaching*, Motion in Two Dimensions, sections 4.9 to 4.11. These can all be found with simple searches.

Planning for the Activity

Time Requirements

- At least one class period (40 - 50 minutes). Allow extra time for variations on their molded clay figures.

Materials needed

For each group:

- laboratory cart
- modeling clay, baseball size
- concrete block or other suitable barrier
- srarting ramp

Advance Preparation and Setup

This experiment requires students to crash a loaded cart into a wall, or other suitable barrier. Test out different barriers (walls, desks, bricks, homemade structures) prior to laboratory day.

Teaching Notes

You might want to show the *Active Physics Transportation* Content Video showing collisions in which a dummy is thrown forward.

The students begin by forming a clay figure of a body with a relatively large head. With the figure seated on the lab cart, allow the cart to be released from various heights or various angles on the ramp. This will simulate the vehicle crashing into a barrier at various speeds. At high speeds, the figure should crash into the barrier head-first. At low speeds, the figure should topple head first, smashing its head into the "dashboard".

Some students may wish to analyze different scenarios. Have the students submit their plans for teacher approval, then allow them to carry out their plans. An example may be to release the cart backwards to demonstrate the rear-end collisions (to be studied later).

Be aware that the ramp needs to be secure on a desk, or the floor as the cart may fall onto the floor or on someone's toes! Remind the students to place down newspaper or some drop cloths while creating their figure.

Students may have the notion that if they were in an accident if they got their arms up in time they would be able to protect themselves. Review with them reaction times, and have them try to bring their hands up to the dashboard level in that time. To further emphasize the danger in this thinking refer to the Additional Activities A following this activity in the Teacher's Edition.

Activity Two

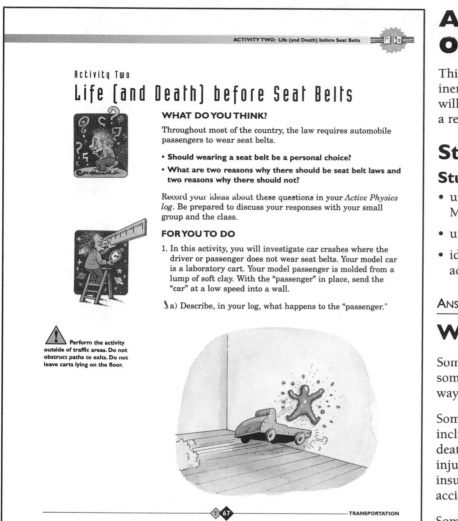

Life (and Death) before Seat Belts

WHAT DO YOU THINK?

Throughout most of the country, the law requires automobile passengers to wear seat belts.

- **Should wearing a seat belt be a personal choice?**
- **What are two reasons why there should be seat belt laws and two reasons why there should not?**

Record your ideas about these questions in your *Active Physics log*. Be prepared to discuss your responses with your small group and the class.

FOR YOU TO DO

1. In this activity, you will investigate car crashes where the driver or passenger does not wear seat belts. Your model car is a laboratory cart. Your model passenger is molded from a lump of soft clay. With the "passenger" in place, send the "car" at a low speed into a wall.

a) Describe, in your log, what happens to the "passenger."

Perform the activity outside of traffic areas. Do not obstruct paths to exits. Do not leave carts lying on the floor.

ANSWERS

For You To Do

1. a) See answer on following page.

Activity Overview

This activity is an investigation into the inertia of an automobile passenger and will lead directly toward the necessity of a restraint system.

Student Objectives

Students will:

- understand Newton's First Law of Motion.
- understand the role of safety belts.
- identify the three collisions in every accident.

ANSWERS FOR THE TEACHER ONLY

What Do You Think?

Some students will think it should and some will think it not. It is an excellent way to open discussion

Some reasons for wearing might include: safety, decrease the risk of death, decrease the risk of serious injury, lower the total cost of health insurance due to decrease in serious accidents.

Some of the reasons for not wearing a seat belt might include: the right to choose to wear or not, might get trapped in the car, the seat belt will do more damage than the accident.

Discussion should try to center around the effects of the accident rather than a debate on the issue of personal choice. Try to bring in statistics from your local police or automobile association to emphasize the risk of injury or death will always decrease over many different accidents. There are always exceptions to the rule, but the facts are that wearing seat belts will decrease the likelihood of serious injury or death.

2

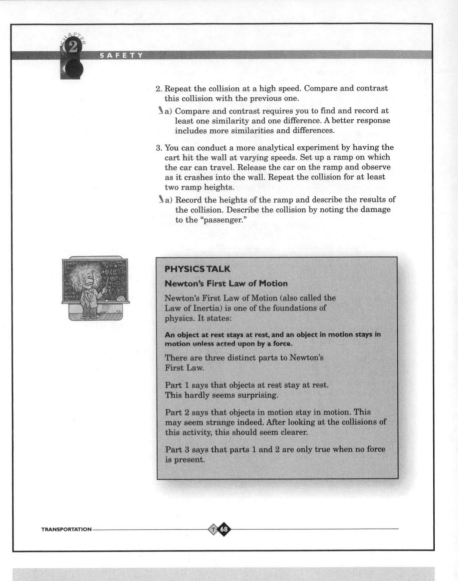

2. Repeat the collision at a high speed. Compare and contrast this collision with the previous one.
   a) Compare and contrast requires you to find and record at least one similarity and one difference. A better response includes more similarities and differences.

3. You can conduct a more analytical experiment by having the cart hit the wall at varying speeds. Set up a ramp on which the car can travel. Release the car on the ramp and observe as it crashes into the wall. Repeat the collision for at least two ramp heights.
   a) Record the heights of the ramp and describe the results of the collision. Describe the collision by noting the damage to the "passenger."

PHYSICS TALK

Newton's First Law of Motion

Newton's First Law of Motion (also called the Law of Inertia) is one of the foundations of physics. It states:

An object at rest stays at rest, and an object in motion stays in motion unless acted upon by a force.

There are three distinct parts to Newton's First Law.

Part 1 says that objects at rest stay at rest. This hardly seems surprising.

Part 2 says that objects in motion stay in motion. This may seem strange indeed. After looking at the collisions of this activity, this should seem clearer.

Part 3 says that parts 1 and 2 are only true when no force is present.

ANSWERS

For You To Do *(continued)*

2. a) The students should note that at a slower speed, the clay model will fall head-first into the front of the cart, or hit the wall with its head. Difference at a high speed would be that the figure will continue moving at approximately the same speed as the cart was moving before the accident. The difference as to why the figure will not continue at exactly the same speed, or that at higher speeds it is more pronounced, is that there is a certain amount of friction between the figure, and the cart. It should be noted also that the greater the speed, the greater damage there is to the figure.

3. a) The higher the ramp, the faster the speed of the cart down the ramp, and the faster the figure will crash into the wall. Therefore, there should continue to be greater damage as the ramp gets higher and higher.

FOR YOU TO READ

Three Collisions in One Accident!

Arthur C. Damask analyzes automobile accidents and deaths for insurance companies and police reports. This is how Professor Damask describes an accident:

Consider the occupants of a conveyance moving at some speed. If the conveyance strikes an object, it will rapidly decelerate to some lower speed or stop entirely; this is called the first collision. But the occupants have been moving at the same speed, and will continue to do so until they are stopped by striking the interior parts of the car (if not ejected); this is the second collision. The brain and body organs have also been moving at the same speed and will continue to do so until they are stopped by colliding with the shell of the body, i.e., the interior of the skull, the thoracic cavity, and the abdominal wall. This is called the third collision.

Newton's First Law of Motion explains the three collisions:

- First collision: the car strikes the pole; the pole exerts the force that brings the car to rest.
- Second collision: when the car stops, the body keeps moving; the structure of the car exerts the force that brings the body to rest.
- Third collision: the body stops, but the heart and brain keep moving; the body wall exerts the force that brings the heart and brain to rest.

Even with all the safety features in our automobiles, some deaths cannot be prevented. In one accident, only a single car was involved, with only the driver inside. The car failed to follow the road around a turn, and it struck a telephone pole. The seat belt and the air bag prevented any serious injuries apart from a few bruises, but the driver died. An autopsy showed that the driver's aorta had burst, at the point where it leaves the heart.

2

ANSWERS

Physics To Go

1. * *You step on the brakes to stop your car.*

You and the car are moving forward. The brakes apply a force to the tires and stop them from rotating. Newton's law states that an object in motion will remain in motion unless a force acts upon it. In this case, the force is friction between the ground and the tires. You remain in motion since the force that stopped the car did not stop you.

* *You step on the accelerator to get going.*

You and the car are stopped. The engine provides a force to turn the wheels, which in turn causes the car to move forward. Inertia will keep you still unless a force acts upon you. This force is provided by the seat back which pushes you forward at the same rate as the car.)

* *You turn the wheel to go around a curve.*

You are moving forward with the car. Your force causes the wheels to turn, the friction of the road on the tires produces the centripetal force necessary to turn the vehicle. Inertia causes you to remain moving in a straight line, where the car (doors, seat belt, seat, etc.) produce the centripetal force to allow you to stay in the car, and move in the curved path. (Review Activity Seven in Chapter 1.)

* *You step on the brakes, and an object in the back of the car comes flying forward.*

The object was moving with the same velocity as the car. The force which caused the car to stop, was not acting on the object. Inertia of the object kept the object moving in a straight path (until it hits the driver or the windshield).

REFLECTING ON THE ACTIVITY AND THE CHALLENGE

In this activity you discovered that an object in motion continues in motion until a force stops it. A car will stop when it hits a pole but the passenger will keep on moving. If the car and passenger have a large speed, then the passenger will continue moving with this large speed. The passenger at the large speed will experience more damage from the fast moving cart.

Have you ever heard someone say that they can prevent an injury by bracing themselves against the crash? They can't! Restraining devices help provide support. Without a restraining system, the force of impact is either absorbed by the rib, skull, or brain.

Use Newton's First Law of motion to describe your design. How will your safety system protect passengers from low speed and higher speed collisions?

PHYSICS TO GO

1. Describe how Newton's First Law applies to the following situations:
   - You step on the brakes to stop your car.

   (Sample answer: You and the car are moving forward. The brakes apply a force to the tires and stop them from rotating. Newton's law states that an object in motion will remain in motion unless a force acts upon it. In this case, the force is friction between the ground and the tires. You remain in motion since the force that stopped the car did not stop you.)

   - You step on the accelerator to get going.
   - You turn the wheel to go around a curve. (Hint: You keep moving in a straight line.)
   - You step on the brakes, and an object in the back of the car comes flying forward.

ACTIVITY TWO: Life (and Death) before Seat Belts

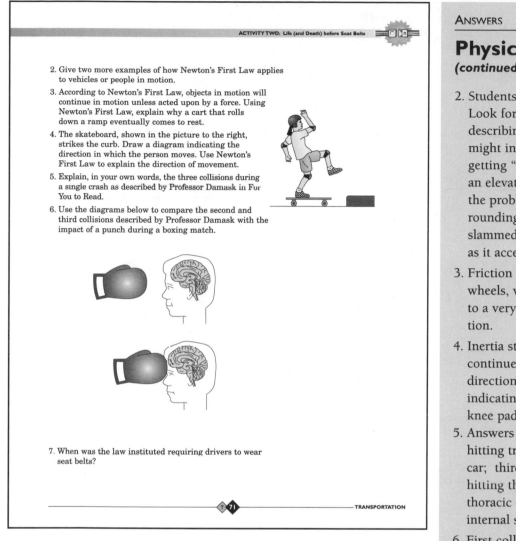

2. Give two more examples of how Newton's First Law applies to vehicles or people in motion.
3. According to Newton's First Law, objects in motion will continue in motion unless acted upon by a force. Using Newton's First Law, explain why a cart that rolls down a ramp eventually comes to rest.
4. The skateboard, shown in the picture to the right, strikes the curb. Draw a diagram indicating the direction in which the person moves. Use Newton's First Law to explain the direction of movement.

5. Explain, in your own words, the three collisions during a single crash as described by Professor Damask in For You to Read.
6. Use the diagrams below to compare the second and third collisions described by Professor Damask with the impact of a punch during a boxing match.

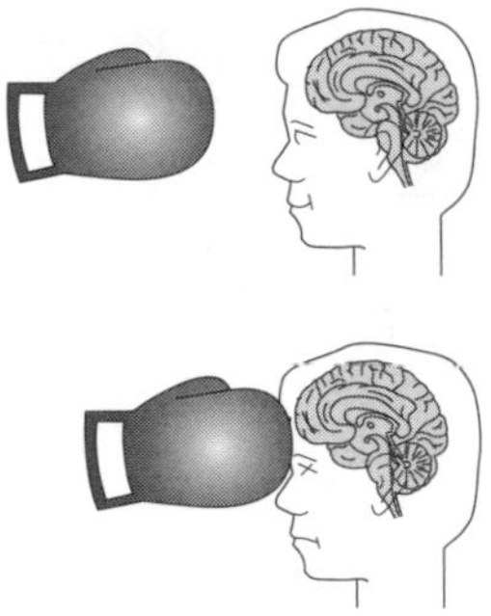

7. When was the law instituted requiring drivers to wear seat belts?

T 71 TRANSPORTATION

ANSWERS

Physics To Go

(continued)

2. Students' answers will vary. Look for sound physics when describing the situation. Some might include, the sensation of getting "heavier" or "lighter" as an elevator starts up or down, the problem of stopping or rounding a curve on ice, being slammed into the seat of a bus, as it accelerates from the stop.
3. Friction between the cart and the wheels, wheels and ground, and to a very small extent the air friction.
4. Inertia states that the person will continue to move in the same direction as the skateboard, thus indicating the need for helmet, knee pads, and gloves!
5. Answers will vary; first: car hitting tree; second: body hitting car; third: internal organs hitting the internal wall of thoracic cavity, or brain hitting internal skull.)
6. First collision: glove hitting head; second collision: head moves backward, and the brain collides with the interior of the skull; third collision: elasticity of the brain attached to the brain stem, causes the brain to move toward the back of the brain colliding with the internal back of the skull.

2

CHAPTER 2 SAFETY

STRETCHING EXERCISE

1. Determine what opinions people in your community hold about the wearing of seat belts. Compare the opinions of the +60 years old and 25 to 59 years old groups with that of the 15 to 24 year old group. Survey at least five people in each age group: Group A = 15 to 24 years, Group B = 25 to 59 years, and Group C = 60 years and older. (Survey the same number of individuals in each age group.) Ask each individual to fill out a survey card.

A sample questionnaire is provided below. You may wish to eliminate any question that you feel is not relevant. You are encouraged to develop questions of your own that help you understand what attitudes people in your community hold about wearing seat belts. The answers have been divided into three categories: 1 = agree; 2 = will accept , but do not hold a strong opinion; and 3 = disagree. Try to keep your survey to between five and ten questions.

Age group:	Date of Survey:		
Statement	Agree	No strong opinion	Disagree
1. I believe people should be fined for not wearing seat belts.	1	2	3
2. I wouldn't wear a seat belt if I didn't have to.	1	2	3
3. People who don't wear seat belts pose a threat to me when they ride in my car.	1	2	3
4. I believe that seat belts save lives.	1	2	3
5. Seat belts wrinkle my clothes and fit poorly so I don't wear them.	1	2	3

2. Make a list of reasons why people refuse to wear seat belts. Can you challenge these opinions using what you have learned about Newton's First Law of Motion?

T 72

Activity Two A

Dropping a Clay Ball to Investigate Inertia

FOR YOU TO DO

1. This could be a messy activity. Place newspaper or other drop cloth on the desks before building the clay balls. Form a ball using 1.0 kg of clay. Using a balance, measure the exact mass of the ball.

a) Record the mass of the ball in your log.

2. Drop the ball from a variety of heights into a hand wearing a baseball glove. Avoid trying to "cushion" the catch, which will ruin the effect of the force of impact. Look away while catching the ball, so you are better able to describe the force qualitatively.

a) In your log record the distance from which the ball was dropped.

b) Describe how the ball felt as it hit the glove when dropped from different heights.

3. The formula for finding the velocity of an object that is falling is:

$v = \sqrt{2gh}$

where $g = 9.81\ m/s^2$,

h is the height from which the ball is released to the glove.

From this formula you can determine the momentum ($m \times \Delta v$) of the object in order to show the increase in the change momentum. Determine the time by averaging the velocities $[(v2 + v1)/2]$, then using that v to find the time in $t = d/v$. Now you can determine the force ($F = m\Delta v/\Delta t$) that is being exerted on their hands as the object is dropped from different heights.

a) Determine the force of the ball for the different heights.

Sample Calculation

Mass of the ball = 1.0 kg; distance from glove to the desk = 1.5 m

- Velocity where $h = 1.5$ m

  $v = \sqrt{2gh}$

  $v = 5.42$ m/s

- Change in Momentum (as the ball goes from the final speed of 5.42 m/s to 0 m/s in the glove)

  $\Delta p = m\Delta v$

  $\Delta p = 5.42$ m/s

- Average velocity

  = (5.42 m/s+ 0 m/s)/2

  = 2.71 m/s

For use with *Transportation*, Chapter 2, ACTIVITY TWO: Life (and Death) before Seat Belts

- Time to stop the ball in 0.10 m

  $t = d/v$

  $t = 0.10 \text{ m}/ 2.71 \text{ m/s}$

  $t = 0.037 \text{ s}$

- Force acting on the glove by the ball

  $F = m\Delta v/\Delta t$

  $F = (1.0 \text{ kg } 5.42 \text{ m/s})/0.037 \text{ s}$

  $F = 146 \text{ N}$

Or about 15 kg (31 lb.) of mass (Every 10 N of force is approximately the equivalent of 1 kg of mass.)

b) What was the speed of the clay ball when dropped from 2.0 m?

c) Estimate what the force might be if the clay ball were dropped from the gym roof (approximate height of 10 m).

If the possibility exists, take the clay ball outside and drop it into a cloth held in a way similar to the firefighters net.

a) The force of an accident can be compared to the forces you felt when you were dropping the ball of clay. Relate your experiences of catching the ball, and how they might compare with the forces that the car and the tree exert on each other during their collision.

4. Make clay balls of various sizes (exact masses are not necessary).

5. Place the balls on the ends of chopsticks so that only the end of the chopsticks is showing, as shown.

6. With the bottom of the chopstick in hand, slam your hand down on the desk. Observe what happens.

a) Why did the clay slide down the chopstick?

b) What stopped the clay once it was moving?

c) What could you do to stop the clay from moving down the chopstick when you hit it on the desktop?

Activity Two B

Life (and Death) Before Seat Belts Part B: Low-Tech Alternative.

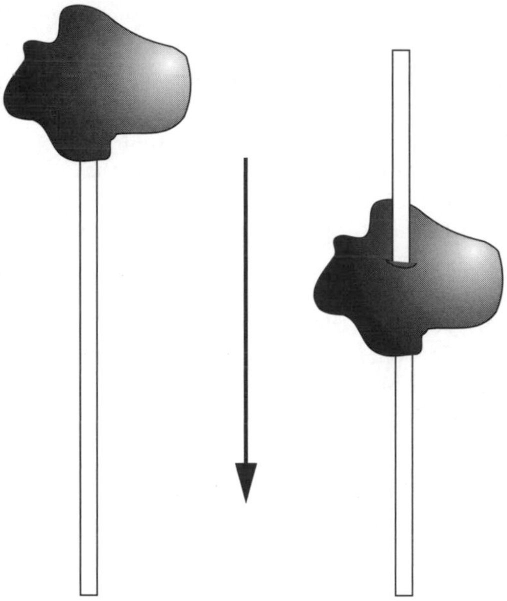

This is a low-tech activity to illustrate Newton's First Law. It is intended to give the students a first hand look at inertia.

Materials needed:

- quantity of play dough or clay
- chopsticks (or similar sticks)

Planning for the Activity

- Students will make clay balls of various sizes (exact masses are not necessary).
- place the balls on the ends of the chopsticks so that only the end of the chopsticks is showing.
- with the bottom of the chopstick in hand, slam your hand down on the desk.
- observe what happens

Time Requirements:

Approximately 30 minutes to complete this activity.

Teaching Notes

As the mass of the ball increases, the students will want to think that the acceleration increases. While the ball appears to accelerate more as it increases its mass, the increases in the mass actually means there is an increase of the force (due to gravity) F_g.

Classroom Management Tips

This could be a messy activity. Remind the students to place newspaper or other drop cloth on the desks before building the clay balls.

Questions:

1. Why did the clay slide down the chopstick?
   A: Inertia of the clay kept the clay moving.
2. What stopped the clay once it was moving?
   A: The friction between the chopstick and the clay?
3. What could you do to stop the clay from moving down the chopstick, when you hit it on the desktop?
   A. Answers will vary. Look for something like seat belts or stops of some kind on the chopstick. Some may say change the friction between the clay and the chopstick (fire it in an oven to harden it), but we are looking for an application to be able to relate it to a moving car.

For use with *Transportation*, Chapter 2, ACTIVITY TWO: Life (and Death) before Seat Belts

ACTIVITY THREE
Life (and Fewer Deaths) after Seat Belts

Background Information

Inertia is the tendency for an object to stay in motion. In order to stop that motion, there must be a force applied to that object in order to accelerate the object or change its velocity to 0 m/s ($a = \Delta v/\Delta t = v_2 - v_1/\Delta t$). For example, for an object moving at 3.0 m/s, is brought to 0 m/s in 1.0 s

$$a = \Delta v/\Delta t$$

$$a = v_2 - v_1/\Delta t$$

$$a = (0 \text{ m/s} - 3.0 \text{ m/s}) / 1.0 \text{ s}$$

$$a = -3.0 \text{ m/s}^2$$

Note that this is a negative acceleration, which we often refer to as deceleration. For the purposes of this course, we will refer to slowing down and speeding up as acceleration. There will be references to negative and positive acceleration.

Newton's Second Law of Motion gives a mathematical understanding of forces and acceleration -- i.e.: changing velocity.

Symbols
v = velocity (m/s)
d = distance (m)
t = time (s)
a = acceleration (m/s)
F = force (N)
m = mass (kg)
Δ = change

Newton's Second Law states that the acceleration of an object is proportional to the force in the same direction, and inversely proportional to the mass.

$$a \quad F$$

$$a \quad 1/m$$

Therefore we can state this proportion as $a = F/m$, or as it is commonly known as $F = ma$.

If you have a wooden crate with nothing in it, it is very easy to push (apply a force to) the box. The empty crate is also very easy (or requires a smaller force) to stop. However, increasing the mass in the box, it becomes increasing difficult to push the box. This is caused by the increase in the inertia of the box. As well, it is very difficult (or requires a larger force) to stop the box.

Newton, after showing that forces cause objects to move (accelerate) asked himself where do these forces come from. This led to his third law, where forces come from other objects. Your hand pushing on a desk exerts a force on the desk. You can see, also that there must be a force acting on your hand because you can see the deformation of the "dent". Also, by applying more force, you realize that it hurts. Therefore, the only conclusion can be that the desk must be exerting a force on your hand. Newton's Third Law of Motion states that whenever an objects exerts a force on another object, the second object exerts a force equal in magnitude, but opposite in direction, on the first object. These are dealt with as action-reaction pairs. There can never be one force on an object without an equal but opposite force on the other

Therefore, your inertia will keep you moving in a straight line unless a force stops your motion. The force comes when your body comes in contact with the seat belt. This net force is enough to accelerate you to a stop.

In the previous activity the students examined the acceleration of a vehicle while stopping in a collision. In this activity, the students are manipulating the restraining device to give different pressures, without changing the forces. The physics involved with this activity is the understanding of how the pressure changes as you increase the area of the restraining device. The pressure is the force per unit area of the contact with the body. They will discover that the greater the area of contact, the more the force is spread out over the body.

$$P = F/A.$$

Therefore, even if the force is great (due to a large acceleration), the pressure on the individual will be much less.

Active-ating the Physics InfoMall

This activity has much in common with Activity Two. So perform searches that will find something new, and perhaps interesting. For example, see what the InfoMall says about crash dummies. One method is to search for "crash"" AND "dumm*", where we are using AND to mean the logical operation (returns hits that contains both search keywords) and the asterisk (wild character). The first hit is "Forensic physics of vehicle accidents," *Physics Today*, vol. 40, issue 3, (1987). You may wish to look this one up yourself.

Another suggestion is to search for "bed of nails". Try it out.

And if you want more problems for your students, don't forget the Problems Place! You can easily find many, many problems about pressure.

Planning for the Activity

Time Requirements

Allow approximately 40 minutes to complete this activity and record the data.

Materials needed

For each group:

- laboratory cart
- modeling clay, baseball size
- concrete block or other suitable barriers
- starting ramp
- wire, approx. 25 cm length
- various widths of ribbon, tape, approx. 25 cm length

For the class:

- *Active Physics Transportation* Content Video (Segment: Crash Dummy)
- VCR & TV monitor

Advance Preparation and Setup

Prepare as you did for the previous Activity. Have several different types of material, as well as large quantities of each available.

Teaching Notes

Students find that the wire will cut more deeply, and that more, thicker supports will do the least damage. In debriefing, emphasis should still be on the fact that even at high speeds, three-point seat belts may still not save lives. There is lots of discussion that can come from this, especially when referring back to the chapter challenge. Again, the emphasis will be on decreasing the force that is exerted on the body by spreading out the force which occurs while the vehicle is stopping. The same force will occur if the body is stopped. The idea of having fatter seat belts is that the greater surface area of the belt allows for a smaller pressure.

As with any activity, a review of proper decorum in the classroom should be warranted. Students may use the clay to throw around the room. If the students are to complete the survey (Question #7 in Physics To Go) they need to have permission to survey other students, or parents. This is a good activity to have the students survey more than immediately around the school. Give them the assignment of surveying some members of their community.

Please note that students may still have the misconception that the forces exerted on the seat belts are not that significant. See the additional activity following Activity Two.

2

NOTES

Activity Three

Life (and Fewer Deaths) after Seat Belts

WHAT DO YOU THINK?

In a collision, you cannot brace yourself and prevent injuries. Your arms and legs are not strong enough to overcome the inertia during even a minor collision. Instead of thinking about stopping yourself when the car is going 30 mph, think about catching 10 bowling balls hurtling towards you at 30 mph. The two situations are equivalent.

- **Suppose you had to design seat belts for a race car that can go 200 mph. How would they be different from the ones available on passenger cars?**

Record your ideas about this question in your *Active Physics log*. Be prepared to discuss your responses with your small group and the class.

Activity Overview

In this activity the students will be investigating the role and requirements of an effective restraint system. They will be simulating different styles of safety belts, and submitting their model to crash simulations as in Activity Two.

Student Objectives

Students will:

- understand the role of safety belts.
- compare the effectiveness of various wide and narrow belts.
- relate pressure, force and area.

ANSWERS FOR THE TEACHER ONLY

What Do You Think?

If you can, go to see the IMAX film *Speedway*. The film talks about how the race cars have changed in the past few decades. Because the speeds are greater than they were, they can no longer build the cars like tiny missiles, which do not crush. They have found, as was mentioned above, that the crush zone allows some of the energy of the collision to be absorbed by the car, rather than the driver. Even in well-protected cars, equipped with shoulder belts, air bags, and padded interiors, if the body of the driver is stopped at certain accelerations, the damage to the interior of the body may be fatal.

Most of the answers the students will come up with will be centered on more of what is already in the vehicle. However, the answers should reflect the idea that the faster you go, the greater protection you will need. Also in the discussion, you can emphasize that it is not only more padding, but rather the reduction of the forces, which will be talked about in this activity. In other words, the stopping from high speeds, into a tree, or the front of your dashboard can be equally dangerous with a tight seat belt on, to the interior organs of the body.

2

FOR YOU TO DO

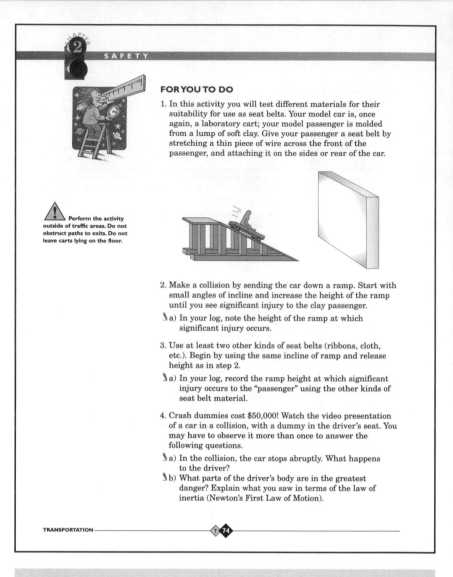

1. In this activity you will test different materials for their suitability for use as seat belts. Your model car is, once again, a laboratory cart; your model passenger is molded from a lump of soft clay. Give your passenger a seat belt by stretching a thin piece of wire across the front of the passenger, and attaching it on the sides or rear of the car.

Perform the activity outside of traffic areas. Do not obstruct paths to exits. Do not leave carts lying on the floor.

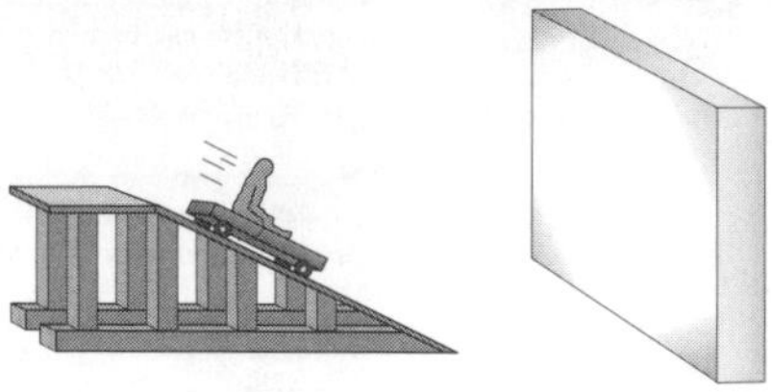

2. Make a collision by sending the car down a ramp. Start with small angles of incline and increase the height of the ramp until you see significant injury to the clay passenger.
   a) In your log, note the height of the ramp at which significant injury occurs.

3. Use at least two other kinds of seat belts (ribbons, cloth, etc.). Begin by using the same incline of ramp and release height as in step 2.
   a) In your log, record the ramp height at which significant injury occurs to the "passenger" using the other kinds of seat belt material.

4. Crash dummies cost $50,000! Watch the video presentation of a car in a collision, with a dummy in the driver's seat. You may have to observe it more than once to answer the following questions.
   a) In the collision, the car stops abruptly. What happens to the driver?
   b) What parts of the driver's body are in the greatest danger? Explain what you saw in terms of the law of inertia (Newton's First Law of Motion).

ANSWERS

For You To Do

1. Student activity.

2.a) Students' responses, but as the height of the ramp is increased, there should be an increase in the significant damage.

3.a) Students' responses.

4.a) The driver continues to move in the direction of the car (inertia) until stopped by the seat belt, (or dashboard).

b) The head is probably in the most danger as it is not secured by anything. In terms of the Law of Inertia, as the car stops, the body continues to move. As the body stops, by the seat belt, the head continues to move. This is where damage can occur and usually happens.

FOR YOU TO READ

Force and Pressure

When you repeated this experiment accurately each time, the force that each belt exerted on the clay was the same each time that the car was started at the same ramp height. Yet different materials have different effects; for example, a wire cuts far more deeply into the clay than a broader material does.

The force that each of the belts exerts on the clay is the same. When a thin wire is used, all the force is concentrated onto a small area. By replacing the wire with a broader material, you spread the force out over a much larger area of contact.

The force per unit area, which is called pressure, is much smaller with a ribbon, for example, than with a wire. It is the pressure, not the force, that determines how much damage the seat belt does to the body. A force applied to a single rib might be enough to break a rib. If the same force is spread out over many ribs, the force on each rib can be made too small to do any damage. While the total force does not change, the pressure becomes much smaller.

PHYSICS TALK

Pressure is the force per unit area:

$$P = F/A$$

where F represents force, measured in newtons (N); A represents area, determined in meters squared (m^2); and P is pressure calculated in newtons per meter squared (N/m^2).

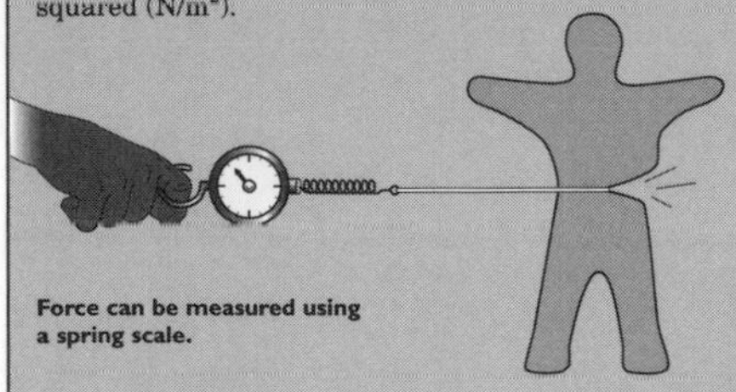

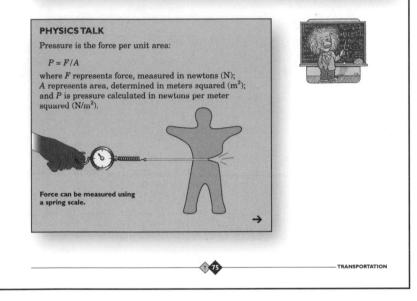

Force can be measured using a spring scale.

→

Example

Why does the boy without snow shoes sink into the snow? The relationship between force and area can be expressed as pressure. Because both boys have the same mass, a constant force of 450 N is applied to the snow. The first boy, wearing snow shoes, stands on a much wider base (2.0 m^2), while the second boy has a much smaller base (0.1 m^2).

Boy A Pressure = $\frac{\text{Force}}{\text{Area}}$ Boy B Pressure = $\frac{\text{Force}}{\text{Area}}$

$P = \frac{450\ N}{2.0\ m^2}$ $P = \frac{450\ N}{0.1\ m^2}$

$P = 225\ N/m^2$ $P = 4500\ N/m^2$

REFLECTING ON THE ACTIVITY

In this activity you gathered data to provide evidence on the effectiveness of seat belts as restraint systems. The material used for the seat belt and the width of the restraint affected the distortion of the clay figure. By applying the force over a greater area, the pressure exerted by the seat belt during the collision can be reduced.

It is important to note that not every safety restraint system will be a seat belt or harness, but that all restraints attempt to reduce the pressure exerted on an object by increasing the area over which a force is applied.

How will your design team account for decreasing pressure by increasing the area of impact? Think about ways that you could test your design prototype for the pressure created during impact. Your presentation of the design will be much more convincing if you have quantitative data to support your claims. Simply stating that a safety system works well is not as convincing as being able to show how it reduces pressure during a collision.

PHYSICS TO GO

1. Use Newton's First Law to describe a collision with the passenger wearing a seat belt during a collision.
2. What is the pressure exerted when a force of 10 N is applied to an object that has an area of
   a) 1.0 m^2?
   b) 0.2 m^2?
   c) 15 m^2?
   d) 400 cm^2?
3. A person who weights approximately 155 lb. exerts 700 N of force on the ground while standing. If his shoes cover an area of 400 cm^2 (0.0400 m^2), calculate:
   a) the average pressure his shoes exert on the ground.
   b) the pressure he would exert by standing on one foot.

ANSWERS

Physics To Go

1. The car is moving in a given direction. As the car stops, the driver or passenger continues to move forward until the seat belt stops them -- a force acts on the body to change the motion from moving relative to the car to stopping with the car. Parts of the body, not directly attached to the seat belt, will continue also to move in the given direction. This is where significant damage to the body, mostly the head, can occur.

2. a) 1.0 m^2

   Using formula $P = F/A$,
   $P = 10$ N/ 1.0 m^2 therefore
   $P = 10$ N/m^2)

   b) 0.2 m^2

   $P = 50$ N/m^2

   c) 15 m^2

   $P = 0.67$ N/m^2

   d) 400 cm^2

   $P = 0.025$ N/cm^2 or 250 N/cm^2

3. a) 17,500 N/cm^2

   b) Double the pressure or 35,000 N/cm^2

2

ANSWERS

Physics To Go
(continued)

4. a) Using approximate values, of weight of 500 Newtons, and area of high heels about 1 cm^2, the $P = F/A$, = 500 N/ 0.0001 m^2, P = 5,000 000 N/m^2

   b) Using approximate values, of weight of 500 N, and area of your hands of about 900 cm^2, the $P = F/A$, = 500 N/ 0.09 m^2, P = 5,555 N/m^2

   c) If your body was about 500 N, and there were 5,000 nails, then there is approximately 500 N / 5,000 nails, or 0.1 N per nail of pressure. In reality, that is probably less the weight of one nail, and if you were to support one nail on your finger it would not penetrate.

5. The force is identical, but on a smaller surface area. Therefore the pressure exerted on your body is greater. It would be enough to cut your body in two pieces.

6. Students answers will vary. Answers might include people who don't use seat belts may end up having greater injuries, therefore increasing the cost of health care, they may lose control of their vehicle more easily, therefore causing more damage to their own vehicle or others. Have the students explore the concept of social responsibility. What constitutes the need for any law? How does the use or lack of use of safety restraints affect us as a society? How do economics affect the passing of legislation in this area?

7. Have students try to survey more people, and not simply their immediate family.

4. For comparison purposes, calculate the pressure you exert in the situations described below. Divide your weight in newtons, by the area of your shoes. (To find your weight in newtons multiply your weight in pounds by 4.5 N/lb. You can approximate the area of your shoes by tracing the soles on a sheet of centimeter squared paper.)
   a) How much pressure would you exert if you were standing in high heels?
   b) How much pressure would you exert while standing on your hands?
   c) If a bed of nails contains 5000 nails per square meter, how much force would one nail support if you were to lie on the bed? With this calculation you can now explain how people are able to lie on a bed of nails. It's just physics!
5. Describe why a wire seat belt would not be effective even though the force exerted on you by the wire seat belt is identical to that of a cloth seat belt.
6. Do you think there ought to be seat belt laws? How does not using seat belts affect the society as a whole?
7. Conduct a survey of 10 people. Ask each person what percentage of the time they wear a seat belt while in a car. Be prepared to share your data with the class.

STRETCHING EXERCISES

The pressure exerted on your clay model by a thin wire can be estimated quite easily. Loop the wire around the "passenger," and connect the wire to a force meter.

a) Pull the force meter hard enough to make the wire sink into the model just about as far as it did in the collision.
b) Record the force as shown on the force meter (in newtons).
c) Estimate the frontal area of the wire—its diameter times the length of the wire that contacts the passenger. Record this value in centimeters squared (cm^2).
d) Divide the force by the area. This is the pressure in newtons per centimeter squared (N/cm^2).

NOTES

2

Assessment: Activity Three

Place a check mark in the appropriate box. Two check marks will be required for one point.
A sample conversion scale is provided below the chart.
Total marks = 10.

Descriptor	Yes	No
Lab Skills		
understands the need to control variables		
knows the manipulated variable		
is able to construct reasonable seat belts		
uses more than two types of materials in constructing seat belts		
uses appropriate materials in constructing seat belts		
runs at least three trials with each model of seat belt		
demonstrates or explains why there is a need for several trials		
rebuilds model as necessary		
Understanding Concepts		
demonstrates understanding of forces		
demonstrates understanding of pressure		
knows which parts of the body are most vulnerable in a collision		
demonstrates an understanding for seat belt laws		
is able to describe a collision of a person with and without a seat belt		
understands the societal impact of using a seat belt		
understands the societal impact of not using a seat belt		
Mathematical Skills		
can calculate the force per unit area (pressure)		
calculates the pressure of the wire		
calculates the pressure of their own weight on their shoes		

Conversion

20 check marks = 10 points
18 check marks = 9 points
16+check marks = 8 points, etc.

For use with *Transportation*, Chapter 2, ACTIVITY THREE: Life (and fewer Deaths) after Seat Belts

NOTES

ACTIVITY FOUR
Why Air Bags?

Background Information

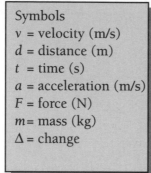

Symbols
v = velocity (m/s)
d = distance (m)
t = time (s)
a = acceleration (m/s)
F = force (N)
m = mass (kg)
Δ = change

Now that we have dealt with forces, how does this have anything to do with accidents? In order to examine accidents, we must first look at momentum. Momentum (p) is the product of the mass (m) of an object and the velocity (v) of that object ($p=mv$). Ask the students which is harder to stop, the 175 pound (80 kg) quarterback running at 4 m/s, or the fullback at 255 pounds (116 kg) running at 4 m/s? Most students will say that the quarterback would be easier to stop. We would say that the momentum of the quarterback is less (m x v) than the fullback (m x v)

momentum of quarterback

$p_{qb} = m \text{ x } v$

p_{qb} = (80 kg) x (4 m/s)

p_{qb} = 320 kg.m/s/s

momentum of fullback

$p_{fb} = m \text{ x } v$

p_{fb} = (116 kg) x (4 m/s)

p_{fb} = 464 kg.m/s/s

We can summarize momentum by stating that the greater the momentum of an object, the harder it will be to stop.

According to Newton's First Law – Inertia, an object in motion will remain in motion unless acted upon by an outside, unbalanced force. Therefore, to stop a moving object (the fullback), we need a force. Newton's Second Law

$F = ma$

states that the acceleration (or change in velocity) will be proportional to the force. Since acceleration is the change in velocity divided by the change in time, we can restate Newton's equation as

$$F = m\ \Delta v/\Delta t.$$

Remove Δt by multiplying both sides by Δt and we now have

$$F\Delta t = m\Delta v.$$

called the impulse (measured in Ns). Impulse is the product of the force applied and the change in time over which the force acted. In other words the force times the time interval is proportional to the change in velocity times the mass.

Therefore, (where $p = mv$)

$$\Delta p = m\Delta v,\ \ [\Delta p = m\ (v_2 - v_1)]$$

or the change in momentum is equal to the mass times the change in velocity.

Substituting Δp for $m\Delta v$ in $F\Delta t = m\Delta v$, we get

$$F\Delta t = \Delta p$$

Therefore we get impulse is equal to the change in momentum. As we analyze the equation, we see that in order to stop an object (change its momentum to zero), there must be a force applied to the object over a particular time. Increasing the time decreases the force and decreasing the time increases the force required to change the same momentum. For example: A bowling ball (m = 16 pounds or 7.3 kg) moving at 5.0 m/s. What is the impulse to stop the bowling ball?

impulse = $\Delta p = m\Delta v$

Δp = 7.3 kg x 5.0 m/s

Δp = 36.5 kg.m/s

Therefore, what is the force required to bring the bowling ball to rest in 1.0 s?

Impulse = Δp, therefore $F\Delta t = \Delta p$, therefore

$F = \Delta p/\Delta t$

F = 36.5 kg.m/s / 1.0s

F = 36.5 kg.m/s^2 or 36.5 N

How much force is then needed to bring the ball to rest in 3.0 s?

F = 36.5 kg.m/s / 3.0 s

F = 12.2 N

How much force is then needed to bring the ball to rest in 0.10 s?

$F = 36.5\ \text{kg.m/s} / 0.10\ \text{s}$

$F = 365\ \text{N}$

You can see as you increase the time needed to stop an object, you decrease the force necessary. As the time decreases, the force increases.

The physics of the air bag is to increase the time required for the object (the driver) to stop, and therefore reduce the force on the driver. The other aspect for which the air bag is designed is that the force, even though decreased, is spread over a larger area. The face slamming into the steering wheel can cause a lot of damage, as compared with the face slamming into an air bag.

Active-ating the Physics InfoMall

Search for "air bag*" and you will not be disappointed. There are several good comments made in various places on the InfoMall, including "Resource letter PE-1: Physics and the environment," *American Journal of Physics*, vol. 42, 267-273 (1974), and "How Things Work" in the Book Basement has a section on air bags (in the 1985 section).

The concept of impulse is introduced in this activity. Searching for "impulse" on the InfoMall provides many great references, including problems your you or your students to work. The textbook *Physics Including Human Applications* has a chapter devoted to Momentum and Impulse (momentum comes up in Activities Six and Eight, especially as it relates to impulse).

Planning for the Activity

Time Requirements

Allow at least one period for the students to design and run the tests on the air bag. If a video camera is used the students may want to take it home to analyze. If there are not enough video cameras to go around, then rotate through the groups, with the other groups analyzing the data they have collected, while the other students may be watching a video, or redesigning their air bags.

Materials needed

For each group:

- camcorder on tripod
- VCR having single-frame advanced mode
- video monitor
- inflatable beach ball or strong garbage bag
- heavy object (rock or coconut)
- landing surface materials having varying hardness (3).

Advance Preparation and Setup

Depending on the material available, you may need to make the equivalent of several different substances to test against the air bag model.

Check proper functioning of the recording device. The VCR must be able to give a clear picture on single frame advance mode. If the students are to use the tape times, they may need additional instructions if they have not used them before. If you are going to use computer software, which digitizes the video, and then allows you to analyze the picture, prior use or training with the software would be an asset, both for the students and the teacher. If there is not enough software, and hardware for all students to use, then a demo would be beneficial to set up for the students in order for them to have a standard to shoot for.

2

Teaching Notes

Air bags are becoming more and more common in vehicles. Poll the students as to whether their family cars have air bags. Ask if they are willing to pay the extra money for them. Have them write the answers in their log books.

Remind the students how to make measurements using the videotape system. Encourage experimentation that includes various impact speeds and different stopping surfaces. If tape timers are to be used review the time interval specifications. Measurements of distances are not necessary; only counting the intervals between when the object touches the bag and when the object stops in order to get the stopping time. When using the tape timer, it may be difficult at first to get good results. Be prepared to use a lot of tape in getting accurate results.

There may be video tapes available which show slow motion air bags actually working. These may be available from your local automobile association, or from a car dealership.

Students should work in groups of three or four. Students will be dropping heavy objects onto surfaces which may cause the object to bounce in different and unpredictable directions, and therefore, should take appropriate precautions to prevent injury to damage to property.

Some students may have heard that air bags have caused suffocation once they inflated. This is an incorrect understanding of how the air bag works. The air bag inflates in about 1/32 of a second, and once inflated, it deflates after about one to two seconds. Other fallacies about air bags are that they impair your ability to see, and they inhibit you from exiting the vehicle. (For more information, visit any car dealer and ask for their information on air bags.) While there is some smoke and dust from the CO_2 cartridge, and some heat associated with the inflation of the airbag, it will not impair your ability to get out of the vehicle. The effectiveness of the air bag increases in conjunction with the seat and shoulder belts, but is not very effective in side impacts.

Local automotive dealers will have safety videos about air bags and ABS brakes. Many dealers will lend them, or may even give a copy to you.

You may also use the local Automobile Association affiliate in your area to give or lend safety videos. Some will even send instructors to give safety talks.

Some local driving companies (taxi, trucking, courier services) may also have safety supervisors who would be able to come to the classroom and talk about safety.

The *Active Physics Transportation* Content Video has excellent footage showing air bags inflating.

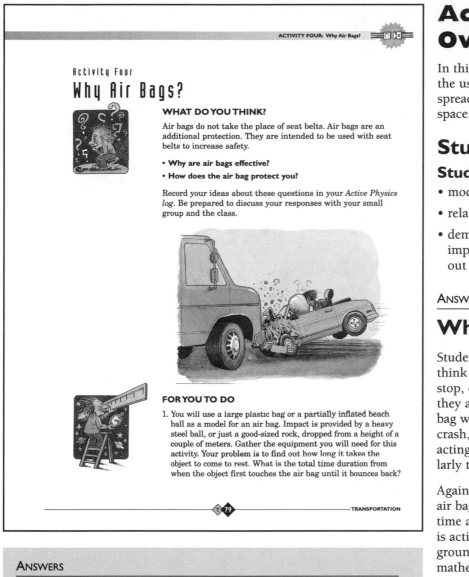

ACTIVITY FOUR: Why Air Bags?

Activity Four

Why Air Bags?

WHAT DO YOU THINK?

Air bags do not take the place of seat belts. Air bags are an additional protection. They are intended to be used with seat belts to increase safety.

- **Why are air bags effective?**
- **How does the air bag protect you?**

Record your ideas about these questions in your *Active Physics log*. Be prepared to discuss your responses with your small group and the class.

FOR YOU TO DO

1. You will use a large plastic bag or a partially inflated beach ball as a model for an air bag. Impact is provided by a heavy steel ball, or just a good-sized rock, dropped from a height of a couple of meters. Gather the equipment you will need for this activity. Your problem is to find out how long it takes the object to come to rest. What is the total time duration from when the object first touches the air bag until it bounces back?

ANSWERS

For You To Do

1. Student activity.

Activity Overview

In this lesson the students will study the use of an air bag and how it will spread the force of the impact over both space and time.

Student Objectives

Students will:

- model an automobile air bag.
- relate pressure to force and area.
- demonstrate that the force of an impact can be reduced by spreading it out over a longer time.

ANSWERS FOR THE TEACHER ONLY

What Do You Think?

Students' answers will vary. Some may think of the air bag as cushioning the stop, or making the stop softer. What they are actually saying, is that the air bag will increase the time in which you crash, therefore decreasing the force acting on your body (or more particularly the head).

Again, students' answers will vary. The air bag protects you by increasing the time and the space over which the force is acting on your body. See the background information for details and the mathematics behind the air bag.

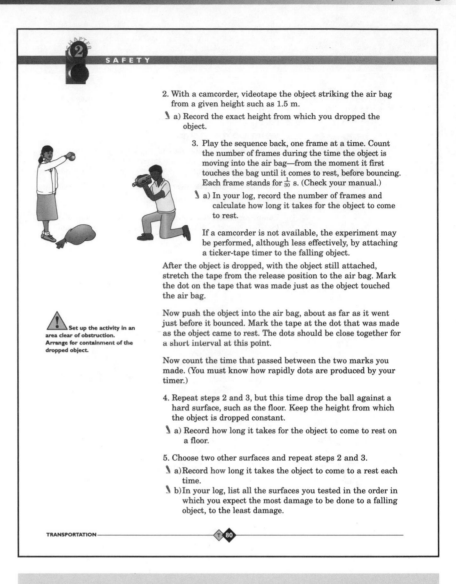

2. With a camcorder, videotape the object striking the air bag from a given height such as 1.5 m.
   a) Record the exact height from which you dropped the object.

3. Play the sequence back, one frame at a time. Count the number of frames during the time the object is moving into the air bag—from the moment it first touches the bag until it comes to rest, before bouncing. Each frame stands for $\frac{1}{30}$ s. (Check your manual.)
   a) In your log, record the number of frames and calculate how long it takes for the object to come to rest.

If a camcorder is not available, the experiment may be performed, although less effectively, by attaching a ticker-tape timer to the falling object.

After the object is dropped, with the object still attached, stretch the tape from the release position to the air bag. Mark the dot on the tape that was made just as the object touched the air bag.

Now push the object into the air bag, about as far as it went just before it bounced. Mark the tape at the dot that was made as the object came to rest. The dots should be close together for a short interval at this point.

Now count the time that passed between the two marks you made. (You must know how rapidly dots are produced by your timer.)

Set up the activity in an area clear of obstruction. Arrange for containment of the dropped object.

4. Repeat steps 2 and 3, but this time drop the ball against a hard surface, such as the floor. Keep the height from which the object is dropped constant.
   a) Record how long it takes for the object to come to rest on a floor.

5. Choose two other surfaces and repeat steps 2 and 3.
   a) Record how long it takes the object to come to a rest each time.
   b) In your log, list all the surfaces you tested in the order in which you expect the most damage to be done to a falling object, to the least damage.

ANSWERS

For You To Do *(continued)*

2. a) Students' response.

3. a) This may vary, with the camcorder. Most are 1/30 s. Students will be noticing, that the greater the time to stop, the less potential damage will be done.

4. a) Students' response. Again the students should be noticing that the greater the time to stop, the less damage will be done.

5. a) Students' response. The harder the surface, the less time, and potentially the greater damage done.
   b) Students' response. This will vary with the types of materials each group uses.

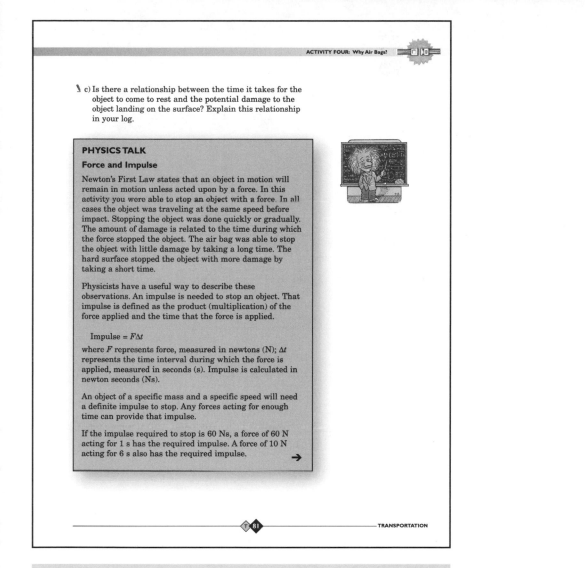

c) Is there a relationship between the time it takes for the object to come to rest and the potential damage to the object landing on the surface? Explain this relationship in your log.

PHYSICS TALK

Force and Impulse

Newton's First Law states that an object in motion will remain in motion unless acted upon by a force. In this activity you were able to stop an object with a force. In all cases the object was traveling at the same speed before impact. Stopping the object was done quickly or gradually. The amount of damage is related to the time during which the force stopped the object. The air bag was able to stop the object with little damage by taking a long time. The hard surface stopped the object with more damage by taking a short time.

Physicists have a useful way to describe these observations. An impulse is needed to stop an object. That impulse is defined as the product (multiplication) of the force applied and the time that the force is applied.

$$\text{Impulse} = F\Delta t$$

where F represents force, measured in newtons (N); Δt represents the time interval during which the force is applied, measured in seconds (s). Impulse is calculated in newton seconds (Ns).

An object of a specific mass and a specific speed will need a definite impulse to stop. Any forces acting for enough time can provide that impulse.

If the impulse required to stop is 60 Ns, a force of 60 N acting for 1 s has the required impulse. A force of 10 N acting for 6 s also has the required impulse. →

ANSWERS

For You To Do *(continued)*

5. c) Students' response. Again, the longer it takes the object to stop, the less damage will be done to the object.

ANSWER

Physics To Go

1. Any combination of F (e.g., 30 N) multiplied by Δt (e.g. 2 s) which give a result of 60 Ns.
2. $\Delta p = F\Delta t$, therefore, $F = \Delta p/\Delta t$,
   a) F = 1000 Ns / 0.01 s, F = 100 000 N;
   b) F = 1000 Ns / 0.1 s, F = 10 000 N;
   c) F = 1000 Ns / 1.0 s, F = 1000 N;
3. When a car stops, there is an impulse (change in the momentum). This impulse ($F\Delta t$) will be transferred to the body in the car as the body's change in momentum is the same. Therefore, the air bag changes the force being applied to the body by increasing the time that the body is slowing down because the impulse does not change.
4. Hitting a brick wall will cause greater damage, as the time that the car stops is smaller, therefore the force is greater than the car hitting a snow bank.

Force F	Time Interval Δt	Impulse $F\Delta t$
60 N	1 s	60 Ns
10 N	6 s	60 Ns
6000 N	0.01 s	60 Ns

The greater the force and the smaller the time interval, the greater the damage that is done.

REFLECTING ON THE ACTIVITY AND THE CHALLENGE

People once believed that the heavier the automobile, the greater the protection it offered passengers. Although a heavy, rigid car may not bend as easily as an automobile with a lighter frame, it doesn't always offer more protection.

In this activity, you found that air bags are able to protect you by extending the time it takes to stop you. Without the air bags, you will hit something and stop in a brief time. This will require a large force, large enough to injure you. With the air bag, the time to stop is longer and the force required is therefore smaller.

Force and impulse must be considered in designing your safety system. Stopping an object gradually reduces damage. The harder a surface, the shorter the stopping distance and the greater the damage. In part this provides a clue to the use of padded dashboards and sun visors in newer cars. Understanding impulse allows designers to reduce damage both to cars and passengers.

PHYSICS TO GO

1. If an impulse of 60 Ns is required to stop an object, list in your log three force and time combinations (other than those given in the Physics Talk) that can stop an object.
2. A person weighing 130 lb. (60 kg) traveling at 40 mph (18 m/s) requires an impulse of approximately 1000 Ns to stop. Calculate the force on the person if the time to stop is
   a) 0.01 s
   b) 0.1 s
   c) 1 s
3. Explain in your log why an air bag is effective. Use the terms force, impulse, and time in your response.
4. Explain in your log why a car hitting a brick wall will suffer more damage than a car hitting a snow bank.
5. There are several other safety designs that employ the concept of spreading out the time interval of a force. Describe in your log how the ones listed below perform this task:
   a) the bumper;
   b) a collapsible steering wheel;
   c) frontal "crush" zones;
   d) padding on the dashboard.
6. There are many other situations in which the force of an impulse is reduced by spreading it out over a longer time. Explain in your log how each of the actions below effectively reduces the force by increasing the time. Use the terms force, impulse, and time in your response.
   a) catching a hard ball;
   b) jumping to the ground from a height;
   c) bungee jumping;
   d) a fireman's net.
7. The speed of airplanes is considerably higher than the speed of automobiles. How might the design of a seat belt for an airplane reflect the fact that a greater impulse is exerted on a plane when it stops?
8. Airplanes have seat belts. Should they also have air bags?

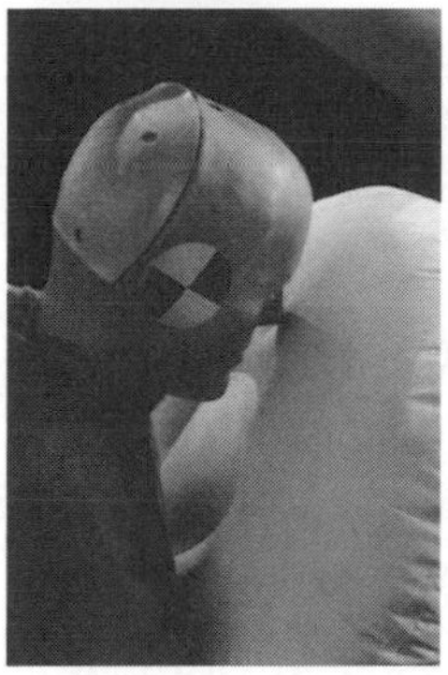

ANSWERS

Physics To Go

(continued)

5. a) The bumper might be mounted on a piston or a spring which will compress when the bumper strikes an object. Even without a spring or piston, the bumper can dent before the rigid frame of the car strikes the object.

   b) The collapsible steering wheel breaks upon impact. Rather than impaling the driver's body on the rigid shaft, the steering column telescopes in, lengthening the time of the impact.

   c) The crush or crumple zones allow the car to compress like an accordion. Previously, the sheet metal parts of the car were welded continuously along the seams, conveying the impact from object to occupants. Now the crumpling of the car increases the time after the front of the car hits until the rest of the car stops.

   d) The padding is not rigid, so as a body hits it, it crushes, lengthening the time for the impulse to be delivered.

6. a) When you catch a hard ball, you use a mitt and you do not hold your arms rigid. The mitt is cushioned and the leather webbing stretches. Your flexed arms ride with the ball. All of this lengthens the time of the impulse, reducing the required force.

   b) When you land on the ground you allow your knees to bend, lengthening the time for your body to come to rest, reducing the required force that will stop your movement.

   c) The bungee cord exerts a force stopping your fall as it stretches. By the time it is fully extended, your speed should be reduced enough so that the jerk of the stop is neither sudden nor severe. The impulse received from the bungee acts over a long period of time.

   d) The net stretches, allowing the victim to stop gradually. The force is the same as if the victim had landed on the ground, but much less destruction since the impulse is less, (due to increased time).

7. Due to the higher speed, the design of a seat belt for the airplane might be similar to the four-point belt that is used by fighter pilots, and race car drivers.

8. Air bags might be a very effective, but expensive, safety feature in a passenger plane. This is especially so because of the absence of a shoulder strap. One could argue that the seat in front of the passenger is not rigid, and acts as a modified air bag.

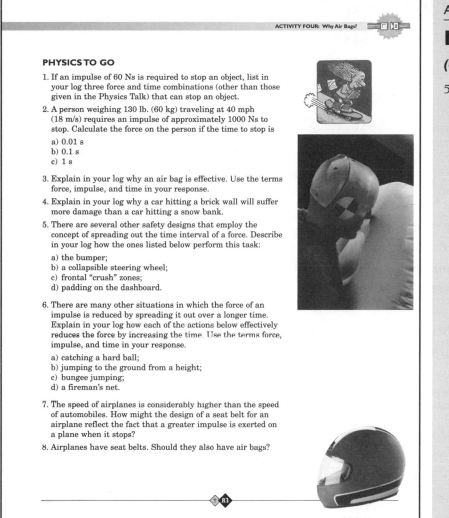

Assessment: Activity Four

Place a checkmark in the appropriate box. Two checkmarks will be required for one point. A sample conversion scale is provided below the chart.

Maximum = 10

Descriptor	Yes	No
Lab Skills		
student understands the need to control variables		
student is able to identify the manipulated variable		
student is able to identify the responding variable		
student is able to accurately record the time required to stop		
student uses more than 2 types of materials in constructing air bags		
student uses appropriate materials in constructing air bags		
student runs at least 3 trials with each model of air bag		
student demonstrates or explains why there is a need for several trials		
student tested at least 3 different surfaces		
Understanding Concepts		
student demonstrates understanding of forces and effects of air bags		
student demonstrates understanding of pressure		
student understands how the air bag inflates		
student relates inertia with the forces an air bag exerts on the body		
student understands need for seat belt use with the air bag		
student relates increased time of stopping with decreased force on body		
student understands impulse and the air bag		
student understands how impulse is related to damage		
Mathematical Skills		
student can calculate impulse given force and different times		
given an impulse and time, student can calculate force		

Conversion

19 checkmarks = 10 points

17+ checkmarks = 9 points

15+ checkmarks = 8 points, etc.

For use with *Transportation*, Chapter 2, ACTIVITY FOUR: Why Air Bags?

NOTES

ACTIVITY FIVE
The Rear End Collision

Background Information

Whiplash is the mechanism of injury, not an injury itself. However, most people associate whiplash with the injury itself. In this activity, whiplash will be referred to as the mechanism of injury, and the injury will be referred to as whiplash effect.

In a head-on collision, the head will continue to move in a forward direction while the body is strapped in, until the chin hits the chest. As there is a sudden movement, there will be minor soft tissue injury, not dissimilar to a mild sprain, but not as in the rear-end collisions.

In the rear-end collision, the head is snapped backward, and then as the collision stops, snapped forward, in a lashing motion (hence whiplash). However, if there is nothing that will stop the head from moving backward (such as a head rest), the head will keep moving as far as possible, very quickly, and doing tremendous damage to the soft tissue. The whipping back and forth will keep doing the damage, can leave the neck muscles very stretched and sore, in minor cases, or torn and not able to function properly, as well as the possibility of fracture cervical vertebrae in severe cases. Again, this will depend on the severity of the accident.

The physics involved with this accident, is again Newton's First Law -- an object (head) in motion will remain in motion unless acted upon by an outside unbalanced force (the elasticity of the muscles in the neck, and the physical motion of the neck). Newton's Second Law, more commonly referred to in the formula $F = ma$, the force involved is proportional to the acceleration of the head. Therefore, if there is a larger vehicle crashing into a smaller vehicle, there will be a larger acceleration. This larger acceleration causes a larger force, which will cause the head to whip backwards with greater force, causing greater injury.

In this activity, car 1 will be released and will collide at the bottom of the ramp with car 2 with the passenger. For this collision we will assume conservation of momentum. Therefore, if the cars are the same mass, there will be conservation of momentum, and the second car will move off with a velocity the same as the first before the collision.

Momentum before the crash will equal momentum after the crash

$$m_1v_1 + m_2 v_2 = m_1v_1' + m_2 v_2'$$

because the first car is stationary before, $m_1v_1 = 0$, and because the second car is stationary after $m_2 v_2' = 0$, then

$$m_2 v_2 = m_1v_1'$$

Now, the passenger in the car, according to Newton's First Law of Motion, will remain stationary unless an outside, unbalanced force acts on it. Therefore, the body as a result of the seat pushing on the back of the individual, will move forward. However, the head remains stationary, and will only go forward after the elasticity of the neck muscles cause the head to snap forward. The result is the whiplash effect and injury.

The extent of the injury will have to do with Newton's Second Law of Motion, more commonly referred to in the formula $F = ma$ (F is the force in newtons, m is the mass in kg, and a is the acceleration in m/s^2). The force is proportional to the mass, and is also proportional to the acceleration of the object. In the case of the collision from behind, the greater the change in momentum, the greater the force acting on the car, and hence the body and head. Therefore, being hit from behind by a motorcycle will cause less damage than being hit from behind by a semi.

Active-ating the Physics InfoMall

Search for "whiplash" and you will find a nice discussion in *The Fascination of Physics*, from the Textbook Trove. This discussion includes some nice graphics.

Newton's Second Law is discussed in virtually every physics textbook in existence, not to mention the InfoMall. Depending on the level at which you wish to present this Law, you may wish to examine the conceptual-level texts, the algebra-based texts, or even the calculus-based textbooks on the InfoMall.

You may wish to look back at what we found in Activity Two regarding forces.

If you want more exercises to give to your students, searching the InfoMall is a bad idea - there are too many problems on the CD-ROM. Searching with keywords "force" AND "acceleration" AND "mass" in the Problems Place alone produces "Too many hits." However, you will find more than enough by simply going to the Problems Place and browsing a few of the resources you will find there. For example, *Schaum's 3000 Solved Problems in Physics* has a section on Newton's Laws of Motion. You will surely find enough problems there to keep any student busy for some time!

For You To Do step 6 mentions ratios. This is one of those areas in which students are known to have problems. Perform a search using "student difficult*" AND "ratio*" for more information. Alternately, try "misconcept*" AND "ratio*". If any of these searches causes "Too many hits" simply reduce the number of stores you search in, or require that the words occur in the same paragraph.

Try similar searches to find student difficulties with the concept of acceleration. You should find, for example, "Investigation of student understanding of the concept of acceleration in one dimension," *American Journal of Physics*, vol. 49, issue 3.

Physics To Go, step 6, asks students to predict the direction a cork will move. If you were to search the InfoMall to find more about the importance of predictions in learning, you would find that you need to limit your search. For example, a search for "prediction*" AND "inertia" resulted in several hits; the first hit is from *A Guide to Introductory Physics Teaching: Elementary Dynamics*, Arnold B. Arons' Book Basement entry. Here is a quote from that book: "Because of the obvious conceptual importance of the subject matter, the preconceptions students bring with them when starting the study of dynamics, and the difficulties they encounter with the Law of Inertia and the concept of force, have attracted extensive investigation and generated a substantial literature. A sampling of useful papers, giving far more extensive detail than can be incorporated here, is cited in the bibliography [Champagne, Klopfer, and Anderson (1980); Clement (1982); di Sessa (1982); Gunstone, Champagne, and Klopfer (1981); Halloun and Hestenes (1985); McCloskey, Camarazza, and Green (1980); McCloskey (1983); McDermott (1984); Minstrell (1982); Viennot (1979); White (1983), (1984)]." Note that students' preconceptions can have a large effect on how they learn something. It is important that they are forced to consciously acknowledge their preconceptions by making predictions.

Planning for the Activity

Time Requirements

Approximately 40 minutes are required to complete the procedure. Longer if the students would like to try to rig up different devices to prevent the injury.

Materials needed

For each group:

- laboratory cart (2)
- starting ramp
- meter stick
- wood piece, 1" x 2" x 2"
- wood piece, 1" x 3" x 10"
- duct tape
- wood piece, 2 x 4 scrap approx. 1 ft long
- balance (to measure mass of wood piece)
- spring scale, 0-10 newton range

Advance Preparation and Setup

Show the students your model of the passenger.

Teaching Notes

This assignment provides an application of the scientific principles of momentum, and Newton's First and Second Laws.

Students will probably be able to articulate the action or anticipated actions. However, it is important that the physics be explained, so as to help them realize that this demonstration can, in fact, be a realistic model.

Give a short explanation as to conservation of momentum. Most students will have a realistic view (from playing billiards, playing marbles, football, or hockey, or other contact sports).

Activity Overview

The students will be comparing the collision of their model "crash test dummy" with real life accidents, in order to analyze the effect of rear-end collisions on the neck muscles. This activity is similar to Activities Two and Three.

Student Objectives

Students will:

- evaluate from simulated collisions, the effect of rear-end collisions on the neck muscles.
- understand the causes of whiplash injuries.
- understand Newton's Second Law of Motion.
- understand the role of safety devices in preventing whiplash injury.

ANSWERS FOR THE TEACHER ONLY

What Do You Think?

Students will likely say that whiplash is an injury to the neck, when hit from behind. See background information for explanation of whiplash injury.

Students will likely say that when you go forward, your body will also move forward, so there is less force acting on the neck. However, when hit from behind, all the force will go into moving the head backwards, due to the body not being able to move due to the seat. This is true to a certain extent, but the primary reason is due to the lashing effect of the head being whipped back and forth, with nothing to support the head in the backwards direction. In the front the chin will hit the chest, thus stopping the head's forward motion.

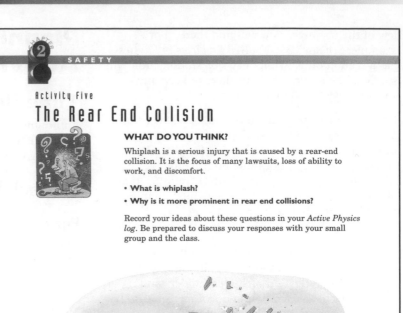

CHAPTER 2 SAFETY

Activity Five

The Rear End Collision

WHAT DO YOU THINK?

Whiplash is a serious injury that is caused by a rear-end collision. It is the focus of many lawsuits, loss of ability to work, and discomfort.

- **What is whiplash?**
- **Why is it more prominent in rear end collisions?**

Record your ideas about these questions in your *Active Physics log*. Be prepared to discuss your responses with your small group and the class.

TRANSPORTATION T 84

FOR YOU TO DO

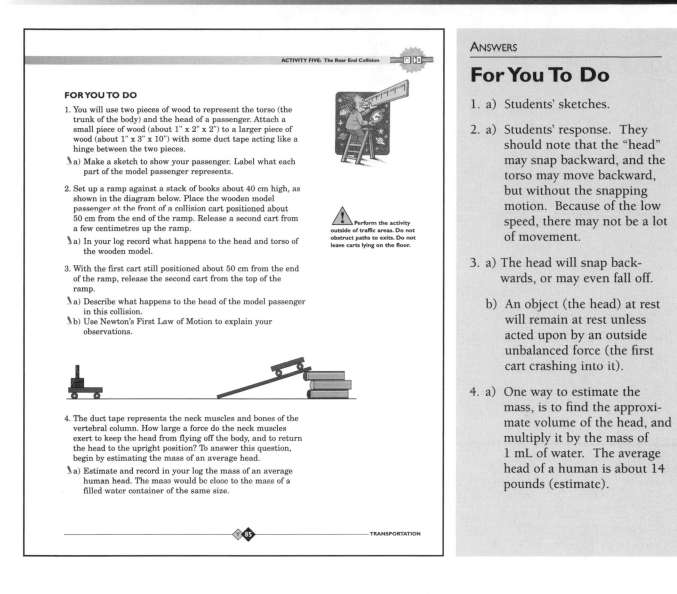

1. You will use two pieces of wood to represent the torso (the trunk of the body) and the head of a passenger. Attach a small piece of wood (about 1" x 2" x 2") to a larger piece of wood (about 1" x 3" x 10") with some duct tape acting like a hinge between the two pieces.
   - a) Make a sketch to show your passenger. Label what each part of the model passenger represents.
2. Set up a ramp against a stack of books about 40 cm high, as shown in the diagram below. Place the wooden model passenger at the front of a collision cart positioned about 50 cm from the end of the ramp. Release a second cart from a few centimetres up the ramp.
   - a) In your log record what happens to the head and torso of the wooden model.

Perform the activity outside of traffic areas. Do not obstruct paths to exits. Do not leave carts lying on the floor.

3. With the first cart still positioned about 50 cm from the end of the ramp, release the second cart from the top of the ramp.
   - a) Describe what happens to the head of the model passenger in this collision.
   - b) Use Newton's First Law of Motion to explain your observations.

4. The duct tape represents the neck muscles and bones of the vertebral column. How large a force do the neck muscles exert to keep the head from flying off the body, and to return the head to the upright position? To answer this question, begin by estimating the mass of an average head.
   - a) Estimate and record in your log the mass of an average human head. The mass would be close to the mass of a filled water container of the same size.

ANSWERS

For You To Do

1. a) Students' sketches.
2. a) Students' response. They should note that the "head" may snap backward, and the torso may move backward, but without the snapping motion. Because of the low speed, there may not be a lot of movement.
3. a) The head will snap backwards, or may even fall off.

   b) An object (the head) at rest will remain at rest unless acted upon by an outside unbalanced force (the first cart crashing into it).
4. a) One way to estimate the mass, is to find the approximate volume of the head, and multiply it by the mass of 1 mL of water. The average head of a human is about 14 pounds (estimate).

2

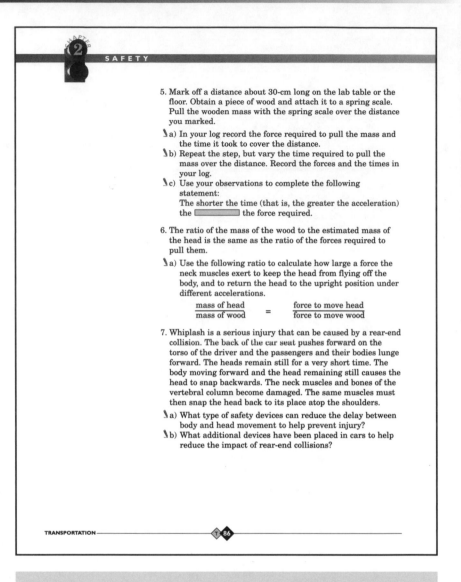

5. Mark off a distance about 30-cm long on the lab table or the floor. Obtain a piece of wood and attach it to a spring scale. Pull the wooden mass with the spring scale over the distance you marked.

a) In your log record the force required to pull the mass and the time it took to cover the distance.

b) Repeat the step, but vary the time required to pull the mass over the distance. Record the forces and the times in your log.

c) Use your observations to complete the following statement:
The shorter the time (that is, the greater the acceleration) the ______ the force required.

6. The ratio of the mass of the wood to the estimated mass of the head is the same as the ratio of the forces required to pull them.

a) Use the following ratio to calculate how large a force the neck muscles exert to keep the head from flying off the body, and to return the head to the upright position under different accelerations.

$$\frac{\text{mass of head}}{\text{mass of wood}} = \frac{\text{force to move head}}{\text{force to move wood}}$$

7. Whiplash is a serious injury that can be caused by a rear-end collision. The back of the car seat pushes forward on the torso of the driver and the passengers and their bodies lunge forward. The heads remain still for a very short time. The body moving forward and the head remaining still causes the head to snap backwards. The neck muscles and bones of the vertebral column become damaged. The same muscles must then snap the head back to its place atop the shoulders.

a) What type of safety devices can reduce the delay between body and head movement to help prevent injury?

b) What additional devices have been placed in cars to help reduce the impact of rear-end collisions?

ANSWERS

For You To Do *(continued)*

5. a) Students' response.

b) Students' response.

c) Students should note that the shorter the time period, the greater the force needed to accelerate the block of wood.

6. a) Students' response.

7. a) Head rests.

b) Rear bumpers also have the collapsing bumpers, which absorb some of the energy of the collision, as well as the crumple zone in the rear of the car. Cars also are equipped with more visible brake lights, to enable the driver behind to see the braking vehicle in front.

FOR YOU TO READ

Newton's Second Law of Motion

Newton's First Law of Motion is limited since it only tells you what happens to objects if no forces act upon them. Knowing that objects at rest have a tendency to remain at rest and that objects in motion will continue in motion does not provide enough information to analyze collisions. Newton's Second Law allows you to make predictions about what happens when an external force is applied to an object. If you were to place a collision cart on an even surface, it would not move. However, if you begin to push the cart, it will begin to move.

Newton's Second Law states:

If a body is acted on by a force, it will accelerate in the direction of the unbalanced force. The acceleration will be larger for smaller masses. The acceleration can be an increase in speed or a decrease in speed.

Newton's Second Law of motion indicates that the change in motion is determined by the force acting on the object, and the mass of the object itself.

REFLECTING ON THE ACTIVITY AND THE CHALLENGE

The vertebral column becomes thinner and the bones become smaller as the column attaches to the skull. The attachment bones are supported by the least amount of muscle. Unfortunately, the smaller bones, with less muscle support, make this area particularly susceptible to injury. One of the greatest dangers following whiplash is the damage to the brainstem. The brainstem is particularly vital to life support because it regulates blood pressure and breathing movements. Consider how your safety device will help prevent whiplash following a collision. What part of the restraining device prevents the movement of the head?

ANSWERS

Physics To Go

1. The huge forces that are associated with the rear-end collision, in conjunction with little or no support for the neck from behind.

2. Inertia. An object will continue to move in a straight path until an outside force acts on it.

3. The passengers on the bus are not moving. They have a tendency to remain at rest even after the bus begins moving.

4. Because the motorcycle has less mass it will move more quickly if struck by a car.

5. The headrest would be most beneficial if you were in a rear-end collision. The passengers and driver are forced backward during the collision.

6. a) The cork will appear to move in the opposite direction to the push. Emphasize to students, that the cork is not moving, but "trying to stay motionless". Inertia.

   b) Opposite to the original push.

PHYSICS TO GO

1. Why are neck injuries common after rear-end collisions?
2. Explain why the packages in the back move forward if a truck comes to a quick stop.
3. As a bus accelerates, the passengers on the bus are jolted toward the back of the bus. Indicate what causes the passengers to be pushed backward.
4. Why would the rear-end collision demonstrated by the laboratory experiment be most dangerous for someone driving a motorcycle?
5. Would headrests serve the greatest benefit during a head-on collision or a rear-end collision? Explain your answer.
6. A cork is attached to a string and placed in a jar of water as shown by the diagram to the right. Later, the jar is inverted.
   a) If the glass jar is pushed along the surface of a table, predict the direction in which the cork will move?
   b) If you place your left hand about 50 cm in front of the jar and push it with your right hand until it strikes your left hand, predict the direction in which the cork will move?

Be sure the outside of the jar is dry so it does not slip out of your hands.

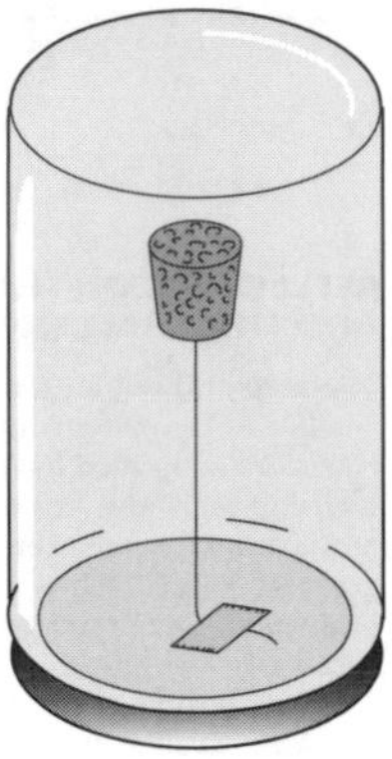

NOTES

2

ACTIVITY SIX
The Bungee Jump (Computer Analysis)

Background Information

In this activity, the students are looking at another application of the impulse/momentum concept. In this activity, however, we must first look at the free falling body. Any object in free fall, has an acceleration of 9.81 m/s^2. Any object, regardless of the mass, will fall at this acceleration.

Aristotle was the first on record to comment on falling bodies. From introspection, he thought that heavier objects fell to the ground faster than lighter objects. He also believed that a falling object gained its velocity immediately upon release, and maintained this speed until it hit the ground.

Galileo, however, thought Aristotle was incorrect. Galileo was the first to show that all things fall to Earth with a changing velocity or constant acceleration. Some attribute the Leaning Tower of Pisa experiments to him, but there is no hard evidence. However, he did many experiments rolling balls down ramps, and dropping of objects from different heights to drive onto stakes. He observed that a rock dropped from a higher height will drive the stake in farther than if dropped at a lower height. He concluded that this must be due to the rock having a greater velocity (and therefore more momentum, although Galileo didn't refer to it is as momentum as such). His ramp experiment showed that every object will accelerate at the same rate if released at the same height. He also recognized, that the friction of air does play a part in free fall, and that is why small massive objects (a stone) appear to accelerate more than large less massive objects (piece of paper).

In our study of falling objects, and most situations in the study of physics, we study falling objects in a vacuum. If we did not, it would be too difficult to analyze the behavior of objects.

In the case of the bungee jumper, she is in free fall for the first part of the jump, until she reaches the end of her rope, and the elastic takes over. The elastic is then applying a force to the jumper, that slows her down (accelerates). If this was a perfectly elastic situation, and there was no flailing of arms and panic, the spring-like motion would continue.

When you look at the data, it is essentially a force-time graph. The area under a force-time graph is the impulse of the motion. Therefore, you can find the force that is required to stop the free fall. Again, we remind ourselves that the greater the time of the impulse, the smaller the force required to slow the person down. This is good, as the smaller forces are easily absorbed by the body, and no injuries are likely to occur. Below is the mathematical derivation of the forces and impulse necessary for the bungee to be effective, and safe, but still be a lot of fun.

While the person is in free fall, the person will have some momentum mv. When the elastic takes over, it will slow the body to a velocity of 0 m/s. Therefore the impulse of the elastic rope must be the same as the change in momentum.

$F\Delta t = m\Delta v$

$F\Delta t = m\,(v_2 - v_1)$, but since v_2 at the lowest point of the fall is 0,

$F\Delta t = mv_1$

Now as the elastic cord takes effect at the beginning $F = 0$ and at the end F = maximum, therefore we assume an average force (F_{ave}). As this force is acting, there is still the force of gravity (Fg), therefore $F_{net} = F_{ave} - Fg$

Substituting ($F_{ave} - Fg$) for F in $F\Delta t = mv_1$,

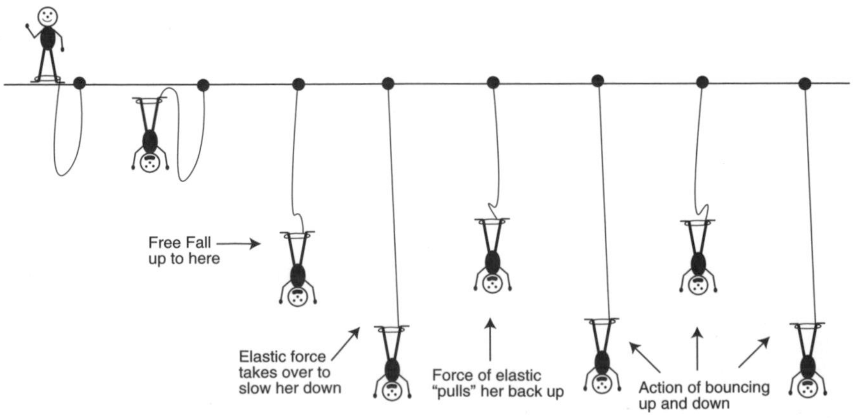
Free Fall up to here
Elastic force takes over to slow her down
Force of elastic "pulls" her back up
Action of bouncing up and down

we get

$(F_{ave} - Fg)\Delta t = mv_1$ ----> where $Fg = mg$

$F_{ave} - mg = mv_1/\Delta t$

$F_{ave} = mg + mv_1/\Delta t$

So we can see that by increasing *t*, we decrease *F*, the force acting on our bodies.

Active-ating the Physics InfoMall

You may wish to investigate the known misconceptions students have regarding momentum. Try a search with momentum AND "misconcept*". One of the hits is "Verification of fundamental principles of mechanics in the computerized student laboratory," in *American Journal of Physics*, vol. 58, issue 10, 1990. This article is also great for using computers for teaching.

This activity uses computers to graph data. You may wish to search for "student difficult*" AND "graph*". This produces several wonderful hits, including "Student difficulties with graphical representations of negative values of velocity," in *The Physics Teacher*, vol. 27, issue 4 on the InfoMall. Also found in that search is "Student difficulties in connecting graphs and physics: Example from kinematics," in the *American Journal of Physics*, vol. 55, issue 6. Don't let these titles make you think that graphs are a bad thing! It is good to be aware that students do not always understand graphs, a valuable tool in the study of physics.

Planning for the Activity

Time Requirements

The time required for this activity should be approximately 40 minutes.

Materials needed

For each group:

- MBL or CBL with force probe
- small doll
- elastic cord
- string
- balance for measuring dolls mass
- ring stand and supports for force probe and doll

Advance Preparation and Setup

Check that the doll is small in size but massive enough to cause measurable forces.

Teaching Notes

The class will probably be able to predict the behavior of the bungee and the string. Encourage them to describe the events in terms of inertia, impulse, force and time. The lesson rests on the ability of the students to interpret the graphical results.

Due to the nature of this experiment, it would be prudent to have alternate activities should you not have enough computers to go around. See the alternative activity following this activity in the Teacher's Edition.

Remind the students of the delicate equipment they are handling

Some students may think that the rope is "pulling" on the person as they jump from the moment they leave the top of the tower. This would be considered an Aristotelian view, where the velocity is at a maximum as they leave the top of the tower. Tell the students to watch carefully as the troll is pushed off. One way to convince them that the troll is accelerating, is to have an identical troll without attachments to the device, and push both of them off and watch their path. It will remain identical until the troll that is attached hits the "end" (where the elastic takes over) part of the rope.

A trip to the local bungee jumping company would be in order. As an alternate, asking the company to video tape the activity, and then analyzing it using computer software, will give good data from which to work.

NOTES

Activity Six

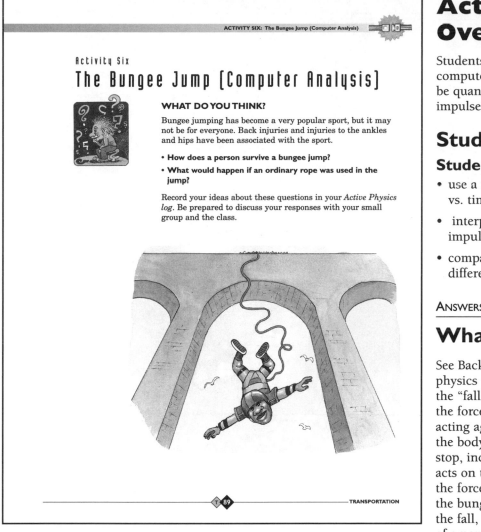

The Bungee Jump (Computer Analysis)

WHAT DO YOU THINK?

Bungee jumping has become a very popular sport, but it may not be for everyone. Back injuries and injuries to the ankles and hips have been associated with the sport.

- **How does a person survive a bungee jump?**
- **What would happen if an ordinary rope was used in the jump?**

Record your ideas about these questions in your *Active Physics log*. Be prepared to discuss your responses with your small group and the class.

Activity Overview

Students will be gathering data using a computer analysis program. They will be quantifying the relationship between impulse, force and time.

Student Objectives

Students will:

- use a force probe to construct a force vs. time graph.
- interpret the area of the graph as impulse.
- compare equal impulses applied by different forces.

ANSWERS FOR THE TEACHER ONLY

What Do You Think?

See Background Information for the physics involved. The person survives the "fall" when the descent is slowed by the force of the elastic bungee cord acting against the force of gravity, where the body will slowly stop. This slow stop, increases the time that the impulse acts on the body, therefore decreasing the force that acts on the body. Without the bungee cord, the stop at the end of the fall, (hitting the ground, or the end of a non-elastic cord) happens very quickly, same impulse acting on a shorter period of time, and increasing the force acting on the body. (Hence the saying...It's not the fall that kills you, but the sudden stop at the end!)

A bungee cord is elastic. The elasticity increases the time over which the impulse is acting, thereby decreasing the force. An ordinary rope would cause the force to increase, as the time is shortened. This would cause an increase in the forces felt by the jumper, and therefore cause damage to the body.

ANSWERS

For You To Do

1.-2. Student activity.

3. a) Students' response.

   b) Students' response.

   c) Students' response.

   d) The maximum force should be greater than the force of gravity (weight).

4. a) Students' response.

CHAPTER 2 SAFETY

Set up the platform so that it is either higher or lower than eye level.

FOR YOU TO DO

1. A force probe is connected to a computer and the concept of impulse and momentum can be used to investigate a bungee jump. Start up the force probe software and perform the probe calibrations necessary to ready the equipment for the measurement. Set the time axis for a maximum of 5 s.
2. Set up the stand and jumping platform as shown in the diagram. Attach one end of the elastic bungee cord to the foot of a small plastic doll on the jumping platform. Attach the other end of the cord to the force probe.
3. Activate the probe by clicking start. As soon as you see the line on the graph, give the plastic doll a gentle push off the platform.
   a) Use the "analyze" tool of the software to zoom in on the region corresponding to the first bounce (the spike) of the bungee jumper. Record the maximum force of the jump and the time duration.
   b) Use the software to determine the area under the spike. This is called the impulse; it is equal to the average force multiplied by the time. Record the value of the impulse.
   c) Measure the mass of the "bungee jumper" in Newtons and calculate its weight. Weight in Newtons (Kg. m/s^2) Mass in Kilograms x 9.8 m/s^2.
   d) How does the maximum force compare to the weight of the jumper?

4. Connect another type of cord to the foot of the "bungie jumper" and the force probe. Repeat step 3.
   a) Record all the measurements for a jump using this cord.

TRANSPORTATION T 90

5. Use the results of your activity to answer the following questions.
   a) How does the maximum force compare between the two cords?
   b) How does the length of the time for the first bounce compare?
   c) How does the impulse (the area under the spike) compare? What did you expect to find? Can you explain the discrepancy?

REFLECTING ON THE ACTIVITY AND CHALLENGE

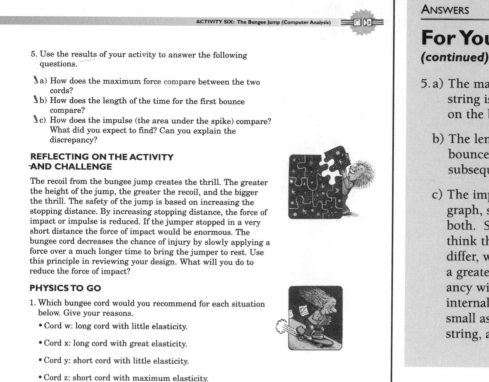

The recoil from the bungee jump creates the thrill. The greater the height of the jump, the greater the recoil, and the bigger the thrill. The safety of the jump is based on increasing the stopping distance. By increasing stopping distance, the force of impact or impulse is reduced. If the jumper stopped in a very short distance the force of impact would be enormous. The bungee cord decreases the chance of injury by slowly applying a force over a much longer time to bring the jumper to rest. Use this principle in reviewing your design. What will you do to reduce the force of impact?

PHYSICS TO GO

1. Which bungee cord would you recommend for each situation below. Give your reasons.
   - Cord w: long cord with little elasticity.
   - Cord x: long cord with great elasticity.
   - Cord y: short cord with little elasticity.
   - Cord z: short cord with maximum elasticity.

   a) This customer is looking for the maximum thrill. She is more concerned with speed and less concerned for safety. She is very fit and has no history of health problems.
   b) This customer is looking for a thrill but is also concerned with his safety. He is looking for a little less speed and is somewhat less fit.

ANSWERS

For You To Do
(continued)

5. a) The maximum force on the string is greater than the force on the bungee cord.
   b) The length of time for the first bounce is greater than the subsequent bounces.
   c) The impulse, area under the graph, should be the same for both. Some students will think that the impulses will differ, with the bungee having a greater area. Any discrepancy will probably be due to internal friction, elasticity, small as it may be, in the string, and calculation errors.

2

ANSWERS

Physics To Go

1. a) Long cord with little elasticity – the long cord will allow her to accelerate to a greater speed, and the little elasticity will give her a very short time of stopping, thus giving her a "jolt". If she wanted a different thrill, the long cord with great elasticity will give her the greater speed, then the great elasticity will allow her to come closer to the ground more slowly, thus giving the impression that she may not stop in time.
   b) This customer should probably go with the short cord and great elasticity. The short cord would give him a lower velocity, and the great elasticity would slow him down with a smaller force being applied to his body, thus not likely to cause any damage.

ANSWERS

Physics To Go *(continued)*

2. Different masses mean different forces of gravity. Therefore, the force exerted by the cord will need to be different in order to stop the jumper before she hits the ground. Think of an ordinary elastic: any time you attach a mass to the end of an elastic, it will stretch. As you increase the mass, the length of the elastic will increase. Therefore, with a greater force (of gravity), the bungee cord will stretch

3. The primary conditions should be that there would be no possible way for the bungee jumper to hit the ground. The elasticity in the bungee cord must be such that force of acceleration, is not enough to "pull" apart the body. If a person had loose joints, or has had numerous soft tissue damage, this force would have to be even smaller still.

4. The stopping distance of the bungee jumper is similar to the crumple zones of cars in that these distances both change the time of impulse. As you increase the time of the crash or stopping, you decrease the force of the jump or crash. ($F = mv/\Delta t$)

CHAPTER 2

SAFETY

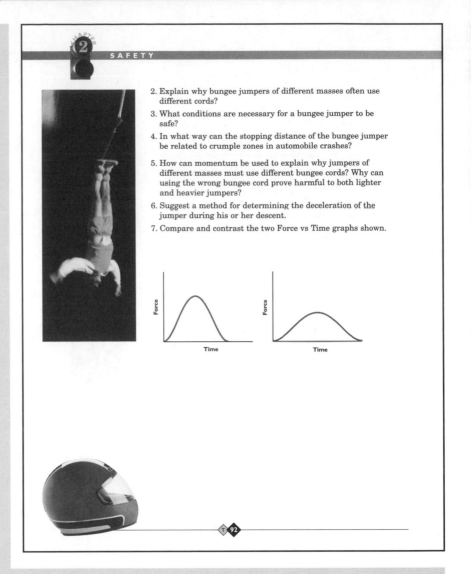

2. Explain why bungee jumpers of different masses often use different cords?
3. What conditions are necessary for a bungee jumper to be safe?
4. In what way can the stopping distance of the bungee jumper be related to crumple zones in automobile crashes?
5. How can momentum be used to explain why jumpers of different masses must use different bungee cords? Why can using the wrong bungee cord prove harmful to both lighter and heavier jumpers?
6. Suggest a method for determining the deceleration of the jumper during his or her descent.
7. Compare and contrast the two Force vs Time graphs shown.

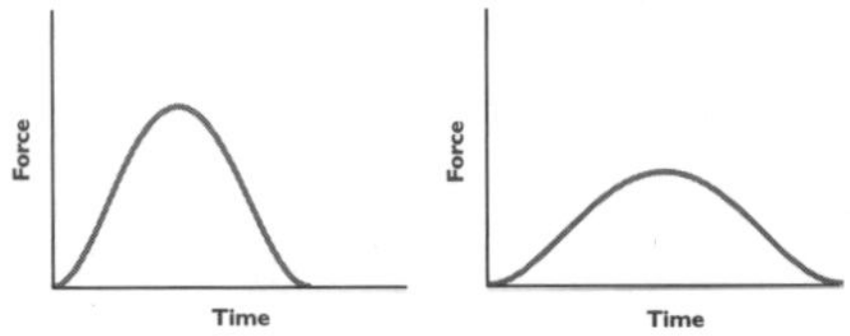

T 92

5. Momentum is the product of mass and velocity. Therefore when you are stopping an object moving, there is a change in momentum. The impulse is the change in momentum. Because the velocities of both a light and a heavy jumper will be the same, and the force necessary to stop the jumper without damage will be the same, then by changing the mass, it must be necessary to change the time taken to stop. ($F\Delta t = m\Delta v$) Because the force exerted by the bungee cord is strictly a property of the cord, it is necessary to change the cord for different masses. (Encourage students to try using different masses and the same elastic, to try to see if they are able to break the elastic.) Using the bungee cord that is designed for heavy jumpers with a light jumper, will be similar to using a non-elastic cord. The impulse is the same, but because the time will be less, the force acting on the body will be greater. Using the light bungee cord with a heavier jumper, will cause the jumper to hit the ground, as it takes a greater distance (time) for the jumper to stop.

6. Deceleration (technically acceleration) can be determined in two ways. One method would involve Newton's Second Law of Motion - ($F = ma$). Knowing the force ($F = m\Delta v/\Delta t$), we can calculate acceleration from $a = F/m$. Another method is calculating the initial velocity (v_i) of the jumper just as the bungee starts to stretch, the time it takes to stretch to the maximum, the final velocity ($v_f = 0$) and the distance, then acceleration can be calculated using the formula $v_{f2} = v_{i2} + 2ad$; $a = -2\ v_i 2/d$.

7. The first graph has a greater force over a shorter time period, and the second graph has a smaller force over a longer period of time. If you measure the area under the graph, you will find the impulse.

Activity Six A

Effects of Mass on Bungee Jumping [Low-Tech]

FOR YOU TO DO

1. Cut fishing line into 0.5-m lengths. You may want to consult a fisherman to find the best knot for tying the fishing line.
2. Attach different types of elastics (length 0.1 m each) to the fishing line.
3. Secure a 0.5 kg mass to the first elastic.
4. Secure the fishing line to a secure spot about 2 m above the ground.
5. Lift the mass to the attachment point and release.
6. Repeat with different masses, for each different elastic.

a) Record your results as either no break or break in the table.

Mass (kg)	elastic		
	weak	medium	strong
0.50			
1.0			
2.0			
10.0			

7. Run at least three trials for each elastic and mass.
8. Inspect the fishing line for damage each time (may need magnifying glass).

a) When picking up the masses with the fishing line, when did the line break?

b) Where was the weakest part of the connections?

c) Which combination with the greatest mass before it broke, worked best? Explain.

Teaching Notes

Time Requirements

About one class period.

Materials needed

- 4-pound-test fishing line
- different elastics (elastic for clothing would be the best, as it can be purchased in large quantities, of different elasticity—try three different strengths first)
- various weights (various masses 0.5 kg, 1 kg, 2 kg, 5 kg, 10 kg)
- variety of methods for attaching masses (fishing leaders, or hooks)
- magnifying glass

The secure setting of the fishing lines may involve a step ladder, or standing on desks. Discourage this as much as possible. If ring stands are used, watch that they don't tip when the masses are large, and they reach the end of the stretch in the elastic.

This activity is a way of showing simply how the mass on the end of a line will eventually break the line, depending on the mass and the elasticity.

This activity is similar to bungee jumping in that the force (the weight of the object—Fg) is reduced by increasing the time that the force is acting on the mass. In bungee jumping, the Fg is reduced by the elastic increasing the time that the force slows down the object or person. (Note: The weakest part of any line or rope is the knot. Be sure the knots are secure!)

To speed things up, have each station set up with several lengths of fishing line precut (0.50 m), and several lengths (0.10 m of elastics). The method of attachment should be secure. If you have open beams, attach a secure rope (or wire) to the beam so that it is about 2 m above the floor. A large ring stand with several books on the base will work, but watch closely, when the masses get large. It is best if the students are also holding on to it.

Answers

1. Generally, as the speed increases, there is a greater and greater force. Thus the line will break with small masses at high accelerations and large masses at low accelerations.
2. The weakest part will most likely be the connections between the various different substances.
3. Answers will vary. Using a 4-pound mass will not break the line. This depends on the age of the line and other factors. Generally, the line is tested higher than the rating. (Have the students check to see if 4-pound test will hold more mass.)

NOTES

2

ACTIVITY SEVEN
Automatic Triggering Devices

Background Information

Air bags and seat belts do save your life, and prevent serious injuries if used properly. If you pull on your seat belt while you are moving at normal speed, it seems as though there is no way the seat belt could stop you from moving forward. Yet, you have probably slammed on your brakes at some point and the seat belt did in fact tighten, and held you in place. However, the air bag didn't inflate. The safety devices in your car cannot be working all the time (you wouldn't be able to see past the air bag), so you must have a triggering device to make sure that the air bag inflates only when it is needed and when it is it will prevent further damage.

In this activity the students will be using their own imagination, ingenuity, and any materials you are able to bring into the classroom. They will attempt to design a device which will operate like the trigger device in a car.

One such design that is used in cars is a cylinder with a steel ball attached at one end to a magnet, and a open circuit at the other end (See diagram). The ball is held in place by the magnet and only dislodges from the magnet at certain accelerations. When it leaves one end and hits the other end, the circuit is then closed, and the air bag inflates inside the car. This acceleration must be such that it would only happen in a collision, where the speed of the car is greater than about 18 km/h (11 mph).

Active-ating the Physics InfoMall

Again, you may want to find what is known about student difficulties with a concept in this activity. One possible search is "student difficult*" AND "circuit*".

Planning for the Activity

Time Requirements

Allow at least 40 minutes for this activity, with the possibility of the students taking their project home to work on. For the presentation of their design, allow approximately 10 minutes for each group to explain their design, and show how it works.

Materials needed

For each group:

- laboratory cart
- flashlight bulb and base
- D-cell
- battery holder
- starting ramp
- concrete block or other barrier

For the class:

- Collection of components such as tape, rubber bands, string, wire, paper clips, metal foil

Teaching Notes

Explore the students thoughts on how a triggering device might operate. One type of the device is shown in the background information. Elicit the conditions under which the device should trigger. The test criterion is purposely vague: that the device must trigger only when the car collides with a large speed and not a slow speed.

Reliability is a key issue. The device that inflates the air bag is a good example of a spin-off from the space program. It is based on a device that demanded 100% reliability: the release mechanism from the lunar launch system.

For a sophisticated class, you may wish to help the class determine the best release points for testing the car by using some kinematics, or through

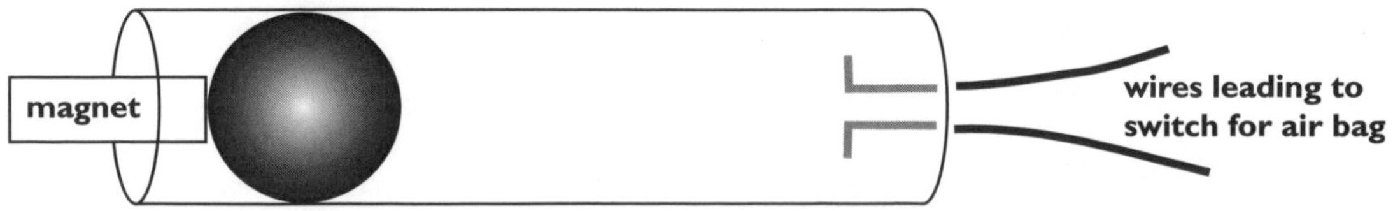

energy conservation, these areas have been explored. A sonic ranger or tape timer may be used in conjunction with your tests.

This activity can lead to increasing amounts of noise and mayhem. Keep students on task with constant monitoring and subtle encouragement while looking at each group. Use groups of four. In groups of three or less, there are generally fewer ideas, and groups greater than five give some an opportunity to blend into the woodwork.

Encourage students to work cooperatively by assigning tasks prior to beginning the activity. The following tasks are designed for groups of four students:

- **Organizer:** helps focus discussion and ensures that all members of the group contribute to the discussion. The organizer ensures that all of the equipment has been gathered and that the group completes all parts of the activity.
- **Recorder:** provides written procedures when required, diagrams where appropriate and records data. The recorder must work closely with the organizer to ensure that all group members contribute.
- **Researcher:** seeks written and electronic information to support the findings of the group. In addition, where appropriate, the researcher will develop and test prototypes. The researcher will also exchange information gathered among different groups.
- **Diverger:** seeks alternative explanations and approaches. The task of the diverger is keep the discussion open. "Are other explanations possible?"

Students will be working with many different electrical devices. Ensure that there are no wires connected to common household circuits. Ensure that the students are only using common dry cell or household batteries.

Some students may think that the triggering device for such safety devices are simple electronic switches. This activity will help them to understand that in order for a switch to be functional for a particular purpose (such as the g-forces that are enough to cause damage to the body, and hence need to have some way to reduce the overall force to the body), that the actual trigger must be linked to the cause of the damage. This is why seat belts are based on a rocker/pendulum switch, which catches the roll that the seat belt is rolled upon, when the forces are high enough -- much like the blinds that when pulling down slowly will slowly come down, but to stop them rolling back up a sharp tug is needed to catch the roll.

2

NOTES

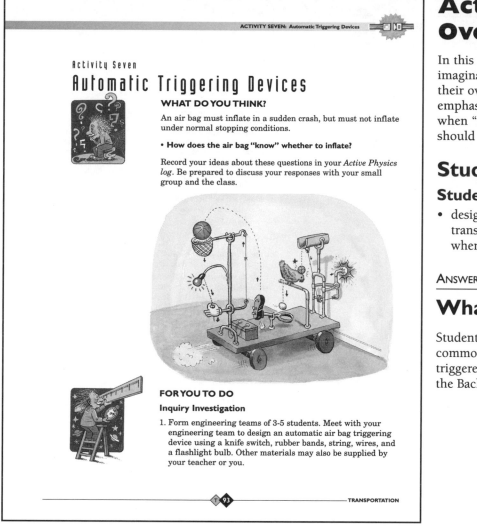

Activity Seven

Automatic Triggering Devices

WHAT DO YOU THINK?

An air bag must inflate in a sudden crash, but must not inflate under normal stopping conditions.

- **How does the air bag "know" whether to inflate?**

Record your ideas about these questions in your *Active Physics log*. Be prepared to discuss your responses with your small group and the class.

FOR YOU TO DO

Inquiry Investigation

1. Form engineering teams of 3-5 students. Meet with your engineering team to design an automatic air bag triggering device using a knife switch, rubber bands, string, wires, and a flashlight bulb. Other materials may also be supplied by your teacher or you.

ANSWERS

For You To Do

All the answers for this section involve students observations and their design of the triggering device.

Activity Overview

In this activity the students will use imagination and creativity to design their own triggering device. The emphasis on this activity should be that when "inventing" something, there should be no limitations, within reason.

Student Objectives

Students will:

- design a device that is capable of transmitting a digital electrical signal when it is accelerated in a collision.

ANSWERS FOR THE TEACHER ONLY

What Do You Think?

Students answers will vary. One common way in which the air bag is triggered, is the method described in the Background Information.

2

2. The design parameters are as follows:
   - The device must turn a flashlight bulb on, or turn it off. This will be interpreted as the trigger signal.
   - The device must not trigger if the car is brought to a sudden stop from a slow speed.
   - The device must trigger if the sudden stop is from a high speed.
   - The car containing the device must be released down a ramp. The car will then strike a wall at the bottom of the ramp.
   - The battery and bulb must be attached to the car along with the triggering device. The bulb does not have to remain in the final on or off state, but it must at least flash to show triggering.

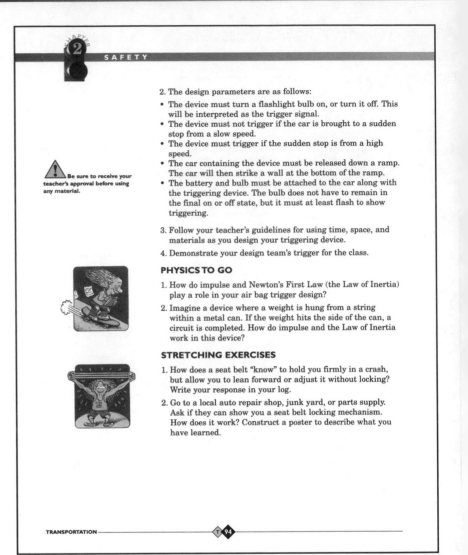

Be sure to receive your teacher's approval before using any material.

3. Follow your teacher's guidelines for using time, space, and materials as you design your triggering device.
4. Demonstrate your design team's trigger for the class.

PHYSICS TO GO

1. How do impulse and Newton's First Law (the Law of Inertia) play a role in your air bag trigger design?
2. Imagine a device where a weight is hung from a string within a metal can. If the weight hits the side of the can, a circuit is completed. How do impulse and the Law of Inertia work in this device?

STRETCHING EXERCISES

1. How does a seat belt "know" to hold you firmly in a crash, but allow you to lean forward or adjust it without locking? Write your response in your log.
2. Go to a local auto repair shop, junk yard, or parts supply. Ask if they can show you a seat belt locking mechanism. How does it work? Construct a poster to describe what you have learned.

ANSWERS

Physics To Go

1. Students' will have individual responses. Impulse is the change in momentum. As the car comes to a stop, the occupants and the triggering device will continue to move in a straight line (Newton's First Law of Motion – Inertia).

2. When in motion at a constant speed the metal pendulum hangs straight down. When the car stops, the pendulum continues to move forward until an impulse, the force of the string and the wall of the can, stop it.

Assessment: Activity Seven

The following rubric can be used to assess group work during Activity Seven: Automatic Triggering Devices.

Each member of the group can evaluate the manner in which the group worked to solve problems in the activity.

Total = 12 marks

1. Low level – indicates minimum effort or effectiveness.
2. Average – acceptable standard has been achieved, but that the group could have worked more effectively if better organized.
3. Good – this rating indicates a superior effort. Although improvements might have been made, the group was on task all of the time and completed all parts of the activity.

Descriptor	**Values**		
1. The group worked cooperatively to engineer an automatic triggering device.	1	2	3
Comments:			
2. A plan was established before beginning and all tasks were shared equally.	1	2	3
Comments:			
3. The group was organized. Materials were collected and the problems were addressed by the entire group.	1	2	3
Comments:			
4. Data was collected and recorded in an organized fashion in data tables in journals.	1	2	3
Comments:			

2

Assessment: Scientific and Technological Thinking

Scientific and technological thinking can be assessed using the rubric below. Allow one mark for each checkmark.

Maximum value = 10

Descriptor	**Yes**	**No**
1. The device (either light on or light off) does not trigger at low speeds.		
2. The device (either light on or light off) does trigger at high speeds.		
3. The device shows innovation and imagination.		
4. Controls, such as release height on ramp, are maintained throughout.		
5. The device is reliable (at least 75%).		
6. Students recognize the need for several trials.		
7. Triggering devices are tested and/or modified prior to final demonstration.		
8. Students identify the role of inertia and Newton's laws in this activity.		
9. Students can identify variables that would trigger the device.		
10. Students are able to explain their device to the class.		

ACTIVITY EIGHT
Cushioning Collisions (Computer Analysis)

Background Information

In this activity the students will be putting into practice the concepts that they have learned in the past few activities. Their task is to design a cushioning device which will reduce the damage that can be done in a collision. They should be looking for cushioning material that will reduce the force as much as possible. The change in momentum will be the same with each velocity, but the force that brings the car to a rest should be as small as possible. Review the impulse/momentum from previous activities (Activities Five and Six).

One other concept that may help in understanding collisions is the Conservation of Energy.

Collisions can be either elastic (energy is conserved) or inelastic (energy is not conserved). The collisions that we study are collisions (in the laboratory) where there is always a conservation of momentum. While there is conservation of momentum (p), there may or may not be conservation of energy. For example, there can be conservation of energy with two billiard balls moving towards each other, and colliding and moving away with the exact opposite speed and direction. This is elastic. However, in the case of most collisions, there is no conservation of energy

In this activity, there will not be a conservation of energy. Therefore, the students will need to design a cushion which will be able to transform as much kinetic energy (energy of motion) as possible to another substance(s). For example, when you have a large ball and you drop it onto a solid floor (such as concrete), it will bounce back. Therefore, there is energy from kinetic energy falling, transferred to potential in the elastic potential energy of the ball in deformation, and subsequently transferred back into kinetic energy to move it upwards. (Assume an elastic collision, and that the ball will bounce back to its original height.)

However, if you were to drop that same ball into a box of sand, then the kinetic energy is transferred to each particle of sand moving in all directions. There is a conservation of momentum in both cases, but not a conservation of energy. In almost all cases of collisions, in reality, there is not a conservation of energy. Energy is transferred to sound, but mostly to heat due to friction of the parts heating up in the collision, and to the deformation of the car parts.

Active-ating the Physics InfoMall

In addition to the information we found previously (on momentum and graphs, for example), you may wish to examine the Problems Place for even more exercises in momentum conservation. Remember, *Schaum's 3000 Solved Problems in Physics* has the problem and the solution. It can be a source for you, as well as a way to provide your students with solved problems for them to study!

Planning for the Activity

Time Requirements

The time for this activity will vary depending on the materials at hand. Allow time to investigate as many different kinds of materials as available, and encourage bringing materials from home. This activity can be introduced (10 minutes) one day and then allow one class (approximately 40 minutes) for the design and measuring. Allow extra time for analyzing the data and graphing the data as necessary.

Materials needed

For each group:

- MBL or CBL with Sonic Ranger
- MBL or CBL with Force Probe
- toy car
- starting ramp
- balance to measure mass of car
- cushioning materials (varieties such as sponge, cotton, paper, packing materials)
- tape for attaching cushions to car

Advance Preparation and Setup

If your materials are limited, use a large-screen monitor to display the data to the class. Prepare a kit for each team consisting of a toy car and a different cushioning material. Each team can prepare one car and run it as a demonstration station.

Try a few sample runs in advance to make sure that the results fall within limits of the available probes. Adjust the height of the ramp accordingly. Demonstrate the operation of the sensors and the software to the class if necessary.

Providing materials produces a certain regularity and predictability to the activity. You may want to present this activity as a challenge a day in advance. The students are sure to bring some unusual cushioning material from home.

Teaching Notes

Replaying the video of auto crashes is one way to engage students in this activity. Ask students to explain and give examples of the three types of collisions that result from a car crash. Previous activities focused on the secondary collision - the occupants with the interior of the car. The tertiary collision - the internal organs of the occupants is not easily tested. Here the focus is on the primary collision - the vehicle with another vehicle or obstacle. How can the effects of this collision be minimized? Students should be encouraged to think of other systems besides sand canisters that are designed to cushion primary collisions such as crumple zones in cars, energy-absorbing bumpers, standardized height bumpers, break-away signs and light poles, types of plantings near roads, buried guard rail ends, shape of curbs or barriers (so-called "New Jersey barriers" are shaped to rub against the tire to slow the car), etc.

In order to help students with the WDYT, demonstrate the operation of the force probe and focus on the impulse graph (force vs. time). The shape of the force spike and its relation to impulse should be discussed again to remind students of the Bungee Jump Activity. Demonstrate how the measurement of the impact force and velocity prior to impact changes when the ramp angle is changed. See if the students understand the operation of the apparatus, make a measurement of the velocity of the toy car before the collision and the impulse during the collision when no cushioning is used. This baseline information (the graphs) should be provided to each lab group or left on the chalkboard during the investigation.

As each group completes the design on the cushioning system, they should test the effectiveness of their system by using the probes at the demonstration work station. Once the students have a printout of the F vs. t graphs, they can return to their regular work stations to analyze the data and figure out ways of increasing the effectiveness of their cushioning system.

The balance is needed to get the mass of each cushioned car in order to calculate its momentum.

Students can work in groups of four, using similar criteria to the previous assessment criteria for group work. This activity will inevitably lead to noise, but busy noise can still be productive noise. Keep students on task by asking them questions such as: Why are you using that material? What are the independent variables? Why are you keeping the height of the ramp the same for this activity? Why are you changing the material?

Refer to the safety notes in previous activities regarding a secure ramp, and objects falling on students' toes.

Students will need to be guided to realize, again, that the increase in the time of the collision is the most important factor here. The change in momentum will always be the same, as the mass of the object never changes, and the velocity should be constant if they are releasing the car at the same height each time they do the trial.

NOTES

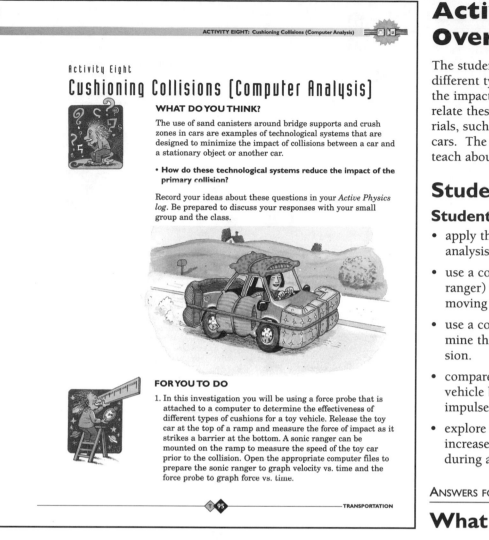

Activity Eight

Cushioning Collisions (Computer Analysis)

WHAT DO YOU THINK?

The use of sand canisters around bridge supports and crush zones in cars are examples of technological systems that are designed to minimize the impact of collisions between a car and a stationary object or another car.

- **How do these technological systems reduce the impact of the primary collision?**

Record your ideas about these questions in your *Active Physics log*. Be prepared to discuss your responses with your small group and the class.

FOR YOU TO DO

1. In this investigation you will be using a force probe that is attached to a computer to determine the effectiveness of different types of cushions for a toy vehicle. Release the toy car at the top of a ramp and measure the force of impact as it strikes a barrier at the bottom. A sonic ranger can be mounted on the ramp to measure the speed of the toy car prior to the collision. Open the appropriate computer files to prepare the sonic ranger to graph velocity vs. time and the force probe to graph force vs. time.

ANSWERS

For You to Do

1. Student activity.

Activity Overview

The students will be analyzing how different types of materials will affect the impact of collisions. They will relate these designs with real-life materials, such as the bumper design on cars. The design of these materials will teach about impulse and momentum.

Student Objectives

Students will:

- apply the concept of impulse in the analysis of automobile collisions.
- use a computer's motion probe (sonic ranger) to determine the velocity of moving vehicles.
- use a computer's force probe to determine the force exerted during a collision.
- compare the momentum of a model vehicle before the collision with the impulse applied during the collision.
- explore ways of using cushions to increase the time that a force acts during a primary collision.

2

ANSWERS FOR THE TEACHER ONLY

What Do You Think?

Looking back to the understanding of impulse and forces, we can say that the impulse is the same in any collision from the same speed -- the car traveling on the highway at 55 mph is brought to rest. However, the car which crashes directly into the bridge support experiences tremendously large forces, as the time of the impulse is very small. The car that crashes into the sand canisters, increases the time of the collision, sometimes many times longer than the first car, which allows the force on the car to be decreased by the same factor. This is similar to the example of the ball falling into the sand.

ANSWERS

For You To Do

(continued)

2.–3. Data will vary.

4. a) Data will vary.

5. a) Data will vary.

Perform the activity outside of traffic areas. Do not obstruct paths to exits. Do not leave carts lying on the floor.

2. Mount the sonic ranger at the bottom of a ramp and place the force probe against a barrier about 10 cm from the bottom of the ramp, as shown in the diagram. Attach an index card to the back of the car, to obtain better reflection of the sound wave and improve the readings of the sonic ranger.

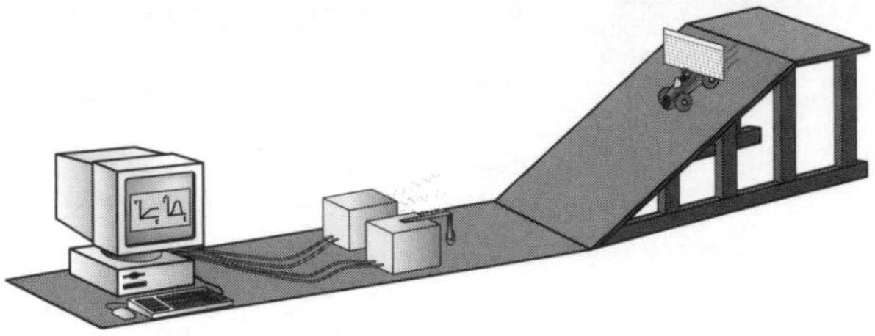

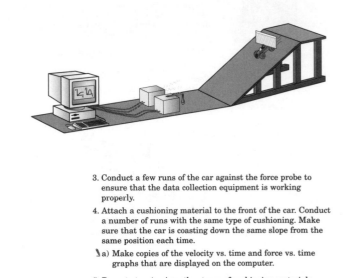

3. Conduct a few runs of the car against the force probe to ensure that the data collection equipment is working properly.

4. Attach a cushioning material to the front of the car. Conduct a number of runs with the same type of cushioning. Make sure that the car is coasting down the same slope from the same position each time.

   a) Make copies of the velocity vs. time and force vs. time graphs that are displayed on the computer.

5. Repeat step 4 using other types of cushioning materials.

   a) Record your observations in your log.

6. Use the graphical information you obtained in this activity to answer the following:

a) Compare the force vs. time graphs for the cushioned cars with those for the cars without cushioning.

b) Compare the areas under the force vs. time graphs for all of the experimental trials.

c) Compute the momentum of the car (the product of the mass and the velocity) prior to the collision and compare it with the area of the force vs. time graphs.

d) Summarize your comparisons in a chart.

e) How can impulse be used to explain the effectiveness of cushioning systems?

f) Describe the relationship between impulse ($F\Delta t$) and the change in momentum ($m\Delta v$).

PHYSICS TALK

Change in Momentum and Impulse

Momentum is the product of the mass and the velocity of an object.

$$p = mv$$

where p is the momentum, m is the mass, and v is the velocity.

Change in momentum is the product of mass and the change in velocity.

$$\Delta p = m\Delta v$$

Impulse = change in momentum

$$F\Delta t = m\Delta v$$

Answers

For You To Do

(continued)

6. a) Data will vary. Generally, students should notice that the force is greater on the collision without the cushioning.

b) Data will vary. If the speeds before the collisions are the same, then the areas under the graphs will be the same.

c) Mass x velocity should equal the area under the force vs. time graphs. The relevant velocity is the velocity at impact, which should be the highest value recorded by the sonic ranger. The area under the graph should equal the change in momentum of the car, since the final momentum is zero. Student answers may vary due to calculation and measurement errors.

d) Data will vary.

e) Impulse is the change in momentum, and is therefore related to the mass and the velocity of the car. Depending on the cushioning, there will be an increase in the time, impulse remaining constant; thus the force acting on the car and individuals inside will be less.

f) Impulse equals the change in momentum.

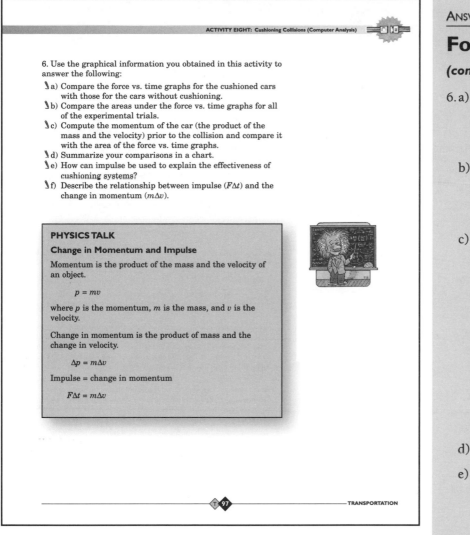

ANSWERS

Physics To Go

1. Helmets use cushioning materials that lengthen the time of impact and thus decrease the force of impact. Note that helmets are designed to break and should not be used again after an accident. A rigid, unbreakable helmet would be useless.

2. The ability of bumpers to withstand collisions at various speeds is directly related to the ability of the bumpers to minimize the force of the impact via cushioning. The intent of the regulation is to protect the consumer from expensive repairs after every fender-bender or parking lot bump. The industry was able to get the regulation changed by arguing that the initial cost of effective bumpers was too high and the added weight contributed to higher fuel consumption. Arguments for another change can be based on consumer preference, cost of injuries, and the development of new materials and technologies that would reduce initial costs.

3. a) $\Delta p = m\Delta v$;

$\Delta p = m \text{ x } (v_2 - v_1)$;

$\Delta p = 1200 \text{ kg x } (0 - 10 \text{ m/s})$;

$\Delta p = 12\ 000 \text{ kg.m/s}$

b) $\Delta p = m\Delta v$;

$\Delta p = m \text{ x } (v_2 - v_1)$;

$\Delta p = 1200 \text{ kg x } (5 \text{ m/s} - 10 \text{ m/s})$;

$\Delta p = 6\ 000 \text{ kg m/s}$

SAFTEY

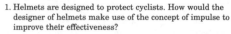

REFLECTING ON THE ACTIVITY AND THE CHALLENGE

What you learned in this activity better prepares you to defend the design of your safety system. The principles of momentum and impulse must be used to justify your design. Previously, you discovered objects with greater mass are more difficult to stop than smaller ones. You determined that increasing the velocity of objects also makes them more difficult to stop. Objects that have a greater mass or greater velocity have greater momentum.

Linking the two ideas together allows you to begin examining the relationship between momentum and impulse. For a large momentum change in a short time, a large force is required. A crushed rib cage or broken leg bones often result. The change in the momentum can be defined by the impulse on the object.

What devise will you use to increase the stopping time for the challenge activity? Make sure that you include impulse and change in momentum in your report. Your design features must be supported by the principles of physics.

PHYSICS TO GO

1. Helmets are designed to protect cyclists. How would the designer of helmets make use of the concept of impulse to improve their effectiveness?
2. The US Congress periodically reviews federal legislation that relates to the design of safer cars. For many years, one regulation was that car bumpers must be able to withstand a 5 mph collision. What was the intent of this regulation? The speed was later lowered to 3 mph. Why? Should it be changed again?
3. If a car has a mass of 1200 kg and an initial velocity of 10 m/s (about 20 mph) calculate the change in momentum required to:

   a) bring it to rest

   b) slow it to 5 m/s (approximately 10 mph)

TRANSPORTATION T 98

4. If the braking force for a car is 10,000 N, calculate the impulse if the brake is applied for 1.2 s. If the car has a mass of 1200 kg, what is the change in velocity of the car over this 1.2 s time interval?
5. A 1500 kg car, traveling at 5 m/s after braking, strikes a power pole and comes to a full stop in 0.1 s. Calculate the force exerted by the power pole and brakes required to stop the car.
6. For the car described in question 5, explain why a break-away pole that brings the car to rest after 2.8 s is safer than the conventional power pole?
7. Write a short essay relating your explanation for the operation of the cushioning systems to the explanation of the operation of the air bags.
8. Explain why a collapsible steering wheel is able to help prevent injuries during a car crash.
9. Compare and contrast the two Force vs Time graphs shown.

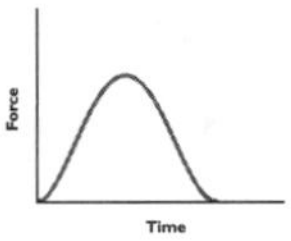

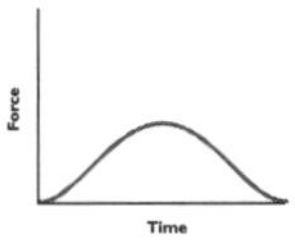

STRETCHING EXERCISE

Package an egg in a small container so that the egg will not break upon impact. Your teacher will provide the limitations in the construction of your package. You may be limited to two pieces of paper and some tape. You may be limited to a certain size package or a package of a certain weight. Bring your package to class so that it can be compared in a crash test with the other packages.

(HINT: Place each egg in a plastic bag before packaging to help avoid a messy cleanup.)

ANSWERS

Physics To Go

(continued)

4. Impulse $\Delta p = F\Delta t$

Δp = 10 000 N x 1.2 s

Δp = 12 000 kg.m/s

change in velocity is Δv therefore:

$\Delta p = m\Delta v$

$\Delta v = \Delta p / m$

Δv = 12 000 k.gm/s / 1200 kg

Δv = 10 m/s)

5. $\Delta p = F\Delta t$

$m\Delta v = F\Delta t$

$F = m\Delta v/\Delta t$

F = 1500 kg x 4.2 m/s / 0.1 s

F = 63 000 N

6. Increasing the time from 0.1 s to 2.8 seconds decreases the force acting on the car (and the driver).

$\Delta p = F\Delta t$

$m\Delta v = F\Delta t$

$F = m\Delta v/\Delta t$

F = 1500 kg x 5 m/s / 2.8 s

F = 2700 N

7. Students' answers will vary.
8. The steering wheel increases the time of contact, and will decrease the force acting on the body. Similar to previous answer.
9. The first graph has a greater force over a shorter time period, and the second graph has a smaller force over a longer period of time. If you measure the area under the graph, you will find the impulse.

2

ACTIVITY NINE
Safety in the Air

Background Information

When designing a safety device it is important to realize that it must be used by ordinary people in sometimes extraordinary situations. Important as it is to design something to attach to a car or airplane, it is as important to be able to effectively communicate your design and its function to the general population. You might have the most fantastic design for a device, but if you cannot explain how to use it, or it can only be used by a small minority, then it is almost useless.

In this activity the students will design a test to help identify certain qualities of individuals who will be able to sit by the exit doors. It will not be designed with the intention of eliminating a particular group of people, but rather identify the qualities that are needed to effectively perform the task of ensuring that the exit is open, secure and safe. The skills that the individuals would need would be identified by the students, and then they will design a test which is easy to administer, and would not cause undue embarrassment.

One thing which should not be overlooked, is to ask for volunteers to take the test, for the purpose of placing them close to the exit. That way, you could eliminate the potential embarrassment.

The tasks that this test would need to cover would be:

- that the passenger have the physical stamina to open the exit door, and store it, and help passengers as needed;
- the ability to read, and understand the written and verbal commands given in the instruction sheet, and by the crew of the airline;
- the ability to recognize danger and the potential for danger before and after the exit door is opened;
- the overall ability not to panic in emergency situations.

Active-ating the Physics InfoMall

While this is a good activity for your students, the InfoMall does not directly address this issue. However, with a little thought, you might find plenty of interesting material that relates to air travel. How fast do planes fly, anyway?

Planning for the Activity

Time Requirements

Allow approximately 40 minutes for the students to design their test, and then about 20 minutes to have the students apply this test to another member of their class. (As an extension, you could have other teachers or members of the staff try some of the tests.)

Materials needed

For the class:

- *Active Physics Transportation* Content Video (Segment: Safety in Air)
- VCR and TV monitor

Advance Preparation and Setup

A creative way to set the mood for this activity is to show the *Active Physics Transportation* Content Video of a flight attendant giving the pre-flight instructions to the passengers on a commercial plane. Alternatively, you may want to act as if the classroom was an airplane: arrange the chairs in rows along a central aisle, position a student assigned in advance to act our the pre-flight instructions at the head of the aisle, collect "Boarding Passes" at the door, have a flight attendant move up the aisle offering candy, etc.

Teaching Notes

You can use the *Active Physics Transportation* Content Video to set the scene for students who have never flown. A careful reading of the Exit seating rules is sure to generate a lot of discussion including comments from students who may have had personal experiences on airplanes. The students will probably focus on the need to lift the exit door, but keep the discussion broader; include the general need for a literate population and the need for good communication skills. One important term in the requirements is "assess". How can a passenger assess - if it is safe to open the door, if the slide is properly engaged, if the safe escape route has been selected? The discussion will touch upon the features of flight and the aircraft itself in addition to human decision making.

CAUTION: Be aware of any hurtful comments or activities that may occur between students. Some students' tests may involve numerous activities that may be potentially harmful. Remind the students of proper and safe lab procedures.

Encourage students to develop a test which is possible for anyone to perform, regardless of sex, race, etc. There may be the tendency to make the test difficult enough to eliminate certain people. The idea is to design the test so that the airline would be able to have at least two or three people available to help at each exit should the need arise. Therefore, the test should be inclusive rather than exclusive.

Activity Overview

This lesson uses the FAA rules for exit row seating to engage the students in a discussion of the human factors involved in technological design.

Student Objectives

Students will:

- critically read a technical document.
- understand the role of communication skills in technological issues.
- assess the role of humans in successful safety design.

ANSWERS FOR THE TEACHER ONLY

What Do You Think?

Students' answers will vary. The requirements should include some of the following:

- physical strength to operate the door.
- physically mobile (no handicapped/incapacitated individuals.
- be able to understand the written instructions.
- be able to initiate necessary procedures.

CHAPTER 2 SAFETY

Activity Nine

Saftey in the Air

WHAT DO YOU THINK?

The excitement of your first plane ride has continued to build and you are not even off the ground. You begin to wonder if that person seated by the exit door is capable of carrying out the responsibilities that the flight attendant has just described.

- **What do you think should be the requirements for sitting in an exit row?**
- **If you were limited to three requirements, what would they be?**

Record your ideas about these questions in your *Active Physics log*. Be prepared to discuss your responses with your small group and the class.

FOR YOU TO DO

1. On the following pages is the safety information of an airline. Read it carefully.

   a) Write down your interpretations of the requirements for sitting in an exit seat.

TRANSPORTATION T 100

ANSWERS

For You To Do

1. a) Students' work.

IT'S ON TIME AIRLINES

Exit Seating

The Federal Aviation Administration (FAA) regulations (14CFR, part 121) outline specific policies and procedures U.S. air carriers must follow concerning exit seating in aircraft. The following content of the rules is being provided for your information and guidance.

RESTRICTIONS

No air carrier may seat a person in a designated exit seat if it is likely that the person would be unable to perform one or more of the applicable functions listed under REQUIREMENTS below because—

1. The person lacks sufficient mobility, strength, or dexterity in both arms and hands, and both legs to
   (A) reach upward, sideways, and downward to the location of emergency exit and exit slide operating mechanismisms;
   (B) grasp and push, pull, turn, or otherwise manipulate those mechanisms;
   (C) push, shove, pull or otherwise open emergency exits;
   (D) lift out, hold, deposit on nearby seats, or maneuver over the seatbacks to the next row objects the size and weight of over-wing window exit doors (approximately 24 1/4"x 39" and up to 53 lbs);
   (E) remove obstructions similar in size and weight to over-wing exit doors (approximately 24 1/4" x 39" and up to 53 lbs);
   (F) reach the emergency exit expeditiously;
   (G) maintain balance while removing obstructions;
   (H) exit expeditiously;
   (I) stabilize an escape slide after deployment, or
   (J) assist others in getting of an escape slide, or
2. The person is less than 15 years of age, or
3. The person lacks the capacity to perform one or more of the applicable functions without the assistance of an adult companion, parent, or other relative, or
4. The persons lacks the ability to read and understand instructions related to emergency evacuation provided by the air carrier in printed or graphic form or the ability to understand oral crew commands, or
5. The person lacks sufficient visual capacity to perform one or more of the applicable functions without the assistance of visual aids beyond contact lenses or eyeglasses or
6. The person lacks sufficient aural capacity to hear and understand instructions shouted by crew members without assistance beyond a hearing aid, or
7. The person lacks the ability to convey information orally to other passengers, or
8. The person has (a) a condition or responsibilities, such as caring for small children that might prevent the person from performing one or more of the applicable functions or (b) a condition that might cause the person harm if he or she performs one or more of the applicable functions.

→

2

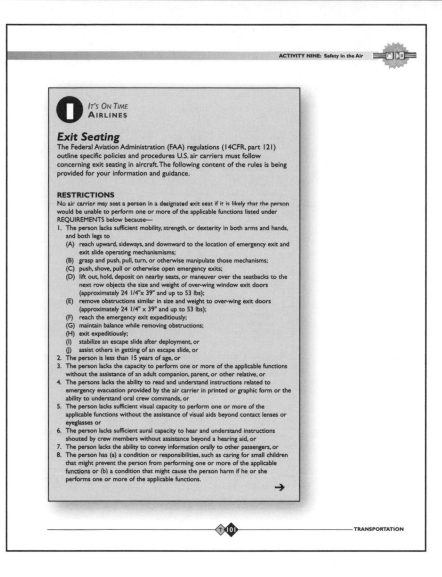

REQUIREMENTS FOR SITTING IN EXIT SEATS

In the event of an emergency in which a crew member is not available to assist in an evacuation of the aircraft a passenger occupying an exit seat may be asked to perform the following functions:

1. Locate the emergency exit;
2. Recognize the emergency exit opening mechanism;
3. Comprehend the instructions for operating the emergency exits;
4. Operate the emergency exit;
5. Assess whether opening the emergency exit will increase the hazards to which passengers may be exposed;
6. Follow oral directions and hand signals given by crew member;
7. Stow or secure the emergency exit door so that it will not impede use of the exit;
8. Assess the condition of an escape slide, activate the slide, and stabilize the slide after deployment to assist others in getting off the slide;
9. Pass expeditiously through the emergency exit; and
10. Assess, select, and follow a safe path away from the emergency exit and aircraft.

Any passengers assigned an exit seat may request reseating if they:

1. Cannot meet the selection criteria above:
2. Have a nondiscernible condition that will prevent them from performing the applicable functions.
3. May suffer bodily harm as a result of performing one or more of the applicable functions;
4. Do not wish to perform these functions.

If you would like to change your seat for a non-exit seat, please see the It's on time agent or flight attendant. U.S. government regulations prohibit an individual from sitting in a designated exit seat if they cannot speak, read or understand the instructions.

Your understanding and compliance with these FAA regulations will be appreciated.

Thank you.

2. Meet with your design team to develop a test that could be used at the airport check-in counter to determine a person's fitness for an exit-door seat. Your test will be applied to a person from outside your group. Be ready to defend the reasons behind your test.

   Consider some of the following questions in designing your test and in evaluating the tests of other groups:

- Does the test cover all essential requirements?
- Does the test provide essential information?
- Does the test address communications skills?
- Is the test quick?
- Does the test avoid embarrassment?
- Is the test necessary?

PHYSICS TO GO

1. The Exit Seating Instruction Sheet is long and complicated. Rewrite it in simpler words on a 5" x 8" card that could be glued to the seat back.
2. Does the Exit Seating Instruction Sheet convey the right information? Translate the English version into another language that you speak or study.
3. What additional requirements might you include on the Exit Seating Instruction Sheet?
4. Look up the statistics concerning accidents. Compare the numbers for the airline industry with those of the automotive industry. Which is a safer means of transportation? Safety is often described in terms of deaths per thousand passenger-miles. Is that a good measure? Is it appropriate for comparing passenger cars to planes? What about other means of mass transit: planes, trains and school buses?
5. Write an Exit Seating Instruction Sheet for a train.
6. Write an Exit Seating Instruction Sheet for a school bus.
7. How would you get the passengers to pay attention to the emergency instructions given by flight attendants at the beginning of each flight?

ANSWERS

Physics To Go

1.-7. Students' work.

ANSWERS

For You To Do

(continued)

2. Students' work.

PHYSICS AT WORK

Mohan Thomas

DESIGNING AUTOMOBILES THAT SAVE LIVES

Mo is a Senior Project Engineer at General Motors North American Operation's (NAO) Safety Center and his responsibilities include making sure that different General Motors vehicles meet national safety requirements. Several of the design features that Mo has helped to develop have been implemented into vehicles that are now out on the road.

"This is how it works," he explains. "An engineer for a vehicle comes to us here at the Safety Center and requests technical assistance with design features to help them meet the side impact crash regulations required by the government. You have to analyze the physical forces of an event, which involves one car hitting another car on the side and then the door smashing into the driver," he continues. "We'll study the velocity, acceleration, momentum, and inertia in an event, as well as the materials used in the vehicle itself."

"The initial energy of an impact from one vehicle on another," states Mo, " has to be managed by the vehicle that's getting hit. Our goal is to manage the energy in such a way that the occupant in the vehicle being hit is protected. You take the forces that are coming into the vehicle and you redirect them into areas around the occupant. The frame work of the car, therefore, is very important to the design, as well as energy absorbing materials used in the vehicle."

Mo grew up in Chicago, Illinois, and has always enjoyed math and science, but he was also interested in creative writing. He wanted to combine math and science with creative work and has found that combination in the design work of engineering. "The nice part of being at the Safety Center," states Mo, "is that you know that you are contributing to something meaningful. The bottom line is that the formulas and problems that we are working on are meant to save people's lives."

Chapter 2 Assessment

Your design team will develop a safety system for protecting automobile, airplane, bicycle, motorcycle or train passengers. As you study existing safety systems, you and your design team should be listing ideas for improving an existing system or designing a new system for preventing accidents. You may also consider a system that will minimize the harm caused by accidents.

Your final product will be a working model or prototype of a safety system. On the day that you bring the final product to class, the teams will display them around the room while class members informally view them and discuss them with members of the design team. At this time, class members will generate questions about each others' products. The questions will be placed in envelopes provided to each team by the teacher. The teacher will use some of these questions during the oral presentations on the next day. The product will be judged according to the following:

1. The quality of your safety feature enhancement and the working model or prototype.
2. The quality of a 5-minute oral report that should include:

- **the need for the system;**
- **the method used to develop the working model;**
- **demonstration of the working model;**
- **discussion of the physics concepts involved;**
- **description of the next-generation version of the system;**
- **answers to questions posed by the class.**

3. The quality of a written and/or multimedia report including:

- **the information from the oral report;**
- **documentation of the sources of expert information;**
- **discussion of consumer acceptance and market potential;**
- **discussion of the physics concepts applied in the design of the safety system.**

Criteria

Review the criteria that were agreed to at the beginning of the chapter. If they require modification, come to an agreement with the teacher and the class.

Your project should be judged by you and your design team according to the criteria before you display and share it with your class. Being able to judge the quality of your own work before you submit it is one of the skills that will make you a "treasured employee"!

CHAPTER 2 SAFETY

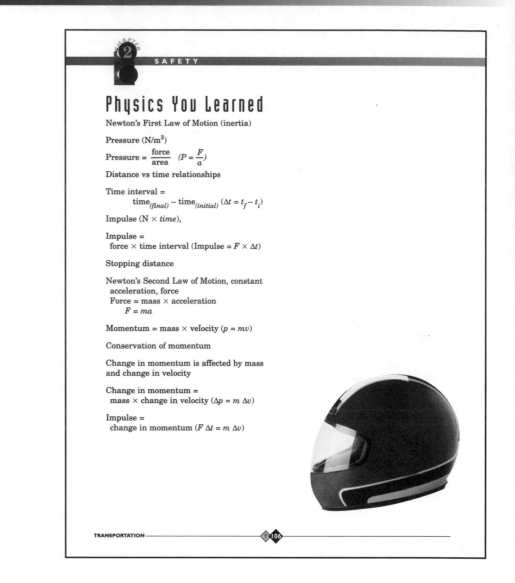

Physics You Learned

Newton's First Law of Motion (inertia)

Pressure (N/m^2)

Pressure = $\frac{\text{force}}{\text{area}}$ $(P = \frac{F}{a})$

Distance vs time relationships

Time interval =
time$_{(final)}$ − time$_{(initial)}$ $(\Delta t = t_f - t_i)$

Impulse (N × *time*),

Impulse =
force × time interval (Impulse = $F \times \Delta t$)

Stopping distance

Newton's Second Law of Motion, constant acceleration, force
Force = mass × acceleration
$F = ma$

Momentum = mass × velocity ($p = mv$)

Conservation of momentum

Change in momentum is affected by mass and change in velocity

Change in momentum =
mass × change in velocity ($\Delta p = m\,\Delta v$)

Impulse =
change in momentum ($F\,\Delta t = m\,\Delta v$)

TRANSPORTATION T106

NOTES

2

Alternative Chapter Assessment Test

Part A: Multiple Choice:

Choose the best answer and place on your answer sheet.

1. Safety belts

a) always protect you from death in an accident

b) seldom protect you from death in an accident

c) increase the chances of you suffering severe injuries or death

d) decrease the chances of you suffering severe injuries or death

2. Seat belts are more effective

a) when used alone

b) when used with shoulder belts

c) when used with air bags

d) when used with shoulder belts and air bags

3. Which of the following are safety features, that have been added to most vehicles in the last ten years?

a) shoulder belts in back seats

b) air bags

c) ABS brakes

d) all of these

4. A seat belt is a safety device used in a vehicle because in a low-speed accident

a) they slow down the vehicle

b) they slow down the occupants in the vehicle

c) they prevent the occupants from flying around inside the vehicle

d) they prevent the occupants from dying

5. In a collision, there are generally more than one collision. Which of the following would describe the collisions of an accident?

a) when the car hits a stationary object, and the occupant hits the dashboard

b) when the car hits a stationary object, the occupant hits the dashboard, and the brain collides with the inside of the skull

c) when the occupant hits the dashboard, and the brain collides with the inside of the skull

d) when the car hits a stationary object, the occupant flies out of the vehicle, and hits the ground and stops

6. Newton's first law is

a) inertia

b) impulse

c) momentum

d) force

7. In order to have a change in inertia, you must have
a) no force
b) balanced forces
c) a force opposite to the object's motion
d) an accelerating force

8. Momentum is the product of
a) mass and acceleration
b) mass and velocity
c) velocity and acceleration
d) force and velocity

9. The reason for having a wide seat belt as opposed to having a thinner seat belt is
a) it is more comfortable when driving
b) it reduces the force on your body when stopping
c) it increases the impulse on your body when stopping
d) it decreases the pressure of the seat belt on your body while stopping

10. Impulse is the same as
a) change in velocity
b) change in impulse
c) change in momentum
d) change in acceleration

2

11. By wearing a seat belt, and a shoulder belt, you are potentially reducing the damage to your body because
a) you are decreasing the velocity of the car
b) you are increasing the impulse of the car
c) you are decreasing the change in momentum of the car
d) you are increasing the time of the impulse of the car

12. A car was travelling at 35 m/s. The car hit a tree, and the crush zone in the car was only 0.40 m. What was the acceleration of the driver of the car?
a) 1521 m/s2
b) 3182 m/s2
c) 7 m/s2
d) 14 m/s2

13. The average speed of a car that is slowing down from 25 m/s to 0 m/s in 3.0 s is
a) 25 m/s
b) 12.5 m/s
c) 8.3 m/s
d) 0 m/s

14. The acceleration of an airplane travelling at 65 m/s that stops on a runway 200 m long in 10 s is

a) 6.5 m/s2

b) 650 m/s2

c) 0.325 m/s2

d) 3.1 m/s2

15. The force to stop a vehicle is supplied by

a) the friction caused by the road against the tires

b) the friction caused by the motor slowing down

c) the friction caused by the brake pads against the moving wheels

d) the inertia of the car

16. The bungee cord works to reduce the force on your body by

a) decreasing the time you are falling

b) increasing the time you are falling

c) increasing the time the elastic part of the cord is slowing you down

d) decreasing the time the elastic part of the cord is slowing you down

17. What is the impulse required to bring a 1000-kg vehicle moving at 25 m/s to a stop in 5.0 s?

a) 25 000 kgm/s

b) 125 000 kgm/s

c) 40 kgm/s

d) 5000 kgm/s

18. What is the momentum of a 75-kg tennis player moving at 6.5 m/s?

a) 488 kgm/s

b) 736 kgm/s

c) 11.5 kgm/s

d) 81.5 kgm/s

Use the following information to answer questions 19 - 21.

A cyclist (mass of cyclist and bicycle is 90 kg) is travelling along a road at 58 km/h (16 m/s).

19. What force is necessary to bring him to rest in 10 s?

a) 56 N

b) 144 N

c) 522 N

d) 14 400 N

20. Where does the force necessary to bring him to a stop come from?

a) no force is necessary, as he will glide to a stop

b) the friction between the road and the tires

c) the friction between the wheels and the brakes

d) friction from wind resistance and the road

21. If time were to change, which time would most likely do the most damage to the cyclist and his bike?

a) 1 s

b) 5 s

c) 15 s

d) 20 s

22. Which of the following would be very important when designing an automatic triggering device?

a) the device must trigger 100 % of the time

b) the device must trigger at high speeds when brought to a slow stop

c) the device must trigger at low speeds when brought to a sudden stop

d) none of these

23. The sand or water canisters you see around bridge supports are similar to air bags in that they

a) are large and protect something hard (cement or dashboard)

b) reduce the impulse of the collision

c) increase the force by decreasing the time of the collision

d) decrease the force by increasing the time of the collision

Part B: Matching

Match the words or phrases on the left with the matching word or phrase on the right.

__ 1. average speed	A. increase the time of collision
__ 2. acceleration	B. final velocity + initial velocity /2
__ 3. impulse	C. change in momentum
__ 4. momentum	D. part of the car to reduce injuries in collisions
__ 5. decrease force	E. reduce energy and therefore velocity in bungee cord
__ 6. friction	F. change velocity divided by change in time
__ 7. crush zone	G. product of mass and velocity
__ 8. inertia	H. Newton's First Law of Motion

Part C: Written Response

Write the answers in complete sentences in the space provided.

1. Describe why seat belts are an important safety device. Be sure to include how physics plays a role.

   A: Answers will vary. Look for seat belts keep the occupant in the car; seat belts slow the occupant down in a more controlled fashion; they spread out the force over a large area of the body, rather than concentrate it in one spot (head on dashboard); they decrease the extent of injury, thus keeping the cost of health care lower.

2. Describe what type of material would make the best kind of seat belt. Include in your answer such qualities as comfort, safety, pressure, cost.

   A: Answers will vary. The ideal type of material, would be inexpensive, have high tensile strength, washable, would decrease the force per unit area (pressure) to the body to an acceptable level, easy to install, readily available materials, be soft to touch so as to be more comfortable, be relatively light.

3. Describe the role of inertia in the three collisions that occur in an accident.

   A: Inertia is the tendency for an object to stay in motion, therefore, when a vehicle stops abruptly (in a collision), the first collision is when the car hits the wall, and the force of the wall causes the vehicle to come to a rest. Because the passenger is in motion, the second collision comes when the force of the vehicle, at rest now, exerts the force against the passenger causing it to come to a rest. The third collision is the force exerted by the inside of the skull, now at rest, against the moving brain.

4. Describe how a parachute works in helping prevent injury to the body. (Be sure to include impulse and force into your answer.)

   A: A parachute will slow down your descent, where the velocity is much decreased. This slower velocity gives a lower momentum ($m \times v$), which therefore lowers the impulse of the parachutist landing on the ground. $F\Delta t = m\Delta v$.

5. Explain why a helmet is designed to break upon impact.

   A: A helmet is designed to increase the time of the collision, therefore decreasing the force of the impact. If the helmet was rigid, then the total force of the collision would be transferred to the head, and serious damage would result.

6. Your baseball coach has been reminding you to stay in contact with the ball and follow through when you hit. Explain why, in terms of the physics you learned about in this chapter, this is important.

   A: The longer (Δt) you can keep in contact (F) with the ball the greater the impulse ($F\Delta t$). Therefore, the greater the impulse, the greater the change in momentum ($F\Delta t = m\Delta v$). (Mass stays constant).

7. Explain how an air bag works. Include the terms pressure, force, impulse, change in momentum.

   A: Answers will vary. An air bag essentially changes the force that is applied to the head during a collision because the time of the collision is larger, and the impulse or change in momentum is the same. Because the air bag has a large surface area, the force is spread out over a large area, causing the pressure on the head to be smaller.

8. You have recently dislocated your shoulder, but it doesn't hurt that badly and you are sitting in the seat next to the emergency exit on the plane. Your friend says that you should change seats with him so that he is next to the seat. Explain why your friend thinks it is a good idea.

   A: Because your need to be able to operate the emergency exit, efficiently, and with a dislocated shoulder, even though it doesn't hurt, may hinder or slow your actions and response time in an emergency.

Alternative Chapter Assessment Answers

Part A: Multiple Choice:

1. d
2. d
3. d
4. c
5. b
6. a
7. d
8. b
9. d
10. c
11. d
12. c
13. b
14. a
15. a
16. c
17. a
18. a
19. b
20. b
21. a
22. a
23. d

Part B: Matching:

1. B
2. F
3. C
4. G
5. A
6. E
7. D
8. H.

2

NOTES

3

Transportation Chapter 3- Journey to the Moon and Beyo

National Science Education Standards

Chapter Summary

Science fiction as a style of writing sets the stage for this chapter. Students are challenged to help any young science fiction fan to learn the difference between science fact and science fiction. They are to write a science fiction story that incorporates a trip to the moon. Then, students must write annotation that explains where the science is true and where the science has been modified to make the story interesting or exciting.

To meet this challenge, students engage in collaborative activities that explore differences in the atmosphere and gravity between the Earth and on the moon. These experiences engage students in the following content from the *National Science Education Standards.*

Content Standards

Unifying Concepts

- Systems, order & organization
- Evidence, models and explanations
- Constancy, change, and measurement

Science as Inquiry

- Identify questions and concepts that guide scientific investigations
- Use technology and mathematics to improve investigations
- Formulate & revise scientific explanations & models using logic and evidence
- Communicate and defend a scientific argument

History and Nature of Science

- Nature of scientific knowledge
- Historical Perspectives

Physical Science

- Motions and forces
- Conservation of energy & increase in disorder

Key Physics Concepts and Skills

Activity Summaries	Physics Principles
Activity One: Weight Change During Takeoff This activity introduces students to real and perceived changes in weight. Using a model elevator and a force probe, they investigate the changes in the measured weight, then generalize this in terms of velocity and acceleration. This introduction to gravity as force sets the stage for activities that focus on air and space travel.	• Physical properties of matter on Earth and in space • Effect of forces on motion
Activity Two: Weightlessness with Gravity Students explore free fall with graphical analysis of data collected in a computer simulation. They then apply the concept of free fall to analyze a variety of situations that vary the factors of mass, drag, and acceleration. Connecting this to sky diving and parachutes expands their understanding of the factors that affect free fall.	• Acceleration due to gravity • Relationship of gravity to free fall
Activity Three: Spreadsheet Games: Free Fall Using a computer simulation that allows comparison of velocity, acceleration, and time of objects with different mass, students investigate the ratio of gravity on the Earth to that on the moon and determine force necessary to move objects on the moon. Reading about how shape affects air molecules an object strikes helps them understand events that appear to conflict with science.	• Gravity and mass on the Earth and moon • Inertial and gravitational mass • Newton's Laws of Motion
Activity Four: Life Without Gravity Students observe and interpret what life is like in zero gravity. Students then brainstorm how common devices could be adapted for use without gravity. They conclude by reading more about daily routines in space.	• Newton's First Law • Technology with and without gravity
Activity Five: Exercise on the Moon Students measure inertial mass and weight. Using the relationships between weight and force of gravity, they are able to compare gravitational mass to inertial mass. They apply this understanding and knowledge of gravitational force on the moon and on Earth to design an exercise program for use in space.	• Newton's Second Law • Gravity and mass on the Earth and moon • Effect of force and gravity on horizontal and vertical motion
Activity Six: The Necessities of Life Looking first at oxygen requirements, students experiment with the differences in oxygen needs at rest and during exercise. They then consider how to obtain oxygen in space and explore how many plants would be needed to provide adequate oxygen for life in space. Other requirements for life in space, including food and water, are then considered.	• Photosynthesis • Fermi problem – oxygen use
Activity Seven: Communication How sound travels is the focus of this activity which involves students in testing sounds in a vacuum and in the classroom. They then read about how sound waves travel in air, water, and through objects. This introduces the need to use electromagnetic waves rather than sound waves to communicate in space.	• Sound waves • Sound in a vacuum
Activity Eight: The Speed of Radio Waves In this concluding activity, students learn more about radio waves that are used to communicate in space. They investigate time delay over several distances, then listen to NASA tapes from space missions to determine the delay that results from extreme distances.	• $d = vt$ where v is the speed of radio waves • Radio waves can travel in a vacuum

3

Equipment List For Chapter Three

QTY	TO SERVE	ACTIVITY	ITEM	COMMENT
1	Class	1	*Active Physics Transportation* Content Video	Segment: Person in Elevator
1	Class	4	*Active Physics Transportation* Content Video	Segment: Life Without Gravity
1	Class	5	*Active Physics Transportation* Content Video	Segments: Drop Hammer/Feather, Exercise on Moon
1	Class	8	*Active Physics Transportation* Content Video	Segment: Speed of Radio Waves
1	Class	3	*Active Physics* Spreadsheet Template	File: Free Fall XLS
1	Class	8	AM radio receiver	
1	Group	2	Balloon-and-Pin-in-Frame Apparatus	See specifications in Teacher's Guide for Activity Two
1	Class	7, 8	Battery or power supply	To operate bell, spark generator
1	Class	7, 8	Bell jar	
1	Group	1, 2	Box to contain mass hanging on scale	Serves as model of elevator
1	Group	2	Camcorder	
1	Group	3	Computer with "Excel" spreadsheet software	Load Free Fall XLS file on each group's computer
3	Class	7, 8	Connecting wires, insulated	
1	Class	8	DC spark generator (induction coil)	
1	Group	1, 2	Device for attaching spring scale to box	Eye screw, or wire through hole in box
1	Class	7	Electric bell	
1	Group	5	Laboratory cart	
1	Group	1, 2, 5	Mass, 1-kg	Able to be hung on spring scale
2	Group	2	Metal washer	
1	Group	2	Paper clip	
1	Group	2	Rubber band	
1	Individual	7, 8	Safety goggles	Wear in presence of vacuum in bell jar
1	Class	7, 8	Safety shield, transparent	Place between students and evacuated bell jar
1	Group	2	Source of water	
1	Group	6	Spirometer with one disposable mouthpiece	
1	Group	5	Spring scale, 0-10 newton range	
1	Group	1	Spring scale, 0-20 newton range	
1	Group	8	Stopwatch	
2	Group	2	Styrofoam® cup	
1	Class	7, 8	Switch	
1	Group	2	TV monitor	
1	Class	7, 8	Vacuum grease	To seal bell jar to base
1	Class	7, 8	Vacuum pump	
1	Class	1, 4, 5, 8	VCR and TV monitor	
1	Group	2	VCR having single-frame advance	

Organizer for Materials Available in Teacher's Edition

Activity in Student Text	Additional Material	Alternative / Optional Activities
ACTIVITY ONE: Weight Change During Takeoff, p. T110	Body Weight on Earth and Beyond, p. 246	
ACTIVITY TWO: Weightlessness with Gravity, p. T118		
ACTIVITY THREE: Spreadsheet Games: Free Fall, p. T124	Graphs For: The Falling Human Problem; Parachute Problem; Free Fall on Earth, Moon and Jupiter, pgs. 268-272	
ACTIVITY FOUR: Life without Gravity, p. T134	Assessments: Participation in Discussion, p. 284 Devices for Spaceship, p. 286	
ACTIVITY FIVE: Exercise on the Moon, p. T142	Assessment: Fitness Program, p. 296	
ACTIVITY SIX: The Necessities of Life, p. T148		
ACTIVITY SEVEN: Communication, p. T153	Morse Code, p. 313	
ACTIVITY EIGHT: The Speed of Radio Waves, p. T157		

JOURNEY TO THE MOON AND BEYOND

Scenario

"Do you know what life is like with a science fiction addict in the house? It is not easy. My little brother thinks our house is a colony on Mars, our garage is a space station, and our car is a star ship. You wouldn't believe the roles that I have had to play just to get some peace and quiet. It's a good thing that my Mom and Dad are good sports, scheduling launch opportunities, spacewalks, and nourishment periods. If you beam over to our place, be sure to refer to the microwave oven as a food replicator. Sometimes it is fun, like when he calls our grumpy, old cat a hostile alien. But it can be rough when he has trouble telling the difference between science fact and science fiction."

Challenge

Science fiction is a very popular style of writing. The bookstores and libraries are filled with science fiction literature. Some of the books and movies such as *Frankenstein*, *2001 – A Space Odyssey*, *Jurassic Park*, *Dr. Jekyll and Mr. Hyde*, *E.T.*, and *Star Wars* have become classics. Not only are the writers of these books or scripts creative writers with wonderful imaginations, but also they are all very knowledgeable about science. It is not uncommon for a science fiction writer or film director to consult with scientists to ensure that the ideas they use are credible. Can you imagine writing a script for a blockbuster, science-fiction movie? If you are successful, you provide entertainment for millions of people and earn lots of money! Some science-fiction movies have even gone beyond entertainment and provided ideas for scientists to develop. To write effectively, you must have good ideas and you must have an accurate understanding of your subject.

Chapter and Challenge Overview

In introducing the Challenge, emphasize the enjoyment of reading science fiction and how understanding the science can help you appreciate the skill of the storyteller. Is the writer able to evoke a sense of reality with unnatural events? Could the author have written a good or better story if the rules of nature were obeyed?

One possible opening might be to read a short story on the theme of outer space. The students may actually have one in their literature anthology if your school uses one. The school library should have collections of stories as well as magazines that include appropriate stories.

The Challenge asks the students to write a story and annotation to the story. You can expect examples in each story to have been mentioned in class, such as, noise in outer space. It is certainly valid, but you might want to include in the Criteria a two-level system for old and new phenomena. Perhaps a list could be posted where students could add ideas as the week goes on.

Perhaps on the day that the assignment is due, you could show a science fiction video and do a similar annotation as a group.

Your challenge is to help my little brother, or any other young sci-fi fan, learn the difference between science fact and science fiction.

- **Write a science fiction story that incorporates a trip to the moon or beyond.**
- **In a separate key to your story (an annotation), you must explain where the science is true and where you have modified the physics for interest or excitement.**

Criteria

You should discuss the criteria for this challenge in your small groups and then with the whole class. For instance, you should discuss:

- **the maximum and minimum length of the story and annotation;**
- **how much of the grade should depend on creativity and interest in the story;**
- **how much should depend on the annotation that relates and describes the real physics in your story and your modifications of physics;**
- **how many physics concepts you should include to receive an "A" for your work.**

Generate criteria that the class can all agree on. Be as specific as possible. A clear understanding of how your project will be graded will make it easier to do the best job possible.

T 109

Assessment Rubric for Challenge: Science Fiction Story and Annotation

Descriptor	5	4	3	2	1
Science Fiction Story					
The length of the story is between the maximum and minimum word requirement.					
The story has a science fiction theme about a trip to the moon or beyond.					
A significant number of physics principles are consistently addressed (either accurately, or inaccurately for interest and excitement). Many of the following physics principles are included: • physical properties of matter on Earth and in space • gravity and mass on Earth and on the moon • acceleration due to gravity • relationship of gravity to free fall • effects of forces on motion (Newton's First and Second Laws of Motion) • photosynthesis • oxygen use • sound waves and a vacuum • $d = vt$ where v is the speed of radio waves • radio waves can travel in a vacuum					
Physics concepts from the chapter are integrated in the appropriate places.					
The story has entertainment value. The story line is creative. The plot is exciting and/or humorous.					
Sentence structure is consistently controlled. Spelling, punctuation, and grammar are used in an effective manner.					
Annotation of Science Fiction Story					
Modifications of physics in the story for interest and excitement have been identified.					
A significant number of physics principles have been addressed. Many of the following physics principles are included and correctly explained: • physical properties of matter on Earth and in space • gravity and mass on Earth and on the moon • acceleration due to gravity • relationship of gravity to free fall • effects of forces on motion (Newton's First and Second Laws of Motion) • photosynthesis • oxygen use • sound waves and a vacuum • $d = vt$ where v is the speed of radio waves • radio waves can travel in a vacuum					

3

For use with *Transportation*, Chapter 3

Assessment Rubric for Challenge: Science Fiction Story and Annotation *(continued)*

Descriptor	5	4	3	2	1
Scientific symbols for units of measurement are used appropriately in all cases. Correct estimates of the magnitude of physical quantities are used as required.					
Physics terminology, symbols, and equations are incorporated as applicable.					
Sentence structure is consistently controlled. Spelling, punctuation, and grammar are used in an effective manner.					

What is in the Physics InfoMall for Chapter 3?

The Challenge and Scenario of this *Active Physics* chapter asks the students to think about science fact versus science fiction. Is science fiction a good way to introduce science concepts to students? If you wonder about such things, you may want to have access to a quick answer. Such information can be found on the Physics InfoMall CD-ROM.

The Physics InfoMall CD-ROM is a huge database containing over 30,000 pages of text and illustrations. While none of this is interactive, the volume of information is impressive. The search engine for finding information within this database is also impressive, and the question posed above gives us a good way to experience this.

There are a small number of ways to explore (or "shop") the InfoMall. The first way is simply to browse - walk in through the entrance, and click on any store to look inside. Depending on what you are looking for, this may work fine. For example, if you are curious what articles appear in the January 1979 issue of *American Journal of Physics*, you can either go to the Articles & Abstracts Attic, then select the desired issue; or you can look through the journal index in the Utilities Closet. Another way to find information is using the search engine. This is useful for finding specific information. Let's use "science fiction" as an example.

After entering the InfoMall, click on "Functions" from the menu bar and select "Compound Search." This will bring up a window which will allow you to specify the search you wish to do. CAUTION: this information is generated on a Macintosh, and may vary slightly from what you will find on a PC. The same CD-ROM works on both platforms, and the database is the same: The interface is a little different. Click the "Search under databases" button and select all databases, then click "Apply," followed by "OK." The search will take less than a minute, and will return all occurrences of the words "science fiction." The first ten hits on the list of search results are all articles. You should check them out - they are on the InfoMall in their entirety. And the text is all live, meaning you can print it, copy it, and even paste it into your own handouts.

ACTIVITY ONE
Weight Change During Takeoff

Background Information

Galileo was the first to show that all things fall to Earth with a changing velocity or constant acceleration. He did many experiments rolling balls down ramps, and dropping objects from different heights driving down stakes. He observed that a rock dropped from a higher height will drive the stake in farther than if dropped at a lower height. He concluded that this must be due to the rock having a greater velocity. His ramp experiments showed that every object will accelerate at the same rate if released at the same height.

Sir Isaac Newton, sitting under his apple tree, observed an apple falling to Earth. From this observation, he thought that if gravity is a force that can act upon an apple from a tree, and that it also will act upon an apple higher (such as on a mountain top), he postulated, that it must also act upon the moon and beyond. The moon travels around the Earth in a circular path, and anything traveling in a circular path has to be accelerating. The force that causes the acceleration, always points towards the center of the circular path. Newton tried to determine the acceleration of the moon, calculating the acceleration of the moon towards Earth. Using the formula $a_c = v^2\ r$ (formula for centripetal acceleration), where a_c is the acceleration of the moon towards Earth, r is the distance between the Earth the moon, and v is the speed at which the moon travels around the Earth, Newton calculated the acceleration of the moon. Because the velocity is in a circle, $v=d/t$ where $d = 2\pi r$, and t is the period (T) of one revolution (27.3 days), we can rewrite the formula as

$a_c = v^2\ r$ or

$a_c = 4\pi^2 r/T^2$ where $T = 27.3\ d = 2.36 \times 106$ s

$a_c = 4\pi^2\ 3.84 \times 10^8\ \text{m}/(2.36 \times 10^8\ \text{s})^2$

$a_c = 0.0027\ \text{m/s}^2$

Newton noticed that this was about 1/3600 of the value of acceleration of gravity on Earth (9.8 m/s^2). The distance to the center of the Earth was known to be about 6400 km, and the distance to the moon is about 60 times that value. Newton noticed that if you squared 60, you would get 3600 which agrees with the inverse square law, i.e.: the force of gravity is proportional to the inverse of the square of the distance from the Earth $F_g\ 1/r^2$ where r = the distances between the two masses. Newton realized, that the masses of the objects would affect the force of gravity as well, and combined this to describe the relationship of $F_g\ m_1 m_2/r^2$ where F_g is the force due to gravity, m_1 is the mass of one object (Earth), m_2 is the mass of the other object (moon) and r is the distance from the centers of these masses. Adding a proportionality constant (G), Newton came up with the Universal Law of Gravitation

$F_g = Gm_1 m_2/r^2$ where G is the Gravitational constant ($6.67 \times 10^{-11}\ \text{Nm}^2/\text{kg}^2$). Newton's Law states that every body in the universe attracts every other body with gravitational force, and is proportional to their masses and to the inverse square of the distance from their centers.

Using Newton's Universal Law of Gravitation, we can determine the acceleration of gravity (g) at different points in the gravitational field around Earth. Knowing the weight of an object (Fg), we can determine the effect of g on the surface of the Earth at a distance r from the center of Earth.

Combining

$F_g = mg$ and Newton's Law

$F_g = Gm_1 m_2/r^2$, give us

$m^2 g = Gm_1 m_2/r^2$ where m_1 is the mass of the Earth, and m_2 is the mass of the object (say an astronaut), and r is the distance between the centers of the masses. Therefore,

$g = Gm_1/r^2$.

We can use this formula to determine the acceleration of any object at any distance from another object. This is known as the gravitational field strength of a producing body (such as the Earth).

In this activity the students will be measuring the relative effects of accelerating up or down, by measuring the local gravitational field strength of an object in an elevator. The best way for students to do this is in an elevator which has a very high speed. While standing on the bathroom scale, they will notice a large weight change on the scale. (The scale really measures the weight of a body. The scale should properly be measured in newtons.) If, however, there is no elevator available, then they can use the box set up in the text book.

When the box is at rest, the 1-kg mass will weigh 9.8 N ($F_g = mg$, where m = 1 kg and g = 9.8 m/s^2). When the box is accelerating upward, the mass will appear to weigh more, and when the box is accelerating downward, it will appear to weigh less. This can be seen in the following formula
$F_{net} = F_A - F_g$, where F_{net} is the accelerating force, F_A is the force applied (or the reading on the scale), and F_g is the weight of the object. If the object is

accelerating upward, then the F_{net} is positive (upward direction is positive, and downwards is negative), and the weight does not change, the reading on the scale (F_A) reads greater than the weight. When the object is accelerating downward, then the opposite is the case, and the F_A is smaller than the weight.

If the F_A is the same as F_g, then we say it has an acceleration of 1g. If the F_A is twice that of the weight, it has an acceleration of 2g. (Another term, that might be familiar to the students is g-force, which is used in training pilots and astronauts.) If the F_A reading is half the weight, then it will be 1/2g.

Active-ating the Physics InfoMall

Activity One is about changes (or apparent changes) in gravity and how we sense such changes. The topic is motivated by the common example of riding in an elevator. This suggests a quick search for the word "elevator" on the InfoMall. Such a search is productive! The first hit is from Arnold Arons' wonderful text *A Guide to Introductory Physics Teaching*, found in the book basement. Arons warns about use of the words "weight" and "weightlessness" in the Elementary Dynamics chapter: "The term 'weight of an object' should be introduced, and then reserved exclusively for the gravitational force exerted by the earth on the object.... Most teachers are aware of the unfortunate use (or misuse) of the word 'weightlessness' in connection with satellites and space vehicles. There is not much we can do about the usage (any more than we shall be able to force people to say 'mass' instead of 'weight' when talking about a number of kilograms of potatoes in a grocery store)." Note that his passage serves two functions: it warns you to avoid confusing related physics concepts, and it demonstrates copying and pasting from the InfoMall into your own documents (as was just done here).

The second hit is "The falling elevator problem," from *The Physics Teacher*, vol. 15, issue 2, 1977. You should read this one. It was inspired by a letter to Ann Landers, and contains many of the responses about safety in elevators. This can lead to classroom discussions, or simply an interesting article to post on a bulletin board for students to read in their spare time.

The third hit is "The measurement of g in an elevator" from *Potpourri of Physics Teaching Ideas* found in the Demo & Lab Shop. This is only one of the books you can find there that are full of great ideas for your class.

Another result from this search is from *Physics: The Excitement of Discovery* found in the Textbook Trove. A short passage from this text says "Riding in an elevator, you can sense an increased force on your feet just as the elevator starts to move upward, and a decreased force when the elevator just starts to move downward. A few seconds after the elevator is in motion, the force on your feet returns to normal. Newton's laws explain these effects. You exert a downward force on the floor (F_f), and the floor exerts an upward force (F_p) on you, the passenger. From Newton's third law, (F_f) equals (F_p) at all times. Your weight (W) is always the same no matter how the elevator moves (see Fig. 3-7). When the elevator is at rest, or is moving with constant speed, the net force acting on you must be zero. Therefore, the upward force (F_p)just balances your weight." The figure mentioned here (Fig. 3-7) is on the InfoMall and can be used in your class, pasted into a handout, or put on transparency for discussion.

As these four examples show, you can find explanations of concepts, pictures, related articles, and pedagogical suggestions with a single search of the CD-ROM. Not included in this example, but still available on the CD-ROM, are demonstrations, homework problems (with solutions if desired!) and catalogs. (And if you ever wondered how those buttons that light up work when touched, even though they are clearly not push-buttons, that can be found in this same search.)

For You To Read mentions Newton's explanation of gravity. Interestingly, Newton wrote that "It is inconceivable, that inanimate brute matter, should, without the mediation of something else, which is not material, operate upon and affect other matter without mutual contact, as it must be, if gravitation, in the sense of Epicurus, be essential and inherent in it.... That gravity should be innate, inherent, and essential to matter, so that one body may act upon another at a distance through a vacuum, without the mediation of any thing else, by and through which their action and force may be conveyed from one to another, is to me so great an absurdity, that I believe no man, who has in philosophical matters a competent faculty of thinking, can ever fall into it." Even Newton did not like the idea of objects affecting one another without contact. This passage is from "Newton and the cause of gravity," *American Journal of Physics*, vol. 26, issue 9, 1958. There is plenty of information on Newton and how he developed his theory of gravitation; see the chapter "Astronomy: A History of Theory: Isaac Newton (1642-1727)" in *Physics for the Inquiring Mind* from the Textbook Trove. There are other sources, and you may wish to look for them.

Note that toward the end of For You To Read, the

General Theory of Relativity is mentioned. The "elevator" search also found "The General Theory of Relativity (Einstein's Theory of Gravitation)" chapter from *An Introduction to the Meaning and Structure of Physics* from the Textbook Trove, in case you want more information.

When Reflecting on the Activity and the Challenge, there is a discussion of blast-off or landing conditions. This is, of course, often called "g forces." A search of the InfoMall locates a short bit called "Acceleration Effects on Living Organisms" and is about launching living organisms in model rockets (insects are suggested). This particular find illustrates one of the problems one may encounter while using the InfoMall - you cannot tell where on the CD-ROM this item exists. The solution is simple. Search for the title (or part of it), and see if it comes up in the table of contents of something you can easily find. In this case, a search for "acceleration effects" indicates that this item is part of the "Projects in Model Rocketry" pamphlet. So you go to the Pamphlet Parlor and ... it is not there. But a scan through the pamphlet titles uncovers "Estes Educator" and you may recognize Estes as a company that makes model rockets. This turns out to be the correct place to look. Does this sound like a lot of work? Granted, it is a bit of extra searching, but it is not without positive side effects. These extra searches often help (or force) you to be more creative or a little broader in your searches.

In Physics To Go question 5, ratios, fractions, and percents are used all in the same question. There are concepts that can cause problems for some students. To investigate this, perform slightly more complicated searches than we have done so far. Try "student difficult*" AND "ratio*". The search engine for the InfoMall interprets the asterisk (*) as a wild character; this search will look for "ratio", "ratios", "ration", "rationing" and so on. This is often a great way to search for both the singular and plural forms of words. The AND (all caps) indicates the "logical AND" in which both words or phrases must be present for the search engine to return a hit. In this example, there could be entire books about ratios on the InfoMall, but if students' difficulties are not mentioned, the InfoMall search engine will ignore the book. As an alternative, you may wish to try "misconcept*" AND "ratio*".

Note that the Stretching Exercises use computers and force probes. Computers are another tool that students can and should use in learning physics. To illustrate this point, notice that computers are mentioned explicitly in the titles for 2 of the first 4 hits from the search suggested above for graphs.

Planning for the Activity

Time Requirements

Allow at least 40 minutes for this activity. If the boxes are pre-made, it will give more time for the students to do many trials, and get more accurate results. If the students have to build the boxes allow an extra 20 minutes. Allow another 40 minutes for the Stretching Exercise activity, with the computer software.

Materials needed

For the class:

- *Active Physics Transportation* Content Video (Segment: Person in Elevator)
- VCR and TV monitor

For each group:

- spring scale - 0 - 20 N range
- 1-kg mass (to hang on scale)
- box to hold mass hanging on scale
- device for attaching scale to box

Advance Preparation and Setup

A cardboard box will suffice but might not be reusable next year. A more rugged device could be a rectangular box constructed of at least 1/4" plywood, about 4" wide. The dimensions must be tall enough to house the spring scale with the suspended mass, and narrow enough for the box to be mounted on a laboratory cart for future experimentation. Suggested dimensions are 15 cm x 30 cm. A cup hook should be screwed into the center of the inner face of one of the narrow sides to support the spring scale and mass. The box should be held together with screws and glue to provide durability. The rear panel of the box should allow a 1.0 cm space on top and bottom for use in later experiments.

Preview the video of the person in an elevator to prepare for any student questions that may arise. Relate the concept of local gravitational field to the weight read on the scale.

The box used for the free fall experiment may be constructed by the students in advance, or may be made in the school wood shop. It is prudent to make several of these boxes to prepare for breakage, or to accommodate multiple lab groups. The box must be tall enough to house a 0 - 20 N spring scale with a 1.0-kg standard mass suspended on it, while hanging from the cup hook. Measure this length before building your boxes.

Cushioning material must be used where the box impacts the floor.

Teaching Notes

Present the WDYT question to the students. The student responses may be explored in class discussion and noted on the board, or individually recorded by students to be re-read at the end of the lesson.

The elevator video is short, but must be viewed more than once to be properly analyzed. It may be necessary to help students review the meaning of "acceleration" and "velocity" as they interpret the video. Data taken from the video is easier to discuss than the data from the dropping box unless it is video-taped, but the box is necessary to make the results real.

The FYTD may be performed by groups, or by the class as a whole, depending on time and available equipment. Make sure to cushion the floor with shock absorbent material to maintain the integrity of the box and of the floor.

Some students might be interested in viewing early astronauts' training films, to see the methods used for training them for situations in which they would be experiencing very large g-forces. If you have the opportunity to bring in astronauts to talk about their training, that would be interesting as well.

Students may see the ups and downs in the elevators, as something unusual, but think of it as simply inertia. As the elevator starts to move, your body wants to stay in one place. Therefore, when the elevator accelerates upward, your body exerts a greater downward force on the scale. Conversely as you stop, your body wants to continue, and consequently will show a lower weight on the scale. Similarly, you get a "funny" feeling in your stomach as you accelerate up and down. You get a similar feeling if you happen to be traveling on a road that has lots of hills and valleys. As you round the top of a hill you get a lighter feeling, and as you round the bottom of the valley, you get a heavier feeling.

Activity Overview

This activity will help the students understand what is meant by a local gravitational field and how it can be altered by motion. The local gravitational field is the elevator, and the motion is in a vertical direction.

Student Objectives

Students will:

- understand the relationship between the acceleration of a frame of reference, and the local gravitational field within that frame.
- identify apparent weight as an effect of accelerated motion.
- relate the increase/decrease of weight with the direction of the acceleration.

ANSWERS FOR THE TEACHER ONLY

What Do You Think?

Answers will vary. There is a net force in the downward direction, which will cause the scale to appear to give a larger reading, or increased weight.

JOURNEY TO THE MOON AND BEYOND

Activity One

Weight Change during Takeoff

WHAT DO YOU THINK?

You are standing on a scale in an elevator on the ground floor. The elevator starts moving up abruptly.

- **What happens to the weight reading on the scale?**

Record your ideas about this question in your *Active Physics log*. Be prepared to discuss your responses with your small group and the class.

TRANSPORTATION T 110

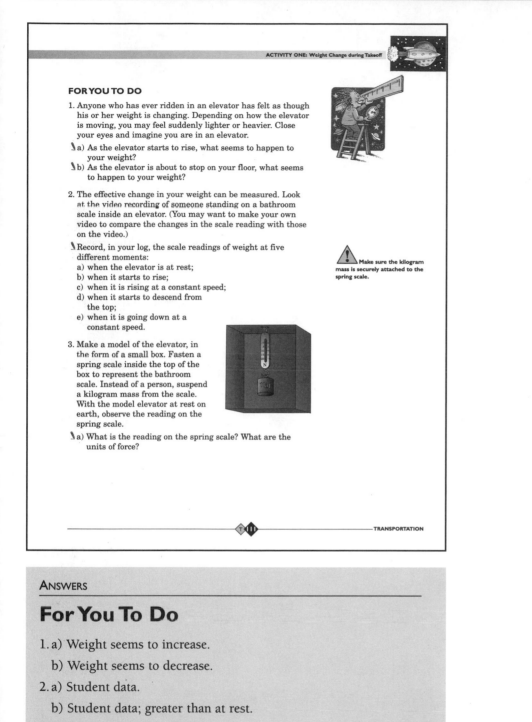

ACTIVITY ONE: Weight Change during Takeoff

FOR YOU TO DO

1. Anyone who has ever ridden in an elevator has felt as though his or her weight is changing. Depending on how the elevator is moving, you may feel suddenly lighter or heavier. Close your eyes and imagine you are in an elevator.
   a) As the elevator starts to rise, what seems to happen to your weight?
   b) As the elevator is about to stop on your floor, what seems to happen to your weight?

2. The effective change in your weight can be measured. Look at the video recording of someone standing on a bathroom scale inside an elevator. (You may want to make your own video to compare the changes in the scale reading with those on the video.)

   Record, in your log, the scale readings of weight at five different moments:
   a) when the elevator is at rest;
   b) when it starts to rise;
   c) when it is rising at a constant speed;
   d) when it starts to descend from the top;
   e) when it is going down at a constant speed.

Make sure the kilogram mass is securely attached to the spring scale.

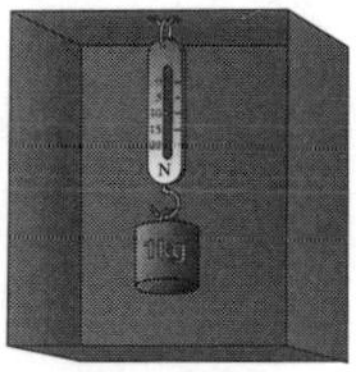

3. Make a model of the elevator, in the form of a small box. Fasten a spring scale inside the top of the box to represent the bathroom scale. Instead of a person, suspend a kilogram mass from the scale. With the model elevator at rest on earth, observe the reading on the spring scale.
   a) What is the reading on the spring scale? What are the units of force?

T 111 TRANSPORTATION

ANSWERS

For You To Do

1. a) Weight seems to increase.
   b) Weight seems to decrease.
2. a) Student data.
   b) Student data; greater than at rest.
   c) Student data; same as at rest.
   d) Student data; less than at rest.
   e) Student data; same as at rest.

   See Background Information for a more detailed explanation.
3. a) The reading on the spring scale should be 9.8 N. The units are in newtons.

3

ANSWERS

For You To Do

(continued)

4. a) As you accelerated the elevator upward, there would have been an increase in the weight (reading on the spring scale), then as you moved it at a constant velocity, return to the at rest reading (9.8N), then as you slowed down the elevator, it should have a reading less than at rest.

5. a) The readings should be opposite to the above #4.

6. a) Student data.

   b) Whenever there is acceleration, there is a change in weight. At rest or moving with constant velocity, the person's weight is "normal". The apparent weight will change whenever there is a change in velocity either going from fast to slow or stop, or going from rest to faster velocity.

   c) When the person is accelerating up.

   d) When the person is accelerating down.

Do not raise the box above the level of your head. Keep all motion away from the plane of your body.

4. Lift the elevator gradually, moving it up at a constant speed, and then stop it.
   a) During this journey of the "elevator," record in your log the changes in the reading of the spring scale.

5. Repeat the movement of the elevator, but start the elevator at the top and have it go down.
   a) Record the changes in the reading of the spring scale in your log.

Do not lift the box so quickly that the kilogram mass becomes unstable.

6. Continue to move the elevator with different accelerations, both up and down, until you feel confident that you know when a scale value does change and when it doesn't change.
   a) Look at the measurements you obtained and generalize the results in your log.
   b) Under what conditions does the person in the elevator experience a change of weight? (Try to explain using the terms *velocity* and *acceleration.)*
   c) Under what conditions is the apparent weight (the weight the scale reads) greater than the "person's" normal weight?
   d) Under what conditions is the apparent weight smaller?

PHYSICS TALK

Velocity is speed with direction, for example, 30 m/s south, or 25 m/s up. Acceleration is defined as a change in velocity over time. Most people think of acceleration as a change in speed. However, acceleration can also be a change in direction.

FOR YOU TO READ

Newton's Explanation of Gravity

You know that things fall to the ground because of gravity. More than 300 years ago, Sir Isaac Newton described gravity as a universal force. Gravity is the force that tends to attract any two masses. Since planets are such big masses, gravity tends to pull objects towards the center of the Earth, moon, or other planets.

Newton recognized that gravity extends beyond Earth. According to Newton's First Law of Motion, objects in motion should continue in motion, in a straight line at a constant speed, unless they are acted upon by some force. But Newton, as others before him, noted that the planets do not travel in straight lines. As early as the time of the ancient Greek philosopher Aristotle, scientists knew that planets orbit in a curved pathway. Newton reasoned that some force must act upon the planets that prevents them from moving in a straight line. He concluded that the force must be the same force of gravity as found on Earth.

According to Newton, every mass in the universe attracts every other mass. The attraction between the masses is proportional to the size of the masses and inversely proportional to the distance between them. That means that the gravitational attraction increases as the mass of objects gets larger. In part, that explains why you would have greater weight on Jupiter than planet Earth. Jupiter has a greater mass than planet Earth and exerts a greater gravitational force. Gravity is so strong on Jupiter (more than 2.5 times as great as Earth) that your legs may not be able to support you. If you weigh 150 lbs. on Earth, you would weigh 380 lbs. on Jupiter. The second part of the relation indicates that the gravitational force decreases as the distance between the objects increases. While traveling far from Earth, you will weigh less owing to this distance change.

How does change in gravity relate to the observations you made in this activity? There are two equivalent ways of describing what happens in an elevator when a scale reading changes. You can account for the scale reading as a "change in weight of the passenger" due to the acceleration of the elevator. You can also account for the scale reading as a "change in gravity within the elevator." If you didn't know that you were in an elevator, there would be no way to determine if the weight change was due to the elevator's acceleration or to a change in gravity. This is one of the ideas in Einstein's Theory of General Relativity!

REFLECTING ON THE ACTIVITY AND THE CHALLENGE

In constructing your science fiction story, think about why an understanding of gravity is important to your story line. You know that the weight of a body or a 1-kg mass changes as a result of the acceleration of the elevator.

Your science fiction story may include a blast-off or a landing sequence. During take-off there is a large acceleration and the occupants in the vehicle will feel much heavier, as you determined in the elevator experiments. How would you describe this in an interesting manner to the readers of your story?

In the old Mercury rocket ships, the acceleration at liftoff was so great that the crew had to wear special pressurized suits and lie down in special couches when the ship took off. In a rising elevator, you might feel your stomach being left behind. In a Mercury liftoff, there was a real danger of internal injury.

Landing on a new planet may also include some descriptions of the lower or higher gravity that you find there. If there is a very large gravity, walking and running will be quite difficult. While traveling through space, you may weigh very little in the capsule because you are so distant from any planet. Including good physics with an interesting story line is your challenge for this chapter.

PHYSICS TO GO

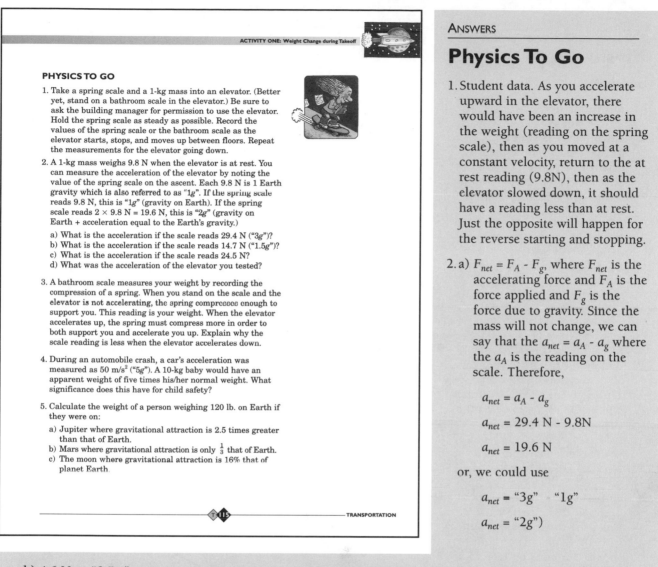

1. Take a spring scale and a 1-kg mass into an elevator. (Better yet, stand on a bathroom scale in the elevator.) Be sure to ask the building manager for permission to use the elevator. Hold the spring scale as steady as possible. Record the values of the spring scale or the bathroom scale as the elevator starts, stops, and moves up between floors. Repeat the measurements for the elevator going down.
2. A 1-kg mass weighs 9.8 N when the elevator is at rest. You can measure the acceleration of the elevator by noting the value of the spring scale on the ascent. Each 9.8 N is 1 Earth gravity which is also referred to as "1*g*". If the spring scale reads 9.8 N, this is "1*g*" (gravity on Earth). If the spring scale reads 2 × 9.8 N = 19.6 N, this is "2*g*" (gravity on Earth + acceleration equal to the Earth's gravity.)
   a) What is the acceleration if the scale reads 29.4 N ("3*g*")?
   b) What is the acceleration if the scale reads 14.7 N ("1.5*g*")?
   c) What is the acceleration if the scale reads 24.5 N?
   d) What was the acceleration of the elevator you tested?
3. A bathroom scale measures your weight by recording the compression of a spring. When you stand on the scale and the elevator is not accelerating, the spring compresses enough to support you. This reading is your weight. When the elevator accelerates up, the spring must compress more in order to both support you and accelerate you up. Explain why the scale reading is less when the elevator accelerates down.
4. During an automobile crash, a car's acceleration was measured as 50 m/s^2 ("5*g*"). A 10-kg baby would have an apparent weight of five times his/her normal weight. What significance does this have for child safety?
5. Calculate the weight of a person weighing 120 lb. on Earth if they were on:
   a) Jupiter where gravitational attraction is 2.5 times greater than that of Earth.
   b) Mars where gravitational attraction is only $\frac{1}{3}$ that of Earth.
   c) The moon where gravitational attraction is 16% that of planet Earth.

Answers

Physics To Go

1. Student data. As you accelerate upward in the elevator, there would have been an increase in the weight (reading on the spring scale), then as you moved at a constant velocity, return to the at rest reading (9.8N), then as the elevator slowed down, it should have a reading less than at rest. Just the opposite will happen for the reverse starting and stopping.

2. a) $F_{net} = F_A - F_g$, where F_{net} is the accelerating force and F_A is the force applied and F_g is the force due to gravity. Since the mass will not change, we can say that the $a_{net} = a_A - a_g$ where the a_A is the reading on the scale. Therefore,

$a_{net} = a_A - a_g$

a_{net} = 29.4 N - 9.8N

a_{net} = 19.6 N

or, we could use

a_{net} = "3g" - "1g"

a_{net} = "2g")

b) 4.6 N or "0.5 g"

c) 14.7 N or "1.5 g"

d) Student data. Be ready to deal with negative "gs". Students should be made to realize that negative in this situation only refers to the direction. Therefore, positive acceleration means upward acceleration, and negative means downward acceleration.

3. The bathroom scale exerts a force upward on you to balance the force of gravity. Therefore, when you are accelerating downward, your scale has to exert less force to support your weight.

4. The apparent weight of the baby would be about 500 N. This represents an equivalent weight of 110 pounds. This means that the baby would be very difficult to stop, by simply holding the baby on your lap. In order to keep the baby safe, a child safety seat, that has been approved, and properly anchored in the car, is the only way to ensure proper safety restraint.

5. a) Weight is 120 pounds on Earth, therefore the weight is 120 x 9.8 = 1176 N. Therefore, their weight is 2.5 times as great or 300 lb.

b) 40 lb.

c) 20 lb.

ANSWERS

Physics To Go

(continued)

6. a) According to the inverse square law, as the object (astronaut) moves farther away, the force changes by the inverse square. Therefore, as the astronaut moves away, the weight will get smaller and smaller.

b) The farther away he is from the center of the planet, the easier it will be to move him away from the Earth. The force will only have to be slightly more than his weight.

c) The weight of the astronaut will be: since F_g is proportional to $1/d^2$ therefore, if we double the original distance, we will reduce the force by 1/22 or 1/4 therefore the force will be 1/4 of the force on the surface (40 lbs).

Using the same logic, then the force at 3 times the distance will be 1/9 the force; the force at 4 times the distance will be 1/16 (22 lbs); the force at 5 times the distance will be 1/25 (8 lbs); the force at 6 times the distance will be 1/36 (5.5 lbs). The graph will be a hyperbola.

d) Answers will vary. Look for well-thought out answers showing understanding of physics.

7. a) It would take less force, and therefore less fuel to launch a spaceship from the moon, compared to Earth.

b) It would take greater force, and therefore more fuel to launch a spaceship from Jupiter, compared to Earth.

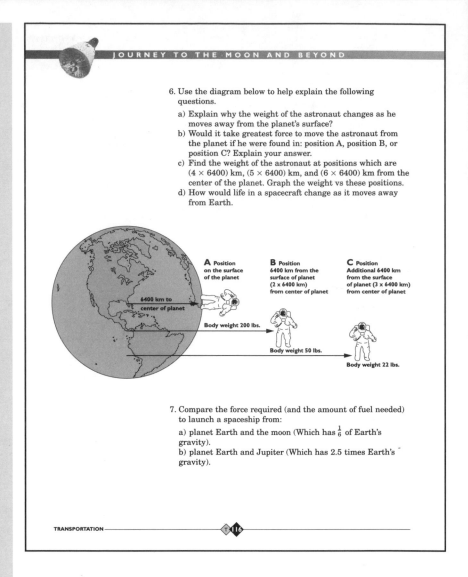

6. Use the diagram below to help explain the following questions.
   a) Explain why the weight of the astronaut changes as he moves away from the planet's surface?
   b) Would it take greatest force to move the astronaut from the planet if he were found in: position A, position B, or position C? Explain your answer.
   c) Find the weight of the astronaut at positions which are (4 × 6400) km, (5 × 6400) km, and (6 × 6400) km from the center of the planet. Graph the weight vs these positions.
   d) How would life in a spacecraft change as it moves away from Earth.

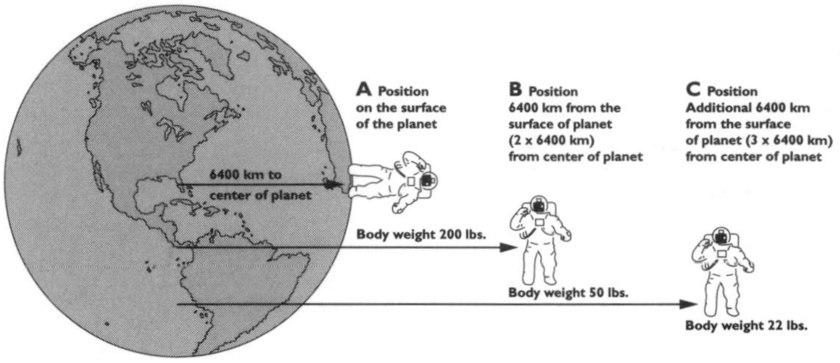

7. Compare the force required (and the amount of fuel needed) to launch a spaceship from:
   a) planet Earth and the moon (Which has $\frac{1}{6}$ of Earth's gravity).
   b) planet Earth and Jupiter (Which has 2.5 times Earth's gravity).

STRETCHING EXERCISES

1. Place an object in a small box to represent a person in an elevator. Attach the box to a force probe connected to a computer. You can either connect the box on top of the probe or suspend it by a string from the bottom. The results will be the same.

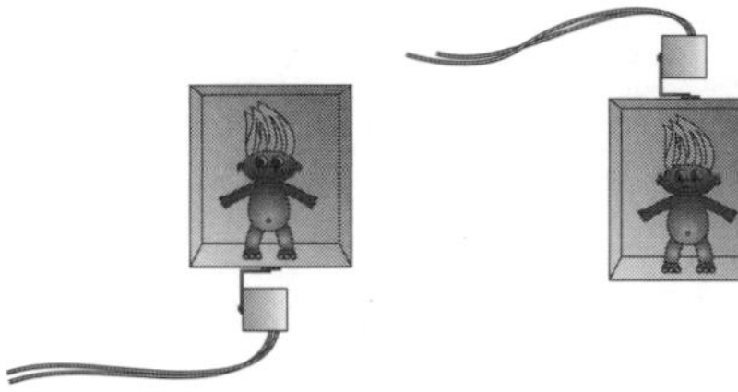

2. Hold the probe stationary and activate the software. The probe will be measuring the weight of the object and box. Start the force probe up and try to maintain a constant velocity. Explain the resulting graph.

Avoid sudden, jerky movements.

3. Hold the force probe with the box about 5 feet above the floor and activate the software. Start the force probe down and try to maintain a constant velocity. Explain the resulting graph.
4. Repeat the last part of the experiment; this time, however, start the force probe down faster. You should notice that the dip in the graph is closer to zero. Under what conditions would the graph reach zero force?
5. Compare the results of the computer testing of the elevator with the videotape experiment.

ANSWERS

Stretching Exercises

1. Student activity.
2. Students answers will vary. Students should observe an increase in the force showing an apparent increase in the weight, then a straight line, showing constant force equal to the weight of the object. The scale should increase above the standing weight, then read the same as if standing on the scale when not moving.
3. Students answers will vary. Students should observe a decrease in the force showing an apparent decrease in the weight, then a straight line, showing constant force equal to the weight of the object. Your weight will show an apparent decrease then move to what your weight would be if standing on a scale when not moving.
4. Students answers will vary. The object will have to drop with the same acceleration as the acceleration due to gravity.
5. Student observations.

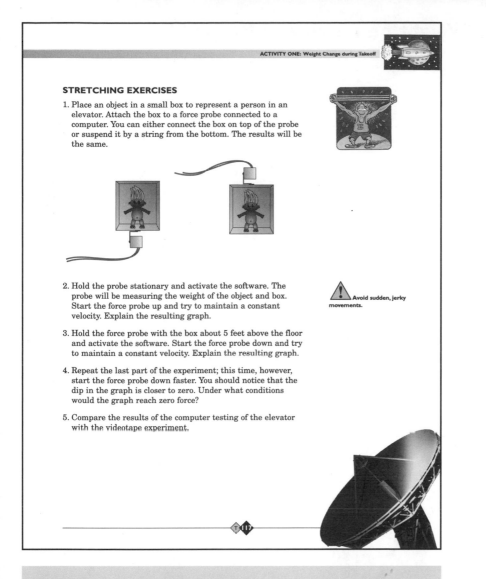

Body Weight on Earth and Beyond

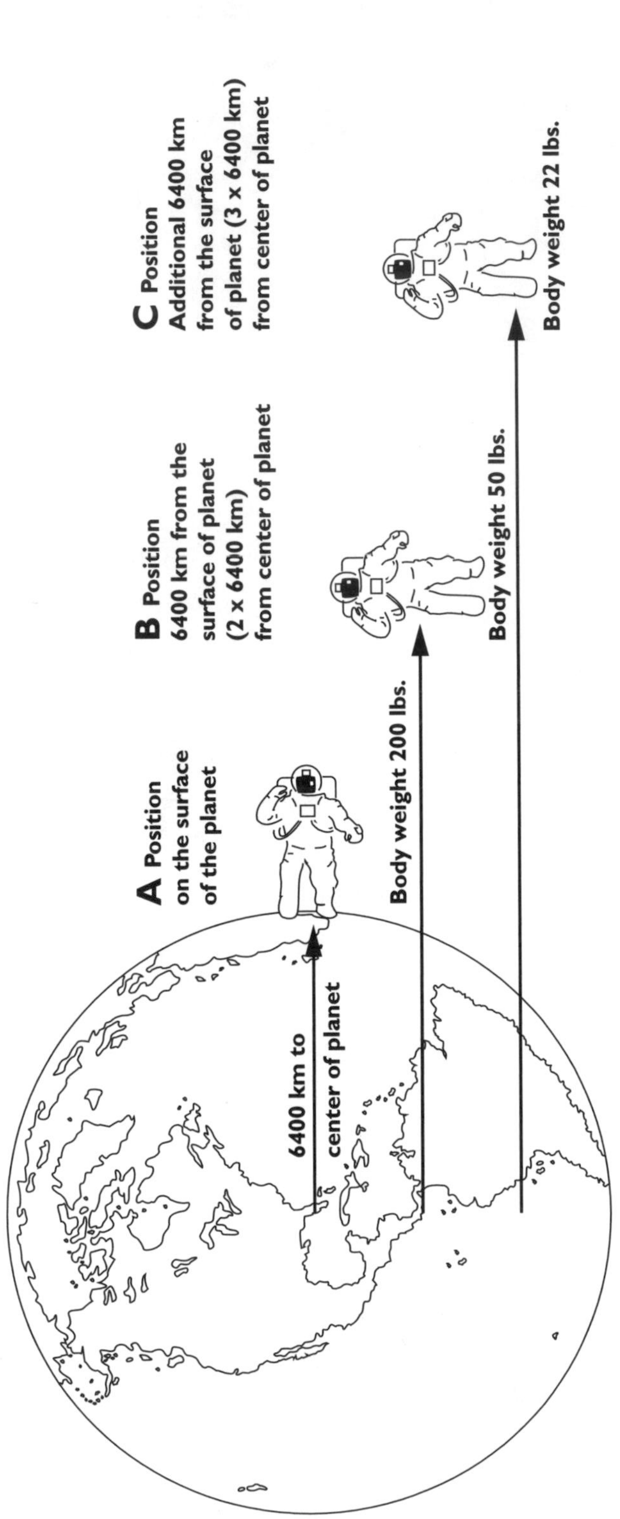

For use with *Transportation*, Chapter 3, ACTIVITY ONE: Weight Change During Takeoff

NOTES

ACTIVITY TWO
Weightlessness with Gravity

Background Information

The term weightlessness most often refers to being able to "float" in space. Weightlessness actually refers to a sensation of no weight relative to a reference point. In the first activities, the students were analyzing the behavior of an object inside an elevator (or box). When the acceleration of the box is the same as the acceleration of gravity, the object appears to be weightless. $F_{net} = F_A - F_g$, is the formula used in the first activity to determine the forces acting on the objects. If the net force acting on the object is the same as the F_A, then the F_g is zero and $F_{net} - F_A = F_g$. When $F_A = F_{net}$ then the apparent F_g is zero.

in the opposite direction

When an object is in free fall, there are no other forces acting upon it (ignoring air resistance) except for the force of gravity. Therefore, the acceleration of that object is going to be 9.8 m/s² ($F = ma$). When we look at objects that are fired horizontally, such as a bullet or cannon ball, we will notice that in the vertical direction, they are in free fall. That is, only the force of gravity is acting on it. Newton also recognized this, and, in a thought experiment, he described how to launch a cannon ball into orbit. Theoretically, if you can launch the cannon ball at a speed great enough and from a height high enough, you would get a trajectory, that would be exactly the same as the curve of the Earth. This would mean that in the first second of travel, the distance the cannon ball drops is

$d = 1/2 \times a \times t^2$

$d = 1/2 \times 9.8 \text{ m/s}^2 \times (1 \text{ s})^2$

$d = 4.9 \text{ m}$

Therefore, because the Earth's curvature is about 8 km per every 4.9 m, the cannon ball would travel 8.0 km and drop 4.9 m in the first second. The speed would have to be 8 km /s or about 29,000 km/h (18,000 mph)!

Newton also recognized that the air resistance would need to be eliminated, and the cannon would have to be placed at about 200 km above the Earth's surface. Newton had the theory, but to build a mountain 200 km above the Earth's surface would be impossible. Since then, we have figured out a way to "create a mountain", and have a "cannon ball" shot out at such a speed that it will in fact go into orbit.

The space shuttle when taking off does not go straight in to the sky in a perpendicular path to the surface, but follows a curved trajectory, such that at some point above the surface of the Earth, the space shuttle starts falling back to Earth. Because the trajectory is the same as the curvature of the Earth's surface, it follows an orbit around the Earth.

Therefore, as an object orbits the Earth, it is really in free fall back to the Earth's surface, but never reaches it. So as far as the astronauts are concerned, they feel about the same in the space shuttle, as we would in an elevator, if the cable were to break, and we would be in free fall (albeit much shorter, and more painful!).

Active-ating the Physics InfoMall

Note that this activity is called "Weightlessness with Gravity." What does it mean to be "weightless"? If you do a search for "weightless*" you will find many references. A short way down the list (Arons' *A Guide to Introductory Physics Teaching*, chapter 3, Elementary Dynamics), you can access this passage: "One can now take up the matter of terminology: When we are in free fall, the gravitational force exerted on us by the Earth has not become zero. What has become zero is the normal force at our feet—the force that we do sense directly. Under these circumstances we experience a strange sensation, one that might be called a "sensation of weightlessness." Hence arises the poor terminology in which the word "weightlessness" is used to describe the situation in a freely falling elevator or in a satellite. We must understand the confusing usage and not interpret the word as literally meaning that the gravitational forces have become zero." As long as both the teacher and the student understand this distinction, nothing is lost or confusing.

What Do You Think? asks students to draw a scale picture of the Earth-Moon system. While there may be plenty of such pictures on the InfoMall (there are 19 textbooks on the CD-ROM, after all), it may not be simple to find one. There are so many occurrences of the word "Earth" that narrowing it down is not so simple. You can search for "Earth" AND "Moon" but that still does not do the trick. Sure, it provides many nice sources of information, but it is not as nice as having students do this themselves. But what numbers should one use for measuring distances? There is, in the Utility Closet, a source for many of the odd numbers a person might want for physics: *Many Magnitudes: A Collection of Useful and Useless Numbers* in "Physics Pfact Potpourri." You should browse through this - there are many numbers that are simply amusing.

For You To Do has several nice activities for students to perform to demonstrate "weightlessness" in free fall. If you want more ideas, simply look to the InfoMall. Search for "weightless*" AND "demo*" to get a list of ideas. However, the first item on the list of results is about optics, and has over 170 references to either "weightless*" or "demo*" and picking out the one you want might be a lengthy process, assuming such information can be found in a section on optics. You can shorten the search further by selecting "Search Hits" under the "Search Category" menu. This will conduct a search only on the hits that were already generated. Now just eliminate "demo*" from your search words, leaving only "weightless*" to search for. (If you do this, the optics reference drops far down the list, with "weightless*" appearing only once, so it is NOT a good choice.) The very first item left on the list is great! It contains some of the same ideas as this *Active Physics* activity, plus more. It also contains graphics that you can use in your own handouts! Some of these are almost identical to the pictures in the *Active Physics* books, and some have explanations and free-body diagrams, too.

Step 4 of For You To Do uses a video camera to analyze the motion of a falling body. This analysis falls into a category often called "interactive video." A search of the InfoMall for "video" AND "analysis" (remember, you need to be creative when selecting search words; these were chosen as an example, but you may find others work better for you) brings up a number of references which illustrate the benefits of such techniques. It might be interesting to note that the first hit from this search produces an article quoting one of the developers of the Physics InfoMall CD-ROM about the use of technology in teaching physics (of course, the InfoMall is also such an example).

Physics To Go mentions the "vomit comet." Search for this on the InfoMall, and you will find a brief discussion, along with a picture. This is part of a discussion of fictional forces, and also addresses objects in free fall.

Planning for the Activity

Time Requirements

The time required for this activity will depend on the video cameras available. It will take approximately 40 minutes to do the experiments, and do enough trials to get reasonable results. Allow another class period for the students to analyze their data, and begin their writeups.

Materials needed

For each group:

- styrofoam® cup (2)
- water source
- paper clip
- rubber band
- metal washer (2)
- balloon and pin in frame apparatus
- model elevator from Activity One
- camcorder
- VCR with stop-frame capability
- TV monitor

Teaching Notes

Present the WDYT question to the students. The student responses may be explored in class discussion and noted on the board, in addition to individually recorded by students to be reread at the end of the lesson.

The FYTD begins by asking students for their predictions about the outcome of the experiment. Remind them not to perform the experiment until they have written their hypotheses.

Have the students work in small groups of three or four. They may do peer assessment as in previous lessons, or may have formative evaluation by the teacher.

Weightlessness is often mistakenly referred to as no gravity. In other words, you appear to be weightless because there is no gravity acting upon you. Students need to recognize that gravity is a force of attraction that happens between any two massive bodies over any distance. As we stand on Earth, we are being "held" to the Earth by gravity. The sun, moon, and all other bodies in the universe are also exerting a gravitational force upon us. However, due to the inverse square law, the effect is almost negligible, even for the sun, and the moon, both of which are relatively close when considering the great distances in the universe. We know that the moon and the sun have a gravitational effect on Earth, as we watch the tides roll in and out.

It is important to show that gravity is a force that affects the movement of all bodies. This can be done showing videos of free fall such as parachuting, and videos of astronauts.

Activity Overview

This lesson will help the students understand the meaning of weightlessness and its connection to free fall and orbits.

Student Objectives

Students will:

- understand how vertical free fall is related to weightlessness.
- understand that a horizontally projected object is in free fall.
- understand that an object may be projected into a circular orbit.
- understand that the weightlessness in an orbiting craft is a result of the free fall motion of the craft.

ANSWERS FOR THE TEACHER ONLY

What Do You Think?

As the radius of the Earth is about 4 times the radius of the moon, the size of the Earth is about 4 times the size of the moon. The size of Earth's diameter is about 30 times smaller than the distance from Earth to the moon.

Students will most likely say that there is no gravity in space. Some students may also say that the shuttle is in between the Earth and moon, so therefore there is "balance" of gravity. However, it is because the shuttle is falling back to Earth at the same rate as the curve of the Earth.

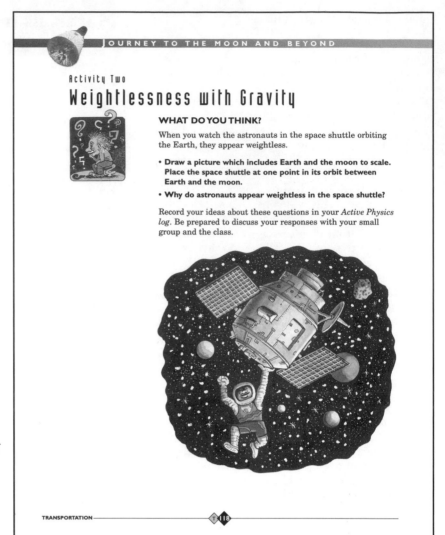

Activity Two

Weightlessness with Gravity

WHAT DO YOU THINK?

When you watch the astronauts in the space shuttle orbiting the Earth, they appear weightless.

- **Draw a picture which includes Earth and the moon to scale. Place the space shuttle at one point in its orbit between Earth and the moon.**
- **Why do astronauts appear weightless in the space shuttle?**

Record your ideas about these questions in your *Active Physics log*. Be prepared to discuss your responses with your small group and the class.

FOR YOU TO DO

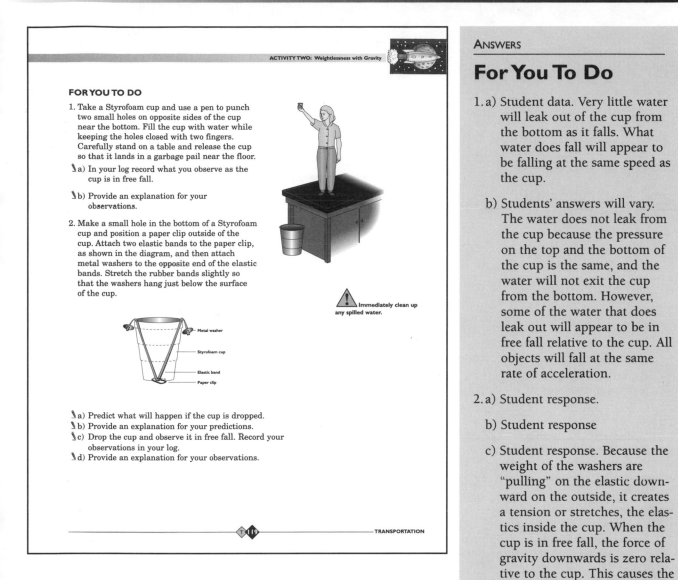

1. Take a Styrofoam cup and use a pen to punch two small holes on opposite sides of the cup near the bottom. Fill the cup with water while keeping the holes closed with two fingers. Carefully stand on a table and release the cup so that it lands in a garbage pail near the floor.
   - a) In your log record what you observe as the cup is in free fall.
   - b) Provide an explanation for your observations.

2. Make a small hole in the bottom of a Styrofoam cup and position a paper clip outside of the cup. Attach two elastic bands to the paper clip, as shown in the diagram, and then attach metal washers to the opposite end of the elastic bands. Stretch the rubber bands slightly so that the washers hang just below the surface of the cup.

Immediately clean up any spilled water.

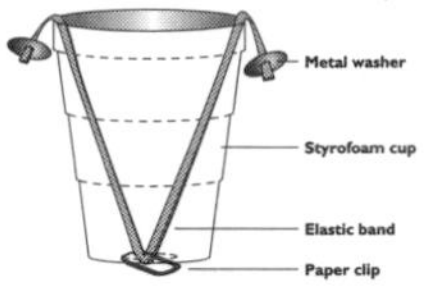

   - a) Predict what will happen if the cup is dropped.
   - b) Provide an explanation for your predictions.
   - c) Drop the cup and observe it in free fall. Record your observations in your log.
   - d) Provide an explanation for your observations.

Answers

For You To Do

1. a) Student data. Very little water will leak out of the cup from the bottom as it falls. What water does fall will appear to be falling at the same speed as the cup.

   b) Students' answers will vary. The water does not leak from the cup because the pressure on the top and the bottom of the cup is the same, and the water will not exit the cup from the bottom. However, some of the water that does leak out will appear to be in free fall relative to the cup. All objects will fall at the same rate of acceleration.

2. a) Student response.

   b) Student response

   c) Student response. Because the weight of the washers are "pulling" on the elastic downward on the outside, it creates a tension or stretches, the elastics inside the cup. When the cup is in free fall, the force of gravity downwards is zero relative to the cup. This causes the elastic, which when stretched creates force, to "pull" the washers back into the cup. While sitting on the desk, the forces or balanced force of gravity down is equal to the force of elastic up.

   d) Students' answers will vary (see 2 c) for explanation).

ANSWERS

For You To Do

(continued)

3. Student work.

   a) Students' response.

   b) Students' response

   c) Students should notice that as they drop the box, the balloon breaks almost instantly.

   d) Again, there are balanced forces between the elastic and gravity. When the box is dropped, the force of gravity relative to the box, is zero, therefore, the weight with the pin, has only the upward force of elastic acting on it. It appears to rise and hit the balloon, breaking it.

4. a) As you drop the box, as soon as you drop it, the scale decreases and will give a reading of zero and will continue to be zero, until it hits the ground. At the moment it hits, the scale will go above the 9.8 N reading. Essentially, the scale is reading "weightlessness" while in free fall.

5. a) Students should observe that the readings will be virtually exactly the same as the readings when dropping the box in free fall.

If any lead dust is created by boring or abrasion, carefully clean it up. Wash your hands.

3. Construct a frame, as shown in the diagram below, and carefully attach two screw eyes to the frame. Loop rubber bands through the screw eyes and attach to a fishing sinker. Hold the sinker with a pair of pliers or tongs. Using another pair of pliers, push a needle into the soft sinker weight. Attach a balloon at the top of the frame with masking tape.

   a) Predict what will happen if the frame is dropped.

   b) Provide an explanation for your predictions.

   c) Drop the metal frame and observe it during free fall. Record your observations in your log.

   d) Provide an explanation for your observations.

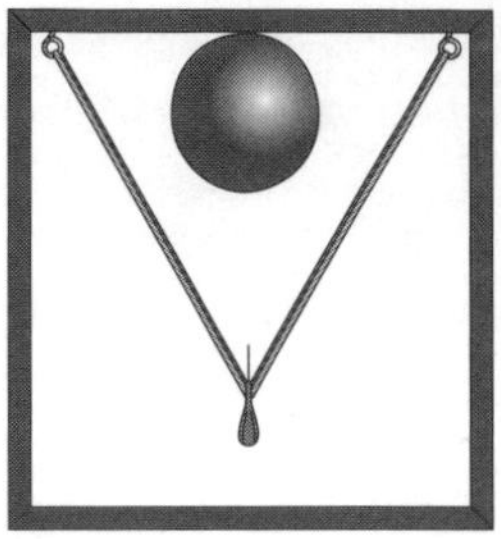

4. Use a model of an elevator with a spring scale and suspended mass similar to the one you made in Activity One, page T111. Set up a video camera to record the box. You are going to drop the box from a height, and record it as it falls. Using stop-action, you can examine the scale readings at all points during the fall.

   a) What does the scale read while the box is in free fall?

   Here are some possibilities:

   - It reads 9.8 N throughout.
   - It starts at 9.8 N and decreases as it falls.
   - It reads zero throughout the fall.
   - It starts at 9.8 N and increases.
   - It starts at zero and increases.

5. Repeat the experiment of the box falling. This time push the box off the table so that it moves horizontally as it falls.

   a) Write the results of this experiment in your log.

FOR YOU TO READ

What is Free Fall?

When the "elevator" box is falling freely, the only force acting on it is gravity, and yet there is no apparent gravity inside the box (the weight is zero). This was the situation when the box was dropped. It was also what happened when the box was shoved horizontally. It does not matter which way the box is moving. As long as the only force acting on the box is gravity, it is in free fall, and gravity seems to disappear inside it.

When a skydiver is falling to the Earth, the only force acting on her is gravity. Does she appear weightless? If she were falling and she dropped a pencil, the pencil would also fall. The pencil would fall as fast as she would. As far as she is concerned, the pencil would be hovering in front of her in midair—the pencil would be weightless.

In the space shuttle, the astronauts are falling to the Earth for days and days. During the time of their fall, they appear to be weightless. The space shuttle orbits the Earth at a height of only 250 km or 150 miles. There is plenty of gravity. But since the only force acting on the space shuttle and the astronauts is gravity (they are falling to the Earth), they appear weightless.

How can something be falling to the Earth (and be weightless) and yet not hit the Earth? Imagine a cannon atop a very high mountain as shown in the diagram. If the cannon shoots a ball horizontally with a small speed, the cannon may land just past the mountain. If the ball is shot with a greater speed, it will land further away from the mountain. If the speed of the ball is greater still, it may fall towards the Earth, but the curvature of the Earth keeps the ball from landing. The ball will continue to fall, but the Earth's curvature keeps the ball above the ground. The space shuttle is falling toward the Earth (and all of the astronauts are weightless) but the space shuttle does not hit the Earth because of its horizontal velocity. It is like the cannon ball shot from the high mountain with a large speed. The diagram shows the path of cannonballs shot from an imaginary high mountain. It also shows orbits that other satellites would have if they could be shot horizontally from even higher mountains. Does it surprise you that the picture was drawn by Isaac Newton in the early 1700s, long before anyone seriously considered space travel? Newton's genius was not that he saw the apple fall from the tree and hit the ground. It was that he imagined the moon also falling, even though he knew the moon would never hit the ground.

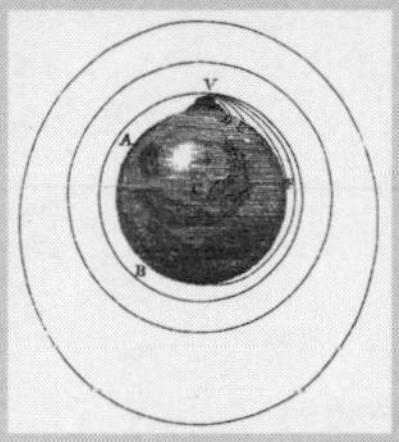

3

ANSWERS

Physics To Go

1. The radius of the Earth is about 26 times the shuttle altitude. To fit the sketch on an 8.5 x 11 page, the Earth would be a circle of radius 10 cm, and the shuttle orbit 0.4 cm larger -- a circle of about 10.4 cm.

2. The scale will read zero. Any orbiting body will be falling back to Earth at the same rate as the Earth's surface falls away. Therefore, while inside an object in free fall, there will "appear" to be no gravity.

3. Students' response. Students may be surprised how many people think that there is no gravity in space.

REFLECTING ON THE ACTIVITY OR CHALLENGE

The longer the spaceflight between Earth and the moon (or beyond), the greater the number of problems faced by the astronauts. As the spacecraft orbits the new planet, weight appears to have disappeared. An analogy can be drawn between a skydiver who drops a pencil while falling to the Earth and the astronaut aboard the spacecraft. The pencil, dropped by the skydiver, appears to float because it falls at the same speed as the skydiver. The pencil would appear to be weightless. As the spacecraft orbits the planet, the astronauts also appear to be weightless. Although gravity still exists, the spacecraft and astronaut are in free fall. Objects float about the spacecraft, much like the pencil would float about for the skydiver.

The feeling of weightlessness presents special difficulties. Many everyday tasks must be rethought. Consider how difficult in would be to pour a glass of milk or the difficulties you would experience going to the bathroom. What kinds of problems are experienced in a weightless environment? What parts of your story can be challenged?

PHYSICS TO GO

1. A scale drawing will show how close the shuttle is to the surface of the Earth. The radius of the Earth is 6400 km (4000 miles). The shuttle orbits at a height of 250 km (150 miles). Draw a scale model showing the size of the Earth and the space shuttle's position relative to it.

2. If a 70-kg astronaut inside a space craft orbiting the Earth at an altitude of 130 miles steps on a bathroom scale, explain why the scale will read zero?

3. Interview five people you know well. Ask them why they think the astronauts appear weightless when they are in the space shuttle. If any of them think it is because there is no gravity there, try to help them change their misconceptions. Use the results of your experiment to help convince them. (This is tough, people do not like to change their minds.)

ACTIVITY TWO: Weightlessness with Gravity

4. Carefully examine the picture of the elevator. If the elevator were in free fall, predict the direction that the balloon and the anvil will move once they are released. Provide an explanation for your prediction.

5. Have you ever hit an air pocket while on board an airplane, and experienced the plane drop? Compare the sensation of hitting a down draft to the way that astronauts feel in a weightless environment.

6. Airplanes can achieve low gravity for periods of 25 s. In Houston, the Johnson Space Center operates a KC-135 aircraft, called the "vomit comet," for astronaut training. The jet is a Boeing 707 with most of the seats removed and padded walls to protect the people inside of the plane. The plane travels in a parabolic flight pattern, first it climbs at a 45° angle, levels off, and then descends at the same 45° angle, before pulling out of the dive, as shown in the diagram. During the flight it ranges in altitude from 7.3 km to 10.4 km.
   a) If a person stood on a scale, indicate which points A,B,C, D, or E would show greatest weight. Explain your answer.
   b) In which part of the flight would the person experience weightlessness? Explain your answer.

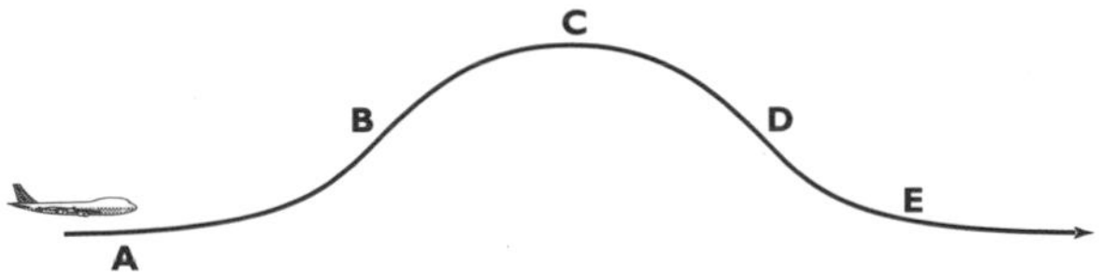

Answers

Physics To Go
(continued)

4. The balloon will stay up, as the force of the balloon is greater that gravity now, therefore, when in free fall, the balloon will exert a net force greater in the upward direction. The anvil, will immediately rise, as the boy is exerting an upward force to counter gravity. When the elevator suddenly goes in to free fall, the boy's grip will cause the anvil to rise, then it will appear to be "weightless".

5. Students' answers will vary.

6. Point A - normal; Point B - slightly higher; Points C and D - weightless; and Point E - heaviest. Points C and D are weightless due to the plane being in a curved path that is falling back to Earth. It will remain in free fall until point E where the weight will increase substantially. This is due to the force on the individual in the plane. Point A - vertical forces balanced; Point B - increased force of the plane on the body upwardly; Point C - sensation of weightlessness due to the plane is now beginning to fall; Point D - the plane is free falling, and towards Point E beginning to come out of the free fall.

ACTIVITY THREE
Spreadsheet Games: Free Fall

Background Information

In this activity students will be using a computer simulation program to simulate free fall experiments. The equations for finding distance and velocity during free fall are $d = v_i t + 1/2at^2$ where d = distance fallen, v_i is initial velocity = 0, t is the time the object has fallen, and a is acceleration = 9.8 m/s^2; and $v_f^2 = v_i^2 + 2ad$, where v_f is the final velocity, v_i is the initial velocity = 0, and a = 9.8 m/s^2 and d is the distance fallen. Another formula that can be used is $v_f = v_i + at$.

The students will be entering the drag factor into their simulation. This is to simulate what actually happens when an object is dropped. The object will free fall until it reaches terminal velocity, which is the speed at which the object no longer accelerates toward the ground but moves at a constant or uniform velocity until it hits the ground. The determination of terminal velocity depends on many factors. The most important of which is the force of the air resistance on the object. This force is dependent on the medium through which it is falling and the size and shape of the ball. Using the equation $F_{net} = F_A - F_f$, where F_{net} is the accelerating force, F_A is the applied force, and F_f is the force of friction acting against the falling object, we can see that when F_A (force due to gravity) is the same as the F_f, then the $F_{net} = 0$. This is terminal velocity.

Active-ating the Physics InfoMall

This activity uses graphs extensively. As mentioned briefly for Activity One, students can have problems interpreting graphs. Search for "student difficult*" AND "graph*" to find a number of references. The first is "Student difficulties in connecting graphs and physics: Example from kinematics, *American Journal of Physics*, vol. 55, issue 6, 1987. There are many other articles in this list that indicate the types of problems students have that teachers should recognize and expect.

The concept of terminal velocity is an important part of this activity. You will not be surprised if a search for "terminal velocity" is suggested. Try it. The first hit ("Fluid resistance and terminal velocity," *The Physics Teacher*, vol. 30, issue 7, 1992) provides ideas for demonstrating terminal velocity with a steel sphere in water, using a computer to measure speed. The second hit is "Parachutes in the classroom," *The Physics Teacher*, vol. 31, issue 1,1993. These articles may give you some great ideas for use in your classroom. There are other hits from this search that you might find useful as well.

The Stretching Exercises involve the design of an accelerometer. If you need ideas for this, the InfoMall is useful again. Simply search the entire CD-ROM using the keyword "accelerometer" and browse through the results until you find something you like.

Planning for the Activity

Time Requirements

Allow at least 1 class period, and even more depending on time. Allow the students to create many different scenarios, changing one variable at a time. Again, judge the time according to the number of computers you have available.

Materials needed

For each group:

- Computer with "Excel" spreadsheet software
- *Active Physics* Spreadsheet Template (File: Free Fall XLS)

Advance Preparation and Setup

Go through each of the scenarios to see how they work, and anticipate the questions the students may be asking throughout the activity. You should also go through and find the answers to the exercises

Teaching Notes

Students can work in groups of two (or three if not enough computers).

Some students will think that an object will continue accelerating forever. When shown pieces of paper falling, they can see almost immediately that the paper is not accelerating and will realize that the surface area affects how much air is "caught" on the way down. The air "slows" down the paper, to its terminal velocity. Crumpling up the paper and dropping doesn't change the mass, but does change the surface area being caught by the air. This might help the students better understand the concept of terminal velocity.

Students may continue to think that objects which are heavier will drop faster than objects that are lighter. However, when shown the paper vs. other objects falling, they should come to a better understanding. Show them an ordinary piece of paper and golf ball, and ask them which will hit the ground first. Most will say the golf ball because it is heavier. Now crumple up the paper as small as you can. When you drop them, they should hit the ground pretty close together. If you have in your possession, a brass or steel set of weights, using a 100-g weight and a 2.0-kg weight will give the same results. The emphasis is that objects will drop at the same rate. Emphasize this by showing different masses with the same acceleration in the computer simulation. Regardless of the mass, the speed of the objects should always be the same at the end of the same time period.

Activity Overview

This lesson provides a quantitative and graphical view of free fall in realistic situations.

Student Objectives

Students will:

- use a spreadsheet to manipulate many variables.
- relate time, distance and speed during free fall.
- evaluate the effect of friction on a freely falling body.
- model free fall on other planets.

ANSWERS FOR TEH TEACHER ONLY

What Do You Think?

Many students will answer that the heavier object will hit the ground first. In fact, all objects will fall at the same rate in a vacuum. A movie clip of Neil Armstrong stating that Newton was right, when he dropped a feather and a hammer on the moon, is available on *Active Physics* video, and could be viewed.

Objects will fall differently (ignoring the air resistance on Jupiter) only due to the different force of gravity on the moon and Jupiter.

JOURNEY TO THE MOON AND BEYOND

Activity Three

Spreadsheet Games: Free Fall

WHAT DO YOU THINK?

Almost 400 years ago, Galileo performed an experiment in which he dropped two objects of different weights off a high tower.

- **Which one do you think hit the ground first?**
- **Would objects fall differently on the moon and Jupiter than on Earth?**

Record your ideas about these questions in your *Active Physics log*. Be prepared to discuss your responses with your small group and the class.

TRANSPORTATION T124

FOR YOU TO DO

In this activity you will use spreadsheets to experiment with what happens during free fall. You can use the copies of the spreadsheets shown in the text, or enter your own data into the spreadsheet program provided by your teacher. The spreadsheet file will enable you to calculate distance, velocity, and acceleration for an object in free fall. The first page of the spreadsheet consists of a set of initial conditions that you can change, along with a units converter. The second page graphs the information. The third page consists of long columns where the values of time, velocity, acceleration, and distance are calculated.

The initial conditions for the problem are the mass of the object that is falling, the acceleration due to gravity and the drag factor. The drag factor is a constant that is used to calculate the value of air resistance on the object.

time	accel	ave vel	new acc	dist fallen	velocity
0.30	9.80	2.45	9.80	0.44	2.94
0.40	9.80	3.43	9.80	0.78	3.92
0.50	9.80	4.41	9.80	1.23	4.90
0.60	9.80	5.39	9.80	1.76	5.88
0.70	9.80	6.37	9.80	2.40	6.86
0.80	9.80	7.35	9.80	3.14	7.84
0.90	9.80	8.33	9.80	3.97	8.82
1.00	9.80	9.31	9.80	4.90	9.80
1.10	9.80	10.29	9.80	5.93	10.78
1.20	9.80	11.27	9.80	7.06	11.76
1.30	9.80	12.25	9.80	8.28	12.74
1.40	9.80	13.23	9.80	9.60	13.72
1.50	9.80	14.21	9.80	11.03	14.70
1.60	9.80	15.19	9.80	12.54	15.68
1.70	9.80	16.17	9.80	14.16	16.66
1.80	9.80	17.15	9.80	15.88	17.64
[illegible]	9.80	18.13	9.80	17.69	[illegible]

Note: To enter a number in the spreadsheet, click in the box, type the number (do not include units or commas) and press enter. *If you get the message, "Locked cells cannot be changed," it means that you did not click in the proper box. Try again.*

On the next pages are a few problems for you to examine with the spreadsheet. The power of the computer spreadsheet is that it allows you to see very quickly the physics in each problem without having to spend time on tedious calculations. By just changing the initial conditions you will be able to see instantly both the numerical and graphical results of those changes.

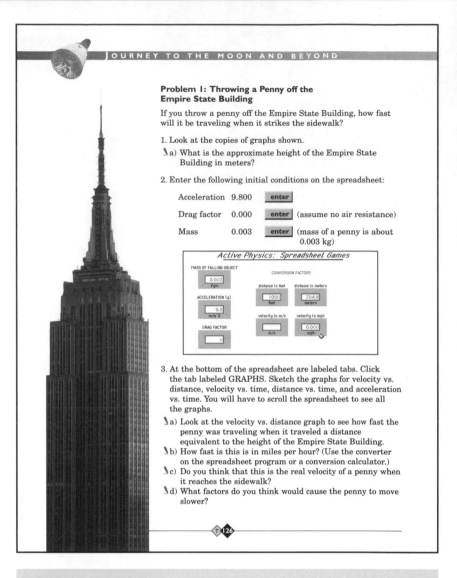

JOURNEY TO THE MOON AND BEYOND

Problem 1: Throwing a Penny off the Empire State Building

If you throw a penny off the Empire State Building, how fast will it be traveling when it strikes the sidewalk?

1. Look at the copies of graphs shown.
   a) What is the approximate height of the Empire State Building in meters?
2. Enter the following initial conditions on the spreadsheet:

Acceleration	9.800	enter	
Drag factor	0.000	enter	(assume no air resistance)
Mass	0.003	enter	(mass of a penny is about 0.003 kg)

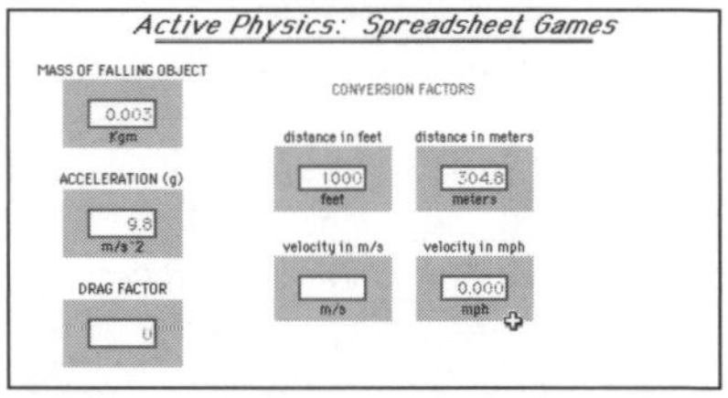

3. At the bottom of the spreadsheet are labeled tabs. Click the tab labeled GRAPHS. Sketch the graphs for velocity vs. distance, velocity vs. time, distance vs. time, and acceleration vs. time. You will have to scroll the spreadsheet to see all the graphs.
   a) Look at the velocity vs. distance graph to see how fast the penny was traveling when it traveled a distance equivalent to the height of the Empire State Building.
   b) How fast is this is in miles per hour? (Use the converter on the spreadsheet program or a conversion calculator.)
   c) Do you think that this is the real velocity of a penny when it reaches the sidewalk?
   d) What factors do you think would cause the penny to move slower?

T 126

ANSWERS

For You To Do *(continued)*

Problem 1:

1. a) From data.

2. Student activity.

3. a) From data.

   b) From data.

   c) From data. Not a real value, as the coin will reach terminal velocity.

   d) Air resistance will stop the penny from accelerating.

4. In reality, there is air resistance on the penny as it falls. Take this air resistance into account. An approximate value for the drag factor for the penny is 0.0001 Ns^2/m^2. Enter this value of the drag factor in the box on the CALCULATION spreadsheet and press enter.

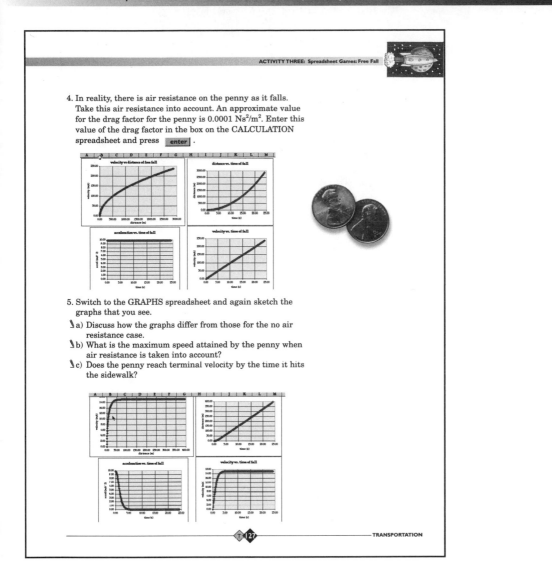

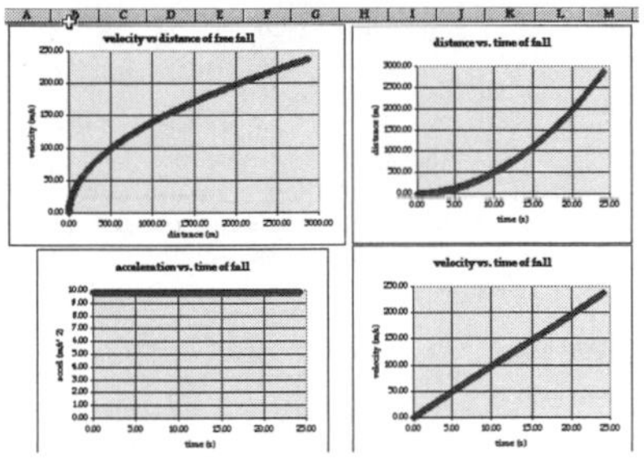

5. Switch to the GRAPHS spreadsheet and again sketch the graphs that you see.

a) Discuss how the graphs differ from those for the no air resistance case.

b) What is the maximum speed attained by the penny when air resistance is taken into account?

c) Does the penny reach terminal velocity by the time it hits the sidewalk?

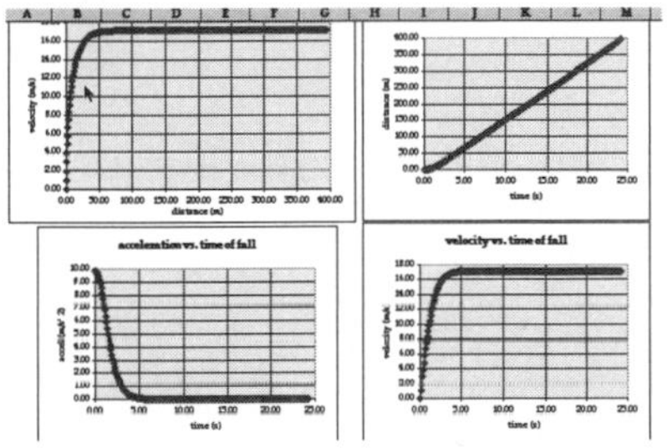

3

Answers

For You To Do *(continued)*

4. Student activity.

5. a) From data.

b) From data.

c) From data. The penny should have reached terminal velocity before it hits the sidewalk.

JOURNEY TO THE MOON AND BEYOND

Problem 2: The Falling Human Problem

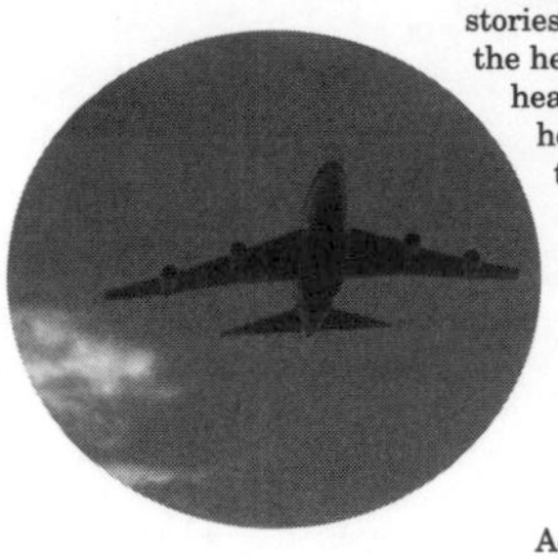

Occasionally you read what seem to be completely ridiculous stories in the supermarket tabloids. One such story might have the headline, "Man Falls from Airplane and Survives!" Is this headline believable? How fast would a person be going when he hits the ground? If the answer is 10 miles per hour, is the story reasonable? What if the answer were about 60, 100, or 1000 miles per hour when the person hits the ground?

1. Use the spreadsheet to determine how fast a person is traveling when he hits the ground. An approximate value of the drag factor for a human is 0.2 Ns^2/m^2. Enter the following initial conditions on the spreadsheet:

Acceleration	9.800	enter	
Drag factor	0.2	enter	
Mass	60.0	enter	(approximate mass of a person = 60 kg)

2. Sketch the graphs.
   a) Do the graphs differ from the penny with air resistance? If so, explain the difference.

3. Now assume the plane is flying at an altitude of 3600 feet. You are going to use the spreadsheet to see how fast the person is moving when he has fallen a distance of 3600 feet.
   a) Use the converter to determine how many meters is equal to 3600 feet.
   b) What is the velocity in meters per second when the person has fallen 3600 feet?
   c) Use the converter to determine the velocity in miles per hour.
   d) Do you think the headline is possible? Discuss your answer.

ANSWERS

For You To Do *(continued)*

Problem 2:

1. Student activity.

2. a) From data.

3. a) From data.

   b) From data.

   c) From data.

   d) From data.

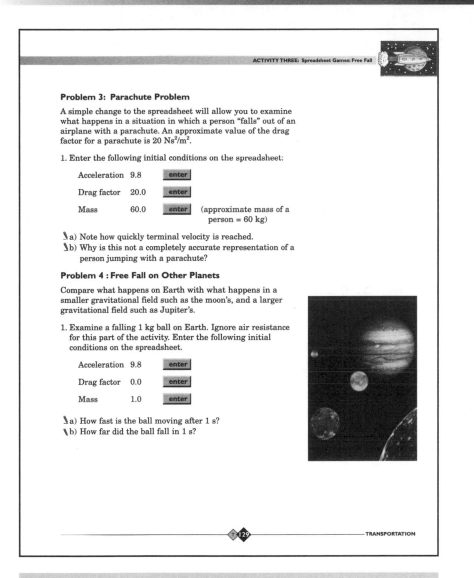

Problem 3: Parachute Problem

A simple change to the spreadsheet will allow you to examine what happens in a situation in which a person "falls" out of an airplane with a parachute. An approximate value of the drag factor for a parachute is 20 Ns^2/m^2.

1. Enter the following initial conditions on the spreadsheet:

Acceleration	9.8	enter	
Drag factor	20.0	enter	
Mass	60.0	enter	(approximate mass of a person = 60 kg)

a) Note how quickly terminal velocity is reached.

b) Why is this not a completely accurate representation of a person jumping with a parachute?

Problem 4 : Free Fall on Other Planets

Compare what happens on Earth with what happens in a smaller gravitational field such as the moon's, and a larger gravitational field such as Jupiter's.

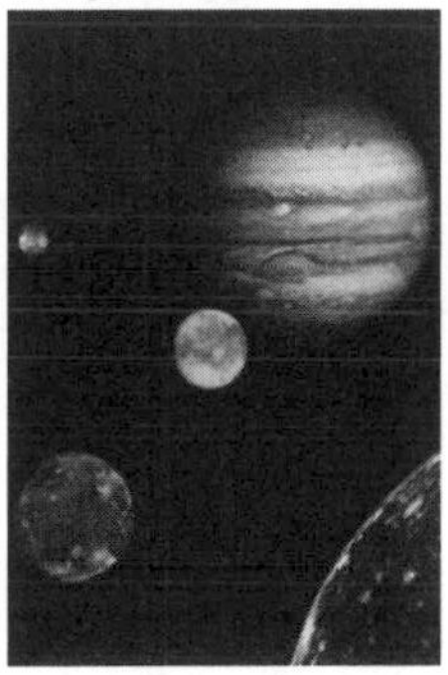

1. Examine a falling 1 kg ball on Earth. Ignore air resistance for this part of the activity. Enter the following initial conditions on the spreadsheet.

Acceleration	9.8	enter
Drag factor	0.0	enter
Mass	1.0	enter

a) How fast is the ball moving after 1 s?

b) How far did the ball fall in 1 s?

3

ANSWERS

For You To Do *(continued)*

Problem 3:

1. a) From data.

   b) From data.

Problem 4:

1. a) From data.

   b) From data.

ANSWERS

For You To Do
(continued)

Problem 4: *(continued)*

2. a) From data. Both velocity and distance will be smaller on the moon than on Earth.

3. a) From data. Both the velocity and distance will be larger on Jupiter than on Earth and the moon.

2. Change the acceleration to 1.6 and press enter. This is the value for the acceleration due to gravity on the moon, 1.6 m/s^2.
   a) Describe how the velocity and distance at 1 s differ from on Earth.

3. Change the acceleration to 25 and press enter. This is the value for the acceleration due to gravity on Jupiter, 25 m/s^2.
   a) Compare the velocity and distance at 1 s with the values for the moon and Earth.

FOR YOU TO READ
Forces on Falling Objects

On Earth, objects accelerate at a constant rate of 9.8 m/s^2. The same object, dropped on the surface of the moon, would accelerate at 1.60 m/s^2. The difference can be explained by the greater gravitational attraction exerted by the greater mass of planet Earth. However, in air, an additional force acts on falling objects. Molecules strike the falling object, slowing its descent. The friction caused by air molecules is often called drag. This helps explain why a flat piece of paper floats to the ground, while one crumpled into a ball falls at a much faster speed. The greater the surface area (such as for the flat paper), the greater is the drag. As objects move through the air they collide with air molecules. The drag force depends upon the size and shape of the object, the density of the air, and the speed of motion.

If you drop a ball, it has very little velocity at the beginning of its descent, and therefore, it will have little drag force. As the ball increases in velocity, the drag force increases. At some time during the descent the drag force will equal the gravitational force. The net force is now zero and the ball falls with a constant velocity (it no longer accelerates). This is referred to as the terminal velocity.

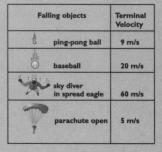

Falling objects	Terminal Velocity
ping-pong ball	9 m/s
baseball	20 m/s
sky diver in spread eagle	60 m/s
parachute open	5 m/s

Objects that move in space do not strike air molecules. Molecules within the atmosphere are held by the Earth's gravitational attraction. As you move away from planet Earth, its gravitational force decreases and there are fewer air molecules that will collide with a spacecraft.

REFLECTING ON THE ACTIVITY OR THE CHALLENGE

Sometimes everyday observations do not appear to be supported by scientific theories. You have observed that objects which have a large flat surface often fall more slowly than objects that appear to be more streamline. For example, a feather appears to fall more slowly than a bowling ball. Yet Newton's physics indicates that mass does not affect that speed at which objects fall. Non-science writers often have difficulties linking everyday observations with scientific explanations. In many cases they abandon scientific theories when they do not support observations.

To explain this inconsistency, consider the fact that as objects move through the atmosphere, they strike molecules of air. Not surprisingly, the shape of the object affects how many molecules it strikes as it falls. Each molecule that strikes a falling object exerts a force on the falling object. Even a small force affects an object in motion. The friction caused by the air molecules, referred to as drag, helps explain why some objects fall more slowly than others. Review your story once again to see why some everyday explanations appear to conflict with scientific theories. How could you maintain the scientific theory and still account for the everyday observation?

PHYSICS TO GO

1. Does a feather fall as quickly as a baseball?
2. Would you be able to throw a baseball farther on Earth or Jupiter? Explain your answer.

ANSWERS

Physics To Go

1. A feather and a baseball will only fall at the same rate when in a vacuum such as on the moon. However, because there is air resistance, the feather will not fall as quickly as the baseball. The mass to surface area is less in the feather so it will reach terminal velocity almost as soon as it has been dropped.
2. You would be able to throw a ball farther on Earth because the horizontal velocity of the ball will not change from the throw on Earth or on Jupiter. Therefore, while the ball is in the air, it will be pulled downward by gravity. Since the force of gravity is larger on Jupiter than on Earth, it will hit the ground faster than on Earth. Therefore, it will travel a shorter distance.

3. Arrange the diagrams so that the scales are arranged from lowest weight to greatest weight.

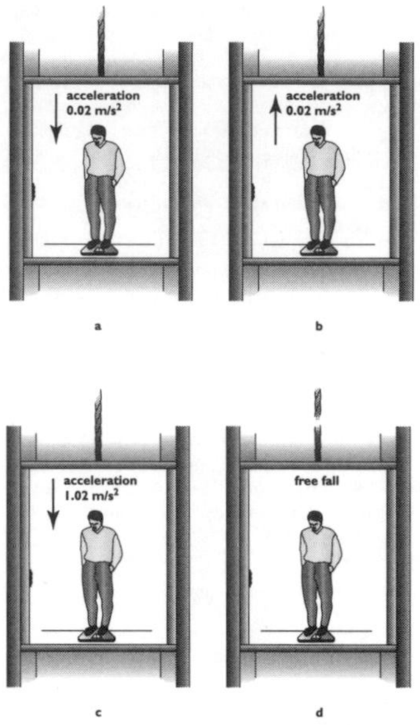

4. Velcro was used to hold objects in place on the space shuttle. Why might objects begin to float around as the shuttle orbits?

ANSWERS

Physics To Go *(continued)*

3. Lowest to highest: d, c, a, b.

4. Although all the objects will be traveling at exactly the same speed, there can be slight vibrations due to the various mechanical objects on board. These vibrations can cause the objects to move around. Bumping of objects, as well as currents in the air can also cause the objects to move around the cabin.

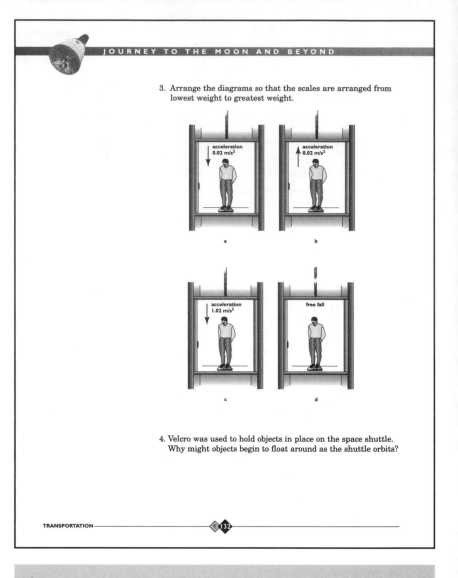

STRETCHING EXERCISES

The diagram below shows a devise that is able to measure the acceleration of a falling body.

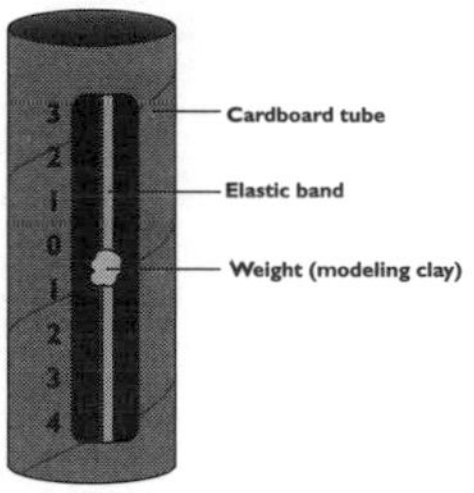

Design and construct an accelerometer that is able to monitor small changes in velocity as might be experienced on the space shuttle.

Problem 2: The Falling Human Problem

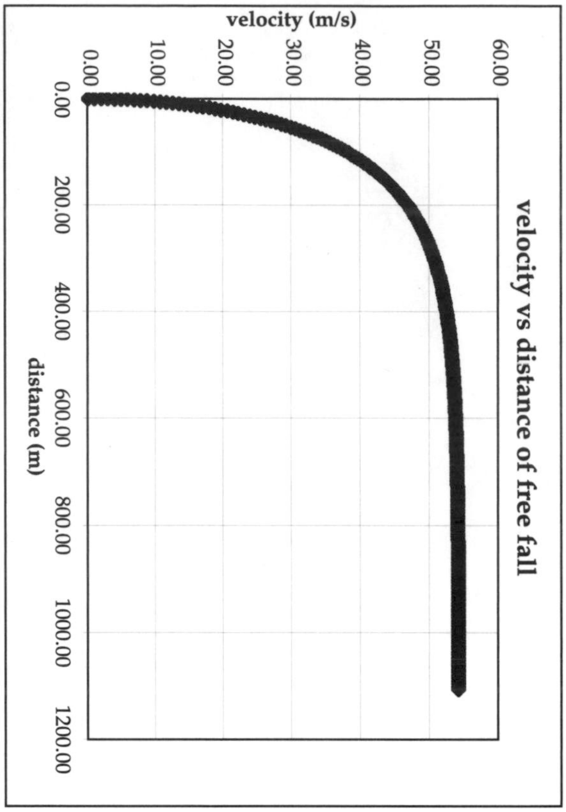

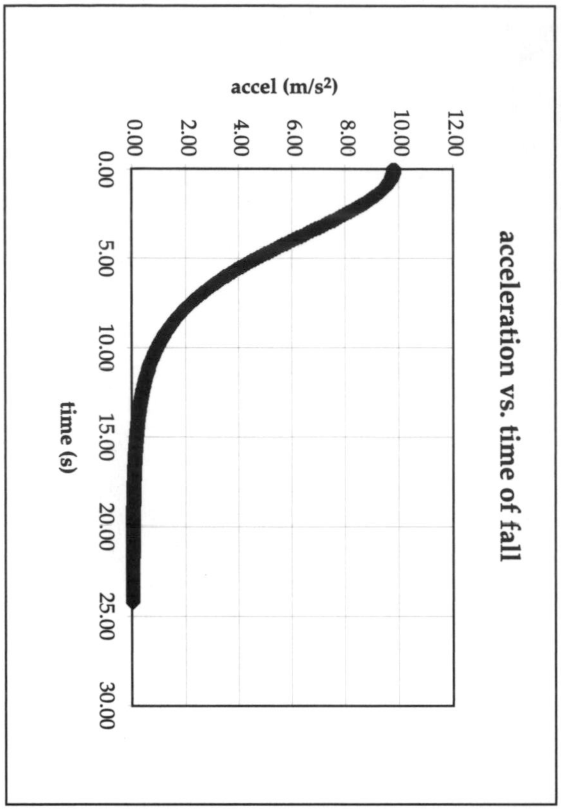

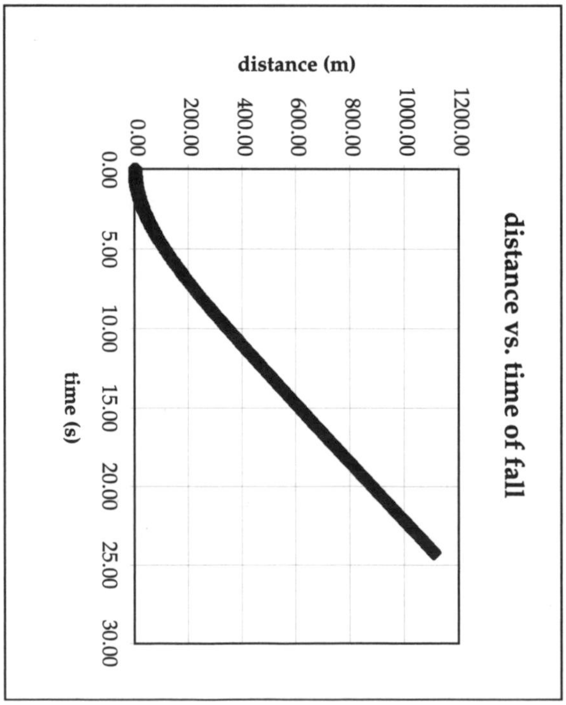

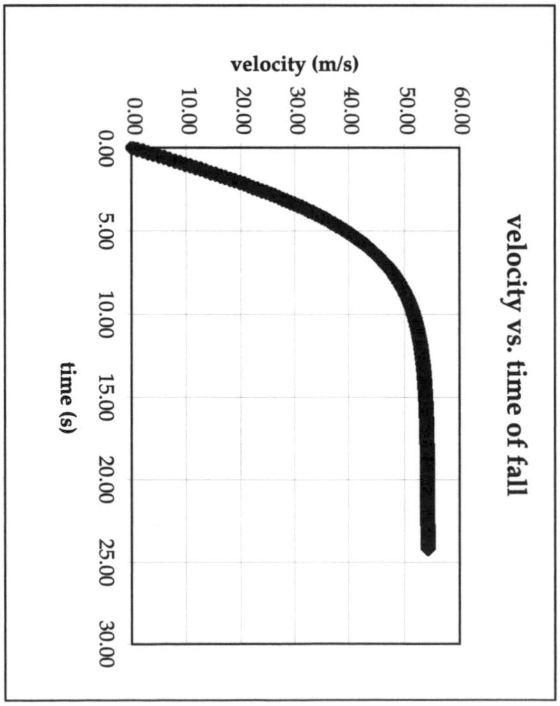

For use with *Transportation*, Chapter 3, ACTIVITY THREE: Spreadsheet Games: Free Fall

Problem 3: Parachute Problem

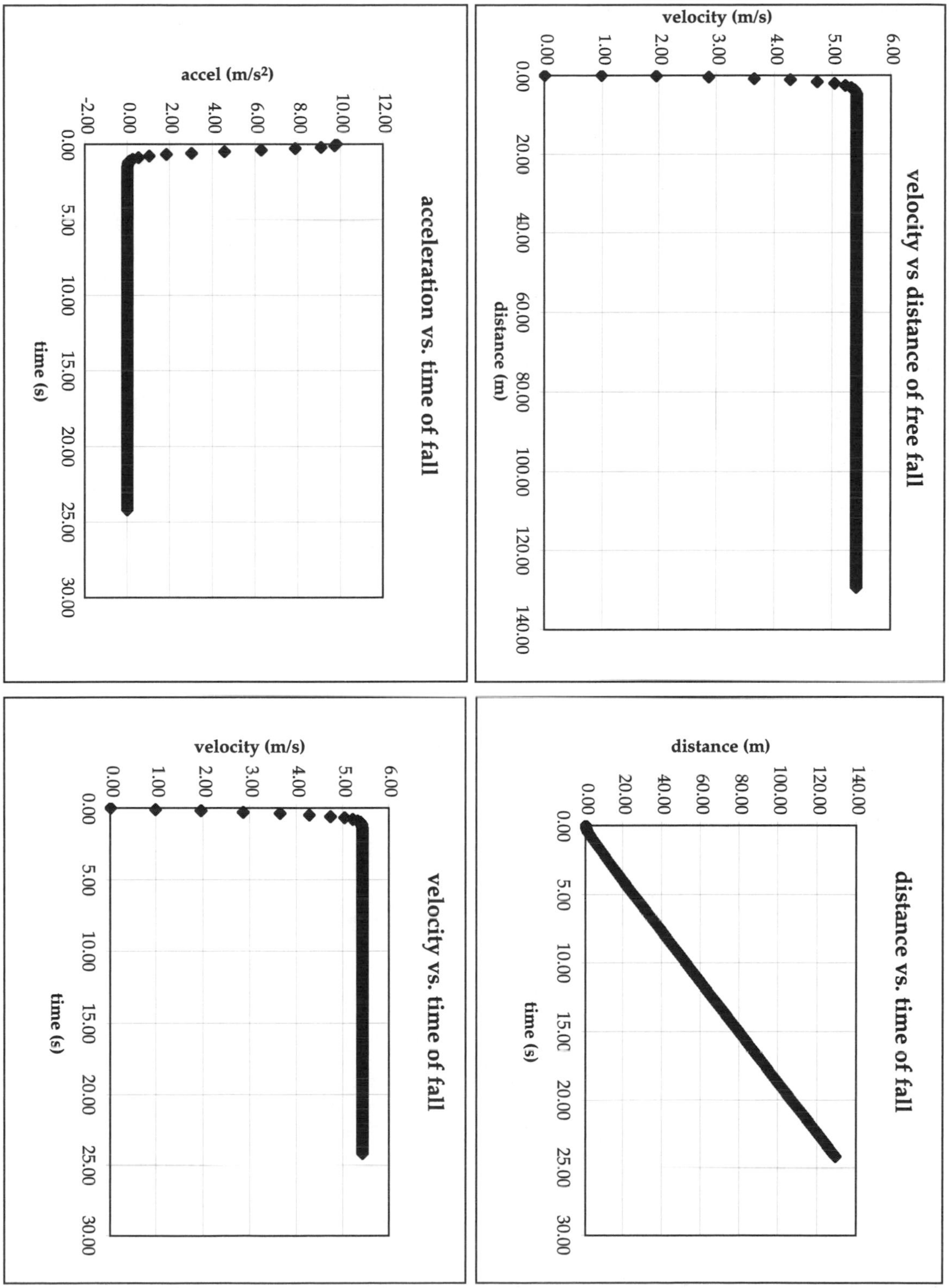

For use with *Transportation*, Chapter 3, ACTIVITY THREE: Spreadsheet Games: Free Fall

Problem 4: 1. Free Fall on Other Planets – Earth

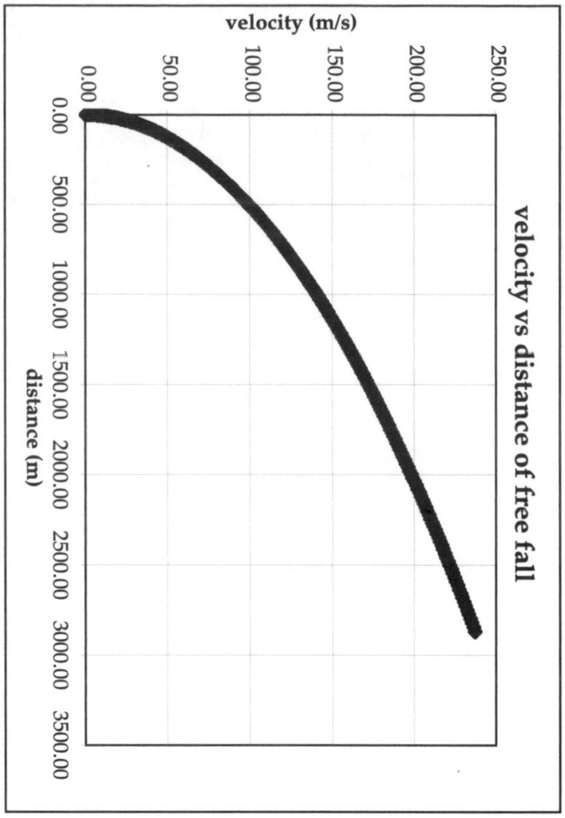

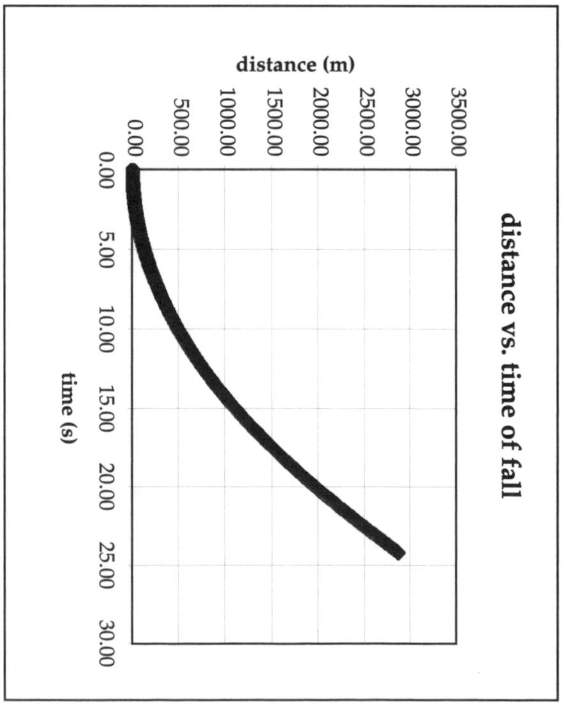

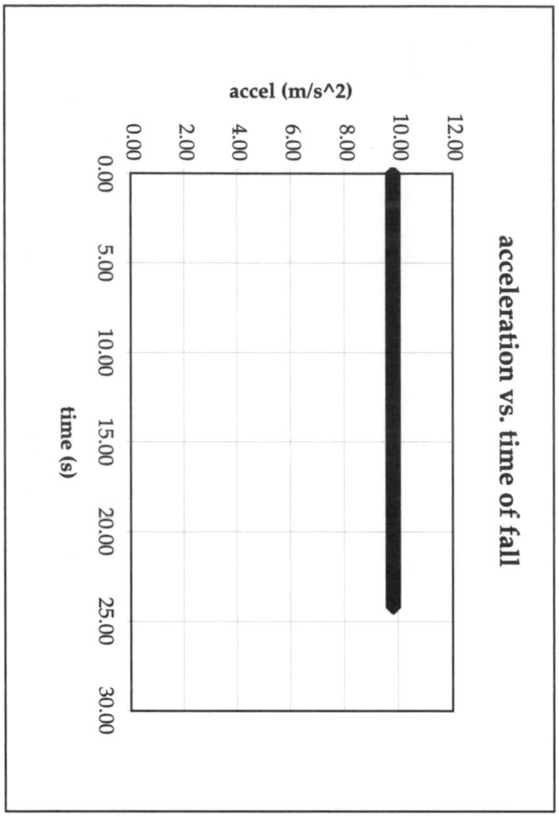

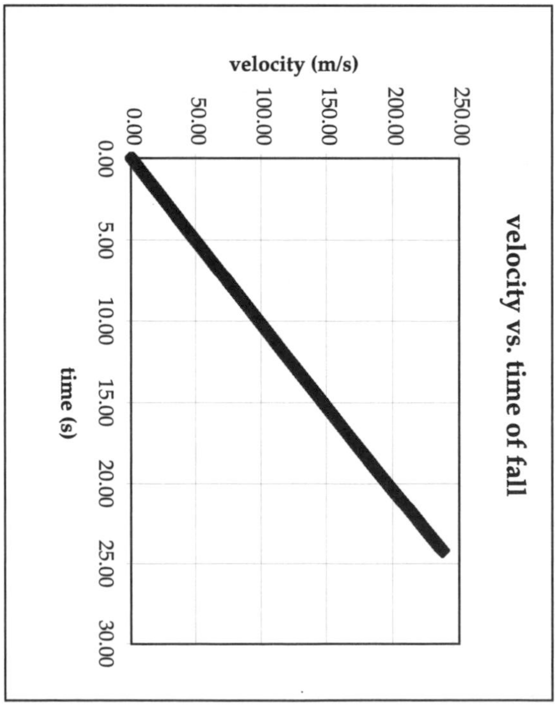

For use with *Transportation*, Chapter 3, ACTIVITY THREE: Spreadsheet Games: Free Fall

Problem 4: 2. Free Fall on Other Planets – Moon

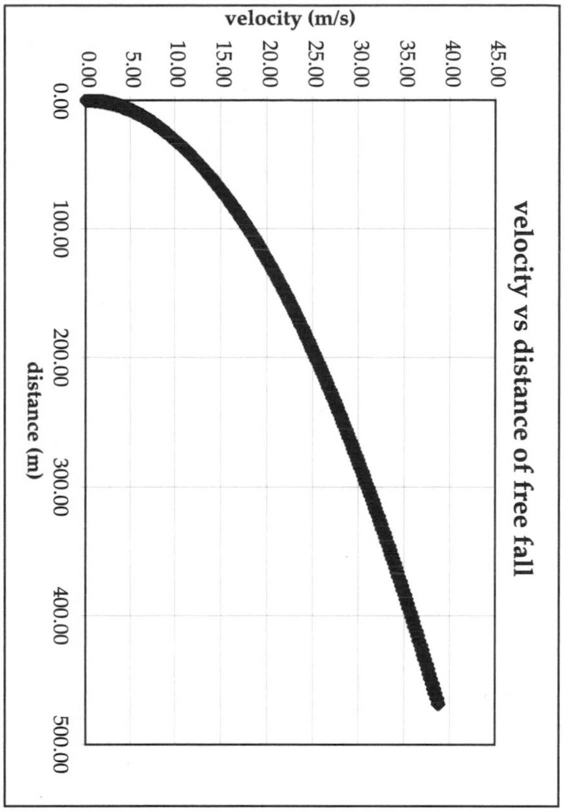

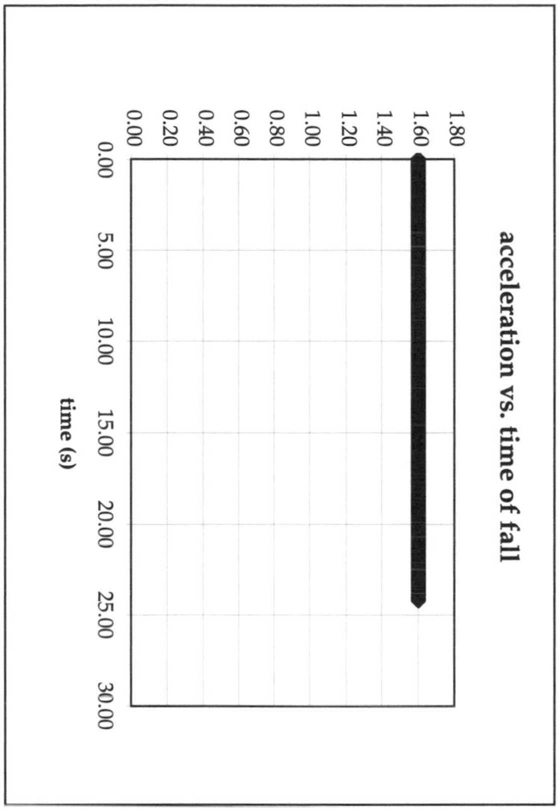

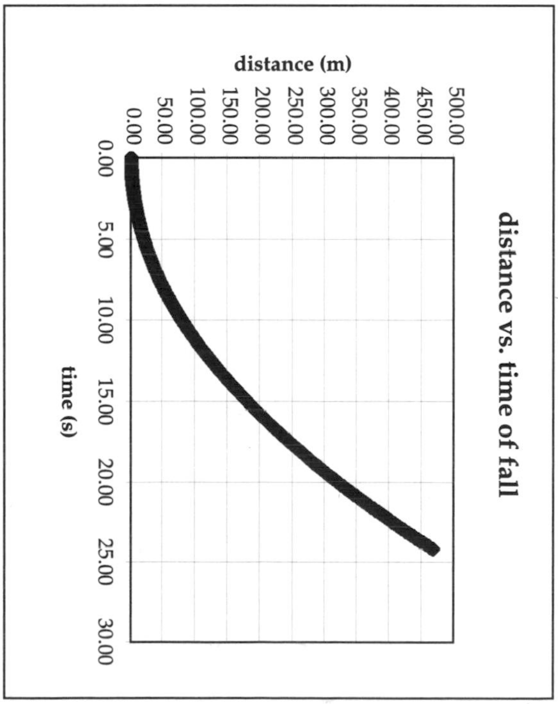

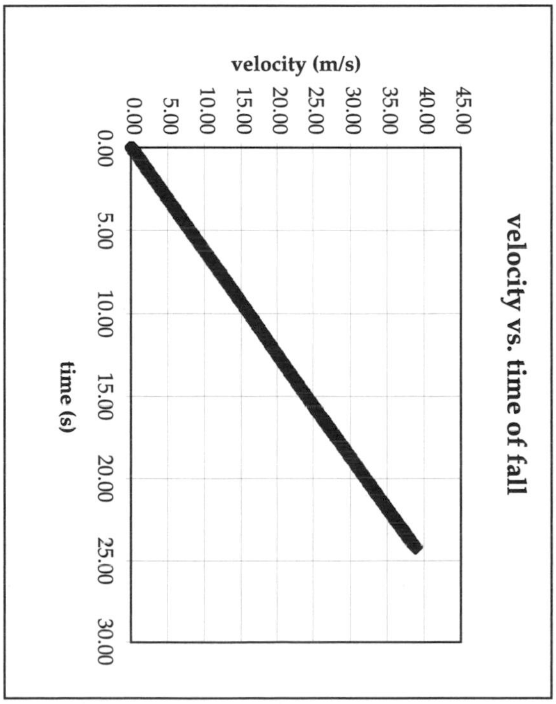

For use with *Transportation*, Chapter 3, ACTIVITY THREE: Spreadsheet Games: Free Fall

Problem 4: 3. Free Fall on Other Planets – Jupiter

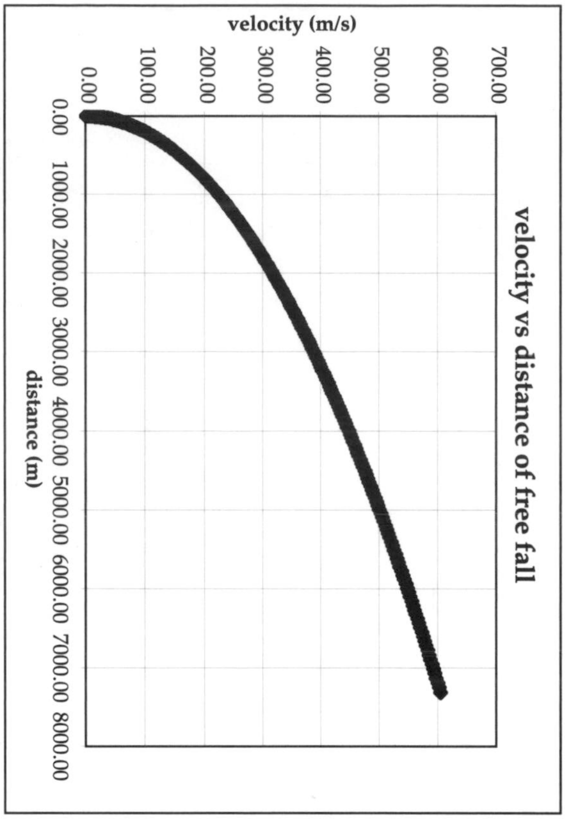

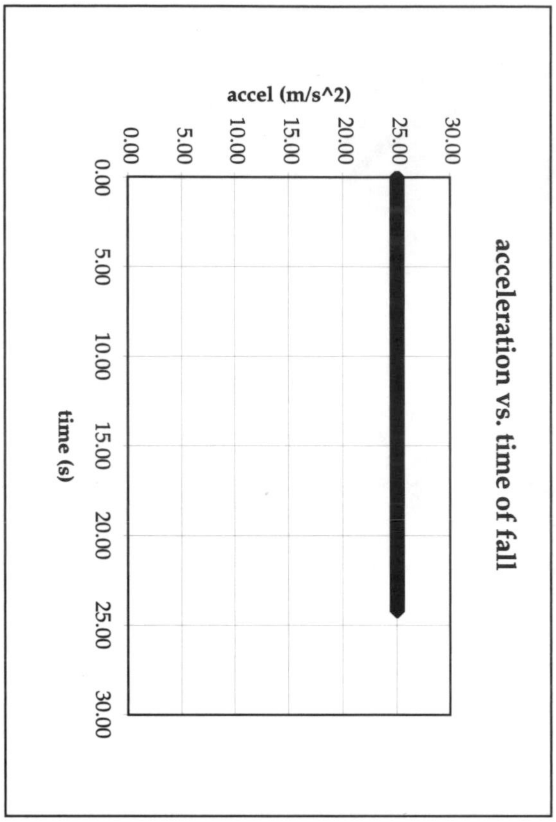

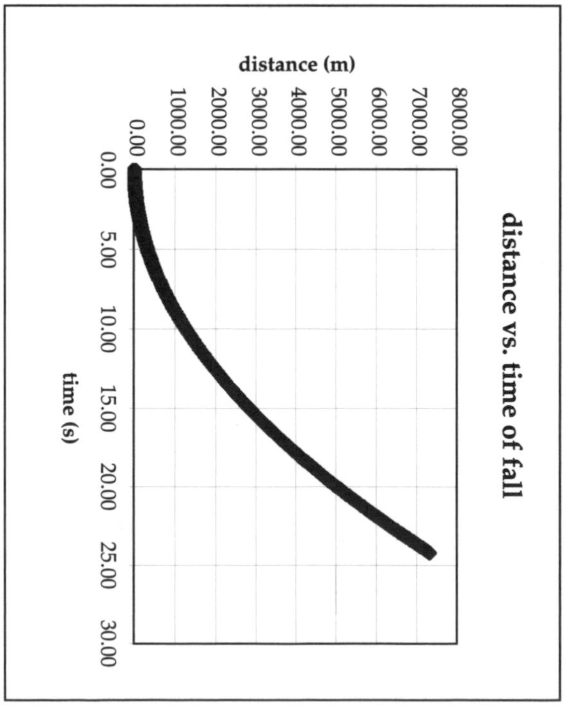

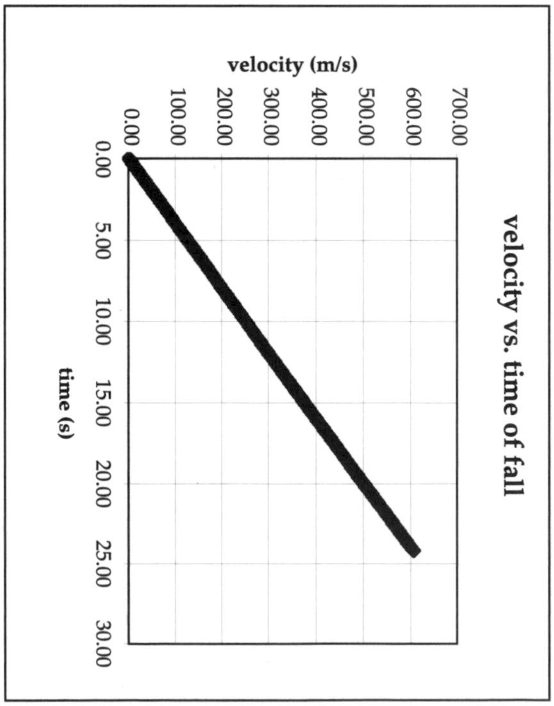

NOTES

ACTIVITY FOUR
Life Without Gravity

Background Information

This activity continues the discussion and investigation of life in zero gravity. Remind the students, that the astronauts are experiencing zero gravity because the spaceship is in free fall back to Earth, but falling in a trajectory that is the same as the curvature of the Earth's surface.

Any liquid in zero gravity will form into a perfect sphere, due to the cohesion of the molecules of that liquid. If you have a slow-motion video of water droplets, you can show the students that water, when in free fall, will form a perfect sphere.

Remind students of Newton's First Law of Motion - Inertia. An object in motion will remain in motion unless acted upon by an outside unbalanced force.

Active-ating the Physics InfoMall

The title of this activity is "Life Without Gravity." It is important to realize that many of the situations we may refer to as "without gravity" really have quite a bit of gravity. Consider astronauts in orbit around the Earth. Do they experience gravity? A search for "astronaut*" AND "force of gravity" AND "orbit" produces a few hits. If you look in Fuller, Fuller, & Fuller's *Study Guide to Accompany Physics Including Human Applications*, you can find a worked-out example for a satellite. The answer is that the gravitational force on a satellite in orbit is 87% of the force at the Earth's surface. That's a lot of gravity! The point of this is that one must be careful when saying something is "without gravity" or "weightless," and the InfoMall contains information on this topic.

For this activity, it is a good idea to revisit our search from Activity Two, in which we used "weightless*" AND "demo*" as our initial keywords, then filtered the search hits for only the word "weightless*" (this eliminated an optics article at the time). The first item on the list was from "Potpourri of Physics Teaching Ideas" found in the Demo & Lab Shop and has a section on the "Physical Effects of Apparent 'Weightlessness'" (which can easily be found by browsing far down the list in the Mechanics section). The second hit on the list is the article "Physics of living in space: A new course," *American Journal of Physics*, vol. 49, issue 8, 1981. The footnotes for this article mentions "Space Settlements: A Design Study," edited by R. D. Johnson and C. H. Holbrow, NASA SP-413, GPO Stock No. 033-000-00669-1 (U.S. GPO Washington, DC, 1977). You may find this interesting. In fact, you should examine many of the items on this list of search hits - many of them apply directly to this activity. This is a hint that even when searching for something, you should keep an eye out for something you may need a little later.

Step 2 of For You To Do asks students to describe some common devices. This brings to mind *Household Physics*, a textbook (from the Textbook Trove) that describes the operation of many items we use on a daily basis. You may get additional ideas for students to investigate. Note that one of the devices is the toilet. This textbook has a section on household water supply and sewage disposal, which seems relevant. See for yourself; there may be more you can use.

Reflecting on the Activity and the Challenge reminds us that astronauts are often nauseated. Why is this so? Search for "astronaut*" AND "nause*" and we get only a single hit: "Fun in Space," , vol. 28, 1960. As if the title is not clue enough that this is not what we want, the passage that includes the desired words is "I believe even the Mercury man-in-space program, in spite of all the nauseating journalistic publicity about the astronauts, has now been converted into a needed research program to study biological problems which must be understood by the time sending men into space becomes a really useful scientific venture." There are a couple of interesting points to be made here. First, even in 1960, it was clear that there were going to be biological problems for people in space. Second, the search engine does a fairly good job of locating words very quickly (the entire CD-ROM was searched in seconds, with the exception of the Keyword Kiosk, which is not useful when you think you know what you want to search for) - note that we asked for "nause*" and found "nauseating." And third, we will not always find what we are looking for on the first try.

If we change the search words to "space" AND "nause*", we find in "The physics of aerobatic flight," *Physics Today*, vol. 40, issue 11, 1987, that "The motion of the inner ear fluids and otoliths can produce disorientation, and even nausea, as the signals about orientation from the eyes don't agree with the inertial orientation signals from the inner ear." So now we can look further if we are interested enough, and find more detail about what it is about the ear that causes this. Of course, you might try "flight" AND "nause*" or "sailing" AND "nause*" as search words. Remember- there are few limits on words you can search for.

A little later in Reflecting on the Activity and the

Challenge, a question is posed as to how a person in space would know if they were gaining or losing "weight"? As we noted a little earlier, sometimes we find things while searching for other things in the InfoMall. It happens that one of the hits we found (but did not discuss directly) earlier addresses exactly this issue. The book (from the Book Basement) is *Teaching Physics: A Guide For The Non-Specialist.* While searching for the meaning of weightless, and conditions of apparent low-gravity, one of the passages that you may have found contained this: "The problem for astronauts who stay in Space for some time, is how to monitor their mass and discover whether they are 'putting on or losing weight'. The solution used in the Spacelab was to arrange a large version of a wig-wag balance with the astronaut sitting in a chair." If you want to find this quickly, you simply search for "wig-wag" and the InfoMall finds only 14 occurrences of this odd word.

Physics To Go question 4 asks about candles in microgravity environments. This is an interesting question, and a demo can help answer it. To find this demo on the InfoMall, you can search for "candle*" AND "space", then refine the search by sorting the Search Hits (under the Search Category button) by only the word "candle*". Try it.

Planning for the Activity

Time Requirements

Allow approximately two class periods to view the videos and design their living quarters, with another period for presentations.

Materials needed

For the class:

- *Active Physics Transportation* Content Video (Segment: Life Without Gravity)
- VCR and TV monitor

Advance Preparation and Setup

Select and preview a video in order to prepare for student questions. Have copies of NASA materials available for the final discussion.

Teaching Notes

One of the environments astronauts will experience is zero-gravity. Ask for some suggestions about this experience, and begin the video. Allow the students about 5 minutes to aggregate their answers.

Proceed directly to the FYTD. Divide the class into groups of four. If they have viewed videos of the space craft, they may have a better idea of the space limitations they are dealing with. Randomly assign two devices to each group for their consideration. The student response should include three parts: a description of the device on Earth, the problems encountered in zero-g and how the innovation solves the problem. Allow at least 10 minutes at the end for presentation of group designs. Compare the best design as chosen by the class with any NASA designs available.

Allow the students to design their devices without correcting obvious flaws, and allow the students to get feedback from the rest of their class when presenting. This will allow for inquiry-type learning, as they will develop their ideas from other input and suggestions.

Keep them on task with constant monitoring and subtle encouragement while looking at each group. Use groups of four. In groups of three or less, there are generally fewer ideas, and groups greater than five give some an opportunity to blend into the woodwork.

Encourage students to work cooperatively by assigning tasks prior to beginning the activity. The following tasks are designed for groups of four students:

- **Organizer:** helps focus discussion and ensures that all members of the group contribute to the discussion. The organizer also ensures that all of the equipment has been gathered and that the group completes all parts of the activity.
- **Recorder:** provides written procedures when required, diagrams where appropriate and records data. The recorder must work closely with the organizer to ensure that all group members contribute.
- **Researcher:** seeks written and electronic information to support the findings of the group. In addition, where appropriate, the researcher will develop and test prototypes. The researcher will also exchange information gathered among different groups.
- **Diverger:** seeks alternative explanations and approaches. The task of the diverger is to keep the discussion open. "Are other explanations possible?"

It may be difficult for some students to understand that life in zero-gravity is very different from life on Earth. They will need to be guided and in some cases to understand that the way we do things on Earth is totally dependent on gravity's effect on us. When they are making their presentations, encourage positive feedback and criticism.

Activity Overview

This lesson is designed to help students understand some of the challenges, difficulties and environment changes that arise in a weightless environment.

Student Objectives

Students will:

- acquire a sense of the differences between functioning in normal gravity and in zero gravity.
- understand some of the physiological problems associated with a zero-g environment.
- appreciate the problems encountered in designing living quarters for a zero-g environment.

ANSWERS FOR THE TEACHER ONLY

What Do You Think?

Eating in our environment so often relies on gravity to help keep things on plates, soup in spoons, liquids in the glass, that eating in a weightless environment changes the rules of table manners.

JOURNEY TO THE MOON AND BEYOND

Activity Four

Life without Gravity

WHAT DO YOU THINK?

Whether you are orbiting Earth in the space shuttle or traveling to the moon or beyond, much of your journey will be in a weightless environment.

- **Why is eating dinner different in a weightless environment?**

Record your ideas about these questions in your *Active Physics log*. Be prepared to discuss your responses with your small group and the class.

TRANSPORTATION — T134

FOR YOU TO DO

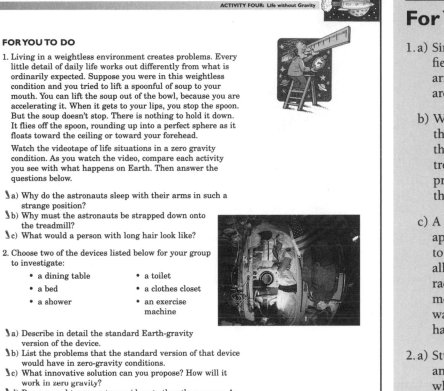

1. Living in a weightless environment creates problems. Every little detail of daily life works out differently from what is ordinarily expected. Suppose you were in this weightless condition and you tried to lift a spoonful of soup to your mouth. You can lift the soup out of the bowl, because you are accelerating it. When it gets to your lips, you stop the spoon. But the soup doesn't stop. There is nothing to hold it down. It flies off the spoon, rounding up into a perfect sphere as it floats toward the ceiling or toward your forehead.

   Watch the videotape of life situations in a zero gravity condition. As you watch the video, compare each activity you see with what happens on Earth. Then answer the questions below.

   a) Why do the astronauts sleep with their arms in such a strange position?
   b) Why must the astronauts be strapped down onto the treadmill?
   c) What would a person with long hair look like?

2. Choose two of the devices listed below for your group to investigate:
   - a dining table
   - a bed
   - a shower
   - a toilet
   - a clothes closet
   - an exercise machine

   a) Describe in detail the standard Earth-gravity version of the device.
   b) List the problems that the standard version of that device would have in zero-gravity conditions.
   c) What innovative solution can you propose? How will it work in zero gravity?
   d) Be prepared to present your ideas to the other groups. As you compare results, try to reach a consensus about the best way to deal with these problems.

ANSWERS

For You To Do

1. a) Since there is no gravitation field in the craft to hold their arms down, and the muscles are relaxed, their arms float up.

   b) Without any local gravity field, there is no other force to push the astronauts feet against the treadmill. The first step would propel the astronaut away from the treadmill.

   c) A person with long hair would appear as if they were attached to an electrostatic generator; all their hair would extend radially from their head. The motion of the head would send wave-like ripples along the hair.

2. a) Students' answers. Look for answers that describe details which may be affected in a zero-g environment. For example, the dining table will have sturdy legs, heavy table top, and possibly supports underneath. Generally, objects used on Earth will be larger, and may have wasted space.

   b) Students' answers. Again, the standard versions will have to be made with gravity in mind, that is the devices will be sturdier, heavier, and bulkier. Anything dealing with liquids, will be a problem of storage.

   c) Students' answers. All devices would be able to made with less structure and bulk, they would have to be attached so as to not float around, devices which need gravity to operate properly (exercise machine or toilet) would have to supply the gravity in another form -- such as suction for the liquid wastes, elastic "tie-down" straps for the exercise machine.

   d) Students' answers.

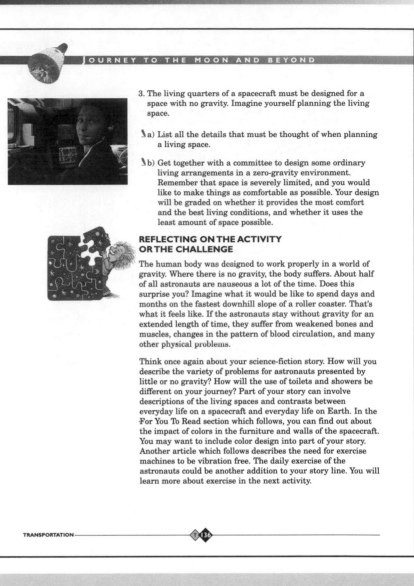

3. The living quarters of a spacecraft must be designed for a space with no gravity. Imagine yourself planning the living space.

a) List all the details that must be thought of when planning a living space.

b) Get together with a committee to design some ordinary living arrangements in a zero-gravity environment. Remember that space is severely limited, and you would like to make things as comfortable as possible. Your design will be graded on whether it provides the most comfort and the best living conditions, and whether it uses the least amount of space possible.

REFLECTING ON THE ACTIVITY OR THE CHALLENGE

The human body was designed to work properly in a world of gravity. Where there is no gravity, the body suffers. About half of all astronauts are nauseous a lot of the time. Does this surprise you? Imagine what it would be like to spend days and months on the fastest downhill slope of a roller coaster. That's what it feels like. If the astronauts stay without gravity for an extended length of time, they suffer from weakened bones and muscles, changes in the pattern of blood circulation, and many other physical problems.

Think once again about your science-fiction story. How will you describe the variety of problems for astronauts presented by little or no gravity? How will the use of toilets and showers be different on your journey? Part of your story can involve descriptions of the living spaces and contrasts between everyday life on a spacecraft and everyday life on Earth. In the For You To Read section which follows, you can find out about the impact of colors in the furniture and walls of the spacecraft. You may want to include color design into part of your story. Another article which follows describes the need for exercise machines to be vibration free. The daily exercise of the astronauts could be another addition to your story line. You will learn more about exercise in the next activity.

ANSWERS

For You To Do *(continued)*

3. a) Students' answers will vary. Look for no waste of space, no sharp corners, everything must be attached, cupboards must have locking doors, privacy for certain activity, beds that fold out of the way when not in use, seat belts for sitting and sleeping, etc.

b) Students' response.

FOR YOU TO READ

Interior Color Testing for Space Station Freedom

Reprinted from *Station Break* (Vol. 4, No. 12, Dec. 1992).

With hundreds of thousands of technical details being determined about Space Station Freedom, one might think the colors used inside would be among the last concerns. But that's not so. In fact some very scientific and detailed testing is under way to select the best color schemes for the space station.

And it's much more than just what looks best. There are many considerations in choosing the space station's colors. Light reflection and absorption, the durability of the finish, integration with the international partners and even the psychological effects are all concerns in color tests.

"What we really are trying to do right now is determine what colors don't work in order to propose some that do," said George Tamas, an industrial designer in Boeing's human-systems division, who has been performing the color testing.

But before colors are determined, other considerations must be made. For instance, the type of finish specified. Although a glossy finish cleans up easily, the glare produced is unacceptable, so a semi-gloss or flat finish will be used. There are also concerns of the paint chipping or flaking, so a two part catalytic paint is needed that will not release unwanted gases into the space station's environment.

When it comes to lighting, foot-candle readings are taken of different colors to determine the amount of reflection. If a color does not reflect a required amount of light, it will not be considered. If a color reflects more light, that means less power for lighting is needed and that power can be used more efficiently in other areas.

"If we're talking about a 50-watt difference, that could be the difference in turning on an experiment or being able to warm dinner," said Tamas.

Boeing's color testing in the US laboratory and living quarters has been under way for two years now in the space station mock-up at Marshall Space Flight Center in Huntsville. The international partners also are conducting their own color tests for their modules. Because Boeing engineers have twice the space to consider, there is more flexibility in their use of colors.

As for the colors, federal standards must be met. Most of those involve various shades of white, gray, and tan. But if approved, additional colors can be used. For instance, inside the living quarters, the wardroom is being tested in shades of red. Because the racks on the space station can be moved, their design and positioning must also be considered in determining their color.

The idea is to use colors that make sense for the area. In the working environment of the laboratory, lighter colors will be used to enhance

→

JOURNEY TO THE MOON AND BEYOND

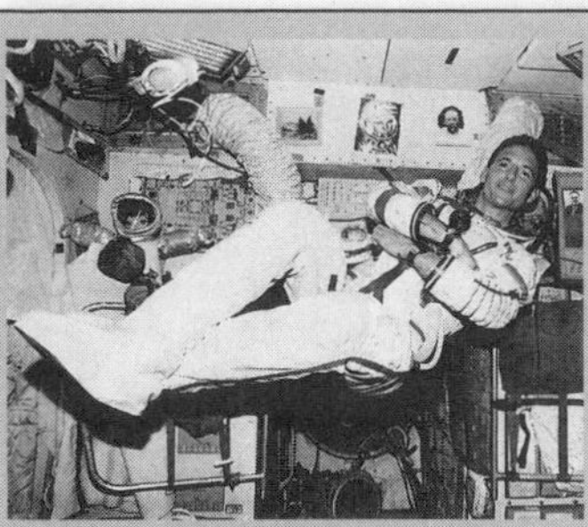

the work environment. Colors that are considered stressful are ruled out. Currently, grays and whites with blue trim are the functional choices. Inside the habitat or "home" for the crew, more cozy, warm colors will be used, giving a sense of security. In the sleeping area, darker, more peaceful shades are the choice.

Gerard Carr, former Skylab astronaut and now a Boeing technical support subcontractor in Huntsville, said coloring is an integral part of Freedom's design. Carr and his fellow crew members spent the longest amount of time yet on an American mission—84 days back in 1973.

"It was like being in the New Mexico or Arizona desert," said Carr. " Everything was finished in earth tones and unexciting, designed not to give any stimulation or distractions."

Carr said based on his Skylab experience, there needs to be some textures also involved in the space station colors.

"The only colors we had on board were the color bars on the wall we used to register the cameras. We really missed color as well as aromas. . .you need the stimulation for a long term in space."

There also is the psychological aspect of choosing the right colors. Great care must be made to avoid eye fatigue, colors that are tiring to look at over time.

Taking Physical Fitness to New Frontiers: Station-Related Cycle Stabilizer to Undergo Shuttle Flight Test

Reprinted from *Station Break* (Vol. 4, No. 5, May 1992).

A major challenge in designing future manned space missions may now be resolved, thanks to some new equipment developed by NASA and Lockheed.

The challenge is the incompatibility of physical exercise and microgravity science. Astronauts must exercise during their missions, but sensitive microgravity experiments conducted on those missions need a spacecraft environment free from disturbance.

The NASA/Lockheed solution is a platform that supports the exercise equipment yet cancels out

→

the vibrations, allowing astronauts to work out strenuously without interfering with science experiments. The device is called the Isolated Exercise Platform (ISEP). The first flight-ready stabilized platform was delivered to Johnson Space Center in January. Its Shuttle debut is planned for June, in the middeck of the Space Shuttle Columbia.

Dr. Damon Smith, Lockheed's stabilized platform chief scientist and project leader, said, "It's desirable that astronauts on the longer Shuttle missions perform hard aerobic exercise daily. Without this exercise, the prolonged absence of gravity could affect the crew's ability to stand upright without dizziness when they return to Earth."

Typically, orbiting astronauts have exercised on a bicycle or treadmill mounted to a Shuttle bulkhead. "When there are no sensitive experiments aboard, this is not a problem," Smith said, "but in the presence of microgravity research such as protein crystal growth, this amount of activity interferes. It's important for space station crew members or voyagers to Mars, who also must counteract the prolonged effects of weightlessness on their skeletal systems. Bones lose calcium during long periods without gravity, and exercise is an effective counter-measure to deal with this loss.

"The conflict between the medical need for exercise and the sensitivity of microgravity experiments has challenged space planners for some time," Smith said. "We think we've solved the problem with the ISEP."

Lockheed designed the first stabilized platform for use with an ergometer, a stationary-cycle device built by the European Space Agency. Future designs will accommodate a treadmill and a rowing machine.

The June flight of Columbia will be STS-50, a 13-day microgravity research mission called United States Microgravity Laboratory1. USML-1 will be the longest Space Shuttle flight to date. Crew exercise is a top priority.

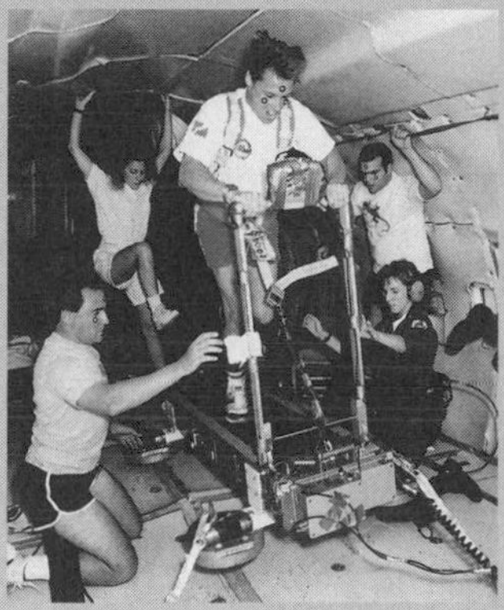

→

3

ANSWERS

Physics To Go

1. A comparison could also be done in the classroom, marking off the dimensions of a space vehicle on the floor with masking tape. Calculating the volume of each person may be difficult, but can be approximated using basic volume of cylinders, or cubes. If a bathtub is available, they could measure their volume by the volume of water they displace.

2.-3. These are short readings designed to connect the aspects of daily life with the space program. You could have a classroom discussion of habitat designs by simply comparing the antiseptic look of many science fiction and real interiors of the type of design presented in a show like *Star Trek: The Next Generation*, which pays close attention to aesthetics.

Weightlessness may be a boon to scientists and manufacturers, but it is a problem for the human body. There is conflict between the body's need for exercise and the demand for a vibration-free microgravity situation. Perhaps automated space laboratories are the solution.

JOURNEY TO THE MOON AND BEYOND

"TV viewers worldwide may be able to look in as the astronauts go through their daily exercise regimen on the ergometer, which will be mounted on Lockheed's ISEP," Smith said.

The stabilized platform consists of four rectangular stabilizers attached vertically to a frame, which rests on shock absorbers called isolators. The ergometer attaches to the frame. The stabilizers hold each corner of the frame stationary. Smith explained, "A motor inside each stabilizer uses inertial stabilization to counteract the disturbances caused by the exercise."

Without stabilizers, a crewmember peddling a stationary bicycle can produce as much as 100 pounds of force, which far exceeds the allowable microgravity disturbance limits set by NASA.

With Lockheed's stabilized platform system, the exercise is expected to cause less than one pound of disturbance force on the Shuttle middeck.

From concept to delivery, Lockheed produced the flight equipment very quickly. Smith said, "We came up with the design only last year and, in about nine months, built, tested and shipped the hardware to Johnson Space Center. We certainly believe this product meets the requirements of NASA's microgravity and life-sciences offices. The successful use of stabilized platforms on USML-1 will show that the needs of both the crew and the microgravity scientists can be accomodated simultaneously on the same spacecraft."

Smith's group is part of the Space Station Freedom office at Lockheed.

PHYSICS TO GO

1. Look up the inside dimensions of the Apollo command module, the space shuttle, or MIR. Calculate the volume per person. Measure your room at home and calculate the volume per person. Compare them.

2. Read the article on page T137, "Interior Color Testing for Space Station Freedom" from *Station Break* (Vol. 4, No. 12, Dec. 1992). Is selecting a paint scheme and composition for a space station very different from doing that for a home or school? Can you make any suggestions for your school based on the NASA findings?

TRANSPORTATION T140

3. Read the article on page T138, "Taking Physical Fitness to New Frontiers" from *Station Break* (Vol. 4, No. 5, May 1992). Describe the two conflicting problems that were solved by the new cycle. What problems might the new cycle introduce to space shuttle designers in the future?

4. Two candles were lit and the flame was observed. How might the observations differ if this demonstration was carried out in a microgravity environment? *(Hint: Would the flame "know" which way is "up" in zero gravity?)*

STRETCHING EXERCISES

Soak 4 bean seeds in water overnight and then position the seedlings in a Petri dish that has been filled with soaking, paper towels. Store the dish in a dark place in the position shown in the diagram.

a) Check the seedling after 5 and 10 days and describe the movement of the roots and stems?
b) Explain your results.
c) Hypothesize how the experimental results would change had this experiment been conducted in a microgravity environment, such as a space shuttle.

3

Assessment: Participation in Discussion

The following is an assessment rubric, designed for informal feedback to the students on their discussions related to their design of the living space. While they are discussing this, the students may want to brainstorm on some of the safety features with which they are familiar.

Descriptor	most of the time	some of the time	almost never	comments
• shows interest				
• stays on task				
• asks questions related to topic				
• listens to other students' ideas				
• shows cooperation in group brainstorming				
• provides leadership in group activity				
• demonstrates tolerance of others' viewpoints				

For use with *Transportation*, Chapter 3, ACTIVITY FOUR: Life Without Gravity

NOTES

3

Assessment: Devices for Spaceship

The following is a rubric to help the students to evaluate each other's projects or designs within their groups. Emphasize to them, that they must be able to justify, in comments, any mark they give. Don't allow the students to just say it is good, bad, or okay.

The students will design two devices that will operate on board a spaceship. They will be able to describe how each device works in normal gravity, and how it will work in zero gravity. After they have designed their devices, they will present their ideas to the rest of the class.

Use the following rating scale: **#4 is excellent, #3 is good, #2 is average, #1 is poor** your group: (circle the appropriate number)				
1. Is able to develop two devices that fit the space requirements. Comments:	4	3	2	1
2. Has an understanding of how the devices work on Earth. Comments:	4	3	2	1
3. Has an undertanding of how the devices work in zero gravity. Comments:	4	3	2	1
4. Can work cooperatively to reach consensus on the designs. Comments:	4	3	2	1
5. Can effectively communicate their ideas to their classmates. Comments:	4	3	2	1
6. Uses scientific terms appropriately. Comments:	4	3	2	1
7. Cooperates well in developing solutions to the problems. Comments:	4	3	2	1

For use with *Transportation*, Chapter 3, ACTIVITY FOUR: Life Without Gravity

NOTES

ACTIVITY FIVE
Exercise on the Moon

Background Information

A review of Newton's Laws of Motion would be in order at this time. Newton's First Law is Inertia. This refers to the fact that an object in motion or at rest has all forces balanced. Therefore, using the formula $F_{net} = F_A - F_g$, an object that is at rest or in constant motion (uniform velocity), will have the forces balanced ($F_{net} = 0$), and the weight of the object (F_g), is equal to (but in opposite direction) to the force being applied(F_A).

Newton's Second Law, can be stated in the form of an equation -- $F = ma$, (where the acceleration is proportional to the force being applied, and inversely proportional to the mass of the object). This can also be referred to as the accelerating force.

Newton's Third Law states that every action force exerted will have a reaction force equal in magnitude, but opposite in direction. Therefore, if we have an object (text book) of $m = 1$ kg, its weight (or F_g) is 9.8 N. This is the gravitational force that is being exerted upon the book by the Earth. There is an equal force on the Earth.

In this activity, the students are distinguishing between the concepts of weight and mass. Mass is the measurement of how much matter or material it has. The mass of an object remains the same in all gravitational situations, whether on Earth, moon or on a different planet in a different solar system.

Weight, on the other hand is the measurement of the force of gravity on a mass. To measure weight, we often place the object on a scale. The Second Law of Motion states that there is a force opposite in direction but equal in magnitude that is pushing on the object opposite to the gravitational force (weight F_g). When we look at the scale, we are really measuring the force that the scale pushes back on our bodies. The weight is affected by the gravitational field (g) of the planet. The mass we measure from the scale is often called the gravitational mass and is in the vertical direction.

Inertial mass is the mass determined by the ratio of the force to the acceleration of that object, and is typically in the horizontal direction. The inertial and gravitational masses of an object are the same.

Newton's Second Law states that if we have an object with mass m, then as we apply the force to it, there is a relationship to the acceleration of that object. In other words, the mass stays the same, and the acceleration varies with the force applied. $F \propto a$, so therefore, as you increase the force, you increase the acceleration ($F = ma$).

To determine the inertial mass of an object, we put the object on a frictionless surface, and pull on it with a given or measurable force. We can then determine the acceleration, ($a = \Delta v/\Delta t$), and using $F=ma$, then determine the mass of the object. Comparing this to the gravitational mass can be done by comparing the unknown object with an object of known mass using a balance beam. If in the same location, the masses are equal, then the weights are equal, since the gravitational field in that location is constant.

The reason why astronauts have to have a very specific exercise program is that they are in a reduced gravity or no gravity environment. Nearly all of our muscles are formed and designed to counteract gravity. Therefore, when we are no longer in a gravity the same as ours (9.8 m/s^2) then our muscles adapt. The astronauts notice, that after extended periods in space, their muscles will atrophy (lose their effectiveness and strength), to the point, that they are not able to stand and walk normally. Since they are in zero-gravity, there is no need to use the muscles needed for posture, as there is nothing to "pull" the body down.

Active-ating the Physics InfoMall

This Activity does a good job of explaining the needed concepts. But you may still have some questions, and the InfoMall is still a great place to look for answers. There are 19 textbooks, after all. And don't forget the article "Physics of living in space: A new course," *American Journal of Physics*, vol. 49, issue 8, 1981, plus the other references we found earlier.

Planning for the Activity

Time Requirements

Allow at least one period for researching the exercise program. Presentations of students programs should take about one period. (Gauge your time to size of groups and number of students in your class.)

Materials needed

For the group:

- kilogram mass
- laboratory cart
- spring scale, 0-10 N range

For the class:

- *Active Physics Transportation* Content Video (Segments: Exercise on the Moon, Drop Hammer and Feather on Moon)
- VCR and TV monitor

Teaching Notes

The WDYT question may seem obvious to some, but is designed to raise the issues of gravity, mass and weight. Newton's insight of universal properties is not shared by all. Use students' misconceptions to explore the topic.

Perform the activity. The point is that when the students hold the kilogram vertically, they are interacting with the object's weight, but when they pull it to the side, they are interacting with the object's mass. Clarify the difference between mass and weight, and point out how easily they are confused on Earth. Compare sitting on someone with bumping into them. The interactions with an object's weight are always vertical.

Calculate your weight on Earth and on the moon. Note that although you weigh less on the moon, a student would still feel the same bump if you nudged him on the moon. If you were to bowl on the moon, it would be easier to lift the ball, but the same force would be required to accelerate it down the alley as on Earth. This will return in the unit *Sports*.

After viewing the video, students will plan a fitness program for a lunar traveler.

Many students may not be involved in active exercise programs. Invite a member of the local professional sports organization such as a trainer or one of the coaches to give an outline of a basic fitness program, or bring in a fitness magazine.

Use a similar structure as previous lessons, by assigning a task to each group member (see Activity Four, Chapter 3).

Students have a problem sometimes with the idea of mass being the amount of material. They will often confuse volume with mass or weight. For instance, they may believe that the larger an object is, the more mass it has.

Activity Overview

This activity explains that mass and weight are two different characteristics of matter, both of which must be considered when launching a rocket, living on the moon or maneuvering in zero-g.

Student Objectives

Students will:

- identify mass as an inertial characteristic of matter.
- identify weight as the force of gravity on an object.
- calculate the weight of known masses.

ANSWERS FOR THE TEACHER ONLY

What Do You Think?

Students answers will vary. Look for some misconceptions about the moon, such as without atmosphere there is no gravity; some may say that because it is so far away there is no gravity. The moon is smaller in both mass and size, and therefore will have a smaller gravitational field strength on the surface.

Activity Five

Excercise on the Moon

WHAT DO YOU THINK?

You have often heard that there is no gravity or less gravity on the moon.

- **Why do you think that this is true?**
- **What would account for less gravity or no gravity on the moon?**

Record your ideas about these questions in your *Active Physics log*. Be prepared to discuss your responses with your small group and the class.

FOR YOU TO DO

1. Attach a 1-kg object and suspend it from a force meter (a spring scale). You are measuring the force that the Earth's gravity exerts on the object. This is called the weight of the object.
   a) How much does the 1-kg object weigh?

2. Put the kilogram mass on a low-friction lab cart. Attach a force meter. The weight of the object is now completely supported by the cart. Attach the force meter, by way of a string, to the cart. Pull in a horizontal direction, so that you get the cart and 1-kg object moving horizontally. The force meter now says nothing at all about the weight of the standard.
   a) When you pull the cart horizontally, you are accelerating the object by exerting a force on it. How much force?
   b) Can you vary the force?
   c) What happens if you increase the force?

Keep the 1-kg object and cart away from the edge of the table or complete the activity on the floor in a cleared area.

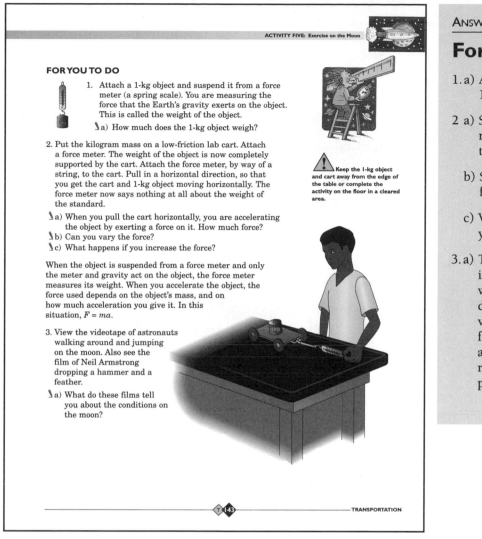

When the object is suspended from a force meter and only the meter and gravity act on the object, the force meter measures its weight. When you accelerate the object, the force used depends on the object's mass, and on how much acceleration you give it. In this situation, $F = ma$.

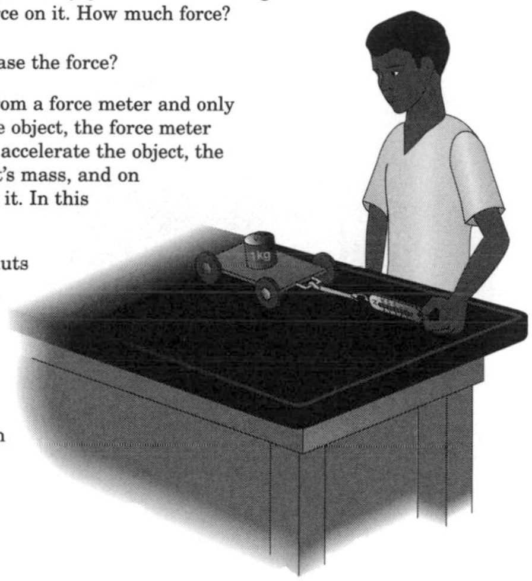

3. View the videotape of astronauts walking around and jumping on the moon. Also see the film of Neil Armstrong dropping a hammer and a feather.
   a) What do these films tell you about the conditions on the moon?

ANSWERS

For You To Do

1. a) At sea level the weight of 1.0 kg is 9.8 N.

2. a) Students' response. Should require a very small force to accelerate it.
   b) Simply pull harder to vary the force.
   c) When you increase the force you increase the acceleration.

3. a) These videos will show that it is easier to move around, which means less acceleration due to gravity. Watching the video about Armstrong and the feather and the hammer would also show that there is no air resistance therefore no atmosphere.

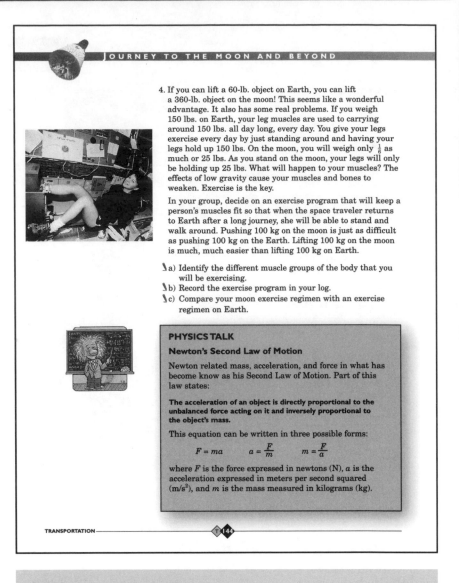

4. If you can lift a 60-lb. object on Earth, you can lift a 360-lb. object on the moon! This seems like a wonderful advantage. It also has some real problems. If you weigh 150 lbs. on Earth, your leg muscles are used to carrying around 150 lbs. all day long, every day. You give your legs exercise every day by just standing around and having your legs hold up 150 lbs. On the moon, you will weigh only $\frac{1}{6}$ as much or 25 lbs. As you stand on the moon, your legs will only be holding up 25 lbs. What will happen to your muscles? The effects of low gravity cause your muscles and bones to weaken. Exercise is the key.

   In your group, decide on an exercise program that will keep a person's muscles fit so that when the space traveler returns to Earth after a long journey, she will be able to stand and walk around. Pushing 100 kg on the moon is just as difficult as pushing 100 kg on the Earth. Lifting 100 kg on the moon is much, much easier than lifting 100 kg on Earth.

   a) Identify the different muscle groups of the body that you will be exercising.
   b) Record the exercise program in your log.
   c) Compare your moon exercise regimen with an exercise regimen on Earth.

PHYSICS TALK

Newton's Second Law of Motion

Newton related mass, acceleration, and force in what has become know as his Second Law of Motion. Part of this law states:

The acceleration of an object is directly proportional to the unbalanced force acting on it and inversely proportional to the object's mass.

This equation can be written in three possible forms:

$$F = ma \qquad a = \frac{F}{m} \qquad m = \frac{F}{a}$$

where F is the force expressed in newtons (N), a is the acceleration expressed in meters per second squared (m/s^2), and m is the mass measured in kilograms (kg).

ANSWERS

For You To Do *(continued)*

4. a) Students should come up with the major leg muscle groups as well as some exercises for the back and abdomen. Their program should reflect a balanced workout for all the groups, with emphasis on maintaining muscle mass and strength.

   b) Students response.

   c) Students will design their program and compare it with one on Earth.

FOR YOU TO READ

Acceleration Due to Gravity on Earth and on the Moon

If you ever get to the moon, you will have to carry around a life-support pack that you could not even lift when you were back home on Earth. It will not be a great burden on the moon. Yet, there is just as much material in that pack when you lift it on the moon as there was when it was loaded into the spacecraft.

On the moon, the mass of all objects is identical to the mass of those objects on Earth. The acceleration due to gravity is considerably less on the moon and objects weigh less. While the hammer and the feather dropped together on the video made on the moon, they did not accelerate downward at 9.8 m/s^2. The acceleration was only 1.6 m/s^2. This low acceleration due to gravity also accounts for the way the astronauts seem almost to float as they walk around.

	Earth	Moon
Acceleration due to gravity	9.8 m/s^2	1.6 m/s^2

How to Tell Mass from Weight

Mass and weight are often confused, but they are quite different. One reason for the confusion is that the same unit is often used for both. When you use the unit "pound," sometimes you are talking about weight and sometimes about mass. In the SI system (the international system of units), weight is a force, so it is measured in the SI force unit, newton. Mass is measured in kilograms.

To make the difference clear, think of the following situation. You are preparing a potato salad for 100 people. About 50 pounds of potatoes will make salad for 100 people. You go to the supermarket and buy a 50-pound bag of potatoes. It is a strain to lift it, but you manage. (When you think about the difficulty of lifting the bag of potatoes, are you thinking about its mass or its weight?) Now suppose you were making the potato salad on the moon. Do you agree that the 50-pound bag of potatoes will still feed 100 people on the moon? The amount of substance in them is the same as on Earth; they have the same mass. When you lift up the bag, however, it is very light. It is no strain at all to get it onto your shoulder. While its mass is the same, it weighs only about 8 pounds. Weight is the force of gravity acting on something. The moon's gravity is much weaker than the Earth's. Everything feels lighter on the moon because the gravitational pull is less than on Earth.

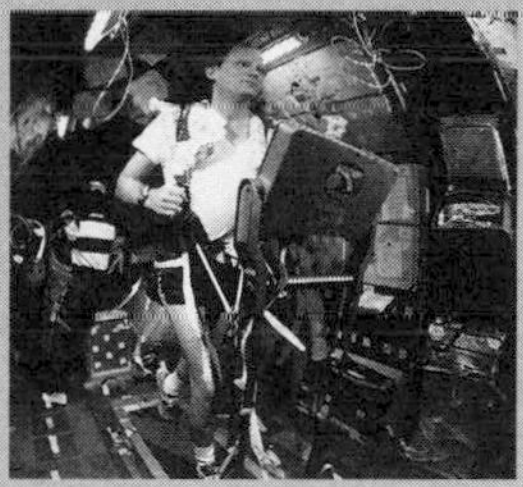

3

ANSWERS

Physics To Go

1. The force that causes acceleration is the net force -- the force in excess of its weight. The accelerating force for the rocket is the same everywhere. On the moon the rocket weighs less than on Earth. The weight of the rocket must be balanced before there is any excess force to do the accelerating.

2. The moon's small gravitational field would put a "bounce" into people's walks, make things easier to lift, etc. On the moon chores such as sweeping or vacuuming would be about the same as on Earth, while lifting the sweepings or the vacuum cleaner would be easier. Playing billiards would be the same for experts, but beginners who hit the balls too low would find the balls jumping off of the table.

3. The large gravitational field of Jupiter makes lifting very difficult but does not affect horizontal motion; if you could lift the cue stick, you could be sure that the balls would not leave the table after you hit them. Walking on Jupiter would be difficult as your feet would feel very heavy. Skating might be the same if you did not try to lift your feet (and if you could keep your head up), but falling would really hurt. Of course we are imagining walking inside of a structure built on Jupiter. Student responses will be creative ideas based on the composition, atmosphere, temperature, etc., of Jupiter which they will have to look up. The focus without further research would be on the large gravitational field.

REFLECTING ON THE ACTIVITY AND THE CHALLENGE

Understanding the effects of the lower gravitational attraction by the moon is important for your story. Lifting objects on the moon will be different from pulling them. Because the gravitational pull is $\frac{1}{6}$ that of Earth, you would be able to lift 6 times the weight on the moon. Just think of the things that you could accomplish! Imagine how you might change a tire on a vehicle.

Also think about how an extended stay on the moon would affect you when you returned to Earth. Because your body weight on the moon has been reduced by a fraction of $\frac{1}{6}$, your muscles are placed under less strain. A musculature and skeleton that must support 150 lbs. on Earth needs to support only 25 lbs. on the moon. Not surprisingly, a skeletal system and muscles which are used much less begin to weaken. Bones that are less dense and a reduced muscle mass will present many problems for a person who returns to Earth. The amount of exercise that you do while recovering must be controlled.

Check your story once again. Have you accounted for short term and long term adjustments to lower gravity? How could you use this principle to make your story even more interesting? Consider the possibilities of doing athletic training on a planet with increased or reduced gravitational force.

PHYSICS TO GO

1. Why does it take a tremendous booster rocket to accelerate a space craft off Earth, but a much smaller rocket to produce the acceleration to get it off the moon. Use Newton's Second Law ($F = ma$) in explaining your answer.

2. Suppose that you lived in a lunar colony. Describe how the difference in weight, but not mass, would affect an everyday activity such as housework, recreation, etc.

3. On Jupiter, gravity is almost 3 times stronger than on Earth (everything weighs 3 times as much on Jupiter). Answer question 2 as if you were in a base on Jupiter.

4. If you were a high jumper, what benefits would be achieved by:
   a) training on Jupiter?
   b) holding the competition on the moon?
5. You must allocate enough fuel to escape the gravitational attraction of the body that it rests upon.
   a) Would more fuel be used by a spaceship to leave planet Earth or the moon? Explain your answer.
   b) In what ways would the allocation of fuel be different if a return trip was to be considered between Earth and Jupiter, rather than between Earth and the moon.
   c) How would docking a spaceship on the moon be different from docking it on Jupiter? Which do you believe would be more difficult? Explain your answer.
6. On Earth determining mass is simple. A spring balance or bathroom scale can be used because gravity is a constant. Measuring mass in space presents a much greater challenge. How would you know if astronauts were receiving the needed nutrition and neither gaining or losing weight?
7. How many different exercise machines would be needed to exercise all of the muscle groups? How could they all fit in the limited space of the ship?

Answers

Physics To Go
(continued)

4. a) By training on Jupiter, you would be training your muscles and developing strength enough to overcome the large gravitational field on Jupiter. If you could jump 1 m on Jupiter, you would be able to jump 2.5 m on Earth.
   b) Just the opposite of Jupiter, in that holding the competition on moon, where gravitational field is 1/6 that of Earth, one would be able to jump 6 times as high on the moon.
5. a) As the gravitational field is less on the moon, there is less force required by the rocket boosters to lift the rocket. Therefore, there would be less rocket fuel required to lift off from the moon.
   b) As the gravitational field is greater on Jupiter, than on the Earth, the fuel required for a return trip to Earth from Jupiter would be much larger.
   c) Docking a spaceship on the moon would be less difficult due to the gravitational field being smaller. Because the field strength is larger on Jupiter, there would a greater force "pulling" on the spaceship as it was docking.
6. In order to calculate weight loss or gain, they could set up an inertial scale. Using this, they could accelerate an astronaut at a known acceleration, with a specific force, and calculate the mass. $F = ma$, therefore, $m = F/a$.
7. The exercise machines used in the space shuttle would have to take up little space. A lot of the exercises would be based on resistance exercise using springs which take up little space.

3

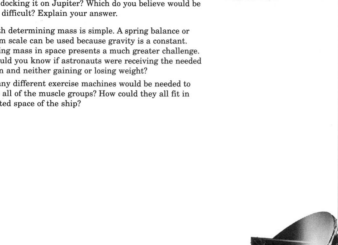

Assessment: Fitness Program

The following is a rubric to help the students to evaluate each fitness program. Encourage them to make comments where appropriate and remind them that they must justify in comments any mark they give. Don't allow the students to just say it is good, bad, or okay.

The students will design a fitness program that will operate on board a spaceship. They will need to take into consideration how an exercise program works in normal gravity, and how it will work in zero-gravity. After they have designed their program, they will present their ideas to the class.

Use the following rating scale: **#4 is excellent, #3 is good, #2 is average, #1 is poor** Your group: (circle the appropriate number)				
1. Is able to develop one program for the astronauts. Comments:	4	3	2	1
2. Has an understanding of what needs exercising on Earth. Comments:	4	3	2	1
3. Has an understanding of how exercising works in zero-gravity. Comments:	4	3	2	1
4. Can work cooperatively to reach consensus on the program. Comments:	4	3	2	1
5. Can effectively communicate their ideas to their classmates. Comments:	4	3	2	1
6. Uses scientific terms appropriately. Comments:	4	3	2	1
7. Cooperates well in developing solutions to the problems. Comments:	4	3	2	1
8. Program has identified the major muscle group. Comments:	4	3	2	1

For use with *Transportation*, Chapter 3, ACTIVITY FIVE: Exercise on the Moon

NOTES

3

ACTIVITY SIX
The Necessities of Life

Background Information

In this activity the students will be looking at the requirement of oxygen for daily life, and the source of the oxygen. On Earth, the atmosphere has about 21% O_2, and less than 1% CO_2. A few billion years ago, when the Earth finally started to cool down, there was little or no oxygen. Ancient plants similar to algae began flourishing and from this explosion of plants, there came a gradual increase in the oxygen, to the present day value. Today the trees and the algae and green plants in the oceans, are providing a fresh source of oxygen. Therefore, the scientists feel that if they can provide the astronauts with the right balance of plants, there will be no need to send oxygen in containers (which are heavy and awkward to transport).

The students will use simple instruments to get an understanding of the amount of oxygen that is needed for space travel, and the amount of oxygen that can be provided by the plants. Given that the plants will only produce 2 L of oxygen per hour per square meter of leaf surface, in full sunlight, and an astronaut will require about 38 L/hour, the size of the plant leaf surface would need to be about 19 m^2. Very quickly it can be seen that it would be rather awkward to have that many plants aboard a spaceship. One would also have to take into consideration the amount of energy required to ensure that there is enough light getting to the plants, and that they are kept at the right temperature.

Active-ating the Physics InfoMall

This activity also does not need much help from the InfoMall. Most of the concepts are clear, or biological. The Stretching Exercises suggest obtaining information from NASA, and we have already seen evidence of one item from NASA: "Space Settlements: A Design Study," edited by R. D. Johnson and C. H. Holbrow, NASA SP-413, GPO Stock No. 033-000-00669-1 (U.S. GPO Washington, DC, 1977), which was in the footnotes to "Physics of living in space: A new course," *American Journal of Physics*, vol. 49, issue 8, 1981.

Planning for the Activity

Time Requirements

The time required for the gathering of data would be approximately 5 - 10 minutes. Again, gauge your time according to the number of spirometers. Allow about one class period to do the necessary calculations.

Materials needed

For each group:

- spirometer with one disposable mouthpiece.

Advance Preparation and Setup

You may find it expedient to have calculators on hand for this activity.

The biology teachers may have a spirometer, even if it hasn't been used for years. Take some care with the mouthpieces; some communities have tough standards or opinions where bodily fluids are involved. Try using the spirometer yourself before the experiment to assess any difficulty in its operation.

Teaching Notes

Begin with the WDYT question. Have the students take some random guesses, and record them on the board. Elicit that this is just one of many such determinations that must be made for a space flight.

Have the student teams begin the FYTD. Point out that calculations of this nature are made easier by doing them one step at a time. Students may need guidance in carrying their calculations through.

Ensure that the spirometer is properly disinfected after each use. Use disposable mouthpieces, and disinfect with alcohol after each use.

Typically, an adult draws in 500 mL of air in each breath. This value can be obtained through rather crude methods using a water bottle or plastic bag. Physiologists are concerned with vital capacity - total possible volume of lungs; tidal capacity - what is normally exhaled, and the expiratory reserve - what is left after a normal exhale. The tidal volume is appropriate here.

Students may come to a better understanding of some of the requirements for traveling in space. It may also allow them to extend that understanding to see the importance of green plants on the planet, not only for the production of oxygen, but using the carbon dioxide, as well as the fact that plants act like a giant filter for toxic gases and elements that are in our atmosphere.

Activity Overview

This activity is designed to develop student awareness of the difficulties in calculating quantities of life-supporting materials needed aboard a space craft.

Student Objectives

Students will:

- calculate the amount of oxygen needed to support a human for one week.
- determine the feasibility of providing the needed oxygen with plants.

ANSWERS FOR THE TEACHER ONLY

What Do You Think?

The students will have a variety of answers. They might be able to estimate how much air they breathe, and then knowing that air is 21% oxygen, they might come up with an estimate

Students answers will vary. Scientists have thought that this is a method for long trips, or space stations, but they are a long way from coming up with a successful plant that would work in all the special environments - low light, artificial light, zero-gravity, low water use, large output of oxygen to space ratio, etc.

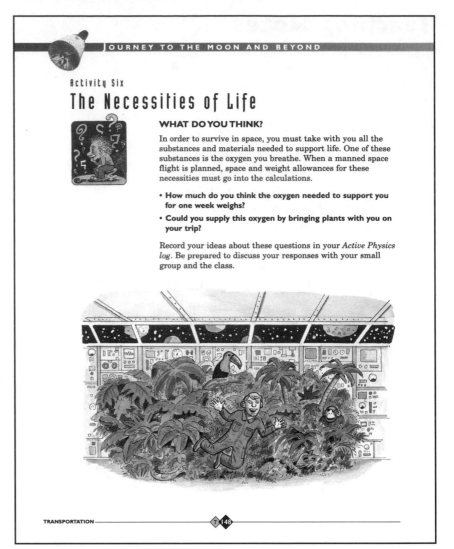

Activity Six

The Necessities of Life

WHAT DO YOU THINK?

In order to survive in space, you must take with you all the substances and materials needed to support life. One of these substances is the oxygen you breathe. When a manned space flight is planned, space and weight allowances for these necessities must go into the calculations.

- **How much do you think the oxygen needed to support you for one week weighs?**
- **Could you supply this oxygen by bringing plants with you on your trip?**

Record your ideas about these questions in your *Active Physics log*. Be prepared to discuss your responses with your small group and the class.

FOR YOU TO DO

1. Count the number of times your lab partner exhales in one minute while at rest and then in one minute after three minutes of vigorous exercise (i.e. running in place).

a) Record the values in your log.

b) Complete at least three trials for each situation and calculate the average. Make a table similar to the following. Record the average under the heading breaths/min, for rest and exercise.

Activity	Breaths/min	Volume/breath mL	Volume/min mL/min
rest			
exercise			

2. The volume of air which you breathe can be calculated using an instrument called a respirometer. Place a disposable mouthpiece in the respirometer and have the subject inhale normally, and then exhale normally into the mouthpiece.

If a commercial respirometer is not available, you may use the apparatus shown in the diagram. Ensure that the rubber tubing is disinfected by alcohol and not used by more than one subject.

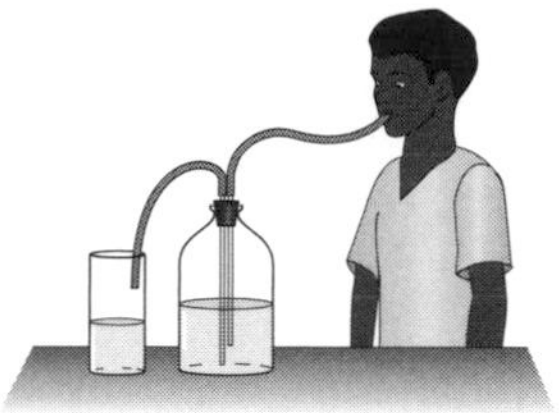

a) Record the volume of air exhaled in the volume/breath column for "rest." It represents a normal exhalation at rest.

ANSWERS

For You To Do

1. a) Student data. Average breaths per min. is about 20 - 25 sitting, and will increase from there.

b) Student data.

2. a) Average volume of breath is about 400 mL.

ANSWERS

For You To Do

(continued)

3. a) This volume should increase.

4. a) There is about 21% of the air is oxygen, so 0.21 x 25 b/min x 400 mL /b = 2100 mL /min or 2.1 L /min.

   Since about 1/3 of the oxygen is used, then 2.1 L / min x1/3 = 0.7 L / min.

   b) Volume in room = l x w x h = 3 x 4 x 3 = 36 m^3. Therefore, in 36 m^3 there is 3,600 L of air. 3,600 L of air x 0.21 = 756 L of oxygen

5. • air breathed every hour 2.1 L / min x 60 min / h = 126 L of air/h

   • 126 L x 0.21 = 26.5 L of oxygen / h

   • 26.5 L x 1/3 = 8.82 l used by the body / h

   a) 26.5 L of oxygen / h

   b) 26.5 L of oxygen / 2L oxygen produced per 1 m2 = 13 m2

   c) No. You would need a greenhouse of plants for each person. Ask students how large a house plant would be needed to provide a square meter of leaf surface. This will help them answer the question.

JOURNEY TO THE MOON AND BEYOND

3. Ask the subject to take a maximum inhalation and then exhale as much as possible into the mouthpiece.

   a) Record this value in the volume/breath column for exercise. It represents the maximum air movement during times of extreme exercise.

4. Use the information you obtained in this activity to calculate the following.

   a) Analysis indicates that air entering the lung contains 21% oxygen, while the air leaving the lung contains 14% oxygen. Indicate how much oxygen is used each minute while at rest, and during excercise.

   b) The volume of air in a space craft is about the same as in an ordinary bedroom measuring 3 m long × 4 m wide × 3 m high. (1 m^3 of gas = 1000 L = 1,000,000 mL) Calculate the amount of oxygen available to the astronauts.

5. In sunlight, green plants produce oxygen. Would it be possible for the astronauts to supply their oxygen needs by bringing a supply of plants with them? You will need the following information to help you answer this question:

   - The amount of air a person breathes every hour (calculate this from your experimental data)
   - Air is only 21% oxygen.
   - In your lungs, $\frac{1}{3}$ of the oxygen in each breath actually gets into the cells of the body.
   - In full sunlight, a green plant emits about 2 L of oxygen per hour for each square meter of leaf surface.

Now you are in a position to answer some questions:

a) How many liters of oxygen does a person use every hour?

b) How much leaf surface area would be needed to make oxygen at this rate, in bright light?

c) Are green plants a practical solution to the oxygen problem?

TRANSPORTATION T150

REFLECTING ON THE ACTIVITY AND CHALLENGE

On Earth you take the exchange of gases for granted. Humans use oxygen and exhale carbon dioxide. Plants, through photosynthesis, exchange the carbon dioxide for oxygen, thereby replenishing the oxygen supply. Supplying astronauts with oxygen is but one of the problems that faces space scientists. As the astronaut exhales, carbon dioxide is released. In low concentrations, carbon dioxide does not create a problem, but as the concentration increases breathing rate will increase. At very high concentrations carbon dioxide will become toxic. The greatest danger that met the ill-fated Apollo 13 was removing the excess carbon dioxide.

The problem of life support becomes more difficult as more astronauts are included on a ship and as they are kept in space longer. Not only do they need oxygen, but the water vapor and carbon dioxide produced during respiration must be removed. Astronauts also need food, water, warmth, and a means to dispose of what goes into the toilets. Also, not only must the necessities for life be transported in a space craft, but the containers that carry them as well.

Look at your story. In 2001, astronauts were frozen to save on food and oxygen. What other solutions exist for saving these necessities on a long journey? What happens if oxygen levels get low? Can some of the potential problems make for a good science-fiction story? How will you realistically account for all the necessities of life? What part of your story is fiction?

PHYSICS TO GO

1. Find the approximate value for the weight of food and fluids you consume in one day. Use this to calculate the approximate weight of the food and water needed to support four astronauts for one week.

ANSWERS

Physics To Go

1. Students response. Weight of the food and fluids can be anywhere around 5.7 kg. 5 kg x 4 astronauts x 7 days = 140 kg of weight (probably too low). This can also be a good exercise to see if students are eating enough food!

ANSWERS

Physics To Go

(continued)

2. Students response. Have them use a food guide or ask for a nutritionist to come to talk about their diet.

3. a) To conserve water, they can make sure there are no antidiuretics (caffeine products), minimize exertion.

   b) Recycling water is important. Other than urine the other most common loss of water from the body is through breathing. There needs to be some kind of dehumidifier to recycle the air, and remove the water, and then recycle it. Other ways would be to reduce long hot showers!

4. Approximatey 20 L per flush; 100 - 150 L per 10 minutes of shower (low flow shower head); 1 L teeth brushing; washing 10 - 30 L; 40 - 50 L for washing dishes, etc.

5. Students responses will vary.

2. Design the perfect food for astronauts. Take into consideration all that you learned, and think about keeping nutritive value high and resulting waste low. Would you enjoy eating this food?

3. Water loss is one of the greatest problems faced by astronauts doing extended space travel. What suggestions could you make that would help astronauts:

   a) conserve water.

   b) recycle water.

4. Make an estimate of the amount of water that you use daily for things other than eating. Brushing your teeth, washing your hands, washing dishes, showers, and the toilet account for a tremendous usage of water. Explain how your daily activities would be changed if your personal water supply was decreased by 90%.

5. Carbon dioxide levels must be controlled during spaceflight. In order to reduce carbon dioxide levels in a space station, a commander rules that only one hour of exercise is permitted daily. Would you agree with the proposed solution? Give your reasons.

STRETCHING EXERCISES

1. NASA has a wealth of available information about space travel. Contact a NASA station for literature that describes the containers for packing food, oxygen, etc., for astronauts to live in space or on a shuttle.
2. Contact a NASA station for literature about design plans for a space colony and long-term missions to the moon or Mars.
3. Read about the Apollo 13 mission and detail the problems involved with gas exchange systems.

NOTES

3

ACTIVITY SEVEN
Communication

Background Information

The development of radio waves came as a result of studying the interactions of electricity and magnetism. Many scientists contributed to the current theories of EMR (electromagnetic radiation).

Hans Christian Oersted, in the early 1800's, was experimenting with electric currents in wires, and noticed that there was a deflection of the compass needle when it was brought near a current-carrying wire. Thus, the discovery that an electric current produces a magnetic field. About ten years after Oersted's discovery, Michael Faraday discovered that if you change the magnetic field, you can induce a current in a wire. Then, in about 1860, James Clerk Maxwell expanded on Oersted's, and Faraday's theories, and proposed a mathematical explanation, that a changing electric field can produce a magnetic field. He went on to explain, that this magnetic field is produced in free space. If the changing magnetic field is producing an electric field, this electric field would also be changing, and therefore, would also produce another changing magnetic field. This continues, each changing field producing another changing field producing another changing field and so on. Thus, the description of the first electromagnetic wave (EM wave). These waves are free to pass through space to infinite distances. Maxwell, however, was never able to prove the existence of these waves, and died before they were produced. Heinrich Hertz, in 1887, used a spark gap generator, and showed that there were waves passing from the generator to an antenna set up on the other side of the room.

Later studies by many scientists revealed that these EM waves behave the same as visible light. Eventually, visible light became known as only a small part of the EM spectrum. The EM spectrum ranges from large wavelengths of several kilometers (e.g.: radio waves) and low energy, to very small wavelengths of 10^{-15} m (e.g.: x-rays and gamma rays) and very high energy.

Since EM waves are produced by changing electric fields, one way to produce a changing electric field is by accelerating charges. The energy of the accelerating charges, will determine the energy of the EM wave. For example, radio waves (low energy) are produced by moving charges of relatively low energy. In the most simple of situations, simply turning an electric current on or off will produce an EM wave. Listen to your radio when turning on an electric drill. You will hear static on the radio.

Active-ating the Physics InfoMall

For sound to travel, a medium is required. The demonstration in step 1 of For You To Do illustrates this. As you might expect, the InfoMall has more information on sound than you will want to use in any single *Active Physics* activity. For example, the demonstration with the bell jar can be done in different ways - including using a microphone inside the jar to overcome any effect due to the jar itself (search the Demo & Lab Shop for "sound" AND "bell jar"). Be careful however, to limit your searches on sound as much as you can - sound is a topic that permeates textbooks and articles, so you will undoubtedly get "Too Many Hits" if you try to search too broadly.

If you desire other demonstrations, there are plenty to be found. If you want explanations on the transmission of sound, note that the textbooks often have entire chapters devoted to this. For example, you may wish to read from "Chapter 17: Sound and the Human Ear" of *Physics Including Human Applications* from the Textbook Trove.

Planning for the Activity

Time Requirements

Because this is an interesting activity, allow time for the students to produce different patterns on the radio, and if time is available, an opportunity to learn Morse code would be an excellent enrichment activity.

Materials needed

For the class:

- vacuum pump
- bell jar
- vacuum grease
- electric bell
- connecting wires
- battery or DC power supply
- safety goggles
- safety shield

Advance Preparation and Setup

Check to see that the vacuum bell jar is large enough to house the doorbell and battery or the spark generator and battery. Test the bell jar for proper seal. Always wear safety glasses when operating this equipment. If the jar does not seal properly, consult the manufacturer's manual. Most bell jars can be made to seal by using grease around the base of the bell. A partial vacuum is good enough to show a reduction of sound, but not all students will be convinced.

If you do not have a DC spark generator, you may use the DC doorbell as the spark generator for the Activity.

Teaching Notes

Explore the WDYT question with the students. Many will express the fact that sound cannot travel in the vacuum of space. Propose to test the hypothesis using the bell jar and proceed to the next part of the Activity.

If you use the doorbell as the spark generator, show the transmission of the radio disturbance both inside and outside the bell jar. This may be done in any order to be effective. You may want to muffle the bell in order to hear the radio clearly.

The FYTD is best performed using a good spark generator which will produce more static than the doorbell. Allow the students to explore with several cheap AM radios while the spark generator is turned on and off. Make sure that the metal cannot contact any live AC connections.

Note: This Activity and the next may run successively over two class periods. If this Activity requires some extra time, allow it to be completed on the next day. The next Activity can be run in slightly under one class period.

Sound waves are mechanical waves, and need a medium though which to travel. Light and radio waves are electromagnetic waves and do not require a medium. Therefore, in space (essentially a vacuum) sound will not travel. The only way a message can go from one point to another is by EM waves. Radio waves, which are a form of electromagnetic radiation (EMR) travel at the speed of light, and behave essentially the same as light. Generally, we refer to visible light as light, even though it is just another form of EMR

If there is time, an enrichment activity might be to have the students learn Morse code, and to bring in a HAM radio operator. This would give the students an opportunity to see what radio can do, other than find the local rock station.

NOTES

Activity Seven

Communication

WHAT DO YOU THINK?

Picture yourself as an astronaut on a spacewalk. You are all alone, floating around in infinite space. No other human being in the history of the world has ever been so alone.

- **Could you use a loudspeaker to communicate with the space ship while on a spacewalk?**

Record your ideas about these questions in your *Active Physics log*. Be prepared to discuss your responses with your small group and the class.

Activity Overview

This activity explores radio waves as a means of communication and investigates some of their properties.

Student Objectives

Students will:

- understand why sound cannot be used from communication in the vacuum of space.
- investigate one means of producing radio waves.
- investigate how radio waves propagate.

ANSWERS FOR THE TEACHER ONLY

What Do You Think?

Students will not likely know this, as they have been inundated with space movies where you could hear the explosions. Therefore, the students will have to overcome this misconception.

3

FOR YOU TO DO

1. Connect a bell jar by a hose to a vacuum pump, as shown in the diagram. Put a doorbell inside the bell jar, and start it ringing. Turn on the pump and listen as nearly all the air is removed from the bell jar.
   - a) What happens to the sound you hear as the air is removed?
   - b) The space between an astronaut on a space walk and the space ship is totally empty. There is no air at all. Based on your observations, can an astronaut on a spacewalk communicate through a loudspeaker? Explain your answer.

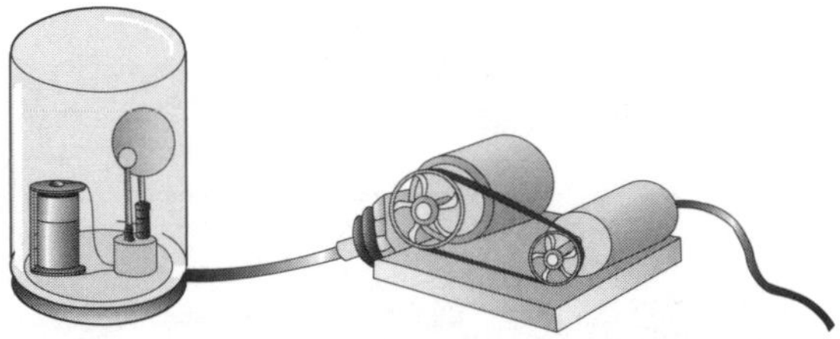

2. Have your partner sit with eyes closed. Snap your fingers above your partner's head. Keep your fingers an equal distance from each of your partner's ears each time you snap your fingers. Snap your fingers in several locations from the front to the back of the head. Ask your partner to guess where your fingers are located.
   - a) Record in your log where your fingers were located, and if your partner was able to correctly identify the position.

ANSWERS

For You To Do

1. a) As the air is pumped from the jar, the intensity of the sound decreases.

   b) A loudspeaker is simply an amplifier, which operates on sound waves. Since the space has no air, there can be no sound traveling through space.

2. a) Student response.

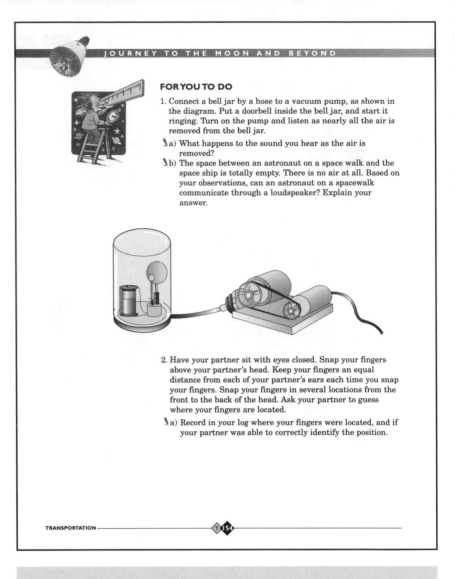

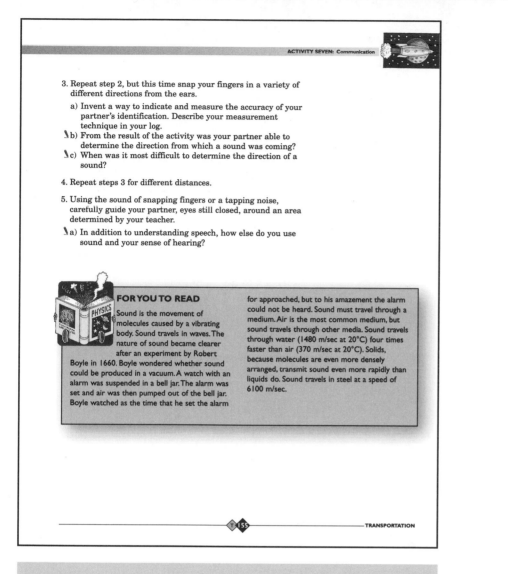

3. Repeat step 2, but this time snap your fingers in a variety of different directions from the ears.
   a) Invent a way to indicate and measure the accuracy of your partner's identification. Describe your measurement technique in your log.
   b) From the result of the activity was your partner able to determine the direction from which a sound was coming?
   c) When was it most difficult to determine the direction of a sound?

4. Repeat steps 3 for different distances.

5. Using the sound of snapping fingers or a tapping noise, carefully guide your partner, eyes still closed, around an area determined by your teacher.
   a) In addition to understanding speech, how else do you use sound and your sense of hearing?

FOR YOU TO READ

Sound is the movement of molecules caused by a vibrating body. Sound travels in waves. The nature of sound became clearer after an experiment by Robert Boyle in 1660. Boyle wondered whether sound could be produced in a vacuum. A watch with an alarm was suspended in a bell jar. The alarm was set and air was then pumped out of the bell jar. Boyle watched as the time that he set the alarm for approached, but to his amazement the alarm could not be heard. Sound must travel through a medium. Air is the most common medium, but sound travels through other media. Sound travels through water (1480 m/sec at 20°C) four times faster than air (370 m/sec at 20°C). Solids, because molecules are even more densely arranged, transmit sound even more rapidly than liquids do. Sound travels in steel at a speed of 6100 m/sec.

ANSWERS

For You To Do *(continued)*

3.-4. a) Student response.

b) Student response.

c) Student response. It will probably be most difficult when the fingers are snapped directly in front of or behind the person.

5. a) Hearing is used to help interpret your surroundings. It aids you in determining the direction, closeness or distance of different objects.

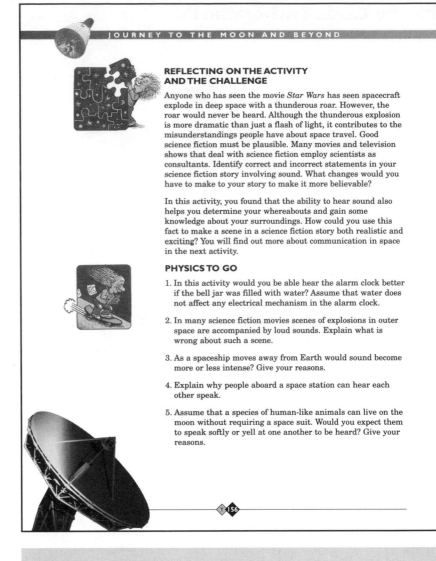

JOURNEY TO THE MOON AND BEYOND

REFLECTING ON THE ACTIVITY AND THE CHALLENGE

Anyone who has seen the movie *Star Wars* has seen spacecraft explode in deep space with a thunderous roar. However, the roar would never be heard. Although the thunderous explosion is more dramatic than just a flash of light, it contributes to the misunderstandings people have about space travel. Good science fiction must be plausible. Many movies and television shows that deal with science fiction employ scientists as consultants. Identify correct and incorrect statements in your science fiction story involving sound. What changes would you have to make to your story to make it more believable?

In this activity, you found that the ability to hear sound also helps you determine your whereabouts and gain some knowledge about your surroundings. How could you use this fact to make a scene in a science fiction story both realistic and exciting? You will find out more about communication in space in the next activity.

PHYSICS TO GO

1. In this activity would you be able hear the alarm clock better if the bell jar was filled with water? Assume that water does not affect any electrical mechanism in the alarm clock.
2. In many science fiction movies scenes of explosions in outer space are accompanied by loud sounds. Explain what is wrong about such a scene.
3. As a spaceship moves away from Earth would sound become more or less intense? Give your reasons.
4. Explain why people aboard a space station can hear each other speak.
5. Assume that a species of human-like animals can live on the moon without requiring a space suit. Would you expect them to speak softly or yell at one another to be heard? Give your reasons.

ANSWERS

Physics To Go

1. Sound will travel through water, about 4 times faster than through air.
2. Sound cannot travel through space, therefore sounds, whether explosions or not cannot be heard in space.
3. As the spaceship moved away from Earth the sound would become less intense, as the air becomes less dense.
4. Inside the space station there is air, so they can breathe, and therefore sound will travel within the space station.
5. As there is no atmosphere on the moon, the creatures would have to use sign language to "hear" each other. No sound can travel on the moon.

Morse Code (American)

USA & Canada landline

1 .--.

2 ..-..

3 ...-. A .- B -... C .. . D -.. E .

4 ....- F .-. G --. H .... I .. J -.-.

5 --- K -.- L __ M -- N -. O . .

6 ...... P ..... Q ..-. R . .. S ... T -

7 --.. U ..- V ...- W .-- X .-..

8 -.... Y .. .. Z ... .

9 -..-

0 . . or - (optional)

A dash time is equal to three times the length of the dot, exception is "L" which is a long dash that is equal to one dot-one dash. Numeral "0" is optional, one dot space dot as in "o", or short dash as in "t".

Question -.. -. "DN"

Comma .-.- "AA"

Period ..--.. "UD"

Colon -.- . . "KO"

SemiC ... .. "SI"

Apostrophe ..-. .-.. "QX"

Begin Bracket ..... -. "PN" (Parenthesis

End Bracket .... "PY" Parenthesis)

Exclamation ---. "MN"

Begin Quotation ..-. -. "QN"

End Quotation ..-. -.-. "QJ"

Capital .. . .-..

Dollar ... .-.. "SX"

AND-& . ... "ES"

3

ACTIVITY EIGHT
The Speed of Radio Waves

Background Information

2000 or more years ago, the Greek scientists of the day (philosophers) thought that light was instantaneous. It wasn't until the 17th century, that Galileo thought that light had a finite speed. In his experiment, using crude instruments of timing, and flame lamps, he tried to prove that light had a finite speed. Galileo went to the top of one hill, and sent his assistant to another. Each had lamps, and Galileo timed the response of his partner's flash, after he uncovered his lamp. His results did show that there was a delay, but he attributed the delay, not to the speed of light, but rather to the reaction times. Although his experiment did not show a finite speed for light, he remained steadfast to the theory that light had a finite speed.

The next attempt to measure the speed of light was made serendipitously by a Danish astronomer, Ole Roemer (1644 - 1710). Roemer made many careful measurements of the orbital period of Io around Jupiter at different times while Earth revolved around the sun. He observed that the times of the orbit of Io was shorter at one time (see diagram time 1) than the orbital time when Earth was in a different position. The first time, Earth was closer to Io and Jupiter, whereas in the second position it is much further. Roemer concluded that the only explanation for this variation in those times of Io's period, could be accounted for by the time it takes light to travel the extra distance from Io to Earth at different times in the orbit of the Earth around the sun. His calculations showed that it took about 22 minutes for light to travel across Earth's orbit, and using these values, with Earth's orbit being about 3.0×10^{11} m, the speed would be about 2.2×10^8 m/s. This is close to the value that we use today (3.00×10^8 m) for the speed of light.

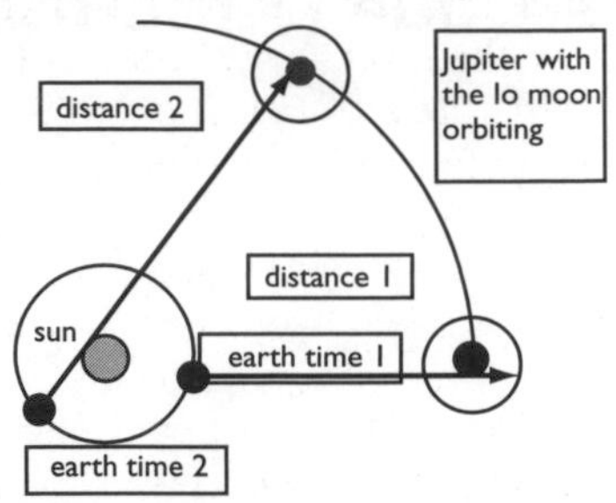

(This diagram is exaggerated for illustration purposes.)

Two other scientists, A. H. L. Fizeau (1849), using a toothed wheel to interrupt the light, and J. B. L. Foucault (1850), using a rotating mirror, also reported a speed of light close to today's accepted value.

However, the first successful land measurement was made in the early part of this century by an American physicist, Albert A. Michelson (the first American to win the Nobel prize). He was able to determine the speed of light to within less than 1/100th of a percent of the current accepted value.

Using an eight-sided mirror, rotating at high speeds, and a 35 km evacuated tunnel, he shone a light onto the rotating mirror, through the tunnel to another mirror, back again to the rotating mirror, and then into a telescope (see diagram). From this experiment, he was able to show that the light did in fact have a finite speed, i.e., that it took a measurable time, to arrive at the telescope.

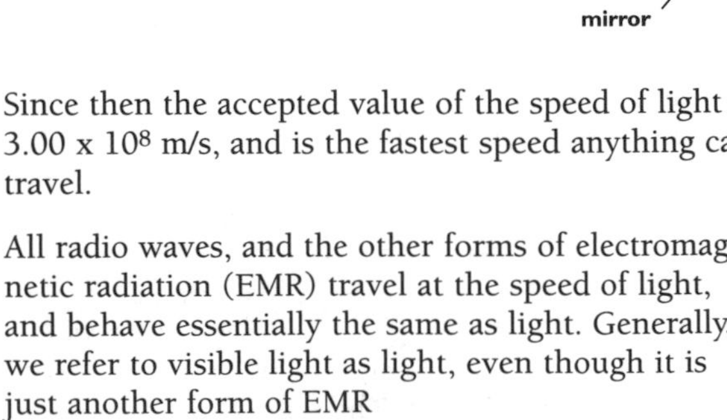

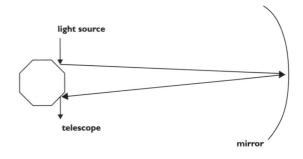

Since then the accepted value of the speed of light is 3.00×10^8 m/s, and is the fastest speed anything can travel.

All radio waves, and the other forms of electromagnetic radiation (EMR) travel at the speed of light, and behave essentially the same as light. Generally, we refer to visible light as light, even though it is just another form of EMR

When calculating the time it takes for a radio wave to travel a distance, we can use the formula $v = d/t$, where v is the speed of light (3.00×10^8 m/s), and d

is the distance that the wave is traveling, such as from Earth to the satellite and back again. Even when watching the evening news, as the anchor is interviewing someone in a different location in the world, via satellite, you can notice a slight delay. The distances we are talking about are about 30,000 km. Therefore, looking at the diagram below, you can see that if the signal goes up to a satellite (30,000 km above the Earth), and then returns to the Earth, 30,000 km away, the total distance covered is about 60,000 km.

$v = d/t$, therefore

$t = d/v$

$t = 60{,}000\ 000\ \text{m}/300{,}000\ 000\ \text{m/s}$

$t = 0.2\ \text{s}$

So, even going from one side of the Earth to the other will give a very slight, but perceptible delay. With this in mind, it is very easy to see how, 2000 years ago, the Greeks believed that light was instantaneous.

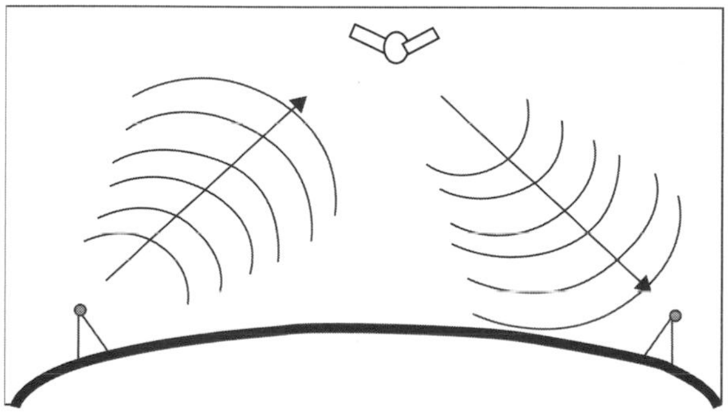

Active-ating the Physics InfoMall

As with Activity Sevev, you will have no trouble finding lots of information on the InfoMall pertaining to radio waves and light. If you want alternate demonstrations, there are MANY to choose from. If you want information, the textbooks are loaded. All you have to do is decide what kind of information you want, the search ("shop") the appropriate store, or select the textbook that explains things as clearly as you desire (there are conceptual texts, algebra-based texts, and calculus-based texts to be found). Maybe you want more information in Heinrich Hertz: look at "Heinrich Hertz and the development of physics," in *Physics Today*, vol. 42, issue 3, 1989. Or look in the textbooks. The Calendar Cart says "02/22/1857 Heinrich Hertz was born in Hamburg, Germany. He was the first to produce and detect radio waves (1888)."

Whatever physics information you may want, whether it is pure physics or how students learn, you can probably find relevant material on this CD-ROM.

Planning for the Activity

Time Requirements

If time permits, go through the video twice, and allow time for discussion.

Materials needed

For the class:

- DC spark generator (induction coil)
- DC power supply
- AM radio receiver
- vacuum pump
- bell jar
- vacuum grease
- connecting wires
- switch
- safety goggles
- safety shield
- *Active Physics Transportation* Content Video (Segment: Speed of Radio Waves)
- VCR and TV monitor

For each group:

- stopwatch

Advance Preparation and Setup

Preview the video and try the experiment to get a feeling for the problems the students will encounter.

Teaching Notes

The WDYT questions appear to expect students to do a calculation, but it is intended to focus their attention on the existence of a time delay.

Have the students proceed with the FYTD. Ask them to devise the best way to time the delay. Hint at the use of multiple timers, averages, and uncertainty. You may want to discuss the uncertainty of their results based on individual, group average and class average measurements.

Devise some questions for the students to consider at the end of the experiment, such as how the time delay would affect the communication between the Earth and a craft at the location of Neptune over 4 billion kilometers away.

Ask about situations where the students can decide if the time delay may or may not be crucial; a NY to CA conversation relayed by satellite vs. a NY to CA link-up of two 486 MHz computers (here the delay is roughly (50 000 mi. / 186 000 mi./s = 0.286 s).

Raise the issue of remote-control operation of space probes. Can the problems of a Mars landing be anticipated and programmed into a computer, can we send commands fast enough, or must we risk human lives on the trip?

There are many videos available about space travel. As this is the last topic of the unit, watching a popular motion picture might be a nice way to wind up the unit. *Apollo 13* is a good movie, as it shows weightlessness, and can open a discussion about how it was filmed. (The actors used the same methods in filming as the astronauts used in training for the space missions.) There are many "B" type movies, where the quality of the movie can open up discussion on the false science being used in the motion picture industry for effect or impact.

It is important for the students to realize that light does have a finite speed, and that they are able to calculate the time in different situations (such as the time it takes light to get from the sun to the Earth). Students may not understand that radio waves and light waves are electromagnetic radiation (or waves) and may need reminding of that fact when talking about the velocity of radio waves and microwaves and x-rays, etc.

One other misunderstanding is that students don't realize that the sun is our closest star.

Alpha Proxima is the next nearest, at 4.3 light-years. This star is very similar in size and luminosity to our sun, and could be one of the stars which may have a planet system. However, at this time there is no positive proof.

NOTES

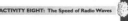

Activity Eight

The Speed of Radio Waves

WHAT DO YOU THINK?

A radio station at one end of your time zone transmits a signal that says, "At the tone, the time will be exactly 3 P.M. — beep!" The signal travels up to an orbiting geosynchronous satellite, and then back down to your radio receiver, a round trip of 50,000 miles.

- **If you live at the other end of the time zone, what time would it be when you hear the signal?**
- **If you asked an astronaut on the moon a question, how much time would elapse before you heard her response on Earth?**

Record your ideas about these questions in your *Active Physics log*. Be prepared to discuss your responses with your small group and the class.

Activity Overview

This Activity will demonstrate that radio waves have finite speed, and will provide a rough measure of that speed.

Student Objectives

Students will:

- measure the speed of radio waves transmitted between the Earth and the moon.

ANSWERS FOR THE TEACHER ONLY

What Do You Think?

Student response. Try to get them to think that there is a finite limit to the speed of light.

Actual delay would be about 0.2 s. Delay for the moon would be about 1.3 (one way).

NOTES

For use with *Transportation*, Chapter 3, ACTIVITY XX: Xxxxxxxxxxxxxxxxxxxxxxx

FOR YOU TO DO

1. You can use a simple system to explore some of the properties of the radio waves that astronauts use to communicate. Such waves are produced any time an electric spark jumps. You can produce radio waves with a simple spark generator. The best way to detect those waves is with an ordinary AM radio, tuned between stations.

   Use a spark generator at one end of the room to make a spark while you listen to the radio on the other end of the room. Have a partner turn the spark on and off.

   a) What do you hear at the spark generator, and at the radio? Are the two sounds the same?

2. Test whether the radio wave will pass through a vacuum by putting the spark generator inside a bell jar and pump out the air using a vacuum pump.

   a) When the air is pumped out, can you still hear the sound of the spark?

   b) Can you still hear the sound coming out of the radio?

   c) What does this tell you about the difference between sound waves and radio waves?

   d) Write a statement giving your conclusions about the ability of radio waves to pass through a vacuum.

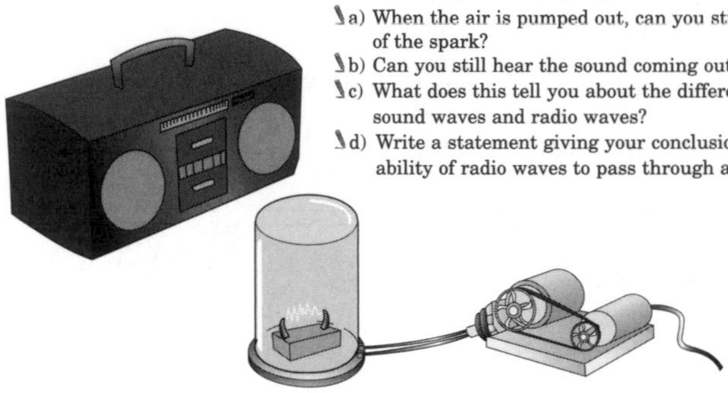

3. Radio waves travel very quickly. If you have ever used a walkie-talkie, you found that the signal seemed to travel to the other walkie-talkies in no time at all. What would happen if the distance between the two walkie-talkies is extremely large, would it be possible to detect a time delay?

ANSWERS

For You To Do

1. a) Sounds will be slightly different. Over the radio there is more static.

2. a) No sound from inside the bell jar will be heard.

   b) Yes.

   c) Radio waves can travel through a vacuum.

   d) Student response.

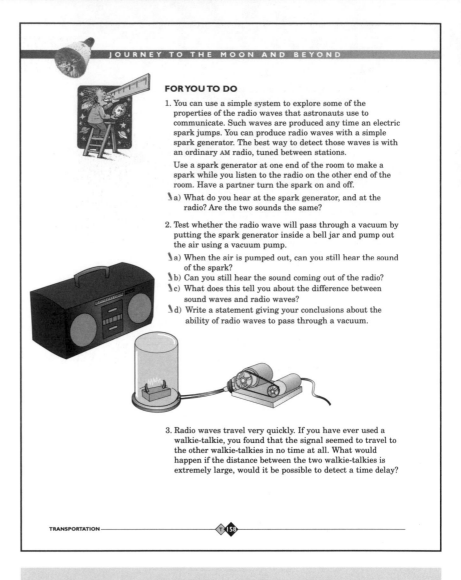

Watch a segment of the NASA film showing communication with astronauts on the moon. When a communication is received, an astronaut is supposed to answer "roger" immediately.

a) Why is there a noticeable delay in the arrival of the answer? Could it be that astronauts do not think as fast on the moon?

4. From the film, you can get an estimate of the speed of travel of a radio signal. Look again at the sequence in which the astronauts on the moon are answering a signal from Earth. When you get the transmission from Earth, answer "roger." Now estimate the time delay between your "roger" and the response from the moon. This is the length of time it took the signal to get to the moon and back. Repeat this until you feel you have a good estimate of the time delay.

a) Record the time delay in your log.

b) Calculate the speed of the signal. The distance to the moon is about 243,000 miles, or 3.80×10^8 m.

REFLECTING ON THE ACTIVITY AND THE CHALLENGE

The fact that radio waves move through a vacuum and that sound waves don't provides an excellent clue as to why communication in deep space uses radio waves. You may want to incorporate some aspect of communication over distance into your story.

Many science fiction movies use earth-bound examples to construct scenarios about communications in space. The delay in receiving and transmitting radio waves over great distances creates problems for the astronauts. The greater the distance, the greater is the delay. Think of how these short delays would affect a crisis situation. You may want to include this feature in your story. This also presents an opportunity to annotate some examples of why the delays are not used. Would the delay slow the delivery of the plot?

ANSWERS

For You To Do *(continued)*

3. Yes it would be possible to detect a delay, but not with ordinary walkie-talkies over small distances.

   a) The noticeable delay is due to the length of time it takes the signal to go to the moon, and then the reply to travel back to Earth.

4. a) Student response (probably about 2.6 - 3.0 seconds).

   b) Student calculation from data.
   $v = d/t$; $v = 3.8 \times 10^8 \times 2 / 2.6$ s $= 3.0 \times 10^8$ m/s

JOURNEY TO THE MOON AND BEYOND

FOR YOU TO READ

Electromagnetic Waves

When Heinrich Hertz first demonstrated the existence of radio waves in 1886, he had no idea that they would turn out to be useful. He was interested only in advancing knowledge of electricity and magnetism. By 1901, knowledge of radio waves had progressed so far that Guglielmo Marconi was able to send a coded signal across the Atlantic Ocean.

Today, these same electromagnetic waves carry radio and television signals. They are used to communicate with satellites and to see objects in the far reaches of outer space. In a microwave oven, they cook your food. Radar determines the exact position of airplanes approaching an airport. A transmitter attached to an eagle enables a biologist to follow its movements.

What else do you know that travels at about the speed of radio waves? The accepted value for the speed of radio waves is 300,000,000 (3×10^8) m/s, or 186,000 miles per second. This is commonly known as the speed of light. At that speed, a radio signal could get from London to New York in a couple of hundredths of a second. All electromagnetic waves—light, ultraviolet, infrared, radio, microwave—travel at this speed.

Sound is not an electromagnetic wave, and does not travel at the speed of such waves. The difference between the speed of sound and the speed of light is apparent whenever you see and hear something that happens at a distance. If you are sitting high up in the stadium to watch a baseball game, you see the ball well on its way before you hear the crack of the bat. Watching target practice from a distance, you see the barrel smoke before you hear the sound of the gun.

Can you think of other examples?

PHYSICS TO GO

1. Find the distances to Mars, Jupiter, the nearest star, and the nearest galaxy. Calculate how long a radio signal would take to travel to these locations. Would conversations with a space traveler be practical in these contexts?
2. If extraterrestrial life were discovered on a planetary system near a star close to Earth, the answer to a question may require 50 years. You would certainly want to have a decent conversation with this intelligent life form. How could you carry out a meaningful conversation given that the radio signal takes so long to get there and back?

ANSWERS

Physics To Go

1.

Mars	1.8×10^{11} m	1.9×10^{-9} light-years	6×10^2 s (10 min)
Jupiter	6.3×10^{11} m	6.6×10^{-8} light-years	2.1×10^3 s (35 min)
nearest star Alpha Proxima	4.1×10^{16} m	4.3 light-years	1.4×10^8 s (4.3 years)
nearest galaxy Andromeda	2×10^{22} m	2×10^6 light-years	6.3×10^{14} s (2×10^6 years)

2. Student response.

3. Explain why radio waves could be used to determine the distance of distant stars.
4. Are there any other technologies around that might be used for communication in years to come?
5. What are the limitations of radio communication and what can be done about them? Why is cable TV used?
6. Is there any limit to the amount of radio communication, that can be used at any time, and what can be done about it?
7. In what ways would modern life be different if you had no access to radio waves?

INQUIRY INVESTIGATION

Find some other properties of radio waves. Use the spark generator and the AM radio. Some of the things you might like to investigate may be:

- How far can the signal from the spark generator be detected? inside the school building? outdoors?
- Can radio waves go through a wall?
- Can radio waves go around the corner of a building?
- Can the radio wave carry the signal through the metal of a can?

Decide on what procedures you will use, and submit them to your teacher for approval. Carry out your investigation.

Write a statement giving your conclusions about the ability of radio waves to pass through a vacuum, around corners, through metal, across distances, etc.

ANSWERS

Physics To Go

(continued)

3 Radio waves have a finite speed. You can determine the distance of a star by bouncing off a radio wave and determining the time it takes to return. However, due to very large distances, and long periods of time between transmission and reception, scientists use stellar parallax to determine stellar distances.

4. Wireless technology, but all types of communication are limited by the finite speed of light.

5. Basic radio communication from land station to land station, is limited by the fact that radio waves can only travel in straight lines. Because the Earth is curved, there must be repeater stations to re-transmit the radio signals to curve around the Earth. Cable is used, as the signal is transmitted to a satellite and back down to Earth to many different communities, then sent through cable lines. This allows the signal to overcome the linear transmission.

6. Radio communication is limited to the number of frequencies that can operate at any one time. If the frequencies become too close, then the transmission from one frequency can overlap and interfere with the transmission of another frequency.

7. Students response.

PHYSICS AT WORK

George Takei

SET A COURSE FOR THE FUTURE MR. SULU

George Takei, as Lt. Sulu, is one of the original Star Trek characters from the television series that began in the late 1960s. He has become, as all the early Star Trek characters have, a science fiction icon.

George believes that imagination and inquisitiveness are the most important factors that move society ahead. And, Star Trek clearly represents that visionary imagination. "Science fiction," claims George "can become fact if we let our imaginations free, free to ask—what if."

"When Star Trek was first conceived by Gene Rodenbury," George explains, "we had scientists from the Rand Corporation to help guide and stimulate our writers and production teams. Gene was a visionary, but he knew that he had to reconcile any problems that might come up between science fiction and science fact."

"Science fiction is a wonderful vehicle to envision new possibilities for society." states George. "And," he continues, "Gene Roddenbury was a true pioneer. He had strong views about human civilization and he created the Starship Enterprise to represent that vision. The Starship Enterprise became a metaphor for the Starship Earth. The bridge of our starship was populated with a wide cultural diversity. At that time on television, it was revolutionary to see that kind of cultural diversity celebrated. In the role that I had the privilege to play, for example, it was the first time that an Asian was depicted on television in an non-servile, non-clownish, non-villain type role. Lt. Sulu was a capable, professional part of the leadership team on the bridge of the Enterprise."

George has written one science fiction novel himself and he explains, "when you write science fiction you have the freedom to create through your imagination another world, a world with its own social and physical reality." He also points out that often what was once considered science fiction later becomes science fact. For example, in 1969, during Star Trek's second season, a man landed on the moon for the first time. "For us on the Starship Enterprise that was rather old hat. We had been 'beaming down' to moons and other planet surfaces for quite a while."

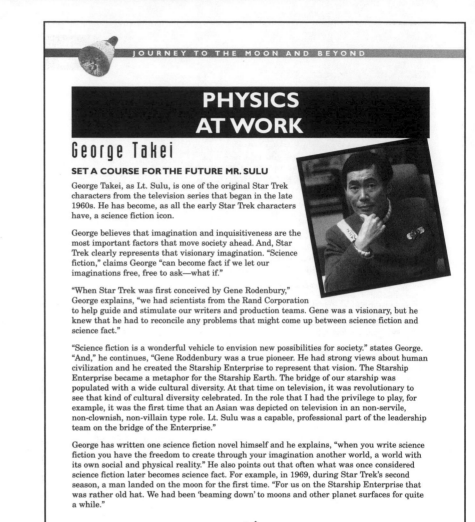

Chapter 3 Assessment

Now that you have finished this chapter, it is time to complete your challenge. You are trying to help my little brother, or any other young sci-fi fan, learn the difference between science fact and science fiction. You may have already started writing a story, and you probably have a number of new and exciting ideas to include.

- **Complete writing your science-fiction story about a trip to the moon or beyond.**
- **In a separate key to your story (an annotation), explain where the science is true and where you have modified the physics for interest or excitement.**

Review the criteria that you agreed on at the beginning of the chapter. Your criteria may have included the following:

- **the maximum and minimum length of the story and annotation;**
- **how much of the grade should depend on creativity and interest in the story;**
- **how much should depend on the annotation that relates and describes the real physics in your story and your modifications of physics;**
- **how many physics concepts you should include to receive an "A" for your work.**

Read over your story. Should it be modified at this point?

Physics You Learned

Free fall

Weight

Apparent weight

Weightlessness

Mass and weight

Technology in zero gravity

$F = ma$

Fermi problem—oxygen use

Sound in vacuum

Radio wave transmission in a vacuum

Speed of radio waves

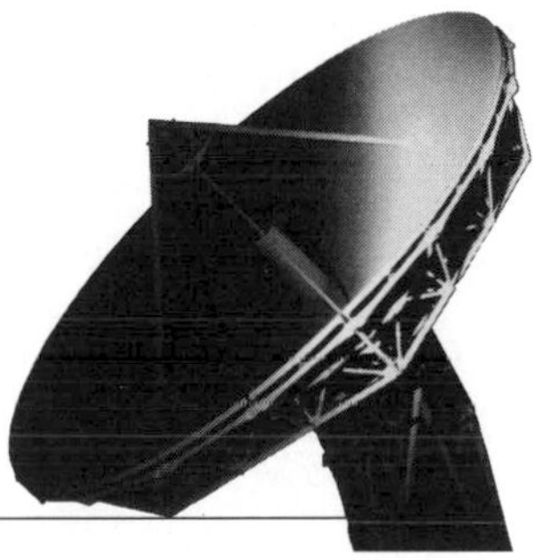

Alternative Chapter Assessment Test

Part A: Multiple Choice:

Choose the best answer and place on your answer sheet.

1. You get into an elevator carrying your handy-dandy bathroom scale. When you step on the scale, you measure your mass in
   a) kilograms
   b) newtons
   c) masses
   d) meters

2. When you step on the scale, and you find that your mass is 60 kg, your weight will be
   a) 60 N
   b) 600 N
   c) 600 kg
   d) 60 kg

3. As you step into the elevator, a friend steps into the elevator with you. Anxious to explain the reason you're carrying a scale into the elevator, you say you are trying to prove that
   a) when you go up in an elevator, you are weightless
   b) when you go down in an elevator, you are weightless
   c) only if you are traveling up or down at a constant speed, will you be weightless
   d) only if the acceleration of the elevator is the same as gravity, will you be weightless

4. You now have a spring scale and a 1.0 kg mass, and want to measures the "g"s of the elevator ride. The "g"s refers to
   a) the velocity of the elevator
   b) the acceleration of the elevator
   c) the guy that fixes the elevator
   d) the speed of the elevator

5. Free fall refers to
   a) the speed at which something falls
   b) the acceleration at which the object falls
   c) the speed which the object begins to accelerate
   d) the cost of falling

6. Newton's Second Law of Motion can be written as an equation. Which equation below correctly describes this law?
   a) $m = Fa$
   b) $m = a/F$
   c) $a = m/F$
   d) $a = F/m$

7. While on a diet, you are instructed to eat only 125 g of meat per day. Knowing that the force of gravity is greater on Earth than the moon, you argue that you should be able to have 6 times that much meat on the moon. Which statement below correctly describes the problem with saying that you can eat 6 times as much meat?

   a) You are not on the moon, so you can't use the gravity of the moon.

   b) You are really only interested in the mass of the meat.

   c) The weight of the meat doesn't change as it is a measure of how much matter is present.

   d) Because you are on the moon, you need to eat more food.

8. The weight of your golf clubs is 500 N on Earth. What would be the approximate weight of these clubs on the moon?

   a) 500 N

   b) 5000 N

   c) 80 N

   d) 800 N

9. If you are pulling a 1.0-kg mass in a car on a frictionless surface, it will be ____________ to pull that same mass on the moon on a frictionless surface.

   a) harder

   b) easier

   c) about the same

   d) none of these

10. You are on a weight training program on Earth, and when you go to the moon in order to keep up with your weight training, you would have to take approximately ______________ as much weight.

    a) the same

    b) twice

    c) one-sixth

    d) six times

11. When watching a video of a skydiver, it appears that the skydiver rises in the air when he opens the parachute. Which statement below best describes the explanation for this?

    a) The skydiver actually does rise because the parachute pulls up on the skydiver.

    b) The skydiver only appears to rise because the videotaper continues to fall.

    c) The skydiver appears to rise due to the parachute slowing the skydiver from a high velocity to a lower velocity.

    d) The skydiver just continues to fall, and the parachute doesn't slow him at all.

3

12. You are given special permission to drop two practice golf balls from the top of the gym. One golf ball has a large mass inside, and the other has nothing but air. Which statement below could be an hypothesis regarding which ball will fall to the ground first?

a) The ball with the large mass will hit the ground first because it is heavier.

b) The ball with no mass will hit first, because it has less air resistance.

c) The ball with the large mass will hit first because the weight is much larger than the air resistance.

d) The balls will probably hit the ground at the same time, because the air resistance will be the same for both.

Use the following information to answer questions 13 - 15.

The amount of air that can be used by an astronaut is critical to the success of the mission. (No air, no astronaut, no mission!) Therefore, scientists spend many years studying different ways of getting the correct amount of air (particularly oxygen) to the astronauts. One source of oxygen could be the use of plants.

Scientists know that about 2 liters of oxygen are produced each hour, for each one square meter of leaf surface (about 10 good-sized house plants).

- air is 21% oxygen
- average volume of air per breath - 400 mL
- average breaths per minute - 25
- about 1/3 of the oxygen gets into your blood

13. What is the total amount of air that is breathed in one hour?

a) 600 mL

b) 600 L

c) 100 L

d) 240 L

14. If an astronaut was breathing approximately 400 L of air every hour, what is the amount of oxygen that gets into the blood?

a) 28 L/h

b) 84 L/h

c) 133 L/h

d) 252 L/h

15. Assuming that the only possible source of oxygen were plants on a spaceship, approximately how many would be needed for four astronauts if each astronaut used 40 L/h?

a) 80 plants

b) 800 plants

c) 20 plants

d) 200 plants

16. Two astronauts are in a space shuttle. What would be the best method of communication they would use if they were both in the cabin?
    a) radio communication
    b) a loud speaker
    c) regular speech
    d) sign language

17. If the two astronauts were trying to communicate, and one of them was on a space walk, they would have to use
    a) radio communication
    b) a loud speaker
    c) regular speech
    d) sign language

18. The speed of radio waves is
    a) the same as the speed of sound
    b) slower than the speed of sound
    c) slower than the speed of light
    d) the same as the speed of light

19. A light-year is
    a) a year where there is more sunshine per hour
    b) a distance used to measure the distances to the planets
    c) the distance that is required for light to travel in one year
    d) the time that is required to travel the distance to the nearest star

20. The nearest star to Earth is
    a) the sun
    b) Alpha Proxima
    c) Andromeda
    d) Alpha Centauri

Part B: Written Response

Write the answers in complete sentences in the space provided.

1. Neil Armstrong dropped a feather and a hammer at the same time, while standing on the moon. When they fell, they hit the ground at the same time. Describe why this happened, and which famous scientist predicted it would happen.

   A: Approximately 400 years ago, Galileo predicted that objects of different masses would fall at the same rate. Newton furthered that study, and came up with his Universal Law of Gravitation. Objects in a vacuum fall at the same rate regardless of the masses. Since the moon has no atmosphere, there is no air resistance, so the feather and the hammer are free to fall at the same rate.

2. Why do astronauts have to have an exercise program in space?

   A: When muscles are not in use, they atrophy or lose their ability to work. After long periods in space, the muscles will get smaller as they are not needed for support of the body or to work against gravity.

3. Describe a typical meal in space. Include the food and the drinks, and how each part of the meal will be served.

   A: Answers will vary. Look for imaginative answers which show an understanding of the problems associated with zero-gravity conditions. Students should be able to recognize the need for closed containers for any liquids. Most of the food is in tubes, or freeze- dried. When water is added to the freeze-dried food, it must be kept in a closed container. If food is allowed to float around in the capsule, it can be dangerous to the functioning of the space shuttle.

4. Read the following statement:

When you are in space there is no gravity.

Comment on the accuracy of this statement.

   A: Answers will vary. Students should recognize that gravity is infinite in its effects, but that the greater the distance from the producing body (e.g., Earth) the smaller the effect. Therefore, gravity is always present, but depending on the distance, in such a small magnitude, the effect is negligible. For an astronaut, orbiting the Earth, the sensation of weightlessness is due to the free fall of the space shuttle back to Earth.

5. When a skydiver jumps from an airplane, she might begin her descent in a spread-eagle position. Explain what advantage this position has for the skydiver.

   A: This position allows the skydiver to descend more slowly. Because she is increasing the wind resistance, this force balances the force of gravity, thus stopping the acceleration downward. She will be moving at a constant velocity, commonly referred to as terminal velocity.

6. Spending long periods in space is difficult to do. What are some of the important things an astronaut will have to remember to bring?

   A: Students answers will vary. Expect answers such as food, air, toiletries. However, look for expanded thinking types of answers. Oxygen instead of just air. Look for examples of the types of foods, as well as the method of preparing and storing.

7. One problem with traveling in space can be providing food and oxygen. What are some other problems a space traveler might encounter?

   A: Many answers will include disposal of urine and feces. However, students should be aware, that water vapor, and carbon dioxide are exhaled, and must be recycled or disposed of.

8. Assume that the amount of oxygen needed for one astronaut to travel for one hour can be supplied by either 20 house plants (mass of 2.0 kg each) or one oxygen tank (mass 20 kg), give one argument in support of each, and one against.

   A: The arguments in favor of the plants, could be that they will last a long time, and their mass is only a one-time cost (in terms of the mass to take off form Earth), and the argument against, is the need for lots of sunlight, water and warmth. The argument in favor of the oxygen bottles could be that the oxygen doesn't need to be watered, will not die, and the argument against would be the very large mass, as the bottles would have to be carried for the whole journey.

9. Explain one major difference in the transmission of radio waves and sound waves.

   A: Students answers will vary. Sound waves will only travel in a medium (e.g., air, water, matter), and radio waves are electromagnetic waves which do not need a medium. Therefore, you can transmit radio waves through a vacuum and space. Students may also refer to the speed of radio waves as very much faster than sound waves.

10. You have developed a remote-controlled vehicle to travel on a distant planet. In order for you to control the movements, you use radio waves. If this planet is 1.5×10^{12} m away from Earth, how long would it take the signal to travel there and back. Show all your work.

    A: The speed of light is 3.0×10^8 m/s, the distance is 1.5×10^{12}m, and time is the unknown. Using the formula
    $v = d/t$
    $t = d/v$
    $t = 1.5 \times 10^{12}$ m / 3.0×10^8 m/s
    $t = 5000$ s or 83 minutes
    Therefore, the time required to go once is 83 minutes, so for the return trip it would be 166 minutes.

11. Using your answer from question 10, what would you need to consider when designing a remote-control vehicle for exploration of this planet?

    A: Students answers will vary. Because there is such a large time difference between the signal arriving at the remote vehicle, and the data returning to Earth, the vehicle should have a very slow speed, referring back to the response time earlier. It would be like a car spotting danger, then not being able to put on the brakes for several hours. The vehicle on the remote planet may also have artificial intelligence, to be able to make decisions about whether or not to stop under certain dangerous conditions (such as cliffs, large rocks, pockets of soft soil, lava flows, etc.).

3

Alternative Chapter Assessment Answers

Part A: Multiple Choice:

1. a
2. b
3. d
4. b
5. b
6. d
7. b
8. c
9. c
10. d
11. b
12. c
13. b
14. a
15. b
16. c
17. a
18. d
19. c
20. a